MONASTIC WISDOM SERIES: NUMBER TWENTY-FIVE

Thomas Merton

Monastic Observances
Initiation into the Monastic Tradition 5

D0861325

MONASTIC WISDOM SERIES

Simeon Leiva, ocso, General Editor

Advisory Board

Michael Casey, ocso

Lawrence S. Cunningham

Patrick Hart, ocso

Robert Heller

Terrence Kardong, osb

Kathleen Norris

Miriam Pollard, ocso

Bonnie Thurston

MONASTIC WISDOM SERIES: NUMBER TWENTY-FIVE

Monastic Observances
Initiation into the Monastic Tradition 5

by
Thomas Merton

Edited with an Introduction by
Patrick F. O'Connell

Preface by
James Conner, ocso

α

Cistercian Publications
www.cistercianpublications.org

LITURGICAL PRESS
Collegeville, Minnesota
www.litpress.org

A Cistercian Publications title published by Liturgical Press

Cistercian Publications
Editorial Offices
Abbey of Gethsemani
3642 Monks Road
Trappist, Kentucky 40051
www.cistercianpublications.org

© 2010 by Order of Saint Benedict, Collegeville, Minnesota. All rights reserved. No part of this book may be reproduced in any form, by print, microfilm, microfiche, mechanical recording, photocopying, translation, or by any other means, known or yet unknown, for any purpose except brief quotations in reviews, without the previous written permission of Liturgical Press, Saint John's Abbey, P.O. Box 7500, Collegeville, Minnesota 56321-7500. Printed in the United States of America.

1   2   3   4   5   6   7   8   9

Library of Congress Cataloging-in-Publication Data

Merton, Thomas, 1915–1968.
  Monastic observances : initiation into the monastic tradition 5 / by Thomas Merton ; edited with an introduction by Patrick F. O'Connell ; preface by James Conner.
      p. cm. — (Monastic wisdom series ; MW25)
  Includes bibliographical references and index.
  ISBN 978-0-87907-025-0 — ISBN 978-0-87907-921-5 (e-book)
  1. Cistercians—Rules.   2. Monastic and religious life.   I. O'Connell, Patrick F.   II. Title.   III. Series.

BX3404.Z5M47   2010
255'.1206—dc22   2010022608

TABLE OF CONTENTS

PREFACE

Fr. Louis (Thomas) Merton gave these conferences on *Monastic Observances* during the years he was Novice Master, from 1955 to 1965. They are based on the book of the *Usages* of the Cistercians of the Strict Observance. These *Usages* were taken from the early Cistercian *Usages* from Cîteaux, as well as the *Usages* of Abbot de Rancé at the Monastery of La Trappe and the *Usages* of Dom Augustin de Lestrange at La Val Sainte in Switzerland. They were first adopted by the Second General Chapter which was held in 1894 after the unification of three Trappist congregations into one Order in 1892. They were subsequently revised after the promulgation of the Code of Canon Law in 1917.

At the time, the Abbot General, Dom Sebastien Wyart, urged those composing the *Usages* to avoid the rigidities and penitential aspects of the "Trappist" heritage and to remain faithful to the Cistercian spirit of the early founders. Both La Trappe and La Val Sainte were known for their penitential spirit and their negativity towards anything merely "human." Unfortunately it took almost fifty years for this evolution to take place, and Fr. Louis himself played a large part in this process. He emphasized in his writings and in his classes for juniors and later for novices that the Cistercian life is a contemplative life rather than simply a penitential life.

These conferences show the ways in which he strove to foster this notion by showing that the observances are not simply rules to be obeyed, but a way of life to be lived out in accord with that primal quality that St. Benedict sought in any candidate to monastic life: "do they truly seek God" (*Rule*, c. 50). As Merton states in the very beginning: "{They must assist our} growth as children of God, {the} formation of Christ in us" (5). The Gospels show Jesus constantly relying on the Father for everything. Whatever he says, whatever he does, comes from the Father. This shows us how we are to live in imitation of him. The monk believes that the observances come to us ultimately from the Father, and in submitting to them and surrendering one's own will, the monk becomes ever more conformed to Christ.

It is interesting to notice that it is in these notes that Merton gives perhaps his fullest teaching on prayer: cf. the section on "THE MORNING MEDITATION" (75–92), supplemented by the section on *lectio divina* and silence (149–83). Together they show us the monastic approach to prayer. Merton believed that "contemplative life" is not merely a juridical term, but a way of life, and that one cannot claim to be a contemplative unless he loves prayer as the way to discover the presence of God in our lives and world. All of the observances must be related ultimately to prayer in order that they may be a way of life and not simply of formalism.

A number of the observances that Merton discusses have been radically changed since his time, due to the period of renewal within the Order and the Church at large. Prime is no longer a part of the divine office. The chapter of faults has been dropped. Many of the penances that he speaks of are no longer in practice. Even the basic observance of silence has been radically changed. And yet what Merton says about these practices conveys valid principles which are applicable at any time. He sees them primarily as ways of cultivating humility of spirit and opportunities to surrender ourselves to God and to the community.

Today the novices are not taught the monastic observances as in the past. But they are exposed to the basic principles found therein. Since 1969, with the Statute of Unity and Pluralism from the General Chapter, uniformity is no longer observed among all of the houses of the Order. Each house is free to determine its own observances and these are drawn up by the particular community. However the observances Merton considers in this volume stand as more than simply a testament to the past. They remain as examples of how monks of an earlier generation approached the monastic life and how they sought to give their lives to God.

We can be grateful to Dr. Patrick O'Connell for his usual diligent research into the conferences that Thomas Merton gave to the novices. His labors, as usual, are thorough and direct the reader to something much deeper than simply the externals. They show us how Merton viewed the observances and how he strove to initiate the novices to a level beyond the canonical level, to a way of living out the Mystery of Christ in their own lives.

Fr. James Conner, ocso
Abbey of Gethsemani

INTRODUCTION

In Cistercian monasteries of the mid-twentieth century it was a standard part of the novice director's duties to give "repetitions,"[1] expositions of the official customs or observances of the Order. Apparently these presentations were frequently little more than what the name suggests,[2] reading or paraphrasing and providing brief comments on the various regulations included in the volume of "*Usages.*"[3] Not surprisingly, when Thomas Merton turned his attention to this topic in his novitiate conferences of the late 1950s, he endeavored to do much more than merely "repeat" for his young charges material that they could easily read for themselves. In this set of conferences, Merton provided an orientation both spatial and temporal to the Abbey of Gethsemani, a brief but comprehensive tour of the "regular places" of the monastery followed by a thorough consideration of the monastic *horarium*, the succession of "exercises" that structure the monastic day (or rather the first part of that day, for in fact at the point where this "Part I" of the *Monastic Observances* course ends he has progressed only as far as the morning chapter, held immediately after the office of prime, and

1. See John Eudes Bamberger, ocso, "Some Features of Monastic Formation," in Augusta Tescari, ocso, Marie-Gérard Dubois, ocso and Maria Paola Santachiara, ocso, eds., *The Cistercian Order of the Strict Observance in the Twentieth Century*, 2 vols. (Rome: Cistercian Order of the Strict Observance, 2008), 2.255-56.

2. See Armand Veilleux, ocso, "Trappist-Cistercian Formation in the Twentieth Century," in *Cistercian Order in the Twentieth Century*, 2.246.

3. *Regulations of the Order of Cistercians of the Strict Observance Published by the General Chapter of 1926* (Dublin: M. H. Gill & Sons, [1927]).

for reasons that will be suggested below, the second part of the
course was never given). Unlike the conferences in which Merton
introduced the novices to the riches of monastic tradition, extending back through the middle ages to the patristic era and from
the Clairvaux of St. Bernard through the Monte Cassino of St.
Benedict to the Egyptian desert of John Cassian and the desert
fathers,[4] these lectures were focused on the familiar setting of
their own monastery and what could quickly become the all too
familiar pattern of their daily life. But like all of the classes that
Merton prepared and presented during the decade of his tenure
as novice master (1955–1965), and perhaps more concretely than
most, the *Monastic Observances* conferences were intended to
reveal the inner dynamic of the monastic vocation, its orientation
toward contemplative union with God with and in the crucified
and risen Christ, as lived out in a community formed and nur-
tured by the *Rule* of St. Benedict. Thus Merton is primarily interested in considering the spiritual significance of the places and
events, the rhythms and rituals that structure the Cistercian life.
This is undoubtedly the most practical series of conferences that
Merton gave to his young charges, but it is marked throughout
by a desire to show how such a framework could and should be
more than a meticulously arranged set of formal activities to
which the monk was expected to conform, how it was developed
to create a balanced integration of work and prayer, a complementary alternation between the public "work of God" in the
liturgy and periods of solitary reflection and meditation, all oriented to deepening communion with God and with one's monastic brothers. For non-monastic readers (and even for monks
who entered Cistercian life in the very different environment that

4. See Thomas Merton, *Cassian and the Fathers: Initiation into the Monastic
Tradition*, ed. Patrick F. O'Connell, Monastic Wisdom [MW], vol. 1 (Kalamazoo,
MI: Cistercian Publications, 2005); Thomas Merton, *Pre-Benedictine Monasticism:
Initiation into the Monastic Tradition 2*, ed. Patrick F. O'Connell, MW 9 (Kalamazoo,
MI: Cistercian Publications, 2006); Thomas Merton, *The Rule of Saint Benedict:
Initiation into the Monastic Tradition 4*, ed. Patrick F. O'Connell, MW 19 (College-
ville, MN: Cistercian Publications, 2009).

followed the Second Vatican Council), these conferences allow
an unparalleled look at daily life behind the enclosure walls at a
point in time just before that life would undergo a radical restruc-
turing. For students of Thomas Merton, *Monastic Observances*
provides an opportunity to watch him introduce aspiring monks
to the traditional way of life in which he himself had been formed
and which he had lived for almost two decades, a way of life that
he deeply valued and loved, even as he continued to struggle
with some of its more problematic aspects.

＊＊＊＊＊＊＊

The presentation of these conferences (which encompass
only about seven hours of the monastic day!) extended in a rather
leisurely and evidently somewhat sporadic pattern over a period
of almost three years, which means that none of the novices could
have been present for the whole series during their novitiate of
approximately two years. So the orientation they provide, useful
as it may have been, could not have been considered essential
for their making sense of the daily routine, which the new monk
in formation would obviously have become quite accustomed to
within a few short weeks at most—clearly the focus was on ex-
ploring the spiritual significance of the various places and exercises rather than simply identifying what they were.

The class must have begun some time during, or just before,
Lent, as on page 6v of Merton's own typescript,[5] which he had
in front of him as he spoke during each conference, one of the
brief notes that he regularly jotted down on the backs of the typed
pages, to remind him about announcements to be made at the
beginning of class, mentions "Lenten books." Nineteen pages
later, on page 25v of the typescript,[6] he makes note of the Solemnity of St. Benedict—not the main feast celebrated (or not celebrated, as it regularly fell during Lent) on March 21—but the
Feast of the Translation of St. Benedict on July 11; and on the same

5. Page 19 of this edition.
6. Page 59 of this edition.

page the date of the Feast of St. Symphorosa and her seven sons—July 18—is also noted. Not until page 31 of the typescript[7] is reached can the year in question be determined: there Merton observes that the Eighth Sunday after Pentecost falls on the first Sunday of August, a correspondence that occurs during the relevant period only on August 4, 1957, so the conferences had begun during late February or early March of that year. The subsequent progression of the course can be traced by means of a number of indications provided by the typescript. On page 44[8] occurs the first of a number of marginal dates made by the typist who was assigned to make a copy of the notes on stencils for eventual distribution to the novices; he had reached this point in the text on "10/26"; Merton's own note four pages later (47v)[9] mentions an exam scheduled for "Fri 20th"—a combination that occurred in December 1957, a date confirmed by notes two pages later (49v)[10] referring to "decorations—Bl Mother Crib Tree". The next typist's note, on page 51,[11] is dated "12/31", but then there is apparently a substantial hiatus in the conferences, as only three pages later[12] the date is "3/17", and five pages after that,[13] "5/2", although the next marginal date, "5/6", is on page 63,[14] four pages afterward. Merton himself refers to the Feast of the Ascension, which was celebrated on May 15 in 1958, in his note on page 66v;[15] subsequent notes refer to the Feast of the Transfiguration (August 6) (73v)[16] and to the (September) ember days (78v).[17] At

7. Page 70 of this edition.
8. Page 100 of this edition.
9. Page 108 of this edition.
10. Page 112 of this edition.
11. Page 116 of this edition.
12. Page 122 of this edition.
13. Page 134 of this edition.
14. Page 142 of this edition.
15. Page 153 of this edition.
16. Page 166 of this edition.
17. Page 177 of this edition; the September ember days were the Wednesday, Friday and Saturday following the Feast of the Exaltation of the Holy Cross (Sept. 14).

this point, these conferences were apparently put aside, since the typist's note on the facing page[18] is dated "3/12", though he apparently did a good deal of catching up on that day since his next note, on page 87,[19] is dated only a day later. Merton's own reference to "Pasternak" on page 82v[20] must be related to the Russian novelist's disappearance from public view, which Merton noted in a journal entry for March 3, 1959;[21] seven pages later (89v)[22] he jots a reminder that there would be no conference on the Feast of St. Joseph (March 19), and on page 92v[23] he mentions "visitation—Father Immediate"—a reference to the arrival of Dom Columban Bissey, the Abbot of Melleray, the motherhouse of Gethsemani, which took place on April 11, 1959.[24] A typist's note on page 98[25] is dated "5/5", but only three pages later (101v)[26] Merton himself refers in a note to the Feast of the Visitation (July 2), so again there must have been a considerable gap in the progression of the conferences. The last few months of the course can be traced by the typist's marginal dating[27] from "Sept 26 '59" (103), through "Sept 28" (105), "10/16" (107), "10-23" (109), "10-26" (110), "1-11" (112), "1-12" (114), "1-16-60" (115), and "1-27" (117—the final page of the typescript).[28] Since the typist, at this

18. Page 176 of this edition.

19. Page 192 of this edition.

20. Page 184 of this edition.

21. Thomas Merton, *A Search for Solitude: Pursuing the Monk's True Life. Journals, vol. 3: 1952–1960*, ed. Lawrence S. Cunningham (San Francisco: Harper-Collins, 1996), 265; see also *Search for Solitude*, 270–71 [7/25/59]—the news that Pasternak had left Moscow of his own free will.

22. Page 198 of this edition.

23. Page 205 of this edition.

24. *Search for Solitude*, 274.

25. Page 215 of this edition.

26. Page 221 of this edition.

27. Pages 224, 227, 231, 233, 235, 238, 241, 245, 250, respectively, of this edition.

28. The differences in the style of the dating notations suggest that there may have been one or even two additional typists who worked on this part of the text.

point at least, was presumably somewhat ahead of Merton's actual presentations, in order that the multigraphed copy of the notes could be distributed to the novices by the time the course was actually concluded, it is therefore probably accurate to assume that the *Monastic Observances* conferences drew to a close some time in early February, 1960. Given the relatively modest length of the text, it is evident that the course would not have extended over such a lengthy period of time if these conferences had been given throughout the entire period on a regular weekly basis. The available dating confirms that there must have been considerable intervals when they were put aside. It is perhaps significant that the time frame for these conferences overlaps that for the initial presentation of the conferences on the Benedictine *Rule*, which Merton discussed between the summer of 1957 and early February 1959,[29] and particularly that datable references for the later part of those conferences are clustered between early September 1958 and early February 1959, the precise period when there is a considerable gap in the *Observances* dating. So it is possible, even likely, that for at least part of this period Merton may have alternated material from these two sets of conferences— moving between the foundational basis of the monastic life in the *Rule* and its practical implementation in the Cistercian observances.

* * * * * * *

There are two significant limitations in the *Monastic Observances* conferences, both resulting from the particular time period in which they were given. The first is that they are incomplete; the second, that they were about to become obsolete.

The text of the conferences proper concludes with the note "End of Part One—Notes on Observances" (250), carrying the obvious implication that they were to be followed by a Part Two, but there is no evidence that Merton ever wrote or delivered this second half of the course. After his tour of the main areas of the

29. See *Rule of Saint Benedict*, xxxv–xxxviii.

monastery, Merton provides a detailed description of the first part of the monastic day, from the beginning of the night office through morning chapter. Along the way he discusses the period of meditation following vigils; the office of lauds; Mass and communion; *lectio divina*; the light breakfast called mixt; and the office of prime. But the activities of the rest of the day, including the little hours of tierce, sext and none, and the later offices of vespers and compline, are not considered, nor is monastic work,[30] the main meal (which would probably have also included some notice of the reading that accompanied it), nor the conventual, or community, Mass, which Merton said he intended to consider at a later point (109). Thus it is clear that the conferences as presented are significantly truncated. It is possible that Merton simply lost interest in the topic, or that the extended period of time devoted to the first part had prompted an indefinite postponement of the second, or that the variety of other courses given during the final five years of Merton's mastership left no room for continuing the *Observances* material. But the text itself provides a more likely explanation. Merton notes as he nears the completion of this first part (226) that the *Usages* were currently being revised, a process that had begun in 1958, mandated by the Cistercian General Chapter of that year.[31] Rather than continuing to cite a text that was about to be superseded, Merton would

30. But see Merton, *Rule of Saint Benedict*, 130–42, which does discuss this topic in detail.

31. See *Cistercian Order in the Twentieth Century*, 1.246, 263–64. See Merton's own September 28, 1964 comments, shortly before the revised *Usages* were published: "Looking through the *Usages* for things that might be dropped as 'artificial'—noticed with alarm that they are all built into the very structure of the life. To take away these observances would be in fact to take away what practically constitutes the 'Trappist Life' for many monks! This is very serious. It seems that there is no real 'adaptation' possible?? That all that can be expected is to preserve what we have in a fairly reasonable and alert spirit—in community: and be at peace away from all this when one is free. It is a problem—probably more easily accepted in French monasteries" (Thomas Merton, *Dancing in the Water of Life: Seeking Peace in the Hermitage. Journals, vol. 5: 1963–1965*, ed. Robert E. Daggy [San Francisco: HarperCollins, 1997], 150).

quite logically have decided to wait until after the new edition
had appeared before continuing his commentary, which referred
continually to the *Usages*. In the event, the process of revision
took considerably longer than had been expected, and the revised
version,[32] issued only in mimeographed form as it was anticipated, rightly, that further alterations in the Cistercian observances would be needed in implementing the renewal called for
by the Second Vatican Council, appeared only in 1964.[33] Merton,
who would resign as novice master to become a full-time hermit
in August 1965, never got around to completing his overview of
the *Observances* during the final year of his mastership.

The changes naturally had a profound impact as well on the
parts of the *horarium* discussed in Part One of the conferences.
Most obvious, of course, was the disappearance of Latin, both in
the Mass and in the Office,[34] a development about which Merton
himself was profoundly ambivalent.[35] But there were numerous

32. *Usages of the Cistercian Monks of the Strict Observance* (Monte Cistello
[Rome]: [Cistercian Generalate], 1964).

33. These revised *Usages* remained in force for only about four years, as the
Statute on Unity and Pluralism, passed by the Cistercian General Chapter of
1969, allowed for "the principle of diverse usages, within specified limits" (John
Eudes Bamberger, ocso, "The Office of Secretary General," in *Cistercian Order in
the Twentieth Century*, 2.79).

34. As early as 1965, the women's monasteries began to use the vernacular
in the office, while in 1966, permission was granted to monasteries in mission
countries to celebrate the office in the vernacular (*Cistercian Order in the Twentieth
Century*, 2.27); general permission was granted by the Congregation of Religious
in December, 1967 (*Cistercian Order in the Twentieth Century*, 2.282-83).

35. As early as September 13, 1957, Merton wrote in his journal: "More and
more I agree with Dom Gregorio. We need the psalms in *the vernacular*. We need
a public prayer that can be appreciated without college courses in Latin, history,
liturgy, etc. etc. A prayer that the *people* can understand. Useless to say that they
are a bunch of fools" (*Search for Solitude*, 118). Yet he himself loved the Latin office
and continued to recite it in the hermitage: see for example his June 10, 1965 letter
to Mother Mary Margaret: "Even though the Church officially and publicly encourages monks to retain the Latin liturgy, I am afraid that there are very many
communities, perhaps the majority in this country, which are seeking the vernacular at any price. They are of course free to ask for this concession, and I am

other significant changes as well to the monastic *horarium*. A period of experimentation that began with the General Chapter of 1967 "left each community free to organize its Office, on condition that it include the various traditional elements and that the 150 psalms be distributed over one or two weeks,"[36] culminating in legislation passed in 1974 that "leaves the choice of the readings, the distribution of the Psalms, and the adaptation of the changed elements to the decision of the Abbot and the community."[37] Private Masses distinct from the daily conventual Mass were replaced by a single concelebrated Mass at which all received communion.[38] The suppression of the office of prime was agreed upon in principle by the 1965 General Chapter, and accepted by the Vatican in 1967.[39] Likewise the daily chapter was no longer held in most houses of the order.[40] The General Chapter of 1967 granted permission for "brief oral communications," so that the dependence on sign language so closely identified with Trappist life in the preconciliar era no longer obtained.[41] The monastic calendar was brought into closer alignment with the Roman calendar.[42] Customary practices like the chapter of faults

---

sure that many will perhaps regret it after they have lost what they had. But this is an irreversible trend, I think, at least in the U.S. For my own part, as I have hopes of a more solitary life, and they seem about to be realized, I think that at least I will be able to keep the old Latin office *privatim*" (Thomas Merton, *The School of Charity: Letters on Religious Renewal and Spiritual Direction*, ed. Patrick Hart [New York: Farrar, Straus, Giroux, 1990], 283–84). See also his August 1966 letter to Dame Marcella Van Bruyn: "I still say the old office. . . . I am going to keep the office in Latin *usque ad mortem*. I read the Vulgate for my *lectio divina*. I am horribly conservative in these respects" (*School of Charity*, 311).

36. *Cistercian Order in the Twentieth Century*, 2.284.

37. *Cistercian Order in the Twentieth Century*, 2.285.

38. *Cistercian Order in the Twentieth Century*, 2.282.

39. *Cistercian Order in the Twentieth Century*, 2.27, 30, 31.

40. Michael Casey, ocso, "Evolution of Cistercian Spirituality," in *Cistercian Order in the Twentieth Century*, 2.236.

41. Casey, in *Cistercian Order in the Twentieth Century*, 2.231.

42. *Cistercian Order in the Twentieth Century*, 2.286-87.

and the weekly use of the "discipline," the penitential practice
of (largely symbolic and ceremonial) scourging, disappeared at
about the same time. By the time Merton resigned as novice master in August 1965 significant changes in the pattern of daily life
in Cistercian monasteries had already begun to be implemented,
and the change to a less uniform system of observances was given
explicit sanction by the adoption of the Statute on Unity and
Pluralism by the General Chapter of 1969. Thus without intend-
ing it, Merton provided in these conferences a vivid valedictory
witness to the traditional pattern of daily life in a Cistercian monastery as it had been lived generally since the medieval era, and
particularly since the reunion of the three congregations of Strict
Observance Cistercians in 1892. It is thus a document of particular
historical interest in preserving, in detail, a record of a lifestyle
just at the point when it was about to undergo permanent and
wide-ranging alteration.[43] This raises the question whether their
value is therefore exclusively, or primarily, historical. To arrive
at a satisfactory answer to this question requires a closer look at
the contents of the *Monastic Observances* text.

* * * * * * *

There is no doubt that some of what Merton is teaching his
novices here is contingent upon the practices that were in force
at the time of writing. A reader familiar with Merton's later essays

---

43. Certain changes in the monastic schedule had already begun to take
place at the time Merton was presenting these conferences, specifically the dis-
continuation of the daily recitation of the Little Office of the Blessed Virgin and
the drastic reduction of the frequency of recitation of the Office of the Dead, from
almost daily to twice a month, authorized by the General Chapter of 1955 (Casey,
in *Cistercian Order in the Twentieth Century*, 2.230), which allowed for more sleep
before the night office and more time for *lectio divina* after it; see Merton's comments on the changes in his journal entry of August 14, 1956 (the day after the
new schedule took effect) (*Search for Solitude*, 64); Merton also mentions the change
in his discussion of the Cistercian daily schedule in *The Silent Life* (New York:
Farrar, Straus & Cudahy, 1957), 119–20.

on monastic renewal[44] and his often sardonic and sometimes scathing comments in his journal and correspondence about what he sees as ossified, deadening routine may be surprised and even dismayed at an apparently complacent acceptance of what in retrospect clearly seem to be outmoded and even potentially harmful aspects of Trappist life. To some extent this can be attributed to the fact that Merton is introducing the novices to monastic life as it was practiced at the time, and so would naturally want to put the best face on even what might be considered the most retrograde aspects of the life. It is surely somewhat unsettling to find that the conferences proper come to their climax with a brief discussion, and justification, of the use of the discipline, the whip employed once a week by each monk to scourge himself (249–50). This is preceded by a longer, very detailed discussion of the chapter of faults, when monks would accuse themselves and one another of various infractions of the rule and usages (215–39), and of the public penances assigned by the abbot to make reparation for various infractions, such as lying prostrate outside the church or the refectory, or having to beg one's food from the assembled brothers, or to kiss each one's feet during mealtime (239–49). Such practices may seem to a contemporary reader disconcerting survivals from a pre-modern era, and Merton's matter-of-fact (though in fact quite nuanced) discussion may strike some as just as disconcerting, if not more so. While it is unlikely that Merton mourned the passing of these customs as he did the disappearance of the Latin liturgy, the impression given by the text is that he wasn't particularly bothered by their continued existence, and even that he regarded agitation for their abolition as somewhat misplaced—a preoccupation with details rather than a concern for authentic renewal. They must be situated in the context of the conferences as a whole to be properly evaluated.

44. Collected in Thomas Merton, *Contemplation in a World of Action* (Garden City, NY: Doubleday, 1971).

The content of these conferences can largely be classified into three interrelated types of material: factual information, practical instruction, and spiritual insight. The first two tend to be time-conditioned to a greater or lesser extent, depending on the particular topic; the third is generally of more enduring significance. The priority from Merton's own perspective of this last category is evident in the brief prefatory remarks with which he begins the *Observances* text (5–6). The words "life," "live," and "living" recur with an impressive intensity in the opening paragraphs: "Our observances are an integral part in our monastic *life*. They must *live*. {They must be} part of a living organism. They must *help us to live*, help our life of charity in the Spirit" (5). The emphasis is on the necessity to discover the spiritual vitality of monastic exercises as the "exact opposite of mere mechanical routine" (5). Merton draws on the traditional Pauline distinction between letter and spirit to indicate the absolutely essential need to discover the inner spiritual meaning of the pattern of monastic life and its various components, of penetrating to the spirit "while carrying out the letter properly" (5). In successive sentences he juxtaposes the dynamic "formation of Christ in us" with a static "formalism" that "stifles the free breath of the Spirit {and} kills the spiritual life" (5), and later the vitality of "monastic tradition" with the deadness of a "traditionalism" that clings to "the old as such" (6). He warns against both the mistaken equation of perfection with "exterior observance for its own sake" (6) and the "sloppiness, laziness, sensuality" (6) that comes with a devaluation and disregard of the outward expression of inner realities, a failure to be "observant" in both senses. Properly understood and properly practiced, Merton emphasizes, the observances are "the visible expression and the outward aid" (5) to a life of prayer, a life of "*fraternal union*" (5), a Eucharistic life, a life "leading to contemplation in the spirit of wisdom and understanding" (6), ultimately a Trinitarian life: "to live in Christ, by charity, in the Holy Spirit, {and} to grow in the works of love—love for God" (5). It is in light of these principles that Merton invites his novices to take a careful look at their new environment and the new pattern of organization that structures their days in this environment.

In introducing the first major section of the course, on the physical layout of the monastery (7–30), he emphasizes both that "Everything about the regular, traditional plan of the monastery has a meaning and a purpose" (7) and that this traditional plan does not entail a rigid, inflexible conformity that forbids all adaptations. In his overview of the monastery as a whole, he begins with a focus, drawn from St. Benedict, on the monastery as *domus Dei*, the house of God, where everything is arranged in such a way as to minimize "preoccupations and anxieties over material things or over anything at all" (8) so that the virtues of peace and love, faith and wisdom, are more easily practiced and made one's own. Again, he highlights the Trinitarian nature of authentic monastic life: "The abbot represents the heavenly Father; the brethren are sons living together in a unity of charity that transcends nature, forming as it were one son, in the bond of the Holy Spirit" (8–9), so that the harmony of the community may mirror "the internal peace and unity of the Three Divine Persons in One Nature" (9).

Turning to the various specific locations that make up the monastic environment as specified in the *Usages*, Merton begins the process of interweaving basic descriptive information with prescriptive instructions on proper behavior and reflections on religious and spiritual meaning, with the last clearly the most important even where it is not the most extensive element. Thus he provides a clear exposition of the fourfold division of the Cistercian church, a description of its various fixtures, a somewhat lengthy excursus on Gethsemani as a minor basilica, details on the set-up of the sacristy and provisions for liturgical books and garb, and even a detailed description of the cemetery as an adjunct to the church. He briefly emphasizes the importance of "reverence and modesty" (11) in church so as not to disturb others' prayer, and will later return to prescribe in detail proper deportment in choir and sanctuary (48–57). But his initial focus is on the laconic but significant statement in the *Rule* that the oratory should be what its name implies, a place of prayer, both communal and solitary, where "[e]verything {is} intended to lift the mind and heart to God" (10). Such a focus is of course self-evident when talking about a church, but the same emphasis is found in the treatment of the cemetery, as Merton follows his explanation of the orientation of the graves with a rather lyrical celebration (reminiscent of his poem "The Trappist Cemetery— Gethsemani"[45]) of the deceased monks as "definitively 'the community'—members with an eternal stability that will never be broken" (17), that should prompt reverence and love in the living brothers and call forth not only prayers for the dead but meditation on the mystery of vocation that brought so many diverse figures, from so many disparate places, to rest together there, as well as on the eschatological fulfillment of that vocation.

Discussion of the cloister combines background information about its relation to the classical atrium and the distinctive functions of its various wings, inspirational quotations from medieval commentators and reflections on its Marian symbolism and associations, and instructions about keeping silence there and in adjacent interior spaces (e.g. "No useless loudspeakers should be blaring in the regular places" [21]). Subsequent descriptions of the auditorium, chapter room, scriptorium, dormitory and refectory are oriented more toward functional information (e.g. the seating arrangements in chapter [24]; the location and function of the "*common box*" [25]) and specific directives (e.g. keeping the scriptorium desk neat [26]; sweeping out the cell [28–29]; proper decorum in entering and leaving the refectory [29]); but the deeper spiritual dimension is not overlooked, as St. Bernard's description of the monastery as a "*schola Christi* and an *auditorium Spiritus*" is associated particularly with the chapter

---

45. Thomas Merton, *A Man in the Divided Sea* (New York: New Directions, 1946), 89–91; Thomas Merton, *The Collected Poems of Thomas Merton* (New York: New Directions, 1977), 116–18. For a discussion, see Patrick F. O'Connell, "Thomas Merton's Wake-Up Calls: Aubades and Monastic Dawn Poems from *A Man in the Divided Sea*," *The Merton Annual*, 12 (1999), 156–63.

room, "where we meet to hear the word of God and where the Spirit of God speaks to our hearts" (23), and the various gestures prescribed in the refectory are associated with the presence of God in the community and the table fellowship of Jesus (29–30).

The transition from this opening "tour" of the regular places to the much more extensive and detailed survey of the first part of the monastic day that will occupy the rest of the conferences proper is effected by what may seem to be a minutely detailed discussion of the monastic bells that announce the various exercises (30–38)—including among much else the names of the three large bells in the church tower (Michael, Thomas and Mary [33]); the very precise note that the bells for vigils are rung "at two twenty-eight or -nine" (35); and an extensive "quiz" (answers provided), about what various types of bell-ringing throughout the day would signal, as a challenge and incentive to practice Merton's directive: "know your bells!" (36). But here too, as in the earlier discussion of the cemetery, the practical details are introduced by a quite lyrical reflection,[46] on bells as the "voice of heaven itself" (31) calling the monk to prayer, uniting him with God and also, in the spirit of John Donne's meditation on those "for whom the bell tolls," to the suffering and dying to whose needs "I must never become indifferent" (31). This section likewise concludes on a similarly reflective note with a brief meditative commentary on the bells for the Angelus, most meaningful when heard "in the midst of ordinary occupations—out in the field," a reminder of "the one great reality of our life, the mystery of the Incarnation and Redemption in Christ" (38).

In discussing the first of the offices of the monastic day, the night vigils (38–75), Merton begins with its spiritual significance, and that of the *opus Dei* in general, as both the monk's work and his rest, his compensation and refreshment, the training and preparation for "more interior prayer which, indeed, accompanies

46. For a similar appreciation of the spiritual role of bells, see chapter XIV of Part One in Thomas Merton, *Thoughts in Solitude* (New York: Farrar, Straus and Cudahy, 1958), 67–68.

the chanting of the psalms and prolongs it" (39). As its name
suggests, vigils is preeminently a time of wakefulness and attentiveness to God. Following St. Bernard, Merton stresses that
while the office includes prayer of compunction and lamentation,
it is above all an expression of praise and gratitude, for one comes
alone before God as a penitent, "immersed in our own shame
and misery" (41), but identified with the community and the
entire Body of Christ in glorifying God with and in Christ. Only
in this spirit are monks "Cistercians in the full sense of the word"
(41) (as distinguished, implicitly, from the "Trappist" emphasis
on penance). Such an approach is conducive to a "contemplative
appreciation" (44) of the psalms as prayed in solidarity with
Christ Himself. As he will later elaborate, providing once again
a Trinitarian understanding of monastic prayer, "Since contemplation is a realization of our union with Christ in the Holy Spirit,
then it is clear that for the divine office to lead to contemplation,
we should strive to realize how Christ sings in us during the
office, and thus become consciously united to Him in His
thoughts and His love and His contemplation of the Father. This
is the work of the Holy Spirit in us" (60).

Having emphasized the spiritual foundation of the office,
Merton can then go on, with the support of Pope Pius XII's encyclical *Mediator Dei*, to call attention to the "importance of rubrics and ceremonies" (45) as the outward expression of interior
worship and as a salutary guard against subjectivism and a de-
bilitating preoccupation with emotional and psychological states,
which are at best a distraction and at worst a serious danger to
spiritual growth. While exaggerated attention to externals can
result in "the contemplation and admiration of our own punctilious zeal" (48), when properly understood and practiced the ceremonies foster an atmosphere of peace and recollection, "save us
from the vulgarity and offensive singularity that inevitably creep
into a too subjective . . . attitude during choral prayer" (48), and
"unite us with the generations of saints and fathers who have
preceded us" (48). With these caveats Merton can move on to the
detailed instructions in the *Usages* on behavior in church, stress-

ing silence and reverence and order, but including such specific details as lowering the seats "only at the moment of sitting down, with the hand nearest the altar (for the sake of uniformity, and {because it is} slightly more reverent, as one turns a little toward the altar instead of away from it)" (54); one may notice even here Merton's concern to show his novices that details which may appear to be rather arbitrary and even picayune do indeed have a meaningful rationale if one gives them due consideration.

After providing this context, both spiritual and practical, for the office, Merton now turns to the actual structure of vigils, interweaving factual information on its progression with meditative reflection on particular texts. The invitatory psalm (94[95]) "sets the tone for the whole office" (62) by its call for "spiritual alertness and attention to God" (63), while various antiphons that accompany it for different feasts and seasons either highlight some aspect of the psalm or connect it to the day's particular celebration.

Merton then guides his audience through the successive segments of the night office: the hymn, borrowed by St. Benedict from the Church of St. Ambrose in Milan; the six psalms with their antiphons, in which the monk participates in "the mystical consciousness of the Church" which contemplates "the divine mystery—the 'reintegration of all in Christ'" (67); the lessons (readings) and their responsories, through which the mind is provided nourishment from the word of God, the writings of the Fathers and the lives of the saints (samples of which Merton provides from the Book of Proverbs, including a reference to his much loved sapiential text of Proverbs 8 in which "Wisdom reveals herself" as "God's own essence in so far as it contains His ideas and His plan for the world" [72], and from St. Ambrose's commentary on "these Old Testament themes of wisdom and folly" as re-visioned "in the New Testament context" [73]); the "*Te Deum*," the triumphant hymn of praise to the Father and to Christ "the King of Glory and conqueror of death" (74), and the briefer "*Te Decet Laus*," that brings vigils to a conclusion (except for the collect prayer and abbatial blessing) with "a beautiful example of the combination of rites, gestures, words and chant to make a perfect act of adoration with our whole being" (75).

The discussion of meditation that follows (75–92) is (along with the complementary section on *lectio divina* still to come) the least dependent on the particularities of the Cistercian *Usages* currently in force, and hence unaffected by revised norms. Thus it is perhaps the material of greatest lasting significance in this entire set of conferences. While it has been frequently, and correctly, pointed out that Merton does not offer a systematic "method" of prayer in his writings, in these instructions to the novices he does provide them with a clear overview of the major stages of meditation and numerous practical suggestions for how to meditate and what to meditate on.

His first point reiterates what he had emphasized at the very beginning of the conferences, that the various activities of the monastic day are not to be looked at as disconnected exercises but as contributing to a unified, holistic experience of life with God. Hence "monastic tradition always associates liturgical prayer with mental prayer. . . . [O]ne leads to the other, normally and naturally" (75–76). A failure to recognize and experience this complementarity is evidence of "an unmonastic approach . . . an unmonastic spirit" (76), and is both an effect and a cause of a disjointed spiritual life. Both psalmody and meditation are oriented to the praise and love of God, both nourished by the word of God and by an awareness of the divine presence; the first is more communal, more involved with the senses and the imagination, the second more personal, more interior, assimilating "the teaching that is given . . . from morning to night" (77) through liturgy, spiritual reading, spiritual direction, "or through *experience* itself" (77). In meditation the word "descends from the lips and mind into the *heart*" (77) (a classic formulation borrowed from the Eastern Church[47]).

---

47. See, for example, Bishop Kallistos Ware, *The Orthodox Way*, revised ed. (Crestwood, NY: St. Vladimir's Seminary Press, 2003), 123: "Normally three levels or degrees are distinguished in the saying of the Jesus Prayer. It starts as 'prayer

Merton then goes on to present what he calls the threefold purpose or triple function of meditation, which in fact lays out the successive stages of development from meditation to contemplation. The purpose of the first level of meditation is to understand and respond to God's saving word as experienced in scripture, in the teaching of the Church, in the events and encounters of daily life. Here Merton succinctly sets out specific topics for meditation: the last things, above all "God's merciful plan" (78) of salvation; the life and passion of Jesus as the source and agency of redemption; the "economy of God's love" (79) in the Church and sacraments, especially the Eucharist; the experience of Christ's love in one's own life; the divine attributes and their "*unfathomable* riches" (79) infinitely transcending their analogies in the contingent sphere of created reality. Merton stresses that while "'thought' or *consideratio*" is central to this first kind of meditation, it "is a matter of affective thinking, of thought impregnated with love and trust and humility" (79), in which thought deepens the affections, and the engagement of the affections reciprocally illuminates "the inner meaning of the truths we behold" (79).

The second function, and second level, of meditation, according to Merton, is for one "to *enter deeply into the school of life itself*, to make his whole life a meditation, a learning from God, a school of wisdom" (80). It moves from a multiplicity of thoughts and ideas to "the *simplicity of the intimate interior embrace which unites us to God in the depths of our being*. . . . a simple, general apprehension of God in faith and love" (80), from clarity and sensible consolation to "*darkness and unknowing*" (80). There is a sense of integration in which all life is experienced in the context of prayer, as "*impregnated with the love and action of God*" (81), the meditative and active dimensions of life mutually enrich one

---

of the lips', oral prayer. Then it grows more inward, becoming 'prayer of the intellect', mental prayer. Finally the intellect 'descends' into the heart and is united with it, and so the prayer becomes 'prayer of the heart' or, more exactly, 'prayer of the intellect in the heart'".

another, and a "meditative way of life" develops that "is *essentially realistic and concrete*" (81) and draws one away from a sterile focus on self.

The *"third and highest function"* (81) or stage of meditation moves "even beyond this unity within ourselves" to a participation "in God's own unity" (82), the apparent disappearance of "any knowing subject" (82) in the all-encompassing divine mystery, which paradoxically is the full realization of one's deepest identity, "the secret of our own being in the mind of God," where, Merton declares, echoing St. Paul (Gal. 2:20), "we 'are' in the fullest sense—so fully indeed that it is no longer we who are but Christ Who lives and is in us" (83). At this level of course one has passed beyond the "normal and ordinary" experience of God and is "over the threshold in the realm of purely mystical prayer" (83) where rules and degrees have lost all relevance and "God alone is the guide and master" (83). Meditation has become contemplation.

After this brief glimpse of the culmination of the process of growth in prayer, Merton returns to practical advice for setting out on the journey, including a warning not to become preoccupied with determining one's "degree of prayer" (84); recognizing that it is not the psychological but the theological effect of meditation, not subjective "lights" and consolations but the deepening of the theological virtues of faith, hope and love, that is the criterion of authentic meditation; realizing that meditation is nourished by appropriate and solid reading, that begins with training the imagination to focus on substantial realities rather than the seductive illusions of worldly existence; praying for divine assistance in learning to meditate, and in overcoming the inertia caused by a lack of deep desire for prayer; making use of visual aids, including prayer before the Blessed Sacrament, and of simple prayer forms like the Jesus Prayer.

While Merton had warned against attempts to "measure" one's success in meditation, he does indicate five "Signs of Progress," but they are all paradoxically linked to letting go of preoccupation with "getting somewhere" (87) in the spiritual life. The first is peace, which is dependent upon abandonment to the loving presence of Jesus and counters all agitation and anxiety with a tranquil acceptance of one's own spiritual poverty. Simplicity, the second sign, is marked by a decrease in the ability "to see and measure what is going on" (88), and a reduction in activity of reason, imagination and the emotions. Obscurity, as St. John of the Cross teaches, is a third sign of progress: the *"inability to make a discursive meditation"* (88) may be, for those who have reached a certain stage in prayer, an indication that a "blind 'turning to' God . . . a semi-passive yielding to grace in obscurity" is now to be "the whole essence of our prayer" (88–89). Purity, the *puritas cordis* taught by Cassian that is a complete surrender of self-will, the "little way" of St. Thérèse that is "unknown and poor, and yet utterly common, for it is the way of the Gospel" (90), is a fourth sign of progress. The final sign Merton mentions is generosity, a "patient and unobtrusive" charity that does not call attention to itself, that goes unnoticed even by oneself. Like all these signs of progress, it "has ceased to measure . . . . It does not compare itself with others. It minds its own business. . . . It has renounced ambition" (90–91).

In this context, Merton brings his teaching on meditation to a close by considering the question of the desire for mystical prayer. While he calls such a desire "perfectly licit" (91), not surprisingly he recommends humility, a sense of proportion that makes love, not mystical experience, the goal, and a sense of humor coupled with common sense. He concludes, "IT IS BEST NOT TO THINK TOO MUCH ABOUT BECOMING A 'MYSTIC.' You are more likely to become one if you forget all about it, and love God" (91). This teaching on meditative and contemplative prayer is certainly consistent with, and comparable to, that found in Merton's published writing, but its specific purpose of introducing the topic to the novices gives it a succinctness and orderliness of exposition not available elsewhere in precisely the same way.

Merton then returns to liturgical prayer with a discussion of the office of lauds (92–103), beginning with the admonition that to suppose that the "graces of contemplation" are to be received only in the context of private prayer is a "fatal illusion" (92).

Liturgical and personal prayer are mutually supportive parts of a continuum leading toward deeper union with God. "The spirit of lauds," in particular, "is a spirit of *contemplative praise*" (92), which "unites the waking of creation with the mystery of Christ's resurrection" (93). As with vigils, Merton combines a description of the constituent elements of this office with his own meditative reflections on particular texts, perhaps in even greater detail as the office is considerably shorter. He identifies the function of the introductory Psalm 66[67] as both focusing on the light of the new day and directing the monk to look forward "toward the great Day of the Lord when the whole earth shall be filled with the glory of the Lord and all nations shall praise Him" (95). Psalm 50[51] (the *Miserere*), which follows, "*the psalm par excellence of Christian compunction*" (96), is recommended as a source for meditation, which Merton models with his brief reflections on the three sections of the psalm, with their respective themes of recognizing and confessing one's sinfulness, experiencing the union of penitence and joy in receiving forgiveness, and celebrating the fruitfulness of penance for one's own life and, through one's example, for the lives of others. After a brief mention of other psalms used at Sunday lauds, Merton turns to the *Benedicite*, the hymn of the three young men in the fiery furnace from the Book of Daniel, which can "too easily become a mechanical routine" but properly serves both as a complement to the *Miserere* and as a way of incorporating all creation, all the "works of the Lord," into the Church's prayer, "our chorus of exultation" (98). He then looks at the three final psalms (148–50), successive hymns of praise that give the office its name and its character, in which redeemed humanity, risen with and in Christ, "is once again the high priest of creation, leading the choir of praise that rises from all creatures to the Father" (99). He advises his charges, in language that surely must have evoked the laughter of rueful self-recognition in oral presentation,[48] that

---

48. Because these conferences were completed before Merton's novitiate classes began to be taped in April 1962, no record of this material as it was actually presented is available. For comparison of written and oral presentation of

it is impossible to invite all creation to share in these divine praises "if we ourselves are still sunk in torpor" (99–100), or to enter fully into the acclamation of God as eternal King if anticipating the conclusion to the long night office tempts the monk "to relax in a mental stupor waiting for it all to end!" (101). He completes his treatment of lauds with the more serious admonition related to the *Benedictus*, the hymn of Zachary praising the God who enlightens those who sit in darkness and guides their feet in the way of peace (Lk. 1:79): "How tragic to sing these words every day and not know what they mean, to go on acting as if we had not received the mercy of God, as if we were abandoned, as if we still needed something, struggling to 'save ourselves'" (103). The *opus Dei* must not be simply a performance, the fulfillment of a duty required by the monastic state. It should be and can be a source of personal and communal illumination and transformation.

Not surprisingly, the longest single section of the *Monastic Observances* conferences is devoted to Mass and communion (104–49), though Merton indicates that he intended to return to the topic later in connection with the conventual or community Mass (109), which would have been part of the second half of the series. It is safe to assume, however, that the focus there would have been largely if not exclusively on the ceremonial aspects of the celebration, since he provides a thorough discussion of the theological and spiritual dimensions of the Eucharist in the context of the "private Masses" discussed here.

The initial section of these conferences on the Eucharist considers the practical issue of making provision for each monk-priest to celebrate a daily private Mass, giving due consideration both to the fact that ordination of virtually every choir religious is "not the normal thing, according to the tradition of the Order" (104), yet certainly had become the norm at that time (though no longer) in Cistercian monasteries, and to the consequent need to provide time in the *horarium* for Mass, theoretically permissible

---

other novitiate courses, see *Cassian and the Fathers*, xlvii–liv; *Pre-Benedictine Monasticism*, li–lxi; *Rule of Saint Benedict*, xlii–xlvi.

during any period set aside for *lectio*, but in practice normally taken care of immediately after lauds. This leads into the related issue of the anomaly of the non-priests customarily receiving communion at these private Masses rather than at the conventual Mass later in the morning, which would entail a longer fast as well as a longer Mass, cutting into work time, as well as raising the whole question of multiple private Masses being celebrated simultaneously, which Merton recognizes as a problem but defends by recourse to the encyclical *Mediator Dei* of Pius XII. He notes, "It is possible that a satisfactory solution to some of these problems might someday be worked out. In practice we have to be satisfied with what we have at the moment" (108). The solution, of course, with relaxation of the fasting laws and especially the reinstitution of concelebration, was much closer than Merton or his audience realized at the time.[49]

Having dealt with these practical issues, Merton then turns his attention to a fundamental understanding of the meaning of the Mass, which has both doctrinal and spiritual dimensions. He is especially careful in this section to provide the novices with a solid grounding in Eucharistic theology, to correct inadequate notions which some of his more pious charges might have brought with them into the monastery, such as the idea that the Mass is principally "a device to produce the Blessed Sacrament" (110) for personal worship, or the "naive and artificial" (111) allegorical approach popular earlier in the century that fancifully associated the parts of the Mass with events of Christ's passion. Merton directs his students' attention to the text of the ordinary of the Mass, with its prayers clearly indicating the central meaning of the Mass as mutual gift, the sacrificial offering of Christ to the Father in praise and thanksgiving (*eucharistia*), and God's gift

---

49. Though ambivalent about concelebration as a manifestation of a unity he did not feel, at least at that point, Merton writes in his journal for July 12, 1965, after concelebrating for the first time: "There is no question that this makes far more sense than the old way (private Mass, then High Mass) for here the community *all* assembles, and most go to communion, and guests are there, etc." (*Dancing in the Water of Life*, 268–69).

of Himself to His people as the Bread of Life and the Cup of salvation, through which "WE IN TURN BECOME THE FATHER'S GIFT TO THE SON AND THE SON'S GIFT TO THE FATHER; AND MORE: GOD GIVES HIMSELF TO OUR NEIGHBOR THROUGH OURSELVES AND TO US THROUGH OUR NEIGHBOR" (119). Merton makes sure the novices are aware of the theological meaning of "real presence" by a systematic outline of erroneous and inadequate understandings and a clear and comprehensive presentation of the traditional doctrine of transubstantiation, including the distinction between sacramental presence and "sensible local and natural presence" with its "vain imaginings" and sentimentality (126) (Christ as prisoner of the tabernacle, etc.).

Doctrinal clarity about Christ's presence in the Eucharist is the foundation for awareness of the effect of communion, becoming one with Christ in His body, soul and divinity, "as intimately united to the Word of God as if He were the soul of our soul and the being of our being" (130), the "mysterious and anticipated realization" of eternal life here and now (131). Merton emphasizes the centrality of joy in this sacramental union, not joy as a superficial emotion but as a deep and abiding awareness of sharing in the divine life through Christ's absolutely unmerited gift of Himself: "it is God Himself who is substantially present to our souls and is Himself their joy" (136). At the same time the Eucharist is both sign and cause of unity with all those who share in the one Body of Christ, and indeed with all those for whom Christ offered His life, to "the exclusion of none" (141). Here Merton emphasizes the intrinsic relationship of Eucharistic communion to issues of poverty, injustice, oppression, "the intolerable scandal of race prejudice" (142):

> The meaning of the Eucharist is not clear, the glory of Christ is not visible in His Church, if it is merely a ceremony by which we display *our union with our friends and immediate neighbors* while at the same time remaining indifferent to those who belong to a different class, a different race, a different society, a different school of thought . . . . No Christian should be able to rest satisfied on this earth as long as there are other

men who are in want, who are abandoned, ill-treated, robbed
and oppressed by other men. Our Eucharistic life has reference
to this greatest of all duties, after our duty to God Himself—
really one and the same duty. (141–42)

Here one of the earliest and most forthright expressions of Merton's "turn toward the world" in the late 1950s is firmly rooted
in a quite traditional Eucharistic theology and spirituality, and
is addressed not to an audience of social activists but to aspiring
monks in a cloistered contemplative monastery. Merton is already
affirming, as he will repeatedly do in the final decade of his life,
that authentic monastic life must be a way of engaging with, not
escaping from, the problems facing the rest of humanity.

This embeddedness in tradition is made more evident by the
fact that he goes on to conclude his teaching on the Eucharist by
providing suggestions on how to make a proper thanksgiving after
communion and instruction on visits to the Blessed Sacrament
throughout the day. Social awareness and traditional devotional
practices are not viewed as in any way incompatible; both flow
from an awareness of the full range of effects of Eucharistic intimacy with Christ.

The separation of the section on *lectio divina* that follows
(149–83) from the earlier section on meditation is somewhat artificial, but it is pedagogically effective in that it reinforces Merton's repeated point about the alternating rhythms of communal
and private prayer creating a complementary unity, and it does
reflect the actual monastic schedule that includes both the short
period for personal reflection between vigils and lauds and the
longer period for *lectio* before prime.

In actuality, Merton's instruction in this section ranges much
more widely than just a discussion of spiritual reading. Beginning
with the importance, not always recognized in the past, of distinguishing between the time of *lectio* and "intervals," the periods
between formal excercises, he declares, "To regard *lectio divina*
as something incidental or unimportant is *to miss the whole point
of the contemplative life*" (150). This leads into a reflection, based

on St. Bernard, on the traditional interpretation of the story of Martha and Mary (and Lazarus) as teaching the priority of the contemplative dimension in monastic life, and on the role of *lectio* in *"provid[ing] us with 'contemplative leisure'"* (153), which "does not imply a neglect of good works" (151) but is opposed to making work an end in itself and to looking for one's identity and worth in one's accomplishments. This, Merton suggests, is the spirit of Babel, a futile effort to be one's own creator, that can only end in "division and confusion" (154).

This allusion to the scene of "wrangling of tongues" (155) leads quite naturally into a lengthy excursus on Cistercian silence (155–67), of course one of the best known characteristics of traditional Trappist life. Merton stresses silence as "a *positive presence*, the presence of Him Who is not heard, so that when all confused sounds and trivial noises are hushed, then the eloquent voice of reality, of God Himself, makes itself heard in peacefulness and silence" (155). He strikes a familiar Mertonian note in pointing out that an atmosphere of authentic spiritual silence incorporates such "good natural sounds" as birds, rain and wind, but should exclude artificial noise such as "the agitation of many machines" as well as the meaningless chatter prevalent in "the world" (155–56). He explores the various implications of the Cistercian rule of silence, emphasizing that it is not a rejection of communion with others, within or without the enclosure, but a preference for *"inner communication* that is higher and better than communication by words" (157), and that it is waived when the needs of charity demand it. He provides a detailed exegesis of the directives in the *Usages* on silence and on the use of signs, to make sure that the novices understand exactly what is required of them in their new way of life. He acknowledges that for novices to exercise their newfound skills in sign-making is normal and natural, and that "the pleasure of useless signs and spontaneous fooling is the *one very definite form of recreation* which is still within reach" (161), but warns that this can become a kind of addiction, and that they should not *"depend on this as a safety valve"* (161). Mention in the *Usages* of the "Great Silence" in force "from the evening Angelus to the end of the collect of Prime" (166) returns the focus to the period of *lectio*, generally about a half hour between the end of Mass and mixt, but more than two hours if one is not at private Mass—Merton's appreciative comments on this period as "a very fine opportunity to do some serious reading and thinking . . . . with its special silence, its relative coolness in summer" (166) seem more applicable to himself than to the novices, as it principally pertains to a priest celebrating the conventual Mass or a later Mass for guests.

At this point there is one more brief detour as he considers the problem of falling asleep during meditation periods, or even in choir, and looks both at causes: spiritual dryness and/or conflicts, psychological unrest, even not being adapted for this vocation—and at solutions (even smelling salts!): generally the need for mental and spiritual balance. He acknowledges that particularly for those without a good grounding in Latin, the long offices can be boring and induce sleep, and that they can be "objectively tedious" at times for others as well, especially when "the poor quality of the chant" (168) drags out some of the responsories (a rare look in these conferences at the imperfect reality of life in the monastery rather than at the ideals at which to aim). A final comment that sleep may be induced by *"reading all the wrong things"* (168) during *lectio* brings the focus back at last to the subject of reading.

The period before prime in the Benedictine tradition is devoted primarily to meditation on scripture.[50] Merton calls attention to the relatively recent official encouragement of scripture reading among all Catholics, and notes, "this applies especially

---

50. Merton's consideration of *lectio* in his conferences on the Benedictine *Rule* takes a broader survey of possible sources for spiritual reading (*Rule of Saint Benedict*, 134–35; see also additional notes 6 and 7 [223–25]). For the traditional connection of *lectio* with *meditatio*, *oratio* and *contemplatio*, see Appendix 1 to Thomas Merton, *An Introduction to Christian Mysticism: Initiation into the Monastic Tradition* 3, ed. Patrick F. O'Connell, MW 13 (Kalamazoo, MI: Cistercian Publications, 2008), 332–40, Merton's discussion of the classic source for this fourfold pattern, the *Scala Claustralium* of Guigo the Carthusian.

to monks. . . . It would be a very sad thing if monks, men of God, men who chant the office, were less able to read and appreciate the scriptures" (173). Thus he emphasizes the importance of learning how to read the Bible, beginning with the observation that though, as the word of God, it is unlike any other book, one best begins to read the Bible as one would any other book, or rather collection of books. He indicates that a meditative or devotional reading of the scriptures needs to be preceded by and grounded in a more objective approach: "Our scripture reading is not always a 'study,' but sometimes it must be" (176). There is a need to understand the literal sense of the scriptures, and to recognize the theological doctrines presented in various books. Merton provides concrete suggestions for various study plans, but stresses that for monks in particular this is not to be a dry intellectual enterprise or a strictly academic exercise. "When one studies wisely and discreetly, his study becomes a recreation, a joy, a help to the spiritual life and to prayer. When one studies unwisely, his study becomes a burden, a curse, a source of weariness and disgust" (179). Study is not to be seen as an end in itself but as a necessary, but not sufficient, preparation for being nourished spiritually by the word of God. "The main point," Merton emphasizes, following St. Bernard, "*is love.* . . . The letter without the spirit is poison" (179–80). Hence the importance in the Benedictine tradition of interiorizing the scriptures, of making them one's own by memorizing them, taking them to heart: "In *meditatio psalmorum*, we enter into ourselves to 'plant,' so to speak, the word of God in the inmost depths of our being" (183). This is the ultimate purpose of *lectio*, and of course it enriches the time of choral prayer as well, as Merton shows by concluding his discussion with reflections on verse 12 of the *Miserere* (Ps. 50[51]), previously considered as a psalm of lauds, in which prayer for a clean heart and a steadfast spirit leads to union with Christ, such that "my heart is hidden in His heart by virtue of the faith and love with which I make this line my own" (183).

Then follow the two briefest sections of the conferences, on mixt (183–87) and on intervals (187–89), both largely but not

exclusively informational. Mixt is the "light refection" taken at
5:45 or 6:00 a.m. (184), to sustain the monk until the main meal at
noon. Merton investigates the etymology and original function
of mixt ("not for everyone" [184]), but then turns his attention to
the brief blessing before and grace after mixt (distinguishing the
two), with further attention to the latter as a time for remembering
benefactors (who often in the past and present provided special
foods), a reminder that "the monk should cultivate *a spirit of gratitude and appreciation* towards everyone" (186). After brief mention
of frustulum, the even more spartan fare provided in place of mixt
on fast days, Merton turns to intervals properly so-called (as distinguished from periods of *lectio*), those brief times "usually
wedged in between two other exercises" to be used "for material
concerns and unavoidable cares" (187–88) like brushing one's
teeth, but which are also opportunities for a quick visit to the
Blessed Sacrament or the cemetery, etc. Here Merton looks ahead
to other intervals throughout the day, noting that while the interval after morning work is occupied for the novices with classes
it provides time for professed monks to shave, cut their fingernails
and the like; the brief interval after Sunday Mass is best spent
prolonging one's thanksgiving after communion, but also allows
for "needs of nature" (188), while the time following afternoon
work, though not actually an interval but a period for *lectio*, "is
the logical time for a shower, or a shave" (188–89), but should not
be frittered away, nor should the time after supper, officially an
interval but "long enough for *lectio*" (189). Thus Merton accounts
for and provides specific instruction about even the least conse-
quential blocks of time during the monastic day.

   What turns out to be the last of the liturgical hours to be
considered by Merton (189–206) is of primarily "historical" interest today, since within a decade the office of prime would be
suppressed, but it seemed to have a good deal of intrinsic attrac-
tion for Merton himself, as having a transitional function, a morning prayer more personal and more oriented toward activity than
the contemplative office of lauds it complements (as compline
will likewise balance vespers at the close of the day). It is transi-

tional even spatially, as its first part takes place in the church while its second moves to the chapter room (and is actually discussed under the general heading of "THE MORNING CHAPTER" in these conferences [198 ff.]). As the first of the "little hours" it sets the basic structure they will follow: hymn, three psalms with a common antiphon, capitulum and versicle, the *Pater Noster* and a brief collect prayer (to be followed for prime only by the readings and sermon in the chapter room).

Merton's affection for prime as a dawn service is evident in his detailed, verse-by-verse exegesis of its opening hymn "*Jam lucis orto sidere*" with its praise of the coming of daylight. Merton's lyrical appreciation here of the hour of sunrise, "one of the most beautiful hours of the day, and one which many people never see or appreciate," is reminiscent of the similar encomium in *Day of a Stranger*.[51] He continues, "It is like the hour of the creation of the world, a new start: the coolness, silence, mist, birds beginning to sing, the sun rising over the woodlands to the east, the cows lowing, brothers starting out on wagons or tractors. It is a great grace for us to be awake, alive, alert at this hour of the day. Remember and regret the days when we did not see the dawn. As the sun rises, *it is natural to pray*" (191–92). He links the hymn to the dawn prayer of Mescalero Apaches, which he quotes, and with "the prayer of the Moslem, prostrate toward Mecca at sunrise" (192), but for Christians the dawn is filled with symbolism of Christ the Light of the World. Liberated from the "*vanitates*" of worldly diversions, the monk is able to respond to "the hills, the fields, the woods, the flowers" as "given us by God as messengers" (193), though the monk is not thereby immune to temptations of "wild schemes . . . silly obsessions . . . dizzy notions" (194) from which he prays in the hymn to be freed. Merton sums up the message of the hymn as: "*the day is a grace given us by God.*

---

51. Thomas Merton, *Day of a Stranger* (Salt Lake City: Gibbs M. Smith, 1981), 51; see also the opening passage of "The Night Spirit and the Dawn Air," the third section of Thomas Merton, *Conjectures of a Guilty Bystander* (Garden City, NY: Doubleday, 1966), 117–18.

Let us use it well" and thereby "make our whole day an act of worship giving glory to God" (195).

The rest of prime (part 1) is treated in more summary fashion. Mention of the psalms of prime becomes the occasion to point out St. Benedict's arrangement of the psalms to include recitation of the entire psalter each week. The antiphons of prime, Merton notes, are the only part of the ritual that pertains to a particular feast. The short scripture reading, or capitulum, alternates between the "splendid, solemn" text of 1 Timothy 1:17 on feast days and the simpler admonition to "Love peace and truth" (Zech. 8:19) on ordinary days: "The ferial text is more ascetic (*bios praktikos*); the festive text is more contemplative (*bios theoretikos*). Meditate on the difference between them and we will see what the Church means by action and contemplation" (197). The versicle, "Rise up O Christ . . ." heralds the coming of the light of salvation, and the collect prayer likewise responds to the new day as a gift of God.

With this, the community processes into the chapter room, where it reassembles "not so much as a choir but as a family" (198), first to hear the martyrology, the announcement of the saints to be commemorated on the following day, a way of recognizing and celebrating not only the particular saints mentioned but the sanctification of time itself. The prayers that follow are oriented principally to requesting help for the day to come, so that "His splendor will shine in our works, without our necessarily seeing or experiencing it" (203).

"The Morning Chapter properly so-called" (206) follows immediately on the last of the prayers of prime, with chapter talks by the abbot and sermons on feast days by other priests in the community. Merton admonishes the novices to regard the abbot's teaching "with the eyes of faith and receive it in a supernatural spirit" rather than taking "too human and exterior a view of his talks and teaching" (209), advice he was not always able to carry out himself.[52] He notes that after a certain period "we may be-

---

52. For critical comments on the abbot's chapter talks, see *Search for Solitude*, 244–45 [1/2/59], 310 [7/26/59], 312–13 [7/30/59]; Thomas Merton, *Turning*

come quite familiar with many of his themes, and feel that we are not getting 'anything new'" (209) (an observation more applicable to himself than to his audience, of course), but concludes by reminding "those who are tempted to be bored with the apparent foolishness and simplicity of the doctrines preached in chapter" (!) of St. Paul's words to the Corinthians (1 Cor. 1:17-24) that the "foolishness" of the Cross of Christ is wiser than the wisdom of men (210). This is followed by a "parenthesis" on preaching which of course would have no direct application to the novices (except the few who were already ordained when they entered) for some years to come, but expresses Merton's own principles for sermons:[53] "be short and to the point" (210)—trying to hold the audience's attention beyond twenty or twenty-five minutes is futile; speak in a "lively, interesting manner," with a seasoning of humor but not a full course of it; don't try to convince those unlikely to agree with you; focus on the Word of God and common doctrine, not idiosyncratic opinions; "avoid what is lofty and obscure, or fantastic and exaggerated; avoid old wives' tales and far-fetched stories of wonders and revelations that tend to make the truth doubtful rather than more persuasive" (211). The fact that Merton mentions these principles, particularly the last, suggests that such topics were not unknown among his confreres! As a kind of appendix to this discussion of chapter talks and sermons Merton raises the issue of whether there is, or should be, an *"official spirituality to which everyone in the house has some obligation to conform"* (211). He is adamant that such a thing does not and should not exist: "To treat spirituality

Toward the World: The Pivotal Years. Journals, vol. 4: 1960–1963, ed. Victor A. Kramer (San Francisco: HarperCollins, 1996), 80 [12/27/60]; *Dancing in the Water of Life*, 144 [9/12/64], 205–206 [2/16/65].

53. For Merton's appreciation of the preaching of Fr. John of the Cross (Wasserman), whom he calls "one of the few men in this monastery who has anything to say in a sermon," see *Conjectures*, 142–43; in the original of this passage, a journal entry for March 30 (Palm Sunday), 1958, he had called Fr. John of the Cross (who subsequently left the community) "really the only one here who has anything to say" (*Search for Solitude*, 186).

as something official and obligatory is to kill it at the root" (211). His subsequent comments suggest that not all members of the community would agree with this assessment, and that there could be a tendency to evaluate and judge others according to how closely they conformed to what an individual or group considered to be the proper standard. While Merton recognizes that a particular house may have its own unique spirit, largely conveyed by the abbot, and that certain qualities characteristic of early Cistercian life, "austerity, simplicity, humility, poverty, love of solitude" (212) are of perennial value, he insists that the Cistercian "spirit" is simply the authentic monastic spirit, that can take many legitimate forms, and that it is the demand for *"absolute conformity"* that is actually "contrary to the spirit of our Order" as it threatens to stifle the action of the Holy Spirit in individual lives (213). Aside from a final explanation of what the expression to "speak of our Order" (213) means—basically to "speak of the way we are keeping our rule" (215), though it also includes news about other houses, recent deaths, etc.—these significant and characteristic reflections on what authentic Cistercian spirituality should mean bring to a close the discussion of the chapter proper. The remaining pages (215–50) focus exclusively and exhaustively on the chapter of faults, a topic of limited interest today but obviously one that needed to be carefully and sympathetically explained to the original audience, who would have found the custom among the most demanding adjustments to be made in the transition from secular to monastic life.

After surveying the historical background for the chapter of faults in the desert fathers, the *Rule* (where only self-accusations are mentioned), the institutionalization of the procedure, including proclamations of others, in the tenth and eleventh centuries, and the exaggerated and hyper-dramatized imposition of penances at La Trappe by de Rancé in the seventeenth century (and at Gethsemani in the late 1800s by Dom Benedict Berger), Merton takes considerable pains to point out the quite circumscribed nature of the chapter of faults in modern Cistercian practice. Not only is it "no longer thought healthy to make use of exaggerated and artificial humiliations" (219); it is recognized that when mis-used, the chapter of faults "can do much harm" to both pro-claimed and proclaimer, who "may be sinning against charity or justice and actively harming his brother's soul" (219–20). He makes clear that the chapter is neither a court of law nor a place for debating the rules nor an opportunity for analyzing others' supposed moral or spiritual defects. Its focus is not on real or imagined sins, but on infractions of rules and usages, which may involve no moral culpability at all. It is a vehicle for "keeping regularity and order in the community," a "purely external" function but "by no means a mere formality" (223); it also "provide[s] an ascetic exercise" both "on the part of the one *pro-claiming* himself or another and on the part of the one *proclaimed*" (224). The irregularities to be proclaimed are violations of the *Constitutions* (quite rare), of the *Rule* (not uncommon) or of the *Usages* (most frequent)—but it is generally a question of exterior faults, deficiencies of observance (Merton references the proper manner of bowing, though his list of irregularities in relation to the Benedictine *Rule* includes more serious lapses): it is not the role of the proclaimer to pass moral judgement on the one pro-claimed, but simply to call attention to a failure of some sort in outward behavior (which may involve an ethical lapse as well, but that is a concern for a superior or a confessor).

Having clarified the matter of the chapter, Merton goes on to take up the manner, the proper procedures for making and taking proclamations, both the actual rituals involved and the appropriate spirit: on the part of the proclaimer, charity, empathy and a maturity of love that excludes "harsh, bitter accusations; exaggerated wording; language that implies contempt or destruc-tive criticism" (232) as well as all mockery or ridicule; on the part of the one proclaimed, humility and attentiveness, lack of resent-ment and gratitude even when the proclamation may seem ten-dentious or made with less than pure motives. Merton concludes on a note of irritation with those agitating to abolish the practice: "Let us accept the chapter of faults as it is, with its imperfections, and be content. The Lord will bless this attitude, much more than the attitude of those who are so eager to change everything that soon they will leave nothing whatever of the Cistercian life intact" (239).

The section on public penances that follows strikes somewhat the same note: "It is possible that the early Trappist reformers exaggerated the importance of public penances, but it is equally likely that we underestimate them" (239). The purpose of these penances, according to Merton, is threefold: to correct the erring brother and so bring healing to him personally, to make reparation for the fault and restore balance and order to the community, and to serve as a reminder to others of the seriousness of faults in relation both to God and to one's fellow monks. The ideal is to see such penances as acts of worship, though Merton acknowledges that "At the present time one feels that they are simply done with the maximum possible good humor. One tries to be a good sport about the whole thing; that is all. Well, that is something, but it isn't very much" (241). He goes on to describe the various penances as found both in the *Rule* and in the *Usages*, from temporary exclusion from common life for grave faults to various forms of kneeling and prostration in public, some no longer possible at Gethsemani because of crowded conditions, but described anyway. This leads into the brief final comments on the use of the discipline, which can be, but seldom is, imposed as a public penance, but is normally a brief "quasi-liturgical" weekly practice, "the only instrument of penance whose use is formally prescribed in our Order" (249). Recognizing that the custom is "a medieval practice, remote from the early spirit of the liturgy," and that it "has its limitations," Merton nevertheless advises the novices that "there is no point in making a big fuss over them. The simplest and most obvious thing to do is to take the penance as it is given to us, in a spirit of humility, mortification and faith" (249). The fact that the *Observances* conferences end with this exhaustive catalogue of penances, rather than with reflections on vespers, compline, and "early to bed," is in one sense accidental and unintended, but as Merton's closing comments point out, it does serve as a salutary reminder to new members of the community "not to take rules lightly and not to disregard the importance of religious observance," while his final sentence puts the emphasis where it belongs when he says that "a spirit of sanity and love" rather than "fear of being caught and punished" (250) must be the true motive for authentic monastic observance.

While the conferences as delivered end here, an appendix entitled "Spiritual Direction in the Monastic Setting" (251–78), not an "observance" per se but certainly part of the customary practice of monastic life, has been added to the mimeographed version of the notes distributed to the students at the conclusion of the course. Not addressed to novices, it may have been included less for them than for formation directors in other houses of the Order who also received copies. With a history of its own that will be discussed below, the appendix is a clearly organized essay consisting of a preface and five parts.

Following the brief preface, which points out that the role of a spiritual director is not to solve all one's problems or to make all one's decisions, but to provide wise guidance that will enhance rather than limit authentic spiritual freedom, the first main section, *"The Life-Giving Action of Jesus in His Church"* (255–58), articulates a broad spiritual and theological framework for direction. Here Merton emphasizes that the grace of Christ is mediated "through the Church and through His visible representatives" (256), requiring submission to authority, not as "a mere arbitrary exercise of human power" (256) but as an agency of freedom, a "liberation from slavery" that "opens the way for us to attain perfection by the free gift of ourselves in love" (256). The Spirit works in the Church through human instruments, both hierarchical and charismatic, as well as directly by interior spiritual transformation.

In this context, he then turns in the second section to the role of *"The Spiritual Director"* (258–61); he puts forth a quite "high" doctrine of the director, stating that *"The spiritual Father is in the place of God to the soul, . . . is, in all truth, Jesus for the faithful Christian. He is a 'sacrament,' a 'mystery' of Christ, in whom the Holy Spirit acts in a very special manner for our sanctification"*

(258–59). He points out that while the director is generally freely chosen, in the context of religious formation the responsibility for spiritual direction of candidates is canonically vested in the novice master, who has both "a *juridical* function to help them decide their vocation, to select or reject them, to form them for their religious life" (259–60) and "a *charismatic* function" (260) to guide their spiritual development. While acknowledging that the master is "human and fallible, and can easily be mistaken" (261), Merton affirms that faith in the working of God's grace through the agency of the master can transcend these limitations and allow the master to be an instrument of authentic spiritual formation and growth.

In section three, *"The Spiritual Father in Monastic Tradition"* (261–66), Merton focuses on the difference between a spiritual director who "simply guides and teaches, according to an externally codified rule, or according to spiritual books" (261), and genuine spiritual fatherhood as understood and practiced in monastic tradition, the role of the *abba* who "makes us sons of God by imparting to us his own life, his own spirit—this is a real participation in the divine paternity" (261). Through love, prayer, discernment, patience and meekness joined with firmness, the father forms spiritual sons, but this is possible only to the extent that the father is himself spiritual, guided by the Holy Spirit not only in his dealings with the directee but in his own life with God.

The fourth and longest section, on *"The Nature and Efficacy of Spiritual Direction"* (267–72), emphasizes that true direction goes beyond guiding the subject away from sin, or general commentary on the spiritual life, or exhortations to virtue, or warnings against hidden tendencies or weaknesses—none of which focuses on the uniqueness of the person being directed. Genuine direction involves manifestation of conscience, "the revelation of one's inmost tendencies . . . *with a view to guidance and support in striving for perfection*" (270). It requires on the director's part an empathetic identification with a "person's interests and inmost strivings" (271) joined with "an objective quality" that can see both the limitations and the potential of the directee in a way that he himself does not (272). Such a perspective is possible only through "charity and paternal affection" that "can give a real inner knowledge of souls" and enables the director to "see that soul through the eyes of Jesus Christ and love him with the heart of Christ" (272).

Such a relationship requires on the part of the directee a complete *"Openness,"* the focus of the final section of the essay (272–78). *"One most know how to manifest one's inner self, and be able to do so with a certain amount of freedom"* (272). This involves the revelation not only of one's sins, temptations and struggles but *"All the movements of our soul"* (273), without any prejudgement of which are good and which are evil. Such openness requires a high degree of trust in the spiritual Father, but above all in God who has appointed him as guide. Honesty of this sort is an aspect of the surrender of one's own will, the "complete self-renunciation" that is essential to "true monastic perfection" (276–77). This humility is a liberation, "freedom from all care, . . . because this docility to the representative of God opens the way for the unimpeded action of the Holy Spirit in the soul, and it is the Spirit Who sanctifies, guides and forms the soul, rather than the spiritual Father, who is merely an instrument and mediator" (277). Such a result is in turn possible only to the extent that the Father himself "strive[s] to be holy and to be a man of prayer" (278). If he does so, and the disciple has the faith to look past the inevitable imperfections of the master and see the action of God's Spirit in him, then "God will surely give great graces through the action of the spiritual Father, graces which the Father himself will scarcely realize, of which perhaps he will know nothing at all. . . . Everything depends upon the faith of the son and of the Father, permitting God to work in them" (278).

Thus Merton tries to adapt the teaching of spiritual paternity, particularly characteristic of the desert fathers, whom he cites repeatedly in this last section, to contemporary monastic formation, in which he himself was so directly involved. The extent to which he was able to put these principles into practice he himself would certainly not presume to judge, but the essay provides clear evidence of his engagement with this dimension of his own vocation, drawing upon his experience as master of students

(1951–1955) and reflecting his early years as master of novices. As such it is a valuable document, though its rather idealized and "entirely supernatural" (278) conception of the spiritual director and his role should not be taken as Merton's "last word" on the subject.[54]

* * * * * * *

The *Monastic Observances* conferences are extant in two versions: the mimeographed copy put together for distribution to the novices in the class and also made available to other houses of the Order, which is found in Volume 15 of Merton's "Collected Essays," the 24-volume bound set of published and unpublished materials assembled at the Abbey of Gethsemani and available both there and at the Thomas Merton Center of Bellarmine University in Louisville, KY; and Merton's own typescript, with extensive handwritten additions, which he had in front of him as he lectured, now in the archives of the Bellarmine Merton Center. The first is a text of 159 numbered pages, headed "OUR MONASTIC OBSERVANCES", preceded by an unnumbered table of contents page headed "MONASTIC OBSERVANCES", and fol-

---

54. On this topic see Thomas Merton, *Spiritual Direction and Meditation* (Collegeville, MN: Liturgical Press, 1960), 3–42; *Introduction to Christian Mysticism*, 251–332; Thomas Merton, "Spiritual Direction," *The Merton Seasonal*, 32.1 (Spring 2007), 3–17; and especially Merton's later essay "The Spiritual Father in the Desert Tradition," first published in 1968 (*Contemplation in a World of Action*, 269–93), which echoes in its title the third section of the appendix here. See also Merton's statement on the eve of his departure for Asia: "The real essence of monasticism is the handing down from master to disciple of an uncommunicable experience. That is to say, an experience that cannot be communicated in terms of philosophy, that cannot be communicated in words. It can only be communicated on the deepest possible level. And this . . . to me is the most important thing. This is the only thing in which I am really interested. There is nothing else that seems to me to have the same kind of primary importance" (Thomas Merton, *Preview of the Asian Journey*, ed. Walter H. Capps [New York: Crossroad, 1989], 34–35). Patrick Bludworth emphasizes the continuing importance of this issue for Merton in his essay "Desert Fathers and Asian Masters: Thomas Merton's Outlaw Lineage," *The Merton Annual*, 17 (2004), 166–94.

lowed by a separately numbered twenty-page appendix headed "SPIRITUAL DIRECTION IN THE MONASTIC SETTING", preceded by its own unnumbered contents page headed "APPENDIX / Contents of: SPIRITUAL DIRECTION IN THE MONASTIC SETTING." The second is a text of 120 pages, all but one of which is typed,[55] headed "OUR MONASTIC OBSERVANCES." The typescript is numbered beginning on page 2 (the page number regularly preceded by "Observances") and running through page 117; the discrepancy in the total number of pages is due to the insertion of page 4a (on the Gethsemani church as a minor basilica), a mispagination in which page 63 is initially typed 62 then altered by hand to the correct page number, but is then followed by a second page also numbered 63 but not altered, nor are the page numbers that follow; and the final two pages of the typescript both numbered 117. Handwritten additions and alterations are found both on the typed pages and on the otherwise blank facing pages. This typescript includes neither a table of contents page nor the appendix on spiritual direction.

Merton's typescript, with its handwritten changes, serves as the copy text for the present edition of *Monastic Observances*. Since the mimeographed version was copied from this typescript, it has no independent authority as a witness to the text, except for the table of contents page, found only there, and the appendix, to be discussed below. All Merton's alterations in the copy text, including both handwritten changes and on-line corrections made in the process of typing (i.e. cancelling a word or phrase and immediately substituting another) are listed in Appendix A, Textual Notes. Thus the interested reader is enabled to distinguish between the preliminary draft of Merton's notes and the revisions made before the conferences were actually delivered. A handful of these additions and alterations that are not incorporated into the mimeographed version, presumably because they were added by Merton after the typist had reached that point in the text, but

---

55. Page 28 (62–65 of this edition), Merton's commentary on the Invitatory Psalm (94[95]).

before Merton himself had commented on the material in class
(since there is no indication that he later revised the notes in anticipation of presenting the *Observances* conferences a second
time), are grouped in a separate section following the initial list.
Errors, whether of omission or of mistranscription, in the mimeographed version of the text are not recorded since they have no
independent authority vis-à-vis the copy text.

The appendix on "Spiritual Direction in the Monastic Setting"
is also extant in two other forms, each entitled "SPIRITUAL DI-
RECTION": a 26-page typescript and a 36-page typescript, both
part of the collection at the Bellarmine Thomas Merton Center;
the text in these two versions is virtually identical (the discrepancy
in the number of pages being due mainly to the difference in
font—elite vs. pica—of the two typescripts), but is considerably
different from that found in the *Monastic Observances* mimeograph. Also extant in the Merton Center archives are two sheets
of reader's suggestions, apparently from an unidentified prospec-
tive publisher, commenting on three essays by Merton: the second
of these is "The Neurotic Personality in the Monastic Life,"[56] written some time before Merton's encounter with the psychiatrist
Gregory Zilboorg at St. John's University in July 1956, since in his
journal for July 29, 1956 Merton notes that Zilboorg severely criti-
cized the article and that he had "engineered" Merton's attendance at the workshop "partly because of the danger of the article
being published and partly because he had sensed my own
difficulties."[57] The third, entitled "Your Will and Your Vocation,"[58]
is dated November 1955. The first is "Spiritual Direction," and
the page references of the reader's suggestions make clear that
the 36-page typescript is being commented on. The three essays,
and quite possibly others (the reader's comments only cover part
of the third essay and presumably were continued on a subse-

---

56. Published in *The Merton Annual*, 4 (1991), 3–19, edited with an introductory note by Patrick Hart, ocso.

57. *Search for Solitude*, 58–59.

58. Published in *The Merton Seasonal*, 34.2 (Summer 2009), 3–11.

quent page or pages, no longer extant, that may have included observations on additional pieces as well), had apparently been collected by Merton in view of possible publication, some time after November 1955, when "Your Will and Your Vocation" was written, but probably before July 1956, since it is unlikely that Merton would have continued to contemplate publication of "The Neurotic Personality in the Monastic Life" after Zilboorg's hostile critique of the essay. Thus the original version of the "Spiritual Direction" essay was probably written some time between October 1955, when Merton became novice master, and the summer of 1956. The "Spiritual Direction in the Monastic Setting" version, found in the *Monastic Observances* mimeograph, clearly represents a revision of this original text; it includes a new "Preface" dated 1958, and is extensively rewritten, resulting in a text that eliminates certain rather extended digressions (on the identity of the "Father" in the Prologue to the Benedictine *Rule* and on the psychological meaning of "transference") and one that gives to the topic a greater sense of flexibility, presumably due to Merton's more extensive experience in direction and increased maturity as developed during the time separating the two versions. Thus the copy text for this appendix is the version found in the *Monastic Observances* mimeograph, and all differences between this and the earlier version are also listed in Appendix A.

All substantive additions made to the text, in order to turn elliptical or fragmentary statements into complete sentences, are included in braces, as are the few emendations incorporated directly into the text, so that the reader can always determine exactly what Merton himself wrote. No effort is made to reproduce Merton's rather inconsistent punctuation, paragraphing, abbreviations and typographical features; a standardized format for these features is established that in the judgement of the editor best represents a synthesis of Merton's own practice and contemporary usage: e.g., all Latin passages are italicized unless specific parts of a longer passage are underlined by Merton, in which case the underlined section of the passage is in roman type; all other passages underlined by Merton are italicized;

words in upper case in the text are printed in small caps; periods and commas are uniformly included within quotation marks; patterns of abbreviation and capitalization, very inconsistent in the copy text, are regularized. All references to primary and secondary sources are cited in the notes. Untranslated Latin passages in the original text are left in Latin but translated by the editor in the notes. Scriptural citations are taken from the Douai-Rheims-Challoner version of the Bible, the edition Merton himself regularly used, as it is a translation of the Latin Vulgate used in the liturgical offices.[59] All identified errors in Merton's text are noted and if possible corrected. All instances where subsequent research and expanded knowledge affect Merton's accuracy are discussed in the notes. A list of suggestions for further reading is included as Appendix B, consisting of other sources in Merton's published works where the topics of this volume are discussed.

* * * * * * *

In conclusion I would like to express my gratitude to all those who have made this volume possible:

- to the Trustees of the Merton Legacy Trust, Peggy Fox, Anne McCormick and Mary Somerville, for permission to publish the *Monastic Observances* conferences;
- to the late Robert E. Daggy, former director of the Thomas Merton Center, Bellarmine College (now University), Louis-

---

59. See the comments of Chrysogonus Waddell, ocso, in the Introduction to the first of numerous selections from Merton's monastic conferences published in the journal he edited, *Liturgy O.C.S.O.*: "As regards the biblical translations, for the purposes of his conferences, Fr. Louis always used the Douay-Challoner version, translated from the Latin Vulgate. He remained faithful to this older translation even long after other modern translations based on the original Hebrew and Greek texts had become almost everywhere standard. This preference was based in part on the fidelity of the Douay-Challoner translation to the Latin texts which were still those of the pre-Vatican II liturgy; and in part it was based simply on the fact that the literary diction of this older translation spoke more to the soul of Merton the poet and literary critic" ("Notes by Thomas Merton for Novitiate Conferences," *Liturgy O.C.S.O.* 24.1 [1990], 41–42).

ville, KY, for first alerting me to the project of editing Merton's monastic conferences, and for his encouragement in this and other efforts in Merton studies;

- to Brother Patrick Hart, ocso, the founding editor of the Monastic Wisdom series, for facilitating my research visits to the library at the Abbey of Gethsemani and for his friendship and guidance in the publication of this series of volumes of Thomas Merton's monastic conferences, as he passes on his editorial responsibilities and begins a well-earned period of *otium monasticum*;

- to Father James Conner, ocso, for many years Thomas Merton's undermaster of novices at the Abbey of Gethsemani, for graciously accepting an invitation to provide the Preface for this volume;

- to Paul M. Pearson, director and archivist of the Merton Center, and Mark C. Meade, assistant archivist, for their gracious hospitality and valued assistance during my research visits to the Center;

- to Colleen Stiller, production manager at Liturgical Press, for guiding this and previous volumes of Merton's conferences through the publication process with grace and efficiency;

- to the Gannon University Research Committee, which provided a grant that allowed me to pursue research on this project at the Merton Center, the Abbey of Gethsemani, and various libraries;

- to Mary Beth Earll of the interlibrary loan department of the Nash Library, Gannon University, for once again providing invaluable assistance by locating and procuring various obscure volumes;

- to library staff of the Hesburgh Library of the University of Notre Dame, especially Sara Weber, and the Institute of Cistercian Studies Collection at the Waldo Library, Western Michigan University, especially Neil Chase, for assistance in locating important materials in their collections;

- again and always to my wife Suzanne and our children for their continual love, support and encouragement in this and other projects.

MONASTIC OBSERVANCES

Contents

End of Part I

Our Monastic Observances

It is important from the beginning to understand what we are doing, in all the observances and practices which we carry out from morning to night. The whole life in large measure {is} made up of these things—they can help or hinder our search for perfection. Everything depends on *how* we carry them out. Our observances are an integral part in our monastic *life*. They must *live*. {They must be} part of a living organism. They must *help us to live*, help our life of charity in the Spirit. {They must assist our} growth as children of God, {the} formation of Christ in us. {They are the} exact opposite of mere mechanical routine, which diminishes and lessens life {and} obscures the image of Christ in us, degenerates into formalism, gradually stifles the free breath of the Spirit {and} kills the spiritual life. {A} wrong understanding and practice of observances leads to {the} wreck of {our} vocation.

A few general principles: we have come here to live—to live in Christ, by charity, in the Holy Spirit, {and} to grow in the works of love—love for God: *prayer*, liturgical and private—{to} enter into the prayer life of the Church (liturgical gestures and rites—liturgical *action*); *fraternal union*, above all Eucharistic—then, in the whole monastic day (work, etc.), cooperation, helping one another to grow in Christ, {through} mercy, forbearance, prayer, instruction and correction (example). The observances are the visible expression and the outward aid to all this—they are supposed to help us, form us, guide us, show us the way. But we must get below the surface, beyond the letter, and while carrying out the letter properly, penetrate to the full spirit. Thus through

5

our observances, which in many cases are sacramentals, we penetrate to Christ Himself as the Head of the Church, living in the
midst of us: "There hath stood one in your midst whom you
know not. . . ."[1] "Truly this is the house of God and I knew it
not . . ."[2]

Our observances have two aspects:

a) for the one learning, there is the exterior, which requires
devoted application and docility;

b) for the one who has learned, there is the interior—the
spirit shining through—received in gratitude and praise, leading
to contemplation in the spirit of wisdom and understanding.

Hence we can see the obvious pitfalls to avoid:

a) Thinking that perfection consists in exterior observance
for its own sake, with its by-products: observing others; {a}
critical spirit; scrupulosity; discord and factions (read St. James
on {a} worldly spirit[3]);

b) Going to {the} other extreme and neglecting the exterior
altogether: sloppiness, laziness, sensuality; lack of zeal; {this}
could greatly harm {the} spirit of faith and diminish the fervor
of our charity; {it} ends in {a} loss of vocation;

c) Subjectivism: trying to put our own interpretation on everything, instead of seeking to see what the Church and the monastic
tradition have to teach us by these things; {this} ends in eccentrici-
ties, vain observance, false spiritualities, fake mysticism;

d) Aestheticism and traditionalism: exaggerated respect for
the old as such; "artiness" {that is a} disguised form of snobbery.

1. John 1:26.
2. Gen. 28:16, 17 (conflated).
3. "Whence do wars and quarrels come among you? Is it not from this, from
your passions, which wage war in your members? You covet and do not have;
you kill and envy, and cannot obtain. You quarrel and wrangle, and you do not
have because you do not ask. You ask and do not receive, because you ask amiss,
that you may spend it upon your passions. Adulterers, do you not know that the
friendship of this world is enmity with God? Therefore, whoever wishes to be a
friend of this world becomes an enemy of God" (James 4:1-4).

I. The Monastery: The Regular Places

We can begin our study of the monastic observances by look-ing at the monastery itself (*Usages*, Bk. VII[4]). Everything about the regular, traditional plan of the monastery has a meaning and a purpose. We should try to understand the meaning of the mo-nastic plan, not necessarily in order to cling slavishly to the letter of the *Usages* on this point, but in order to see why the regular places exist, what they are for, and see whether or not we are failing to achieve any of the purposes for which they were insti-tuted. Seldom, if ever, does one find a monastery that corresponds exactly in every detail to the plan laid down in the *Usages*. This plan is a pattern to which one will conform, in each case, with certain changes and adaptations which make it possible to achieve the end intended in each particular situation.

Hence we need to know *why* we have these regular places and what purpose they serve:

1. The monastery. For St. Benedict, the monastery is first of all the *house of God*, *domus Dei*, the place of peace in which every-thing is ordered according to wisdom, and where in an atmo-sphere of love and faith the monk can work out his eternal salvation by a life of prayer and labor and virtue, in silence with his brethren. *Nemo perturbetur neque contristetur in domo Dei* (*Rule*, 31[5]). Peace in the house of God {is} insured by the fact that ev-erything is done at the right time and in the right way so that no one is overburdened or distressed by the heedlessness or selfish-ness of any individual or group. Hence the monks in charge must be wise, for the house of God must be wisely ruled: *Domus Dei a sapientibus sapienter administretur* (*Rule*, 53[6]). Hence, {the} first

---

4. *Regulations of the Order of Cistercians of the Strict Observance Published by the General Chapter of 1926* (Dublin: M. H. Gill & Sons, [1927]), 139–50 (nn. 282–305).

5. "so that no one may be troubled or vexed in the house of God" (*The Rule of St. Benedict in Latin and English*, ed. and trans. Justin McCann, osb [London: Burns, Oates, 1952], 82/83).

6. "And let the house of God be administered by prudent men in a prudent manner" (McCann, 122/123, which reads ". . . *sapientibus et sapienter* . . .").

principle {is}: everything in the monastery plan is *ordered wisely*, to prevent useless distraction, worries, cares, agitations, to help a life of prayer and simplicity, to cut down preoccupations and anxieties over material things or over anything at all, in order that the brethren may live together in peace and hear the voice of God. The Fathers compare it to the ark, a safe refuge in the deluge of this world (St. Ambrose[7]). The monastery itself, says Peter the Venerable, forms us by its silent instruction. *Ipsa [cella] sola eloquentius omnibus magistris tacendo te doceat (Letter 20).*[8] It is a refuge from the judgement of God; it is like Segor to which Lot fled from Sodom.[9] William of St. Thierry {says} the monastery is a paradise in which we prepare for heaven by doing the things that will be done is heaven: *Vacare Deo, frui Deo.*[10] It is the dwelling place of a FAMILY, says St. Basil.[11] The abbot represents the

---

7. See J. P. Migne, ed., *Patrologiae Cursus Completus, Series Latina*, 221 vols. (Paris: Garnier, 1844–1865), vol. 14, col. 374CD (*De Noe et Arca*, 9.30, where the reference is to good living, not to monastic life in particular), vol. 15, col. 1587B (*Expositio Evangelii Sancti Lucae*, 2.92, where the reference is to the Church as a whole rather than to the monastery) (subsequently referred to as *PL* in text and notes).

8. "May the cell itself by its silence instruct you more eloquently than all teachers" (*PL* 189, col. 90C).

9. I.e. Zoar (Gen. 19:23); see Peter Damian, *De Perfectione Monachorum*, 7: "*Nimirum melius est quidem salvari animam in Segor, quam sulphureo in Sodomis igne consumi*" ("It is certainly better for the soul to be saved in Segor than to be consumed in the fire and brimstone of Sodom") (*PL* 145, col. 302B).

10. "To make time for God, to enjoy God " (*Epistola ad Fratres de Monte Dei*, 1.4 [*PL* 184, col. 314A]).

11. This is not in fact an especially prominent image in Basil: but see *Short Rules* 190: "One who *is born of the Spirit* according to the voice of the Lord (cf. John 3:8) and has received *power to become a child of God* (cf. John 1:12), is ashamed of kinship according to the flesh and owns as his relatives those who are of the *household of faith* (cf. Gal. 6:10)" (Anna M. Silvis, *The Asketikon of St Basil the Great* [New York; Oxford University Press, 2005], 377); see also Philip Rousseau's reference to Basil's *Homily Exhorting to Holy Baptism*, in which the sacrament is seen as bringing about "the intimacy of those sharing a common household" (Philip Rousseau, *Basil of Caesarea* [Berkeley: University of California Press, 1994], 179), although this statement is not directly or exclusively referring to monasticism.

heavenly Father; the brethren are sons living together in a unity of charity that transcends nature, forming as it were one son, in the bond of the Holy Spirit. Hence, the monastery is a place of unity in which men live together, mirroring on earth by their harmony and peace the internal peace and unity of the Three Divine Persons in One Nature.

2. The Regular Places in the *Usages*: Book VII of the *Usages* has eight chapters, dealing with the church, cloisters and chapter room, then with the scriptorium, the dormitory, refectory, kitchens and workroom, and finally the calefactory.[12] We must distinguish here what is essential from what is not essential. The church is the very *raison d'être* of the whole monastery. It is the true House of God, the place where we offer Him sacrifice and praise, where we meditate most often, where we recollect ourselves in silence with the Eucharistic Christ. The cloister is traditionally the heart of the family life in the monastery. In modern houses this center of balance has shifted. The chapter room {is} the center of the community as such. These three give us the very essence of the monastery. They fulfill essential functions. {The} refectory, dormitory {and} kitchen are also essential since the monk has a body as well as a soul. {The} scriptorium has become in modern times the real center of family life, replacing the chapter room and cloister. The calefactory[13] is generally obsolete.

The layout of the regular places: the *Usages* say nothing about the location of the church. Traditionally it is *oriented* and occupies either the north or south side of the monastic quadrangle. {For} the cloisters, the *Usages* prescribe:

a) One part to be devoted to the reading before compline. Here there should be a statue of Our Lady, *in the middle* (288);[14]

---

12. C. 1: "Church," 139–42 (nn. 282–87); c. 2: "Cloisters," 142–44 (nn. 288–91); c. 3: "Chapter Room," 144–45 (n. 292); c. 4: "Scriptorium," 145 (nn. 293–94); c. 5: "Dormitory," 146–48 (nn. 295–99); c. 6: "Refectory," 148–49 (nn. 300–302); c. 7: "Kitchens and Scullery," 149 (nn. 303–304); c. 8: "Calefactory," 150 (n. 305).

13. I.e. the warming room.

14. *Regulations*, 142–43.

b) On one wing of the cloisters we have the following places: chapter {room}, auditorium and calefactory, in that order.

Nothing else is said about the exact location of the regular places, but traditionally the refectory is on the opposite side of the quadrangle from the church, the dormitory of the religious is above the chapter room, etc. The west side of the quadrangle traditionally was reserved for the brothers and the cellarium,[15] but nothing is said about this in the *Usages*. Considering the *Usages* alone, a great deal of latitude would be allowed in monastic planning. N.B. when a monastery is planned, the plan has to be approved by the architectural commission of the General Chapter.

3. *The Church of the Monastery*:

a) The *Rule*: *Oratorium hoc sit quod dicitur*: a place of silence and prayer, where a monk not only joins his brethren in the solemn choral praise of God, but can also retire to pray in silence and solitude at any time (*Rule*, 52[16]). Everything prescribed in the *Ritual*[17] and *Usages* is supposed to further this one purpose of the church. Everything {is} intended to lift the mind and heart to God. It is the House of God (read Guardini, *Sacred Signs*, p. 39[18]).

---

15. I.e. the storeroom(s).

16. "Let the oratory be what its name implies" (McCann, 118/119).

17. *Rituale Cisterciense ex Libro Usuum Definitionibus Ordinis et Caeremoniali Episcoporum Collectum* (Westmalle, Belgium: Ex Typographia Ordinis, 1948).

18. Romano Guardini, *Sacred Signs*, trans. Grace Branham (St. Louis: Pio Decimo Press, 1956), 39: "Notice how as you cross the threshold you unconsciously lift your head and your eyes, and how as you survey the great interior space of the church there also takes place in you an inward expansion and enlargement. Its great width and height have an analogy to infinity and eternity. A church is the similitude of the heavenly dwelling place of God. Mountains indeed are higher, the wide blue sky outside stretches immeasurably further. But whereas outside space is unconfined and formless, the portion of space set aside for the church has been formed, fashioned, designed at every point with God in view. The long pillared aisles, the width and solidity of the walls, the high arched and vaulted roof, bring home to us that this is God's house and the seat of his hidden presence."

In turn, we should behave in church with a reverence and modesty which make prayer easy for all others who happen to be there. Even {those} working in church should work with reverence and recollection, in {an} atmosphere of silence and peace. Everywhere God is present, but in a very special way in church.

b) Legislation of the Order: all the churches of the Order are dedicated to the Blessed Virgin (*Usages*, 282;[19] *Ritual*, I, III, 1;[20] *Instituta*, I, 1[21]—one of the oldest statutes of the Order). {The} importance of this {is that} in church we gather around the Virgin Mother (contrast {the} Benedictines, {who focus on} the Glorious Christ). All churches {are} constructed in the form of a cross "like our Mother Cîteaux."[22] {This is the} traditional Gothic plan. (Explain the regular divisions of a Gothic church: nave, transepts, choir, ambulatory, apse, etc.)

c) Fourfold division of the Cistercian church (*Usages*, 283;[23] *Ritual*, I, III, 1 and 2, etc.[24]):

1. {The} *presbytery* {is} one or two steps above the rest of the church (*Rit.*[25]); {for the} *high altar*, one must be able to pass around the back; {the} high altar {is} one or two steps above the presbytery floor (*Rit.*[26]). {A} statue of {the} Blessed Virgin behind {the} high altar {is} prescribed only in {the} *Usages*,[27] not in {the} *Ritual*: why? {because of the} ancient Cistercian ban on all statues; {the}

---

19. *Regulations*, 139.

20. *Rituale*, 4.

21. This is the reference as given in the *Rituale*; it is in fact c. 18 of the *Instituta* of 1134 (*In Statutorum Annorum Precedentium Prima Collectio*) (Joseph Marie Canivez, ed., *Statuta Capitulorum Generalium Ordinis Cisterciensis ab Anno 1116 ad Annum 1786*, 8 vols. [Louvain: Bureaux de la Revue, 1933–1941], 1.17).

22. *Regulations*, 139 (n. 283), which reads: "like that of our Mother, Cîteaux."

23. *Regulations*, 139.

24. *Rituale*, 4.

25. *Rituale*, 4 (I, III, 2).

26. *Rituale*, 4 (I, III, 2).

27. *Regulations*, 139 (n. 283).

credence; tierce stalls {are} *infra gradum altaris* (*Rit.*[28]); {a} crucifix, six candlesticks and two "sanctus candlesticks" {are} prescribed in {the} *Usages* (283).[29] {The} *Ritual* (I, ɪᴠ, 3) says sanctus candlesticks *possunt haberi*,[30] and refers to {the} General Chapter of 1463. {The} *Ritual* allowed a hanging ciborium.[31]

2. {The} *choir* {is equipped} with stalls, seats, and desks (called "forms": *Rit.*[32]). The *Ritual* says the whole seat is called the *misericord*;[33] {the} *Usages* attach this title to the little seat on which we lean when bowed over.[34] {The} *novices' choir*, {located} below the forms, {is} traditionally without forms, and with a bookstand out in the middle.

3. {The} *retrochoir*, separated from the choir by a *screen*, is the choir of the sick. {The} jube[35] {is} in the middle of the screen. The sick have a regular choir.

4. {The} *nave* {is} separated by another screen (*similiter separatur a retrochoro*: *Rit.*[36]). Choir stalls, etc., for {the} brothers, altars *de beata* and *pro defunctis*[37] {are located there}.

d) The lamps: {there are} "three principal lamps":[38] 1—{above the} presbytery step; 2—{in the} choir; 3—{in the} nave ({the}

28. "below the level of the altar" (*Rituale*, 4 [I, ɪɪɪ, 2], which reads: "*Infra vero . . .*").

29. *Regulations*, 140 (n. 283), which reads: "a large candelabrum is placed on each side at the foot of the steps" (the term "sanctus candlestick" is not used).

30. "are permitted to be had" (*Rituale*, 6, which reads: "*possunt etiam* [also] *haberi*").

31. *Rituale*, 5 (I, ɪɪɪ, 8).

32. *Rituale*, 4 (I, ɪɪɪ, 3).

33. *Rituale*, 4 (I, ɪɪɪ, 3).

34. *Regulations*, 140 (n. 283)

35. I.e. the ambo or lectern.

36. "it is separated in the same way from the retrochoir" (*Rituale*, 4 [I, ɪɪɪ, 5]).

37. "for the Blessed [Virgin Mary]; "for the dead" (i.e. the altars where daily Masses were celebrated in honor of Mary [and for the intentions of members of the Order and benefactors] and for the dead: see *Regulations*, 141 [n. 283], *Rituale*, 4 [I, ɪɪɪ, 5]).

38. *Regulations*, 141 (n. 284).

brothers' choir) (or {the} infirm choir: *Rit.*[39]); two others {are} permitted before other altars (*propter conversos vel hospites*: *Rit.*[40]). {It is} evident that these lamps were originally for light, and not just votive lights.

e) Cleanliness (*Rit.*[41]): the church should be kept clean; nothing that does not befit the sanctity of the church should be found there; animals should not enter.

Our church is a minor basilica: what is that? {The} original meaning of the word {was} royal judgement hall. A basilica is a church which because of its *historical importance, its renown, or its splendor*, is singled out for special distinction by an indult of the Holy See or by immemorial custom. The dignity of the basilica is signalized usually in the title itself and what it implies, and the use of the decorative insignia of the umbrella and the bell, which are carried in all processions and remain in the sanctuary. *Major basilicas* are the four more important churches of Rome— St. Peter's, St. John Lateran, St. Paul's Outside the Walls, and St. Mary Major. Others hold that the churches of St. Francis and St. Mary of the Angels at Assisi are major basilicas. It would also seem *a fortiori* that the Basilica of the Holy Sepulchre at Jerusalem and of the Nativity at Bethlehem would be major basilicas, though canonists do not mention them. In any case, only a very ancient and universally important church would ever be considered a major basilica. There are numerous *minor basilicas*—for instance in places of pilgrimage: v.g. Lourdes, Lisieux. There have been other minor basilicas in our Order: v.g. Aiguebelle[42] and Orval[43] (though sentiment in the Order has not been favorable

---

39. *Rituale*, 5 (I, ɪv, 1).

40. "for the laybrothers and guests" (*Rituale*, 5 [I, ɪv, 1], which reads: ". . . *conversos et* . . .").

41. *Rituale*, 5 (I, ɪɪɪ, 6).

42. Cistercian abbey in southeastern France, founded in 1137.

43. Cistercian abbey in southern Belgium, originally founded in 1070 and affiliated with the Order of Cîteaux in 1132; it was shut down in the aftermath of the French Revolution and reestablished in 1926.

to attaching this kind of dignity to one of our churches). Before
Gethsemani, the following churches were erected to this dignity
in the U.S.: Our Lady of Victory, Lackawanna, NY (1926);[44]
St. Mary, Minneapolis (1926);[45] St. Josaphat, Milwaukee (1929);[46]
Baltimore Cathedral (1937);[47] Immaculate Conception, Conception, MO (1940).[48] Ours came in 1949. Since then there have been
quite a few others, for instance, St. Vincent's, Latrobe.[49] The bull
"Inter vastam solitudinem" of May 3, 1949, granted us this title
(*AAS* [1949], 446[50]). It says in part: "The Abbey of Gethsemani
stands in a vast solitude surrounded by forests, a wilderness
which brings peace to the heart and raises the mind to the contemplation of divine things."[51] There follows a brief sketch of the
history of the abbey, then a fulsome description of the monastery,
{the} guest house, surrounded by "most fragrant gardens,"[52] the
"ancient semi-gothic structure" with its "admirable fabric,"[53]
pictures, and stained glass windows, the splendor of the offices,
the retreats for clergy and laity, the great number of sacred relics,
etc., etc. {It} names the various bishops who supported the petition, and grants the title with all annexed privileges.

44. Shrine built by Fr. Nelson Baker just south of Buffalo, NY, consecrated
and named a minor basilica in 1926.

45. Co-cathedral of the Minneapolis/St. Paul Archdiocese, built between
1907 and 1915.

46. Parish and shrine, dedicated in 1901, staffed by Conventual Franciscans
since 1910.

47. Basilica of the National Shrine of the Assumption of the Blessed Virgin
Mary, Baltimore's original cathedral, the first in America, built between 1806 and
1821.

48. Abbey church of the Benedictine community of Conception, dedicated
in 1891.

49. Abbey church and parish of St. Vincent Archabbey, originally dedicated
in 1836 and taken over by the Benedictines upon their arrival ten years later.

50. *Acta Apostolicae Sedis*, 41 (1949), 446–48.

51. "*Inter vastam solitudinem animis afferentem pacem mentibusque caelestium
rerum contemplationem, . . . nemore circumdata exstat . . .*" (*AAS*, 446).

52. "*fragrantissimis circumdata hortis*" (*AAS*, 446).

53. "*antiquae semigothicae structurae . . . fabrica, picturae, tabulae sunt admi-
randae*" (*AAS*, 446).

f) *The Sacristy* (*Usages*, 285–286[54]): "The Sacristan shall conform to the customs of our Fathers, who recommend simplicity
in our churches" (*Usages*, 552[55]). This is a very broad statement
—so broad that it is often completely ignored. In general, it means
simplicity in choice of vestments, vessels, ornaments, etc., plain-
ness {through} avoidance of the showy, {the} peculiar, but above
all, avoidance of vulgarity and bad taste. {There should be} "safe
and suitable cupboards" (*Usages*, 285[56]). "It is well to put lavender
or other fragrant plants into the cupboards . . . in order to keep
them free from insects" (552[57]—today: DDT[58]). "The cupboards
and drawers of the sacristy should be frequently opened in fine
weather."[59] In a word, {there is emphasis on the} importance of
cleanliness, neatness, and a salubrious atmosphere in the sacristy.
There should be a *piscina*.[60] There should be one or more *wash
basins with running water*, "with towels":[61] "three towels: one for
the priest and sacred ministers before Mass, the second for the
same after Mass, and the third for the other ministers" (*Usages*,
552[62]). {In} the crypt, stations of the cross {are} for seculars only.

g) *Liturgical Books—Sacred Objects*: {there should be} enough
for all. {A} spirit of poverty {is} stressed by the *Usages* (286): "The
religious {. . .} should have nothing *exclusively* for their use, such
as a chalice, or missal, etc., so that they may not be tempted to
regard these objects as their own property."[63] Hence we have *only*

---

54. *Regulations*, 141.

55. *Regulations*, 261.

56. *Regulations*, 141.

57. *Regulations*, 261.

58. For Merton's renunciation of DDT, see his letter of January 12, 1963 to
Rachel Carson (Thomas Merton, *Witness to Freedom: Letters in Times of Crisis*, ed.
William H. Shannon [New York: Farrar, Straus, Giroux, 1994], 70–72).

59. *Regulations*, 261.

60. I.e. a sink "to receive water which has been blessed or has been used
for ablutions" (*Regulations*, 285 [n. 141]).

61. *Regulations*, 141 (n. 285).

62. *Regulations*, 262.

63. *Regulations*, 141, which reads: ". . . chalice, a missal, . . ." and includes
a clause between "religious" and "should".

albs assigned to individuals, for obvious reasons—other things are given out at random; chalices and books are assigned to each altar and the priests change from week to week.

h) *Cemetery* (*Usages*, 287[64])—{the} *Ritual* prescribes[65] that no one shall be buried in the churches except a king or a bishop. In the old days saints were buried in the churches, v.g. Sts. Bernard and Malachy at Clairvaux. Abbots {were buried} in the chapter room, brethren in the cemeteries. This rule was not too strictly followed in the past (cf. {the} *Menology, passim*[66]). The cemetery *may be* divided into three parts (*Usages*, 287[67]): priests, monks, brothers. Here there is no division. {The} only distinction {is that} priests {are} buried with their feet to {the} west, others with feet to {the} east (*Usages*, 500[68]). {The} cross being at the head, the priests have their cross at {the} west end of {the} grave, others at {the} east {end}. It is surrounded by a wall or quickset hedge (haie vive);[69] box or hawthorn, etc. is okay. Crosses {are} of wood or iron, "painted black or white,"[70] {with an} inscription bearing the name, rank and date (choir religious in Latin, brothers in English). {On} the sanctity of the cemetery, cf. {the} rite for blessing of {a} cemetery {in the} *Ritual*.[71] It is especially consecrated to God, as a place which speaks symbolically of the fact that *He is the keeper, the protection and the hope of all*. Here the bodies of the faithful *rest*, waiting for the last day. They await *the day when they shall be re-united* to their glorified souls. The cemetery is indeed a very im-

64. *Regulations*, 141–42.

65. *Rituale*, 5 (I, iii, 9).

66. *Menologium Cisterciense a Monachis Ordinis Cisterciensis Strictioris Obser-vantiae*, ed. Séraphin Lenssen, ocso (Westmalle, Belgium: Ex Typographia Ordinis, 1952); this is a collection of brief biographical notices, arranged by date, of notable deceased members of the Order (a mimeographed English translation was produced at Gethsemani in 1955).

67. *Regulations*, 142.

68. *Regulations*, 236.

69. *Regulations*, 142, which does not use the French term.

70. *Regulations*, 142.

71. *Rituale*, 354–63 (VIII, x).

portant part of the community, and those in the cemetery still form part of the community; indeed they are definitively "the community"—members with an eternal stability that will never be broken. Hence {there should be} great reverence and love for the cemetery and for those whose bodies rest there. The cemetery should remind us not only of the fact that we must one day die, but primarily and above all that our bodies will one day be reunited with our souls in glory, if we are faithful to our vocation. The cemetery is a place of rest—in what sense? First, {it is} protected against the evil spirits. It is guarded by its own guardian angel. Then {it is} a place where bodies rest in hope, then a place which symbolizes Christ Himself, the protection and "rest" of the faithful. Some prayers from the *Ritual* for the blessing of a cemetery:

> Lord God, shepherd of eternal glory, light and honor of wisdom, guardian and strength of prudence, health of the sick, strength of the healthy, consolation of the sorrowful, life of the just, glory of the humble, we earnestly beseech Thee that this cemetery of Thy faithful servants may be protected by Thee from every defilement of evil and attack of the spirits of darkness. We beg Thee to purify and bless it, and to grant without ceasing perseverance in truth [*sinceritatem perpetuam*] to the bodies of those who come to this place, and that those who have received the sacrament of baptism and have persevered in the Catholic faith until the end of their lives and in the course of time have ended their days and commended their bodies to rest in this cemetery, may receive the everlasting reward of heavenly joy, both in body and soul, when the angels sound their trumpets. Through Christ Our Lord . . .[72]
>
> Lord Jesus Christ, Who didst form the human body from earth to repair the gaps in the ranks of the angels and Who hast assumed this very body to Thyself for our Redemption, who dost cause the body to return to dust by reason of man's sin, and Who wilt raise it again from dust

---

72. *Rituale*, 357–58 (Merton's translation).

unto immortality, we beg Thee to consecrate this plot of
ground for burial by the blessing which flows from the mystery of Thine own burial. And we beg Thee to grant that
those who have been buried together with Thee in baptism,
and who by nature of the flesh are here to be buried together,
may in the hope of Thy Resurrection rest in the mercy of
Thy Redemption . . .[73]

How much theology {there is} in this wonderful prayer. All these
truths are present in the sacred ground of the cemetery, and we
should not cease to learn them from it.

Visiting the cemetery: N.B. {the} indulgences {that are given}:
seven years for a visit to the cemetery any day of the year, applicable only to the poor souls, {under the} condition {of} prayer,
even mental, for the dead; during the octave of All Souls, for the
same {exercise, there is a} plenary indulgence each day, under
the usual conditions. {Visiting the cemetery is} a good daily practice, but especially on Sundays or {on a} day of recollection:

a) to pray for the dead, especially those we ourselves have
known. True piety, an essential virtue of the monk, renews the
eternal bond that binds us to our brethren, a certain spiritual
affection which is a great grace {and} aids in compunction; while
we pray for them, we may also believe that they pray for us,
especially since so many are saints high in heaven.

b) {it} makes us think of the mercy of God, of the mystery of
our vocation, to walk among these quiet graves among the
wooded hills of our solitude. How many have come from far to
end here by mysterious ways, led by God's Providence. {There
is} humility {in} realizing that our ways are not God's ways, and
how many of us, if left to ourselves, would have ended anywhere
but in a monastery.

c) {it reminds us of our} hope of eternal reward and the final
coming of the Kingdom {and gives us} strength to continue on

73. *Rituale*, 358 (Merton's translation).

the way of our own vocation, {fostering} "preparation for death" in hope rather than in shuddering.

The cemetery is indeed important to a Trappist, but not in the sense of the popular legend of digging a bit out of the grave each day, etc. {In} *our cemetery*, the big cement cross {marks} the mingled remains of the founders—*abbates in pace*[74]—some of the monks and brothers. Our Blessed Mother presides over the cemetery. {Note} the silence of summer evenings in the cemetery. *Pax Domini . . .*[75]

The Cloisters {are} the center of the monastic family life, the normal place of reading and meditative prayer (with the church). The cloister is ideally an open arched walk around the four sides of an enclosed garden. All the main regular places are normally supposed to open on to the cloister. It corresponds to the patio in the houses of Mediterranean lands. To understand the cloister we must think of those dwellings. They present a bare and austere front to the outside, almost without windows. Once inside the house, all is different—there are flowers, fountains, statues, rooms opening out into the central court, etc. {This is} the atrium of the ancient Romans. The cloister with its "préau" or "garth" should normally then be a place of (1) silence; (2) light; (3) peace; (4) shelter; (5) delight ({an} enclosed garden[76]). {According to} St. Peter Damian, "the cloister on all four sides turns inward and away from the world, that the very location should show you that you must turn away from the noise and manners of the world."[77] Historically, the cloister in ancient Benedictine monasteries was divided up for various purposes. One wing, usually the north, along the church, was the reading place of the monks. Another was for the novices, another for students. The west wing

---

74. "fathers [resting] in peace".

75. "Peace of the Lord [be always with you]" (*Missale Cisterciense* [Westmalle: Ex Typographia Ordinis Cist. Strict. Obs., 1951], 228; *Missale Romanum*, 28th ed. [Turonibus: Sumptibus et Typis Mame, 1952], 358).

76. Song of Songs 4:12.

77. *De Perfecta Monachi Informatione*, 10 (*PL* 145, col. 729C).

was for material business. The monk was known as a *claustra-lis*—one who lived in the cloister. For a *claustralis* to return to the world was for a dweller in heaven to fall into hell (Peter of Blois).[78] "*Nulla vita fidelior, nulla simplicior, nulla felicior, quam eorum, qui humiliter in claustris degunt, abjectione sua gaudentes*" (John of Salisbury).[79] *The Usages* (288[80]) prescribe a statue of Our Lady in the part of the cloister where the compline reading takes place (normally the part along the church). Our Lady presides over the community. The statue is a material sign of the fact. But the very nature of the cloister itself, as a garden enclosed, reminds us that Our Lady surrounds us with her own silence and peace and brings forth Christ in our souls as we read quietly in the cloister. The cloister itself is a symbol of Our Lady, Mediatrix of all grace. Hence the importance of a real cloister. However, the spirit of the cloister pervades our scriptoriums and gardens. *To preserve silence in a special way* (*Usages*, {290}[81]), we do not speak in the cloister (*Usages*, 328[82]). The cloister should be regarded as sacred. A special permission of the abbot is required before an outsider can enter the cloister. The doors which lead from the guest house or any other outside place to the cloister must be kept shut, or even locked if necessary. There must be no door through which an outsider can freely enter into the inside of the monastery. This goes also for the gardens. If guests are to be taken through, (a) we must NOT bring them in when the community is at *lectio*; (b) we must NOT speak to them there, any more than we do in church, chapter or refectory (*Usages*, 328[83]). In order to keep the cloister quiet and peaceful, great attention should be paid to

---

78. *Epistola* 142 (*PL* 207, col. 426C).

79. "There is no life more faithful, more simple, more happy, than that of those who humbly dwell in the cloister, rejoicing in their own lowliness" (*Poly-craticus*, Bk. 7, c. 21 [*PL* 199, col. 695D], which reads: ". . . *qui in claustris fideliter degunt, et humiliter abjectione . . .*").

80. *Regulations*, 142.

81. *Regulations*, 143 (typescript reads: "*Usages*, 289").

82. *Regulations*, 159.

83. *Regulations*, 159.

silence when working in {the} refectory, with plates, milk cans, etc. No useless loudspeakers should be blaring in the regular places. Walk quietly, close doors quietly, be quiet on the stairs.

The Auditorium (grand parlor) (*Usages*, 291[84]): the cloister is a place of silence; but in the heart of the monastery there must also be a place for necessary speaking. All speech cannot be avoided and it is not desirable that it should be avoided in the monastic life. We have to be realistic on this point; otherwise there will be evasions and stupidities—people getting into the cloister closets to exchange a few words, because no regular speaking place is to be found. {The} purpose of the "grand parlor"[85] (grand parloir) {is therefore}:

1) brief communications with the superior;
2) distribution of work ({the} tablet for announcing work belongs here);
3) hence it is the place where the work shoes are kept, and where the cowls are left before one goes to work;
4) postulants wait here before being called into chapter for clothing;
5) novices say the *De Profundis*[86] here when dismissed early from chapter.

Nothing is said in the *Usages* about {a} washroom, etc. In a modern monastery plan, an intelligent solution to various problems presented would be to have a medium-sized "auditorium" next to the chapter room for brief communications, distribution of work, etc., and then below in the basement have the washrooms, toilets, etc., of the choir religious, easily accessible. The *auditorium* could then be a simple and dignified speaking place, from which one would go downstairs to the washrooms, etc. "Other smaller speaking parlors"[87] are permitted in different

---

84. *Regulations*, 143–44.
85. See *Regulations*, 143 (n. 291).
86. Psalm 129[130]: "Out of the depths [I cry to you, O Lord] . . ."
87. *Regulations*, 144 (n. 291).

parts of the house besides the grand parlor. (Reference is then made to n. 325 which says, "As far as possible, we speak only in the places appointed for speaking."[88]) An important aspect of our rule of silence {is that} we should be able to speak when necessary, and places for speaking should be provided. Outside these places we should be strict about not speaking—that is, around the house. *Recognized places of speaking* {include}:

1) {the} prior's room;
2) {the} foot of {the} infirmary stairs ({the} reason: the old cellarer's office was once there);
3) {the} foot of {the} dormitory stairs (but there should not be large groups of brothers gathering there to talk to the cellarer—they should go to their own grand parlor);
4) {the} singing rooms;
5) {the} corridor outside the infirmary refectory.

Places where we tend to be careless about silence {include}:

1) the sacristy (n. 328: "We can only speak in the sacristy on *urgent* matters"[89]);
2) the walks between the main building and the shops, {the} brothers' novitiate or steel building; it is absolutely an abuse of speech for religious to walk in a group, or in twos, along these walks from the main building to the shops, speaking to one another there when they have a speaking permission—this is a very bad habit and ruins monastic discipline;
3) the cemetery, {which should be} a place of strict silence—only the most necessary signs should be made there; this applies also to the woods where we are allowed to go for *lectio* or prayer.

Around the novitiate there should be little speaking in the library, none in the scriptorium; we should avoid it if possible at the foot of the chapel stairs and especially outside the religious grand parlor.

88. *Regulations*, 157.
89. *Regulations*, 159 (emphasis added).

The Chapter Room (*Usages*, 292[90]): according to St. Bernard,[91] the whole monastery is a *schola Christi* and an *auditorium Spiritus*. But this is especially true of the chapter room where we meet to hear the word of God and where the Spirit of God speaks to our hearts. We have to cultivate a spirit of faith then, in our sessions in chapter, but also later on, when we may have occasion to speak there, we must realize that it is a sad thing to become a scandal to little ones by the aridity and emptiness of one's words to them in this place. The chapter room should be the center of *regular life and discipline* in the monastery. It is here that the *Rule* is explained, that it is daily read aloud at prime, that it is applied in the form of fraternal correction. The spirit of St. Benedict should reign in the whole monastery but above all in the chapter room. As we enter the chapter room we should have in our hearts the substance of what the Church prays for in the Collect of St. Benedict's feast (and of the Feast of St. Stephen Harding): "Stir up, O Lord, in Thy Church, the Spirit Whom St. Benedict served that we, being filled with the same Spirit, may devote our energies to love what he loved and practice what he practiced."[92] It is all too true that the spirit of a community is reflected by the atmosphere of the community chapter. Here souls are formed, but here also they can be warped. Here vocations can be strengthened—and they can be destroyed. A few words of reminder, on the spirit of St. Benedict—it is marked above all by the following characteristics: discretion, reverence, simplicity, piety, wisdom, charity. It is the spirit of supernatural family life in which the members live as brothers under a common father, who represents Christ Himself. The bonds of union in this family depend entirely on obedience and humility in the spirit of religion and of faith. The monastery is not a barracks, or a social club, or a concentration camp, or a sanatorium, or a reform school (even on the

---

90. *Regulations*, 144–45.

91. *In Nativitate S. Joannis Baptistae*, 1 (*PL* 183, col. 397D, which reads: "*auditorio spirituali*").

92. *Missale Cisterciense*, 390 (March 21: Feast of St. Benedict); 464 (July 16: Feast of St. Stephen Harding, for which "*beatus Stephanus, Abbas*" replaces "*beatus Benedictus, Abbas*"); these are not found in the *Missale Romanum*.

pattern of Boys' Town![93]) or a small-time backwoods college. Let us see that the atmosphere of such institutions does not creep into our community.

Legislation {provides that}:

1) {The} abbot's seat {is} to the east, surmounted by a cruci-fix[94]—to remind us that the abbot holds the place of Christ. A moderate bow is always made to the crucifix when we (a) enter; (b) leave; (c) pass through the middle of the chapter room. This is a special reverence which is proper only to the crucifix in the chapter room, and implies an act of faith in the authority of the abbot as representative of Christ.[95] Hence there is no reason for extending this practice to other places where it is not prescribed. It is *not prescribed* in the scriptorium. But it *is* prescribed in the refectory (*Usages*, 300[96]). Here again, however, the crucifix is normally over the abbot's place (nothing explicit in the *Usages*, but it seems to be constant in every monastery).

2) {The} prior {is} at {the} abbot's right, {the} subprior on his left.

3) {There are} *stalls or* benches for the religious.

4) There may be different levels, in which case the novices are on the "lower step."[97]

5) {The} private box may be in chapter, or under the seats in the cloister. (In point of fact there are now private desks in the scriptorium.)

6) What exercises are prescribed for the chapter room? prayers of prime, explanation of the *Rule*, chapter of faults, consultation of the community (or other reunions) "whenever the

93. The residential facility for boys founded in 1917 by Fr. Edward Flanagan (1886–1948) in Omaha, NE, made famous in the 1938 Spencer Tracy film of the same name.

94. See *Regulations*, 144 (n. 292).

95. See *Rule*, c. 2: "*Christi agere vices in monasterio creditur*" ("He is believed to act in the place of Christ in the monastery") (McCann, 16/17).

96. *Regulations*, 148.

97. *Regulations*, 144 (n. 292).

abbot thinks fit,"[98] votes, vestition of novices, temporary profession, absolution of apostates, opening and closing of visitation,
preaching of sermons, reading of visitation cards—and the *Usages*
add "etc."[99] In the early days of the Order, confessions were heard
in the chapter room.

The Scriptorium (*Usages*, 293–294[100]): two brief paragraphs
are devoted to what is actually, in most of our monasteries, the
place where the religious usually make their *lectio divina*. These
paragraphs deal with the scriptorium and {the} common box:

a) {The} text of the *Usages* {says of the} *scriptorium*, "besides
the place of lecture [this is a bad translation—the English word
"lecture" is not a correct translation of the French word "lecture,"
which means "reading"] there *may be* a room called the
Scriptorium."[101] It is a place to which the religious are free to go
to write and take notes during the time of *lectio*. In some monasteries there are no seats—just desks at which one stands. The
same silence is observed there as in the cloisters, *a fortiori* when
it is the usual place of reading. This rule of silence also applies to
the gardens and other places where the monks are allowed to read
(as they are allowed at Gethsemani). {The} *common box* may be in
the scriptorium or elsewhere ("according to local circumstances"[102]).
It is a cupboard containing books, writing materials, and sewing
materials for the common use of the religious. The text adds "etc.,"
meaning other things useful to the monks may be kept there.

b) *Commentary*: in the early days of the Order the scriptorium
was a place reserved for the copyists of manuscripts. No one else
was allowed to go there; even the cantor, in charge of the copying
work, could only go to the entrance and deal with the copyists
there. It was a place of rigorous silence (this goes back to the

98. *Regulations*, 145 (n. 292), which reads: "whenever he thinks fit".
99. *Regulations*, 145 (n. 292).
100. *Regulations*, 145.
101. *Regulations*, 145 (n. 293) (emphasis added).
102. *Regulations*, 145 (n. 294).

Instituta of 1134[103]). It was not necessarily a room, but a separate small cloister or arcade. Later a common reading room was tolerated. The *armarium* or common box was ordinarily at the corner of the cloister near the entrance to the church. It is now customary to have, in the scriptorium, an *individual desk* for each monk. With the growth of reading and the increased number of books, it is usual for the common box to be well supplied with books. The *Usages* prescribe, regarding the books, {that} they should deal "only with spiritual subjects or the study of the sacred sciences."[104] They should be sufficiently numerous, and "well chosen,"[105] renewed from time to time according to need. In other words, the common box should contain standard, up-to-date books for which there is likely to be a considerable demand. There should be especially good *reference material* and especially abundant material on the scriptures and on the spiritual life, as well as on the *Rule* and the Order. {This encourages the} laudable habit of looking things up and checking in reference books, especially before proclamations. Other books can safely be left in the library to be called for—v.g., biographies, etc. Two points should be emphasized regarding the monk in the scriptorium: *poverty*, or simplicity, and *silence*. We have individual desks, practically the only place where we can accumulate odds and ends that can practically become "possessions." In his desk, the monk will normally have {a} pencil and pen, a few notebooks, one or two books given him for his personal use (perhaps even more if need be), a holy picture tacked on the inside of the lid, maybe. But one should not accumulate snapshots of the family (though this is all right within reason) or all sorts of miscellaneous junk, set aside "for a rainy day." Keep your desk neat. Do not leave things on top of the desk outside the time of *lectio*. {In respect to} silence, conversational signs should *never* be made in the scriptorium, only the most necessary signs. *Do not salute.* Do not distract your

---

103. C. 85 (Canivez, 1.32).
104. *Regulations*, 145 (n. 294), which reads: "only be such as deal with . . ."
105. *Regulations*, 145 (n. 294).

brother in his *lectio*. {Be} quiet in moving around, careful not to knock over stools, etc.

The Dormitory (*Usages*, 295–299[106]): these paragraphs prescribe how the cells should be, how we should conduct ourselves in the dormitory during the night and also outside the time of sleeping; emphasis is laid on cleanliness; and finally the *meridian* is discussed.

295[107]—*cells and bedding*:

1) the cells are separated by partitions, {which} can be the whole height of the room;

2) only a curtain {is} in front;

3) {there is a} nameplate of the religious;

4) the couch {consists of} planks and {a} straw mattress, {a} straw pillow, {and} blankets according to need;

5) other furniture {includes} {a} crucifix, holy water stoup, holy pictures (here they are standard and uniform), one or two hooks; you cannot add holy pictures of your own choice; clothes hangers {are} okay, with permission. We do not hang clothes over the wall of the cell during {the} daytime, and do not hang them so that they go over into the neighbor's cell.

296–298[108]—*Rules*:

1) {We are} always covered when we go about in the dormitory, except for work. {The} reason for this {is} modesty and recollection. {There is} no need to cover when we are sweeping there, {as} we are generally alone at such a time.

2) {There should be} no signs, except to superiors or by their orders.

3) Do not stand on the couch (or look over the partitions).

4) Permission {is} required to go there at all, *a fortiori* to take extra rest.

---

106. *Regulations*, 146–48.
107. *Regulations*, 146.
108. *Regulations*, 146–47.

5) {The} light {is} to burn all night (cf. {the} *Rule*[109])—enough to see to get around.

6) No other lights may be used except by the officers—Fr. Master, {the} subprior, and here also the bellringer. It would be a violation of {the} *Rule* to take a flashlight to the dormitory in order to read.

7) We sleep in the habit—including the cowl unless dispensed. Novices always remove the cloak; {the} night cowl {is} permitted, {the} scapular also; shoes {are} always removed; socks {are} okay to remove. {There may be} dispensations for summer.

8) Once we are in the dormitory for rest, no one should leave without a special need. {It is} not allowed to get up and go wandering around. No one {is} allowed to get up early and go down to choir before the bell. No visits to {the} Blessed Sacrament {are to be made} during the night. {We must be} quiet in entering and leaving during {the} time of sleep—remove shoes (even on the stairs).

9) Make the couch daily after chapter, or Fridays after the discipline.

10) {The} curtain {is} always closed when we are in {the} cell, always open when we are out of it.

11) It is not permitted to draw aside the curtain of another's cell under any pretext whatever—except only superiors, {the} infirmarian, {the} wardrobe keeper—and when waking another for the night watch (do not knock on {the} cell, but shake the mattress); if we knock on {another's} cell, we wait until he appears.

12) {There is} separation of juniors from one another ({cf. the} *Rule*[110]), and of monks from brothers.

Cleanliness:[111] {the cell should be} swept once or twice a week, {with a} general clean-out once or twice a year, in good weather, when {the} floor is washed, mattresses {are} put out in {the} sun,

109. *Rule*, c. 22 (McCann, 70/71).

110. *Rule*, c. 21 specifies that the beds of the younger monks are to be placed among those of the older members of the community rather than grouped together (McCann, 70/71).

111. See *Regulations*, 147 (n. 298).

blankets aired, etc.—Rev. Father announces {the time for this} in chapter. Other points {include} air, screens in summer, urinals, {and} especially the fire escapes!

Meridian (siesta) (*Usages*, 299[112]) {is} no longer prescribed; {it is} permitted in summer for those who wish, ordinarily {lasting} half an hour. Others should not walk around in {the} dormitory when some are taking their rest. Some may have reason to get permission for extra rest at some other time. In general, always be quiet in and around {the} dormitory, and do not use {the} singing room without first checking to see that the cells are empty.

Refectory (300–302[113]):

1) No one enters {the refectory} outside of meal times. The refectory is not a passageway. No one should go in and look at the relief board, for instance, without a truly valid reason. {Practice} mortification.

2) We must always wear {the} cowl or cloak when eating, unless dispensed on account of {the} heat (then also, wear them if in work blouse). Our meals are acts of religion, in which a certain decorum is called for. Washing hands at the door tends to be a formality, but we should be clean already. When entering the refectory, do not make a great ceremony out of the way you use the towel, or do not drag it in after you so that the one behind you can't catch it. {Show} simplicity and decorum in everything, to preserve a supernatural and peaceful atmosphere during meals, in which one can nourish the body without too much distraction for the soul.

3) Bows to {the} crucifix {are to be made} when arriving at {one's} place, when crossing, when leaving (explain: all {bows are} moderate). Again {there should be} a certain simple decorum about our conduct. All these small gestures, without destroying the essential simplicity of our conduct in the refectory, are an acknowledgement of the presence of God *in the community*, {and a} respect for Jesus Who sits down to eat in the midst of His disciples, not

112. *Regulations*, 147–48.
113. *Regulations*, 148–49.

physically, but in the mystery of charity. "Where two or three are gathered together . . . there am I in the midst of them."[114]

4) The head table: superiors represent Jesus—guests also.

5) Poverty in the refectory {is evident in} no tablecloths, nothing "special"; great simplicity {is practiced} to avoid useless work, for one thing. {There is} one row of religious at each table. {This makes for} greater recollection, not facing each other across the table, {providing} an element of solitude. {The} reader's pulpit {is located} in the obvious place, where all can best hear (n.b. loudspeakers: do not leave them on during times when no one is there). The set-up for each religious {includes} spoon, etc., napkin.

Kitchens ({and} *Workrooms*):[115]

1) {There are} two kitchens—one for {the} community and one for guests. Meat {is} never prepared in {the} community kitchen, even for the sick.

2) No one enters {the kitchen} without special permission, except cellarers, {the} guestmaster, and {the} infirmarian (and of course cooks). {It is} a place of silence where even those who ordinarily have permission to speak cannot speak unless another permission is granted.

THE MANNER OF ANNOUNCING THE EXERCISES
(Book II, chapter 2[116])

This short section has two parts: {the} first one[117] on the bells, when and how they are to be rung, and the second[118] on the Angelus. Before we start considering the daily exercises themselves, we must pause to talk about the bells by which they are announced. We should have a great love and reverence for the bells. They are to us, first of all, the *voice of God*. They are the voice

114. Matt. 18:20.
115. See *Regulations*, 149 (nn. 303–304).
116. *Regulations*, 36-42 (nn. 67–83).
117. *Regulations*, 36-41 (nn. 67–81).
118. *Regulations*, 41-42 (nn. 82–83).

by which God makes known His will to us. They speak to us of
His love. They call us to show our love for Him by doing His
will. They call us to heaven. They summon us to make acts of
faith and to renew our offering of ourselves to God. They remind
us that if we are faithful to our vocation we will without any
doubt dwell happily with God forever in heaven. Hence they are
the very voice of heaven itself. Heaven opens its windows to us
momentarily every time the bells call us to prayer. The bells call
us to all our exercises, but *above all to prayer and to Holy Mass.*
Hence at the first sound of the bell, we should always respond:

a) in a spirit of *faith*—{we must} *realize Who is calling us*, and
that we are called by these bells to perform the greatest work
possible for man on earth. Each time we hear the bells ring we
should *first of all be thankful for our vocation*, and in a general way
realize the importance of fidelity—for this bell is not calling me
only to this or that hour of the office, but to heaven itself, the
reward for performing faithfully whatever duty is being announced. If we go to choir like the Magi following the star to
Bethlehem, we will truly find God in our prayer.

b) in a spirit of *love for souls*—the bells are the *voice of the
Church*, a kind and solicitous Mother, calling us to pray for souls
and obtain grace for them, both the living and the dying. Remember John Donne's meditation on the tolling bell:[119] when the bells
ring for one who is dying they are ringing for me also, for we are
all "part of" one another. The bells of my monastic church ring
for those who suffer and die in all parts of the world and who
need my prayers. I must never become indifferent to their need!

---

119. John Donne, *Devotions upon Emergent Occasions* (Ann Arbor: University
of Michigan Press, 1959), Meditation 19: "No man is an island, entire of itself;
every man is a piece of the continent, a part of the main. If a clod be washed away
by the sea, Europe is the less, as well as if a promontory were, as well as if a
manor of thy friend's or of thine own were: any man's death diminishes me,
because I am involved in mankind, and therefore never send to know for whom
the bell tolls; it tolls for thee" (108-109). This passage is of course the source of
the title for Merton's own *No Man Is an Island* (New York: Harcourt, Brace, 1955).

c) in a spirit *of obedience* we should immediately put aside whatever we are doing and hasten to do the will of God (cf. {the} *Rule*, c. 5: obeying *"in auditu auris"*[120]). Thus we make reparation for all the disobedience of mankind—for all the hearing of evil things. *Relinquentes* statim quae sua sunt *et voluntatem propriam deserentes* . . .[121] St. Bernard says[122] that self-will is what fills hell. *The bells call us to abandon our own will, hence they deliver us from slavery;* they are the voice of liberty and joy, calling us to the freedom of the sons of God! How sad to remain attached to what we are doing! From the time of the Desert Fathers it has been regarded as a sign of a good monk, that at the first sound of the bell he stops what he is doing, even leaving unfinished a letter he may be tracing or a word he is writing. Realize that we give glory to God by our promptitude, by the alacrity with which we prefer His will, and the call to prayer, to anything else. Only if there is a definite indication that He wills something else for us, should we not go immediately where the bell calls. Charity however constitutes a higher obligation, but we must not be too quick to think that charity or obedience demand that we stay away from choir. There must be a *serious* reason.

The Blessing of Bells in the Rituale[123] tells us of the many graces brought to us by the bells, as sacramentals. They protect us first of all against the devil, against temptations and phantasms, against storms, and they impart an increase of devotion. Simply to listen to the bells in the right spirit and to think what the sound means is already a perfect preparation for prayer. The grace of the bells is in particular an increase of faith—*crescat in eis devotio fidei.*[124]

---

120. "as soon as the ear has heard"; McCann, 32, which reads: ". . . *Obauditu auris* . . ." (a quotation from Ps. 17[18]:45).

121. McCann, 32/33: "immediately abandoning their own affairs and forsaking their own will."

122. *In Tempore Resurrectionis*, 3.3 (*PL* 183, col. 290A).

123. *Rituale*, 363–67 (VIII, xi).

124. "May the devotion of faith increase in them" (*Rituale*, 365).

READ Psalm 76,[125] several verses of which are important in this blessing; and finally the Gospel of Martha and Mary,[126] read at the end of the blessing, {is} important for our contemplative life: we hear God if we hear His bells!

Usages #67: How many bells are prescribed? "two church bells, {. . .} of different dimensions"[127] (one large and one smaller); a bell for the dormitory; one for the refectory. We have here three bells in the church tower: Michael, Thomas, and Mary. The old small bell from the church is now the dormitory bell. In the refectory, is a handbell really sufficient? The only time the refectory bell is rung is for the "second table" (cf. *Usages*, 457[128]—here in the chapter on the *reader*, who rings the bell in the refectory for the second table after the bell in church has finished ringing the

125. "I cried to the Lord with my voice; to God with my voice, and he gave ear to me. In the day of my trouble I sought God, with my hands lifted up to him in the night, and I was not deceived. My soul refused to be comforted: I remembered God, and was delighted, and was exercised, and my spirit swooned away. My eyes prevented the watches: I was troubled, and I spoke not. I thought upon the days of old: and I had in my mind the eternal years. And I meditated in the night with my own heart: and I was exercised and I swept my spirit. Will God then cast off for ever? or will he never be more favourable again? Or will he cut off his mercy for ever, from generation to generation? Or will God forget to shew mercy? or will he in his anger shut up his mercies? And I said, Now have I begun: this is the change of the right hand of the most High. I remembered the works of the Lord: for I will be mindful of thy wonders from the beginning. And I will meditate on all thy works: and will be employed in thy inventions. Thy way, O God, is in the holy place: who is the great God like our God? Thou art the God that dost wonders. Thou hast made thy power known among the nations: with thy arm thou hast redeemed thy people the children of Jacob and of Joseph. The waters saw thee, O God, the waters saw thee: and they were afraid, and the depths were troubled. Great was the noise of the waters: the clouds sent out a sound. For thy arrows pass: the voice of thy thunder in a wheel. Thy lightnings enlightened the world: the earth shook and trembled. Thy way is in the sea, and thy paths in many waters: and thy footsteps shall not be known. Thou hast conducted thy people like sheep, by the hand of Moses and Aaron."

126. Luke 10:38-42.

127. *Regulations*, 36, which reads: ". . . bells, which, according to the tradition of our Fathers, should be of . . ."

128. *Regulations*, 213.

grace. This ringing of the grace is done by the *junior professed* for the space of a *Pater*. The reader in the refectory should then ring the bell for the second table for the space of a *De Profundis* but a few clangs are considered sufficient. This rule really presupposes a bell in a belfry over the refectory, which can be heard all around the monastery, so that gatekeepers, etc. can know that it is time for their dinner.) The refectory bell prescribed in the *Usages* is distinct from the handbell on the abbot's table.

#68:[129] *The Bell for Rising*: {the} *Usages* prescribe that the bell-ringer provide light and open the church, and then {he} rings the dormitory bell for the space of a *Miserere*.[130] The rising bell is now rung *fifteen minutes before* the bell for the night office. How do we rise in the morning? Why the extra time? We sleep clothed in order to be able to go to church without delay. This is the main idea we should have on rising: our *call to pray in the night* while the world sleeps. *Prayer should be the first idea in our mind*, from the first moment of waking. This is important—much depends on the way our day begins. If we are slow and sluggish in turning to prayer, and spend a lot of time and thought on our physical comfort and bodily needs, these will gradually come to take up too much of our attention and our ardor for prayer will be cooled. Obviously, certain needs must be taken care of. But this is not a time for elaborate attention to the body; wash quickly and hasten to church in a quiet, peaceful way. The extra time is given so that we may get to church peacefully. Rushing defeats the purpose of our early rising, unsettles the mind. But it is good to be in church a few moments before the office begins, quiet, awake, at peace, ready to give our whole heart to the one thing necessary, prayer and the praise of God. Avoid an elaborate routine of private prayers in the cell upon rising: holy water, a few ejaculations, {a} kiss {of the} crucifix etc. {are fine}, but the simpler the better. Do not build an elaborate private ritual on top of the prescribed observances and prayers. Avoid racing one another to church—{this} induces {a}

---

129. *Regulations*, 36.
130. Ps. 50[51]: "Have mercy [on me, O God] . . ."

natural spirit and self-love. In summer a change of clothing or a certain amount of dressing is usually necessary.

The Bell for the Beginning of Vigils, and for Offices in General: {for} vigils, at two twenty-eight or -nine, different bells {are rung} according to the rank of the feast, until the signal of the superior {is given}. {For} lauds {the bells are rung}:[131]

a) on feasts of twelve lessons and over—at *Te decet laus;*[132]

b) {on feasts of} under twelve lessons—at the end of the meditation;

c) on ferial days, when lauds is said with prime, {the} first bell {is the} large, {the} second small (as for prime ordinarily).

#69:[133] {The} general rule for the *first bell* for offices {is as follows}:

a) All offices have a first bell, provided that there be a half hour's interval before the office. The exception to this rule is *compline*, which has no first bell. Why? because the compline reading is sufficient warning and preparation.

b) Offices which do not have a first bell are either preceded by sleep (as the night office—in effect the dormitory bell is {the} first bell for the night office) or by work (for instance there is no first bell for vespers when work ends less than half an hour before the office), or by another office or a community Mass. This is a practical point to remember, because frequently we are listening for the first bell for vespers on days when (due to {the} office of {the} dead, for instance), the office begins too early for there to be a first bell.

c) In what does this first signal for office consist? always {the} large (or middle, or two, or all three bells) rung for the space of a *Miserere*, always fifteen minutes before {the} office except in {the} case of tierce and High Mass, when the first bell is a half hour before. At this time the deacon and subdeacon prepare the altar.

---

131. See *Regulations*, 36 (n. 68).
132. See below, n. 302.
133. *Regulations*, 36–37.

Note (#71) the *three tolls for tierce* "to summon the ministers of the altar and to announce the assembling in choir."[134] A custom of the house here however makes it regular for the community to be already assembled and to open the books at the three tolls. However if one is not present in choir for the three tolls he is not really "late" according to the *Usages*. But one should be careful not to develop a habit of arriving after the three tolls.

Remarks: know your bells! When a novice begins his novitiate, he generally judges everything by the novitiate bell, but this is only a convenience that is permitted us. It is useful indeed, but to live merely by the little bell is in fact not to know the language which the monastery bells speak. The *first bell* is the one that should really prepare us for office. For the professed, this is the time to think of getting ready: when one hears the first bell for vespers, for example, he may well put away his books and start for church to make a visit before the office; or he may give himself another few minutes of reading, allow time for necessary errands on the way to church, and be there as the little bell rings in the cloister. One should not wait until the little bell, unless he is certain that he will have nothing to do except put away his book and start for church. The little bell does not allow time for anything more than this. When one is not in choir, for instance in the infirmary, he can tell by the church bells what is going on; or if one has to remain out of the office for some other reason, similarly, he is united to the community by the bells, if he is near enough to hear them.

Examples: what do the following mean? At the ablutions of the conventual Mass, {the} small bell rings for {the} space of a *Pater*—for sext, to follow. {The} bell tolls during the *Magnificat*[135] of vespers—{for} Benediction to follow. {The} bell tolls during the *Salve*[136] from the beginning to *Eia ergo*[137]—{for} Benediction after

---

134. *Regulations*, 38.

135. "[My soul] magnifies [the Lord]" (the hymn of Mary from Luke 1:46-55).

136. The compline hymn, *Salve Regina* ("Hail, holy Queen").

137. "[Turn] then, [most gracious advocate] . . ." (beginning of the second part of the *Salve Regina*).

{the} *Salve*. (What bell would be rung, or how, if Benediction is to take place isolated from any office? "It is announced a few minutes beforehand *more solito*."[138]) {The} large bell rings at the end of canonical compline, from *Custodi nos*[139] to *Deo Gratias*[140]—for {the} *Salve* to follow. {In the} middle of {the} last psalm of tierce, {the} bell rings until the *capitulum*[141]—{for the} procession to follow (two bells {signals a} solemn procession, i.e., stations or solemn litanies). If these same bells are rung from the *capitulum* of tierce to the end of the *Pater*, they are for the conventual Mass (solemn if more than one bell). But if there is a procession?—then the bell for Mass is rung as the community reenters church. From {the} *Sursum Corda*[142] to {the} *Sanctus*[143]—i.e. during the preface of conventual Mass, major or minor, when {the} community assists (no bell {is} tolled for {a} minor Mass said *privatim*[144]), the bell is tolled. Suppose it is the middle of the morning work, and a small bell rings for the space of a *Pater*—it is a private Mass of some religious. {If a} small bell {is} *tolled* for a *Pater* and {a} large bell *tolled* four times—{it is} Rev. Father's Mass. Supposing about three-thirty you hear the large bell ring for the space of a *Miserere*?— what else could it be besides the end of work?—reception of a special guest. At the end of prime, the small bell rings for the space of a *Pater*—for chapter. What if the large bell rings at the same time, for the same space? {The} brothers come to chapter. Supposing it is nine-thirty in the morning of a work day, and you hear the large bell ring twice, for the space of a *Pater*, with a short pause in between—{it signals} extreme unction or viaticum. If the large

138. "in the customary manner" (*Regulations*, 37 [n. 70]).

139. "Guard us, Lord, [as the apple of your eye]" (*Breviarium Cisterciense Reformatum*, 4 vols. [Westmalle, Belgium: Typis Cisterciensibus, 1951], *Pars Vernalis*, 170–71 etc.]).

140. "Thanks be to God."

141. I.e. the scripture reading in the office.

142. "Lift up your hearts" (part of the introductory prayers of the preface of the Mass).

143. "Holy, [holy, holy]" (the conclusion of the preface).

144. "privately".

bell rings *three times* for the space of a *Pater*, with a short space in between, then it is for prayers for the agonizing (at the same time the infirmarian should strike the tablet). If the *large bell is rung and the small bell is tolled*, it indicates either a solemn office of the dead, or a solemn Mass for the dead, or the presence of a dead monk in the house (see #76 for the times when this is done[145]), or a funeral (of a monk or brother). ({The} small bell only {is} rung for {the} death and funeral of {a} guest or familiar.) N.B. according to #74 the two bells can be rung *whenever the superior thinks proper*.[146]

The Angelus {is} rung after the night office, before dinner, and after *Salve*. In choir, {one is to} turn in choir and go on the knuckles and say the Angelus in secret; Saturday night and Sunday, say it standing; during Paschal Time, {the} *Regina Coeli*[147] {is} said standing. We stand in token of joy at Christ's victory and in honor of His Resurrection. In the early days of the Church, when the triumph of the Resurrection was uppermost in the mind of Christians, all usually prayed standing, and it was considered wrong to kneel or prostrate at all on Sundays or during Paschal Time. The *Angelus* tends to mean more to one who hears the bell in the midst of ordinary occupations—out in the field. It is a joy to find oneself reminded by Holy Church of the one great reality of our life, the mystery of the Incarnation and Redemption in Christ. At the end of our office, the *Angelus* sums up all our prayers. It is the last reminder of the ancient *oratio* when the monk prostrated and prayed silently after the psalms; {it is} a joy and a privilege to pray bowed down low to the earth—a moment of union with Our Lady—more conscious and more fervent.

The Night Vigils

The monastic day begins immediately with several hours of prayer, showing that the monk is *essentially and above all a man of*

---

145. *Regulations*, 40.
146. *Regulations*, 39.
147. "Queen of Heaven [rejoice]," the Marian prayer that takes the place of the Angelus for daily recitation during the Paschal season.

prayer. The night office, made up of vigils and lauds, is one of the principal parts of the monastic day of prayer, second only to the conventual Mass. Its importance cannot be overestimated. Our esteem for it cannot be too great—hence a few reflections to help us understand what the night office really is. If we do not appreciate the office, we will not truly be monks or men of prayer. Why? as Bouyer rightly points out (*Meaning of Monastic Life*,[148] p. 130), *prayer is not only our work but our rest*. We have not only consecrated ourselves to a life of prayer and sacrificed all else in order to give ourselves to this; but also prayer is, or should be, our compensation for all that we have sacrificed. *If it is not*, then we will tend to seek compensation elsewhere, and this is not licit. The monk must then seek fresh strength, joy, new life, in his monastic prayer. This is clear from the very fact that we rise in the night to pray while other men sleep. They are refreshed by sleep; we are refreshed by prayer. (True, we have had sufficient sleep, for this too is willed by God.) If we *do not* find refreshment and new strength in prayer, then we will sleep indeed. The office is not the whole prayer life of the monk. It is only part of that prayer life. But it is the great school of monastic prayer. The monk formed and taught by the chanting of the psalms, especially in the night, is made ready for deeper and more interior prayer which, indeed, accompanies the chanting of the psalms and prolongs it. Hence the wisdom of uniting a half hour of meditation with our night office. No time could be more appropriate or more fruitful, although perhaps in the beginning it is hard to make a good meditation at that time. As we draw more fruit from the office our meditation also becomes easier and better. At the same time the value of our office depends on the seriousness and fruitfulness of our *lectio divina*.

Some Points about the Night Office:

1. The night office is a "holy vigil"—a time of wakefulness and prayer in which we alone are up while all the rest of the

---

148. Louis Bouyer, *The Meaning of the Monastic Life*, trans. Kathleen Pond (London: Burns & Oates, 1955).

world sleeps, or engages in sin. The darkness and silence of the night are especially favorable to prayer. All other concerns are set aside. Outside {are} the silent woods. In other parts of the monastery the brothers engage in light work in common, with spiritual reading going on, so that their work is also a meditation. In choir, the monks praise God and especially rehearse His great works—the *magnalia Dei*[149]—in the psalms. The memory of the Church, wakeful, goes over the great works of God.

2. It is a *common vocal prayer* in which the use of words, chant, the simple ceremonies and the presence of the monastic community all incite to fervor and aid prayer. Above all it should aid praise. Lauds is the culmination of the night office and it is nothing but pure praise of God. The strength and purity of our prayer come from *unity of faith and charity* more than mere physical presence in the same place. St. Ambrose says: *Multi minimi dum congregantur unanimes, fiunt magni: et multorum preces impossibile est ut non impetrent.*[150] We must realize the strength and worth of the prayer of the Church which is the prayer of Christ, for the all-important fact is that when we are united together in *the prayer which expresses our common faith* Christ Himself prays in us by the voice of His Spirit. Let us get rid of the obsession with our own poor works and prayers as individuals and realize the tremendous power of our solidarity in Christ. Then we will truly begin to pray: lack of firm faith in this great truth is precisely what makes our prayer so vague and sometimes so pointless. The monastic community is never so truly a community as when it prays in common, or rather, more accurately, when *it praises and thanks God* in common. St. Bernard points out (Sermon 11 *In Cantica*, n. 1-2[151]), when we do penance, we act as isolated individuals

149. "great works of God" (Acts. 2:11).

150. "While they are gathered together and of one mind, even a few are many and become powerful, and it is impossible that the prayers of many not obtain [what they ask]" (*Commentaria in Epistolam ad Romanos*, 15, from the anonymous "Ambrosiaster" rather than St. Ambrose himself; *PL* 17, col. 177D, which reads: "*Multi enim minimi . . .*").

151. *PL* 183, cols. 824B–825C.

rather than as members of a community in the sense that each one tends to feel himself isolated in his own sins. This is a rather acute psychological point, and worthy of close attention, for it shows that we *cannot* become Cistercians in the full sense of the word if we are exclusively engaged in lamenting our faults and shortcomings in such a way as to be practically "individualists" cut off from the others, and immersed in our own shame and misery. The true psychology of the divine office is that of *unity in a common gratitude* to God—it is a *Eucharistic* spirit, to put it simply. "Those who engage in thanksgiving are occupied with God alone and think of Him alone, and *for that reason they truly dwell together in unity*" (St. Bernard, *loc. cit.*[152]). Again, {this is} an instance of Bernard's acute psychological insight. As long as we go to choir as individualists, occupied with our own cares, our own little anxieties and preoccupations, even though we may be praying and doing penance, we do not enter fully into the great stream of praise and prayer which is the full expression of the Church's life in the monastic community. As long as we fail in this, we are not fully occupied with God either. Exclusive concern with God means a spirit of thanksgiving and praise which divert our attention from self and from individual concerns to give our whole heart to God, and *by that very fact* we become united with those who do the same. Then we can truly say, "*Ecce quam bonum et quam jucundum habitare fratres in unum.*"[153] This unity and fervor are *helped* by unity and order in the chant, and when the chant is beautiful our hearts are more easily lifted to God in gratitude, provided that we let the chant enlighten our minds to a deeper understanding of the sacred text. (Mere sensible pleasure in the chant actually does very little to help prayer—it tends rather to create passionate attachments to technical opinions and preferences, which make true peace in choir all but impossible). St. Bernard concludes: "NOTHING SO CLEARLY REPRESENTS ON EARTH

152. *PL* 183, col. 824C.
153. "Behold how good and pleasant it is for brothers to dwell in unity" (Ps. 132[133]:1), quoted by St. Bernard, *In Cantica*, 11.1 (*PL* 183, col. 824C).

THE CONDITION OF THE DWELLERS IN HEAVEN, AS THE FERVOR OF THOSE WHO PRAISE GOD" (*loc. cit.*[154]). This devotion is however a special grace of God, the *unguentum pietatis*,[155] which anoints our hearts with a divine and celestial joy, and makes us enter fully into the prayer of the Church—finding in it the sure way to true contemplation. We must ask for this grace, but meanwhile we must be content to struggle generously. *Material attention* to the words and to the chant is of course absolutely necessary, at least as a starting point and a foundation. We do not always have to be explicitly *conscious* of the material aspect of the choir—God forbid. The purpose of the material attention is to give us an habitual grasp of the basic material elements of the office so that we can handle them spontaneously and without special effort or concern, meanwhile devoting our minds to the higher and more important significance of the divine praises, and above all uniting ourselves to God Himself to Whom we are singing. St. Bernard however insists on material fervor in choir, generosity in giving our voice, in attention to the words we sing, but above all in order that we may "taste" the spiritual "honey" of the divine meaning hidden in the wax of the "letter" (Sermon 7 *In Cantica*, n. 4-5[156]).

Needless to say, this is also a time when we practice "watching." This is an important ascetic practice, requiring often considerable sacrifice and self-control. We should not merely be negative about this duty, and "not sleep," because if in fact we are merely negative and passive we *will* sleep in choir and elsewhere. The great thing is to cultivate a fervent devotion and attention to God and the things of God and the desire to enter deeply into these holy things will give us positive motives for keeping awake. Of course, we must carefully avoid all negligence and sloppiness. We shall consider the ceremonies and postures later. The essence of "watching" is not just in keeping physically

154. *PL* 183, col. 824B.
155. *In Cantica*, 10.(title), 4; 12.(title), 7, 10 (*PL* 183, cols. 819C, 821A, 828A, 831D, 832D).
156. *PL* 183, cols. 808A–809B.

awake, but in keeping our mind on spiritual things—the night office is a time when we learn this above all. *Our night vigils are also a battle against the spirits of evil.* The warlike character of many of the psalms we recite in the night hours is to be understood by the fact that we are the watchmen placed on the walls of the City of God while others sleep, and we are engaged in a spiritual war with the enemies of man and of God. Note the *eschatological character* of the night vigils. Jesus said he would come like a thief in the night;[157] {see also} the parable of the wise and foolish virgins.[158] This *coming of Jesus* is a matter of supreme importance to the contemplation of the Church. She looks for an *event*, not for a *mere psychological state*. We rise in the night thinking of the day when we will rise up from the sleep of death. *Super muros tuos, Jerusalem, constitui custodes.*[159] Our fervor and attention are important from this point of view above all. *Much depends on the fervor* of our prayer not only for ourselves and for those we love, for our community and the Order, but also for the whole Church. It is true that the Church's prayer is of great dignity and value in itself. It is true that we are united to the Mystical Christ, Whose prayer cannot fail to be pleasing in the sight of God. But at the same time, we cannot remain passive and inert, for much depends on us. Particularly much depends on our *love* for God and that means love for His will. It has been said that the contemplative exercises in the Church a "ministry" of prayer and penance. It is certainly true that by our prayer in choir, for the whole Church, we are playing a most important part in the affairs of the Church and of Christendom, gaining graces for souls and for nations, and for priests everywhere. A little thought about these things will often help us to pay greater attention and to be more generous in self-sacrifice when it is required. However, the fact remains that the prime purpose of the divine office is not *petition*

157. 1 Thes. 5:2.

158. Mt. 25:1-13.

159. "Upon your walls, Jerusalem, I have stationed watchmen" (Is. 62:6) (*In Cantica* 77.4 [*PL* 183, col. 1157A]).

even for the graces needed by souls and by priests, but *praise and thanksgiving* to God because He is God and because "His mercy endureth forever."[160] Also we must not take too materialistic an attitude towards our choral duties: it is not simply a question of time we have "put in" or the volume of sound we have contributed, or the amount of exercise we have given to our vocal cords that counts. Some people feel they have done much when they have "sung a sackful" (according to the story of Caesar of Heisterbach[161] who saw the devil in a Cistercian monastery gathering into a sack the notes sung by those who were in love with the sound of their own voices). The importance belongs above all to the love of our hearts, our humility, our spirit of prayer, and before all else our *adoration* of God. The modern fashion is to consider adoration above all as a matter of kneeling in silent prayer before the Blessed Sacrament exposed. But the divine praise in choir is a much more ancient and traditional and profound form of adoration. In conclusion, St. Benedict, with his usual simplicity, gives us the basic dispositions with which we should go to choir to praise God in the night hours. We should attend first of all to *the divine presence*, for God is "more present" (*maxime tamen*[162]) when we are in choir. Hence we must remember to serve the Lord in fear that is filial respect and love. We must sing "wisely"—*psallere sapienter*[163] in its fullest meaning embraces a contemplative appreciation of the spiritual sense of the psalms. St. Benedict means at least the attention required to understand what we are singing: *sic stemus ad psallendum ut mens concordet voci.*[164] This may be taken at least in the broad sense that if one

160. Ps. 135[136] *passim.*

161. Caesarius of Heisterbach, *The Dialogue on Miracles*, trans. H. von E. Scott and C. C. Swinton Bland, 2 vols. (London: Routledge, 1929), 1.204-205 (Bk. IV, c. 9); Caesarius says "a certain religious" saw the demon, not himself.

162. *Rule*, c. 19 (McCann, 66).

163. Ps. 46[47]:8 (*Rule*, c. 19 [McCann, 66]).

164. "Let us so stand while praying the psalms that our minds are in harmony with our voices" (*Rule*, c. 19 [McCann, 68], which reads: ". . . *mens nostra . . . voci nostrae*").

does not fully understand the psalms he must at least not cherish any dispositions of heart which would be contrary to the general idea of the praise of God alone and above all, for His greatness and love. Then, too, St. Benedict invites us to recall the presence of the angels, the union of our choir with the choirs of heaven and with the Church triumphant (see *Rule*, c. 19[165]).

The Ceremonies Observed in Choir (*Usages*, Bk. III, nn. 84–144[166]):

1. *The Importance of Exterior Ceremonies*: the whole importance of rubrics and ceremonies lies in the fact that they *express* man's interior worship of God. What does this mean? In order to appreciate the value of ceremonies, we must remember that our public worship is essentially an expression of interior dispositions, and not merely of subjective dispositions of individuals, but of the objective prayer and worship of the Church. Hence, ceremonies, like words, have a twofold function:

a) to help the individual to grasp what the Church means to express, and to enter into it;

b) to help all in common, who "mean" interiorly the same thing, to express that meaning outwardly in unison, so that all together, body and soul, give God the manifest and public glory which belong to Him in the world.

A few principles from *Mediator Dei*: "The worship rendered by the Church to God must be, in its entirety, *interior as well as exterior*."[167] Comment: liturgical worship is *all* interior and *all* exterior—not partly interior, partly exterior, sometimes one, sometimes the other, first exterior then interior (n.b., even the times when we pray in silence, the position in which we do so, and the

---

165. McCann, 68: "*in conspectu Divinitatis et angelorum ejus*" ("in the sight of the Divine One and his angels").

166. *Regulations*, 43–66 (cc. 1–9).

167. *Encyclical Letter of His Holiness Pius XII on the Sacred Liturgy* (Vatican Library Translation) (Washington: National Catholic Welfare Conference, 1948), 11 (#23).

silence itself, has also an exterior function). There is no time in the liturgy when one can say that the interior *alone* is what counts, and there is also no time when one can say that the exterior *alone* is sufficient. {A} twofold error {can occur}: those who misuse the principle that God must be adored "in spirit and in truth"[168] to say that interior worship is sufficient {have a} wrong understanding of the New Testament use of the word *spirit*; *pneuma* does not exclude matter; it embraces both the (spiritualized) body and the soul. St. Paul says[169] {that} our body must be holy because it is the temple of the Holy Ghost {and therefore} that we must use the members of our body as instruments of justice and praise of God, to repair for having used them for sin. Pope Pius XII continues and gives his reasons why the body must participate with the soul in divine worship: "the nature of man as a composite of body and soul requires it to be so."[170] "Divine Providence has disposed that 'while we recognize God visibly, we may be drawn by Him to the love of things unseen.'"[171] Comment: these words, from the preface of the Nativity, call to mind the whole economy of the Incarnation—the Word, having become flesh, has divinized man's human nature, and the bodies of those united to Christ must participate in the same divinization, which expresses itself in the praise of Christ in us, and through us, using our voices and our bodies. The Mystical Body thus continues on earth the worship offered by Jesus to the Father. That our members belong to Christ is clear from 1 Corinthians 6:13-17. "Every impulse of the human heart expresses itself naturally through the senses."[172] "The worship of God is social."[173] "Exterior worship reveals and emphasizes the unity of the Mystical Body, feeds new fuel to its holy

168. John 4:24.

169. 1 Cor. 6:15-20.

170. *Mediator Dei*, 11–12 (#23), which reads: ". . . composite body . . ."

171. *Mediator Dei*, 12 (#23).

172. *Mediator Dei*, 12 (#23), which reads: ". . . heart, besides, expresses . . ."

173. *Mediator Dei*, 12 (#23), which reads: "the worship of God, being the concern not merely of individuals but of the whole community of mankind, must therefore be social as well."

zeal, fortifies its energy, intensifies its action from day to day."[174]
He quotes Cardinal Bona[175] ({a} Cistercian): "Although the ceremonies themselves can claim no perfection or sanctity in their
own right, they are, nevertheless, the outward acts of religion,
designed to rouse the heart to veneration of the *sacred realities*."[176]
Bona adds that pious and well-ordered use of Christian ceremonies is an expression of the faith of the Church, and a sign of faith,
a confession of faith, which distinguishes true from false piety
and the true Christian spirit from heresy. Hence, to sum up, our
bodies have a noble vocation and a great dignity. They share in
the vocation of the soul to glory. They help immensely in the
formation of our spiritual life, both as individuals and as a community. In a fervent and well-ordered community, where ceremonies are properly understood and practiced in subordination to
the deep, inner realities of the spiritual life, they have a great
formative power. They help our prayer. We must learn to use these
ceremonies, as well as the chant, etc., precisely for this, for our
spiritual formation and to nourish our inner life. But note that the
activity of the body in the liturgy *itself forms part of our inner life.*
Pope Pius XII concludes (*Mediator Dei*, nn. 24–27) {that} the interior
element in divine worship is the *chief element*: "Otherwise religion
amounts to mere formalism, without meaning and without
content."[177] "It is an error to think of the liturgy as merely the
outward or visible part of divine worship or as an ornamental
ceremonial . . . or to think that it consists solely of lists of laws
and prescriptions."[178] Not only then is the union of body and soul

174. *Mediator Dei*, 12 (#23), which reads: ". . . day by day."
175. Giovanni Bona (1609-1674).
176. *Mediator Dei*, 12 (#23), which reads: "rouse the heart, like signals of a
sort, to . . ." (*De Divina Psalmodia*, c. 19.3.1) (italics added).
177. *Mediator Dei*, 12 (#24), which reads: ". . . religion clearly amounts . . ."
178. *Mediator Dei*, 12 (#25), which reads: "It is an error consequently and a
mistake to think of the sacred Liturgy as merely the outward or visible part of
divine worship or as an ornamental ceremonial. No less erroneous is the notion
that it consists solely in a list of laws and prescriptions according to which the
ecclesiastical Hierarchy orders the sacred rites to be performed."

in divine worship itself a highly spiritual activity, but, by so doing, we unite ourself to the worship offered to the Holy Trinity by Jesus Christ in His Church, and this, says Pope Pius XII, "IS THE MOST EFFICACIOUS MEANS OF ACHIEVING SANCTITY."[179] {It is} needless to say how important it is, then, to understand the liturgy, to perform the ceremonies well, according to the mind of the Church. Obviously the mind of the Church is not that we should perform these ceremonies with our minds fixed on ourselves and absorbed in the contemplation and admiration of our own punctilious zeal. We are supposed to perform the sacred ceremonies in such a way as to forget ourselves, rise above ourselves, lose all thought of drawing attention to ourselves, and abandon ourselves to the tide of prayer which surges through the whole Church.

In general, the ceremonies and prescriptions surrounding our choral prayer are meant to produce the following effects:

a) Peace, silence, recollection: the ceremonies aid us in *controlling* the restive and impatient movements of the undisciplined body, directing them to God in such a way that the body does not interfere with the soul but helps it (note the difficulty of recollection, sometimes, when one kneels long in mental prayer, and the strange positions the body sometimes gets into; contrast a well-ordered liturgical service).

b) Reverence, gravity, seriousness, "fear of the Lord": {a} sense of the *presence* of God.

c) Decorum and good taste: to observe the rubrics well, and the rules of chant also, will save us from the vulgarity and offensive singularity that inevitably creep into a too subjective (and somewhat distracted) attitude during choral prayer.

d) The rubrics and ceremonies (this is not often thought of) are *organs of tradition* and they unite us with the generations of saints and fathers who have preceded us in praising God since the time of the Apostles. Our ceremonies, needless to say, form us in the spirit of the Order and make us visibly one with our fathers.

---

179. *Mediator Dei*, 13 (#26) (emphasis added).

Entering the Church: everything the monk does should be a prayer—the way he stands, sits, walks, talks, keeps silence, smiles—all should reflect the interior peace and simplicity of a child of God. But at the same time, if he tries in the wrong way to "cultivate" a pious and spiritual appearance in all these things, he will by no means make his acts "prayers" but only expressions of vanity and self-conceit—or else of strain and tension. The fact remains that if a monk *walks* well, he will tend to pray better. If he walks into church as a monk about to pray, he will already be prepared for the divine office. There are certain things which the *Usages* necessarily take for granted: that one already knows how to walk, how to stand, how to turn his head, look up, look down, in a human and religious way, not like an automaton or a sub-human being. Read Guardini, *Sacred Signs*, 25 ff. ("walking"[180]), 21 ff. ("standing"[181]).

180. "Walking,—how many people know how to walk? It is not hurrying along at a kind of run, or shuffling along at a snail's pace, but a composed and firm forward movement. There is a spring in the tread of a good walker. He lifts, not drags, his heels. He is straight, not stoop-shouldered, and his steps are sure and even. There is something uncommonly fine in the right kind of walking. It is a combination of freedom and discipline. . . . And when the occasion is religious, what a beautiful thing walking can be! It is a genuine act of divine worship. Merely to walk into a church in reverent awareness that we are entering the house of the Most High, and in a special manner into his presence, may be 'to walk before the Lord.' . . . Walking is the outward mark of man's essential and peculiar nobility. It is the privilege of man alone to walk erect, his movement in his own power and choice. . . . But we are more than human beings. We are, as the Bible calls us, the generation of God. . . . [Through the Eucharist,] our work, our recreation, our pleasures and our pains, are all taken up into the Christ-life. The consciousness of this mystery should pass in all its joyous strength and beauty into our very manner of walking" (*Sacred Signs*, 25–27).

181. "The respect we owe to the infinite God requires of us a bearing suited to such a presence. The sense that we have of the greatness of His being, and, in His eyes, of the slightness of our own, is shown outwardly by our kneeling down to make ourselves small. But reverence has another way of expressing itself. . . . Standing is the other side of reverence toward God. Kneeling is the side of worship in rest and quietness; standing is the side of vigilance and action. It is the respect of the servant in attendance, of the soldier on duty. . . . We may feel at times a sort of constraint in kneeling. One feels freer standing up, and in that case standing

a) walking to church: the novices go in "community"—quietly, recollected; there is a definite spiritual and psychological effect, a *grace* that comes with entering the church in procession. We should try not to miss this (cf. {the} Benedictines and their "station"[182]—an excellent preparation for the office; *the reason why we do not have a station* is that it is presupposed that most of the choir will already be there in church in advance, praying in silence and preparing their hearts in this way for the divine office). Avoid rushing to choir at the last minute. Avoid making signs on the way to church, and especially near the church door.

b) *Usages*, 84: "Before entering the church we uncover."[183] When we go to church covered in community, many uncover too soon. Uncover near the church door, near the statue of St. Joseph— not at the chapter room; "arrange habit becomingly"[184] refers especially to the hood. {A} house custom {is} not arranging one another's hoods.

c) Taking holy water (entering the door: read Guardini, *Sacred Signs*, 37-40[185]): why do we take holy water? as a *purification*

---

is the right position. But stand up straight: not leaning, both feet on the ground, the knees firm, not slackly bent, upright, in control. Prayer made thus is both free and obedient, both reverent and serviceable" (*Sacred Signs*, 21–23).

182. "Remote preparation for prayer is recommended by all the masters of asceticism. The speak to us also of a proximate and immediate preparation; and our Constitutions have provided for it by securing us before each choir duty the few minutes, 'statio' in the cloister. These are precious minutes, and it would be hard to exaggerate their importance, for then do we tune the soul, our spiritual instrument. We should therefore have the good sense not to pursue in the 'statio' questions or lines of thought which we have begun; nor should it be a place for conversation or any sort of intercourse" (Paul Delatte, osʙ, *The Rule of St. Benedict: A Commentary*, trans. Justin McCann, osʙ [New York: Benziger, 1921], 186–87).

183. *Regulations*, 43.

184. *Regulations*, 43 (n. 84), which reads: "arrange our habit . . ."

185. "When you step through the doorway of a church you are leaving the outer-world behind and entering an inner world. . . . Behind the church doors is an inner place, separated from the market place, a silent, consecrated and holy spot. . . . Between the outer and the inner world are the doors. They are the barriers between the market place and the sanctuary, between what belongs to the world at large and what has become consecrated to God. . . . Do not rush

of our heart, {a} reminder of our *baptismal consecration* to God, our baptismal vows to renounce the world and Satan and serve God alone, a reminder that by baptism we are buried together with Christ in death, and that we live a risen life in Christ; therefore we should seek the things that are above. This wonderful act of faith in the cross and the resurrection, and in the fact that we ourselves are temples of the Holy Trinity, should never be performed merely mechanically, but with deep inward love and gratitude to God Who dwells in us. We take holy water and make the sign of the cross (*Usages*, 111): "We make the sign of the cross gravely, with the body *erect*";[186] we give the sign of the cross its *"full extension."*[187] What is said in n. 111 about covering the hand with the border of the cloak or sleeve of the cowl is not to be interpreted as if we did this when taking holy water—or at least we do not get the sleeve of the cowl wet when taking holy water (n.b. n. 111 adds that no signs of the cross are made in common exercises unless explicitly prescribed, "except at the beginning of work,"[188] from which it is clear that a sign of the cross at the beginning of work *is not prescribed* but permitted; *lectio divina*, hearing a private Mass, etc. do not count as a common exercise and the monk is not obliged to limit himself then to signs of the cross "prescribed in the usages").

Other points in n. 84: never pass through the church, or in and out, without kneeling for a moment (explain what to do when passing an altar where the consecration is taking place,[189] where communion is being distributed,[190] or between {the} consecration

---

through the doors. Let us take time to open our hearts to their meaning and pause a moment beforehand so as to make our entering-in a fully intended and recollected act" (*Sacred Signs*, 37-39; see also n. 18 above).

186. *Regulations*, 54 (emphasis added).

187. *Regulations*, 54 (emphasis added).

188. *Regulations*, 54.

189. "prostrate" (*Regulations*, 44).

190. "we kneel down and wait until the last has communicated, unless the communicants are very numerous" (*Regulations*, 44).

and communion[191]). 85:[192] which door to enter—why do we enter from the end of the choir not occupied by the abbot and seniors? What is the difference in the choir when the seniors are in the Mass stalls, and in the office stalls? In the office stalls, *emphasis is on the community and the abbot presiding*—the salutations indicate this, and fit in with this; in the Mass stalls, all is directed toward the altar and here too the salutations correspond to the situation. 86-87:[193] {for} the salutations on entering choir, in general these various bows and the way in which one goes to his stall are recognitions of the presence of God on the altar {and} in the community. Instead of going straight to the stall, one goes "by a gradual ascent"[194] at each step of which one takes cognizance of the dignity of the place and of those who are present in it, and also of one's own position in the community. This is *not a mere matter of protocol*—it is an education in reverence and in awareness. (Explain the bows in detail.) 88:[195] when to occupy the stall of a religious who is late. 89:[196] saluting the abbot in his stall: n.b. {the} difference between saluting the abbot as an "object" and as a "person"—for instance on the way to the jube. What is the meaning of a bow? Would you bow to a person who had his back turned to you? Is not a bow a recognition of a dignity as *present*? What is the difference between the presence of a person and the presence of an object? {What is the proper protocol} when there are several abbots in choir? (still n. 89[197]).

nn. 90–92:[198] *behavior in church*: what is meant by "reverence" (90[199])? It contains both the notions of fear and of love, the fear of offending a loved and worshipful person. What do we rever-

191. "genuflect" (*Regulations*, 44).

192. *Regulations*, 44.

193. *Regulations*, 44–45.

194. Not a direct citation from the *Usages*.

195. *Regulations*, 45.

196. *Regulations*, 45.

197. "we only salute the one who occupies the abbatial stall" (*Regulations*, 45).

198. *Regulations*, 45–47 (c. 2).

199. *Regulations*, 45.

ence in God? especially His *holiness*, His *mystery*, His *power*, His *mercy*. It is possible in practice for a "religious" person to be in the presence of God, to speak of God, to pray to God, to sing to God and to praise God—all as if God did not exist and never existed. God has become merely an "object," a "notion." We must always keep alive the sense of His presence as a *Person in mystery*; not as a He or an It, but as the "You" to Whom "I" ("we") speak. Paradoxically, we can lose the sense of God just by *knowing too much about Him*. Knowledge *about* God tends to be dangerous, necessary though it may be—it ends by taking us away from the mystery in which alone He is truly confronted and loved and known. The other point is to remember His infinite transcendency, and our complete helplessness to do anything for Him, or to serve Him as He desires, or to pray well, without the action of His divine Spirit in us. One of the functions of interior trial and temptation in our life is to preserve the real sense of God's infinite holiness and of our need for Him.

Silence in church: two points are stressed in the *Usages* (n. 90[200]):

a) *Avoid unnecessary noise*: everything should be done to cut down on noise in church; silence is essential to the atmosphere of reverence and prayer: loud coughing, throat-clearing, careless banging of books, etc. destroy the exterior reverence proper to the house of God. If we were really *penetrated* with a reverential sense of God's presence, we would more easily avoid these things. But as it is, our "sense" of God, while sincere, remains too often abstract and "mental" and does not reach out to take possession of our whole being. Outside {the} time of office, even during work time, be considerate—n.b. however, don't exaggerate (walking on tiptoe).

b) *Signs* are strictly forbidden in church—more strictly than anywhere else; {they are} only made to prevent some *considerable* fault or confusion. Note—it is not said that we should, or can, make signs to tell others what to do, to instruct others. It is of

---

200. *Regulations*, 45.

course necessary that guardian angels[201] instruct their charges (but this should be prepared as much as possible outside of church) but one novice should avoid telling another what to do. Repeat: {signs are allowed only} to avoid a *considerable* fault or confusion. When summoning someone to leave office (cf. 312[202]), first ask permission of {the} superior in the usual way, then make {a} sign to the one who is to leave.

Walking in church {is} always in ceremony. Why? How does "walking in ceremony" express greater reverence? {It} presupposes the wearing of *a cowl*—long sleeves; exceptions to this rule {are} when others carry books or etc.: why? {With regard to} walking when others are bowed down or out of the stalls (n. 92[203]), at such times we do not walk in *choir* without necessity. Stop at {the} *first stall on your own side* and conform to {the} posture of {the} choir: why? reverence and common sense—bowing, or standing out of the stall, is {a} sign of special reverence, recollection, attention, and for one to be walking through the choir would contradict this (exception: {the} servant of {the} church lighting {the} lamps). Do not push past {the} hebdomadary[204] or invitator or subinvitator when they are fulfilling their functions ({the} reasons {are} obvious). Only the cantors can sing when away from the proper stall and circulating in choir: why? In general, avoid unnecessary moving around in choir; be prepared beforehand, get the books you need, etc.

Other points: raising and lowering the *seats* {should be done} noiselessly[205] (beware {of} oblate cloaks!). Lower only at the moment of sitting down, with the hand nearest the altar (for the sake of uniformity, and {because it is} slightly more reverent, as one turns a little toward the altar instead of away from it). {With regard to} *books*, open {them} and prepare the office before begin-

---

201. I.e. a more experienced novice assigned to introduce a newly arrived novice to the monastic routine.

202. *Regulations*, 153.

203. *Regulations*, 47.

204. I.e. the priest celebrating the conventual Mass for a given week.

205. See *Regulations*, 46 (n. 91).

ning; charity and good order demand this: {it} shows appreciation for the dignity of the choral prayer to which "nothing is to be preferred."[206] Novices should cultivate this habit from the very beginning. Closing {of} books {is done} at the *per omnia*[207] of the last collect {for} Mass,[208] lauds, vespers, and {the} office of {the} dead; at the versicle of other hours—again, for the sake of uniformity and reverence. Be especially careful of silence when closing the books.

Order and Rank in Choir (93–100[209]): why {the} emphasis on order and rank in a monastery? Is this not contrary to the Gospel? cf. Matthew 23, where Jesus, speaking against the scribes and pharisees, warns His disciples to avoid imitating them who "love the first places at feasts and the first chairs at synagogues. . . . They love to be called by men rabbi, etc." (read Matt. 23:2-12[210]). In this passage Jesus is *condemning the love of honors*. But He does not condemn honor itself. The more one is united to Christ in sanctity or in office, the more he becomes humble and the servant of all, yet at the same time the more he is worthy of honor in so far as *Christ in honored in him*. "He that heareth you heareth me,

206. "*Ergo nihil operi Dei praeponatur*" (*Rule*, c. 43 [McCann, 102]).

207. I.e. "*per omnia saecula saeculorum*" ("through all the ages of ages"), the concluding words of the collect prayers.

208. See *Regulations*, 46–47 (n. 91).

209. *Regulations*, 47–48 (c. 3).

210. "The Scribes and the Pharisees have sat on the chair of Moses. All things, therefore, that they command you, observe and do. But do not act according to their works; for they talk but do nothing. And they bind together heavy and oppressive burdens, and lay them on men's shoulders; but not with one finger of their own do they choose to move them. In fact, all their works they do in order to be seen by men; for they widen their phylacteries, and enlarge their tassels, and love the first places at suppers and the front seats in the synagogues, and greetings in the market place, and to be called by men 'Rabbi.' But do not you be called 'Rabbi'; for one is your Master, and all you are brothers. And call no one on earth your father; for one is your Father, who is in heaven. Neither be called masters; for one only is your Master, the Christ. He who is greatest among you shall be your servant. And whoever exalts himself shall be humbled, and whoever humbles himself shall be exalted."

and he that despiseth you despiseth me."[211] St. Paul (Romans 12:10) says we should all love and honor one another ("with honor preventing one another"—a phrase taken up by the *Rule*[212]). And {in} Romans 13:7 {he says}, "Render therefore to all men their dues, tribute to whom tribute is due . . . honor to whom honor [is due]." If this is true of secular princes, how much more for priests and religious superiors who represent Christ. The monks' view of the universe conforms to that of the Fathers who saw in all things a *hierarchical structure*. The Church is made up of visible hierarchies which represent the invisible and spiritual hierarchies of the angels, and form one great organism with the invisible hierarchies.[213] Indeed, the whole universe surrounds the throne of God. Closest to the mystery of God Himself are the spiritual beings who contemplate Him, and in the outer circles are the hierarchies of men who are illuminated by the angels and who transmit to one another the understanding of the mystery of God. The whole function of the ecclesiastical hierarchy is to bring about the divinization of men by purification, illumination and union with God.[214] Let us remember the mystery that God's sanctifying action *reaches us through other men*. All this is then represented by the order and rank of monks in choir. {*Usages,*} 93:[215] the place of highest dignity in our choir is on the *epistle side* of the choir. (Note: this is illogically reversed in the sanctuary.) The next highest is at the head of the gospel side. Hence the abbot stands on the epistle side, the prior on the gospel side, and the

211. Luke 10:16.

212. *Rule*, c. 72 (McCann, 160).

213. The reference is to the *Celestial Hierarchy* and *Ecclesiastical Hierarchy* of Pseudo-Dionysius; for a summary see Thomas Merton, *An Introduction to Christian Mysticism: Initiation into the Monastic Tradition* 3, ed. Patrick F. O'Connell, Monastic Wisdom [MW], vol. 13 (Kalamazoo, MI: Cistercian Publications, 2008), 139–42.

214. See *Ecclesiastical Hierarchy*, 5.I.3,7; 6.III.5-6 (Pseudo-Dionysius, *The Complete Works*, ed. Paul Rorem, trans. Colm Luibheid, Classics of Western Spirituality [New York: Paulist Press, 1987], 235–36, 238–39, 247–49).

215. *Regulations*, 47.

other religious follow according to three principles: (a) seniority; (b) orders; (c) office. Of these, the second is obviously the most important, in view of the hierarchical superiority of the *priest* over the plain monk. What "hierarchies" are conceivable in our choir? (1) abbots, equivalent to bishops (bishops themselves sometimes visit us); (2) priests; (3) deacons, etc., other orders; (4) monks; (5) novices; (6) laybrothers; (7) oblates; (8) postulants and other lay persons; (9) penitents (the excommunicated, etc.: cf. *Rule* of St. Benedict[216]). Practical points to remember in nn. 93–100 {include}: the stall in front of the abbot's and prior's stall {is} *left empty* during {the} office.[217] Never occupy {the} abbot's or prior's stall during office, in their absence.[218]

The Ceremonies Observed in Choir (101–111[219]): let us now look at the ceremonies of the office and at the office itself. The night office begins. The bell rings, we open the books, and stand in the stalls *turned towards the altar*. This is one of the standard postures: attention, alertness, readiness to serve: "Speak, Lord, for thy servant heareth."[220] READ Isaias 6:1-9,[221] the great theophany of the

---

216. See *Rule*, c. 44: "How the Excommunicated Are to Make Satisfaction" (McCann, 105, 107), which specifies that the one excommunicated is excluded from choir and prostrates himself outside the oratory during the office until the abbot permits him to return, at which point he is assigned a place in choir as decided by the abbot.

217. *Regulations*, 48 (n. 93).

218. *Regulations*, 47 (n. 93).

219. *Regulations*, 49–54.

220. 1 Sam. 3:9, 10.

221. "In the year king Ozia died, I saw the Lord seated on a high and lofty throne, with the train of his garment filling the temple. Seraphim were stationed above; each of them had six wings: with two they veiled their faces, with two they veiled their feet, and with two they hovered aloft. 'Holy, holy, holy is the Lord of hosts!' they cried one to the other. 'All the earth is filled with his glory!' At the sound of that cry, the frame of the door shook and the house was filled with smoke. Then I said, 'Woe is me, I am doomed! For I am a man of unclean lips, living among a people of unclean lips; yet my eyes have seen the King, the Lord of hosts!' Then one of the seraphim flew to me, holding an ember which he had taken with tongs from the altar. He touched my mouth with it. 'See,' he said, 'now that this has touched your lips, your wickedness is removed, your sin

prophet Isaias. This reading should give us a deep insight into the spirit with which we should appear before God, at the night office especially—the majesty and power of God, praised by the seraphim (the monk's praise is the most characteristic feature of his *bios angelikos*[222]—"angelic" vocation—along with his virginity). The passage concludes: "I heard the voice of the Lord saying, 'whom shall I send' . . . And I said, 'Lo, here am I, send me.'" This is the spirit with which we stand facing the altar. Also, when we chant facing one another in choir, we are like the seraphim in the vision crying "*one to another,*" *sanctus, sanctus, sanctus.*[223] Note here that the "Thou and I" approach of Martin Buber,[224] taken up by Bouyer,[225] is not too absolute. We do in fact chant to one another about God, in the third person.

The Antiphon of the Blessed Mother: we prostrate on our knuckles. It is beautiful and fitting that the day of the Cistercian and all his hours of the *opus Dei*[226] (except compline, which ends with the *Salve*) should begin with this act of profound homage to Our Lady. Bowing on the knuckles {is} peculiar to our Order in the main, a deep reverence, prostrating our whole being before God

---

purged.' Then I heard the voice of the Lord saying, 'Whom shall I send? Who will go for us?' 'Here I am,' I said; 'send me!" And he replied: Go and say to this people: Listen carefully, but you shall not understand! Look intently, but you shall know nothing! . . ."

222. "angelic life".

223. "holy, holy, holy" (Is. 6:3).

224. Martin Buber, *I and Thou*, trans. Ronald Gregor Smith (Edinburgh: T. & T. Clark, 1937); Merton is reading this book in late April, 1958: see Thomas Merton, *A Search for Solitude: Pursuing the Monk's True Life. Journals, vol. 3: 1952–1960*, ed. Lawrence S. Cunningham (San Francisco: HarperCollins, 1996), 192–93 [4/20/58], 195–96 [4/24/58].

225. "If it is to be *truly* God whom we seek, we have to seek him as a person. Martin Buber . . . has expressed this very adequately: a person is only sought as a person, in dialogue. It is only in the 'I to Thou' relationship that the person remains personal for us. Someone of whom we get into the habit of speaking as 'he' is no longer a person for us. Whether we realize it or not, 'he' is no more than a thing" (*Meaning of the Monastic Life*, 8).

226. "the work of God"—i.e. the Divine Office (*Rule*, cc. 7, 22, 43, 44, 47, 50, 52, 58, 67 [McCann, 46, 70, 102, 104–106, 108, 116, 118, 130, 152–54]).

in thanksgiving for the great mystery of the Incarnation. *O admi-rabile commercium. Creator generis humani, animatum corpus sumens, de Virgine nasci dignatus est, et procedens homo sine semine, largitus est nobis suam deitatem.*[227] {There is a} concentration upon the won-derful mystery of God's love: it is an *admirable* exchange; the greatness of the mystery takes us out of ourselves. He has taken our flesh and given us His divinity—all the more marvelous since He has emptied Himself that by His poverty we might be made rich. We begin the praise of God with this remembrance of the entire meaning of His great work in the world, the mystery of our redemption and deification in Christ. This is our proximate preparation for the office—praise should flow naturally and spontaneously from the thought of this great mystery of God's love for us. Then, after {this comes} a silent recitation of the *Pater, Ave* and *Credo*[228]—{a} moment of deep recollection and gathering together of our faculties, in order to praise God—not just {a} mechanical repetition of words without thought. {Note the} im-portance {of the} presence of God, and {the need for} reflection on what we are about to do—even if we cannot always pay too much attention to the very familiar words we recite. Try however to think of the words, normally—so too throughout the office.

The *Deus in Adjutorium*:[229] we stand out of the stalls in cere-mony, facing the altar. This {is} one of the most solemn postures, {which} indicates total surrender to God and {the} complete gift of ourself to His service and praise. We become all praise, and we *stand* to praise Him, because we are men, His sons, proud of our dignity and our vocation. There is a great nobility about our work of praise, and this immediately becomes clear with the *Deus in adjutorium*, which is solemn and fervent and prayerful. Above

227. "O marvelous exchange. The Creator of the human race, taking on an animate body, deigned to be born of a Virgin, and coming forth as man without human seed, conferred on us his own divinity" (Vespers Antiphon for the Feast of the Circumcision [*Breviarium Cisterciense, Pars Hiemalis*, 304]).

228. The Our Father, Hail Mary and Creed.

229. "O God, [come to my] assistance" (Ps. 69[70]:2; see *Rule*, c. 18 [McCann, 62]).

all, think what it means: how we need the help of God to accomplish the slightest good; especially also the thrice repeated *Domine labia mea aperies*,[230] which should bring home to us our need for grace at this solemn time. We should take this prayer seriously.

The Office Begins: St. Benedict's office begins with the *Domine labia mea aperies*. Unless God gives us the Holy Spirit to pray in us, our office is worthless in His sight. But since the Church prays here, and the prayer of the Church is always heard, then God does indeed.open our lips, and does indeed give us the Holy Spirit. It is the Spirit Who prays in us, Christ who prays in us by His Spirit. *Mediator Dei* says: "By assuming human nature, the Divine Word introduced into this earthly exile a hymn which is sung in heaven for all eternity. He unites to Himself the whole human race and with it sings this hymn to the praise of God. As we must humbly recognize that 'we know not what we should pray for, as we ought, the Spirit Himself asketh for us with unspeakable groanings.' Moreover, through His Spirit in us, Christ entreats the Father."[231] Then the Holy Father quotes St. Augustine: "We recognize in Him our voice and His voice in us."[232] Since contemplation is a realization of our union with Christ in the Holy Spirit, then it is clear that for the divine office to lead to contemplation, we should strive to realize how Christ sings in us during the office, and thus become consciously united to Him in His thoughts and His love and His contemplation of the Father. This is the work of the Holy Spirit in us, "opening our lips"—not only our lips but the inner depths of the spirit—to pray to God. It is not sufficient that we pray with our lips alone, but we must pray with our inmost heart. Spiritual understanding of the psalms {is} necessary, and for this the purification and mortification proper to the monastic life should help to prepare us, but also our reading and study of scripture. Pope Pius XII continues, remarking that the objective dignity of the Church's prayer calls

---

230. "Lord, open my lips" (Ps. 50[51]:17; see *Rule*, c. 9 [McCann, 50]).
231. *Mediator Dei*, 51 (#144), quoting Rom. 8:26.
232. *Enarratio in Psalmum 85*, 1 (*Mediator Dei*, 51 [#144]).

for a correspondence on our part: "earnest devotion in our souls. For when in prayer the voice repeats those hymns written under the inspiration of the Holy Spirit and extolls God's infinite perfections, it is necessary that the interior sentiment of our soul accompany the voice so as to make those sentiments our own in which we are elevated to heaven . . . etc."[233] He quotes St. Benedict, *Rule*, c. 19 here.[234] Read all *Mediator Dei* n. 145.[235] {In} conclusion (n. 146): "on this depends in no small measure the efficacy of our prayers."[236]

Domine quid multiplicati sunt . . .[237] Then we recite Psalm 3, *recto tono*.[238] It is a *preparatory prayer*. READ Psalm 3,[239] a magnificent morning prayer. It is obviously chosen first of all because of line 6 (*Ego dormivi et soporatus sum, et exsurrexi quia Dominus suscepit*

233. *Mediator Dei*, 51 (#145), which reads ". . . Holy Ghost . . ."

234. McCann, 68; see the following note.

235. "To this lofty dignity of the Church's prayer, there should correspond earnest devotion in our souls. For when in prayer the voice repeats those hymns written under the inspiration of the Holy Ghost and extolls God's infinite perfections, it is necessary that the interior sentiment of our soul accompany the voice so as to make those sentiments our own in which we are elevated to heaven, adoring and giving due praise and thanks to the Blessed Trinity: 'so let us chant in choir that mind and voice may accord together.' It is not merely a question of recitation or of singing which, however perfect according to norms of music and the sacred rites, only reaches the ear, but it is especially a question of the ascent of the mind and heart to God so that, united with Christ, we may completely dedicate ourselves and all our actions to Him" (*Mediator Dei*, 51 [#145]).

236. *Mediator Dei*, 51 (#146), which reads: ". . . no small way . . ."

237. "Lord, how many [are my adversaries]," the opening verse of Ps. 3.

238. "in a direct tone," i.e. a single note.

239. Why, O Lord, are they multiplied that afflict me? many are they who rise up against me. Many say to my soul: There is no salvation for him in his God. But thou, O Lord, art my protector, my glory, and the lifter up of my head. I have cried to the Lord with my voice: and he hath heard me from his holy hill. I have slept and have taken my rest: and I have risen up, because the Lord hath protected me. I will not fear thousands of the people surrounding me: arise, O Lord; save me, O my God. For thou hast struck all them who are my adversaries without cause: thou hast broken the teeth of sinners. Salvation is of the Lord: and thy blessing is upon thy people."

me[240]), but also because of the night office's character as a struggle against the forces of evil (*Quid multiplicati sunt qui tribulant me . . .*[241]), and above all because of the confidence and hope in God which is the theme of the psalm. Our night office is *an office of struggle and hope*, a flame of hope rising up in the spiritual darkness of the world, before the presence of the hidden God.

Multi dicunt animae meae non est salus ipsi in Deo ejus . . .[242] From all sides the world insidiously whispers its message of despair and unbelief—not openly and explicitly, but there are so many human and unworthy things we do which implicitly declare that we trust more in human means than in God. Our office is the time to purge our hearts of all unworthiness and "be converted" to our God Who alone is our salvation. "Salvation is from the Lord and His blessing is upon His people." The psalm introduces us to the naked poverty and insecurity of the human soul left to itself and also shows us that God Himself is our garment and our strength.

The Invitatorium—Psalm 94—{is} a psalm of processional entrance to the Temple {and} prostration before the Holy of Holies. Here the office really begins. This whole idea is probably an original invention of St. Benedict.[243] The two invitators stand at the presbytery step, before the dark sanctuary—a most solemn reminder of the presence of the All-holy God. The Invitatory sets the tone for the whole office; and that tone is *invariably* one of praise, but also secondarily of *repentance* and *compunction*, and preparation for a day of holiness. *Praise* is primary: Exultemus *Domino;*[244] Jubilemus *Deo salutari nostro*[245] (the *rock* of our salvation). We come to stand before Him *"in confessione"*[246]—*confessio*

---

240. "When I lie down in sleep, I wake again, for the Lord sustains me."
241. "Why have those who trouble me grown numerous?"
242. "Many are saying to my soul, 'There is no salvation for him in God.'"
243. *Rule*, c. 9 (McCann, 50); see Pius Parsch, *The Breviary Explained*, trans. William Nayden, cssr and Carl Hoegerl, cssr (St. Louis: B. Herder, 1952), 155.
244. "Let us sing joyfully to the Lord" (Ps. 94[95]:1).
245. "Let us acclaim God [the rock of] our salvation" (vs. 1).
246. "[Let us greet him] with thanksgiving" (lit. "in confession") (vs. 2).

laudis[247] above all. Why do we praise Him? because of His greatness (*Deus magnus Dominus*[248]); because of His mercy (*Non repellet
Dominus plebem suam*[249]); because of His power as our Creator (*In
manu ejus sunt omnes fines terrae . . . Ipsius est mare . . .*[250]). Penance
{is also important}: in view of the greatness and holiness and
goodness of God, we are also aware of our own nothingness and
misery, our need to cast ourselves down, to *adore*, to *implore* Him
(*Ploremus coram Domino qui fecit nos*[251]). Yet our prayer is confident
and full of love, for we recognize that we are His people and "the
sheep of His pasture."[252] Hence {we show} *vigilance*. The last two
sections are in effect a call to spiritual alertness and attention to
God and a recalling to mind of the faults of the Fathers in the
desert who did not understand His wonders. Attention to His
will {is required}—not to be one of those who *"errant corde."*[253]
(For the temptation in the desert, see Exodus 17:1-7 and Numbers
20:2-13.[254]) All these things will be recounted in the psalms. In
reciting the psalter we will be spiritually passing through the Red
Sea and the desert; we must be alert to the "great works" of God,
and forge ahead in our journey to *enter into His rest*. Parsch says:
"The invitatory is a cry to wake up. It is the herald, announcing
tersely what the feast is about."[255] {This focuses on} the *kerygmatic*
character of the liturgy—a statement of a glorious *fact* that calls
for our *acclamation* today (*hodie*[256]). God reveals Himself to us anew

247. "a confession of praise".

248. "the Lord [is] a great God" (vs. 3).

249. "the Lord will not cast off his people" (vs. 3 [Vulg.]).

250. "In his hand are all the ends of the earth . . . His is the sea . . ."
(vss. 4, 5).

251. "Let us weep before the Lord who made us" (vs. 6).

252. vs. 7.

253. "go astray in their heart" (vs. 10).

254. In these passages the Israelites murmur against the Lord because they
are without water, and are given water from the rock; the incidents take place at
Massa (Ex. 17:7) and Meriba (Ex. 17:7, Num. 20:13), mentioned in the psalm (vs. 8).

255. Parsch, 155.

256. vs. 7.

each day (cf. *St. Benedict, Prologue*[257]). We hail God our Savior as our Lord and our King. This *acclamation of the Divine Word* is a great work of salvation. The seed is sown and springs up in our heart. Dom Hilaire Duesberg says, "Chanting the invitatory psalm is not a job for lazy people and those with heart trouble should be persuaded not to undertake it, because in it one picks up the whole world to carry it away into the cycle of sacred praise."[258]

The invitatory antiphon varies according to the feast or season, stressing the mystery or some part of Psalm 94: Christmas: *Puer natus est nobis, venite adoremus;*[259] Epiphany: *Christus apparuit nobis, venite adoremus;*[260] {I} Sunday {of} Lent: *Ploremus coram Domino qui fecit nos;*[261] Easter, etc.: *Alleluia;*[262] Assumption: *Venite adoremus Regem Regum, cujus hodie ad aethereum Virgo Mater assumpta est coelum;*[263] All Saints: {*Regem regum Dominum, venite adoremus: Quia ipse est corona Sanctorum omnium*};[264] Martyrs: *Regem martyrum Dominum;*[265] Sundays after Pentecost: *Adoremus Dominum qui fecit*

257. "The divine voice crieth daily to us: *Today if ye will hear his voice, harden not your hearts*" (McCann, 6/7, quoting Ps. 94[95]:8).

258. Hilaire Duesberg, "Le Psaume Invitatoire (Ps. 95)," *Bible et Vie Chrétienne*, 12 (Dec. 1955–Feb. 1956), 86: "Ce n'est pas un métier de paresseux que de réciter le psaume invitatoire et l'on devrait en détourner les cardiaques, car il s'agit de prendre en charge le monde entier pour l'entraîner dans le cycle de la louange sacrée" (Merton's translation).

259. "A child is born to us; come let us adore" (*Breviarium Cisterciense, Hiemalis*, 236, which reads: "*Christus natus . . .*").

260. "Christ has appeared to us; come let us adore" (*Breviarium Cisterciense, Hiemalis*, 350).

261. "Let us weep before the Lord who made us" (*Breviarium Cisterciense, Vernalis*, 174, which reads: ". . . *coram Domino Deo nostro* [our God] . . ."); copy text reads "III".

262. *Breviarium Cisterciense, Vernalis*, 305 (repeated six times).

263. "Come let us adore the King of Kings whose Virgin Mother has been raised to heaven today" (*Breviarium Cisterciense, Pars Aestivalis*, 570).

264. "Come, let us adore the Lord, the King of Kings; for He Himself is the Crown of all the saints" (*Breviarium Cisterciense, Pars Autumnalis*, 427 [antiphon left blank in copy text]).

265. "[Come let us adore] the Lord, King of martyrs" (*Breviarium Cisterciense*, 48*).

nos;[266] Common of Our Lady: *Sancta Maria Dei Genitrix Virgo, intercede pro nobis.*[267]

The General Structure of Vigils: after the *invitatorium*, vigils follows a standard pattern that varies accidentally according to the dignity of the feast. But there are always the same elements. On big feasts there are three nocturns, and twelve lessons with twelve responsories. There are also generally twelve antiphons—one for each psalm, and a thirteenth for the canticles of the third nocturn. On ferial days and "feasts of three lessons" there is no third nocturn. In the first nocturn there may be three lessons and responsories, or there may be only a short lesson and a *responsorium breve.*[268] The night vigils always include the following elements:

1. *The hymn*—at the beginning. Most hours of the office begin with the hymn (except vespers and compline). A hymn is a *song of praise* as well as a prayer. Note that in our breviary the element of petition is often most emphatic in the hymns. Hymns were brought to the Western Church from the East by St. Hilary.[269] St. Ambrose is the Father of Western hymnody, hence the dignity and strength of many of the hymns of the breviary composed by him. Ambrose is a great poet—simple and laconic, without artifice, but his verse has a great nobility and strength. The Church of Milan was, then, a center of hymnody from the beginning. Rome was very slow in adopting hymns into her office. St. Benedict took the custom of singing hymns in the office from St. Ambrose and the Church of Milan—hence in the *Rule* a hymn is often called an *"Ambrosianum."*[270] The regrettable "revision" of the ancient

266. "Let us adore the Lord who made us" (*Breviarium Cisterciense, Aestivalis*, 19).

267. "Holy Virgin Mary, Mother of God, intercede for us" (this is actually the versicle for the capitulum for vespers ["*Dei Genetrix, intercede pro nobis*"] [*Breviarium Cisterciense*, 170*]; the antiphon for vigils is "*Ave Maria, gratia plena: Dominus tecum*" ["Hail Mary, full of grace; the Lord is with thee"] [*Breviarium Cisterciense*, 170*]).

268. "a short responsory".

269. See Parsch, 137.

270. *Rule*, cc. 9, 12, 13, 17 (McCann, 50, 54, 56, 62).

hymns {took place} under St. Pius V: the humanist Ferrari first composed new hymns, then under Urban VIII a team of four Jesuits revised and "purified" the old hymns of St. Ambrose, making them extremely stuffy and heavy and robbing them of most of their poetry.[271] Fortunately in the monastic and Cistercian breviaries we still retain the old Ambrosian texts. Parsch comments on the "revision": "We know today that this 'correction' was nothing more than gross barbarism. What the humanists pedantically labeled 'mistakes,' were, in fact, quite idiomatic peculiarities of popular, late-Latin poetry" (*The Breviary Explained*, p. 138). (Discuss the matins hymns for Sundays.[272])

　　2. Six psalms with six, or three, or one antiphon: the psalms and antiphons are the main part of the office. We shall discuss

271. See Parsch, 24–27, 138.

272. There are a dozen different Sunday matins hymns over the course of the year—Advent: "*Verbum Supernum Prodiens*" ("Heavenly Word Proceeding") (*Breviarium Cisterciense, Hiemalis*, 176); Sunday within the Octave of Christmas: "*Christe Redemptor Omnium*" ("Christ, Redeemer of All") (*Breviarium Cisterciense, Hiemalis*, 235–36); Sunday within the Octave of the Epiphany: "*Hostis Herodes Impie*" ("Herod, Impious Enemy") (*Breviarium Cisterciense, Hiemalis*, 373); Second Sunday after Epiphany through Quinquagesima Sunday, and Sundays of November: "*Aeterne Rerum Conditor*" ("Eternal Creator of All Things") (*Breviarium Cisterciense, Hiemalis*, 20); First Four Sundays of Lent: "*Summi Largitor Praemii*" ("Giver of the Highest Reward") (*Breviarium Cisterciense, Vernalis*, 174); Passion and Palm Sunday: "*Pange Lingua*" ("Sing Out, My Tongue") (*Breviarium Cisterciense, Vernalis*, 239–40); Easter and five following Sundays: "*Chorus Novae Jerusalem*" ("Choir of the New Jerusalem") (*Breviarium Cisterciense, Vernalis*, 305); Sixth Sunday after Easter: "*Aeterne Rex Altissime*" ("Eternal King Most High") (*Breviarium Cisterciense, Vernalis*, 362–63); Pentecost: "*Jam Christus Astra Ascenderat*" ("Now Christ Had Risen to the Stars") (*Breviarium Cisterciense, Vernalis*, 390); Trinity Sunday: "*Summae Deus Clementiae*" ("God of Highest Mercy") (*Breviarium Cisterciense, Aestivalis*, 174); Corpus Christi and Second Sunday after Pentecost: "*Sacris Solemniis Juncta Sint Gaudia*" ("On this Sacred Feast Let Joys Be Joined") (*Breviarium Cisterciense, Aestivalis*, 194); Third through Sixteenth Sundays after Pentecost, and Sundays of October: "*Nocte Surgentes Vigilemus Omnes*" ("Rising in the Night, Let Us All Keep Watch") (*Breviarium Cisterciense, Aestivalis*, 20). Merton is probably thinking particularly of the "*Aeterne Rerum Conditor*," by St. Ambrose, the so-called "Cockcrow Hymn" (see Parsch, 143–46 for a discussion).

them in greater detail perhaps. Meanwhile it is sufficient to say that in the psalms we have the Church "ruminating" on all the words of God, and penetrating deeply into her unceasing contemplation of the divine mystery—the "reintegration of all in Christ" (*instaurare omnia in Christo*[273]) which is the sum total of all divine revelation. The psalms are a compendium of the whole scriptures. *The Church wants to go through the whole psalter once a week*, in order to be constantly meditating on the mystery. The Church herself is the mystery of Christ. In meditatively chanting the psalms, we are as it were the conscience, the mystical consciousness of the Church, aware of herself as the mystery of Christ, the Body of Christ, the City of God—aware too of her incomplete and imperfect state, her condition as a pilgrim in the exile of this world, her longing for eschatological fulfillment, the new Creation, the New Jerusalem. *The antiphons* are important in so far as they show us how the Church takes each psalm, what aspect of the mystery she sees in that particular psalm and in that particular office. {For} examples, see the antiphons used with Psalm 18—in {the} Office of Virgins and the Blessed Virgin Mary (*Nigra sum*[274]); in {the} Common of Apostles (*In omnem terram . . .*[275]); {for} Christmas (*Tamquam Sponsus Dominus procedens de thalamo suo*[276]). ({This} psalm {is} used also in {the} Ascension, {the} Sacred Heart, {the} Holy Angels.) Line 6 (*In sole . . .*[277]) is borrowed as an antiphon for {the} Immaculate Conception, etc., etc.

3. *The Lessons and Responsories*: in addition to the hymns and psalms, which are especially prayer and praise, the office also consists of readings and responsories—nourishment of the mind with texts from the word of God, from the writings of the Fathers, and from the lives of the saints. The Church *meditates* on these

---

273. Eph. 1:10.

274. "I am black [but beautiful]" (Cant. 1:5) (*Breviarium Cisterciense*; 111*).

275. "In all the earth" (Ps. 18[19]:5) (*Breviarium Cisterciense*, 4*).

276. "He comes forth like a bridegroom from the bridal chamber" (Ps. 18[19]:6) (*Breviarium Cisterciense, Hiemalis*, 238).

277. "[He has pitched a tent] in the sun" (*Breviarium Cisterciense, Hiemalis*, 491 [second antiphon for the first nocturn]).

texts as she reads them, and the function of the responsories is usually to deepen the understanding of the texts and draw more fruit from them. The practice of reading from the scriptures goes back to the Jewish meetings in the synagogues. Jesus Himself read a "lesson" from Isaias in the synagogue of Nazareth and expounded it to the people (READ Luke 4:14-21[278]). This brings to mind the great truth that all the lessons somehow or other bring us to Christ, Who is the center of the scriptures and the object of the teaching of all the Fathers; and it is Jesus Who lives in His saints. Every time the Church reads the scriptures publicly it is Jesus Who reads them and says: "This day this scripture is fulfilled . . ." Listening to the lessons, not only try to understand them but try to find Christ in and through them. This does not mean strained allegorism and forced applications, but allowing the Holy Spirit to show us how Jesus is revealed to us in all these different ways—if only by the growth of grace and virtue in our own souls. The lessons contribute powerfully to the growth of His life in us. *Note*: the order of *lector* {is instituted} especially to provide the reader with special graces to read as an instrument of God for the promulgation of the divine message. {The} lectorate {is a} function proper to the priest, an *alter Christus*.[279] The lector is an *alter Christus* as far as *reading* is concerned. In reading ancient manuscripts, a special skill was required, since punctuation did not exist or was not clear. Lectors were also cantors;

---

278. "And Jesus returned in the power of the Spirit into Galilee; and the fame of him went out through the whole country. And he taught in their synagogues, and was honored by all. And he came to Nazareth, where he had been brought up; and according to his custom, he entered the synagogue on the Sabbath and stood up to read. And the volume of Isaias the prophet was handed to him. And after he opened the volume, he found the place where it was written, *The Spirit of the Lord is upon me because he has anointed me; to bring good news to the poor he has sent me, to proclaim to the captives release, and sight to the blind; to set at liberty the oppressed, to proclaim the acceptable year of the Lord, and the day of recompense*. And closing the volume, he gave it back to the attendant and sat down. And the eyes of all in the synagogue were gazing on him. But he began to say to them, 'Today this Scripture has been fulfilled in your hearing.'"

279. "other Christ."

{they} sang the texts now sung as gradual and alleluia (perhaps they would sing a whole psalm after the epistle, solo). Read from the rite of ordination of lectors: "Endeavor therefore to read the word of God, that is, the sacred lessons, distinctly and intelligibly, without any mistake or falsification, so that the faithful may understand and be edified and that the truth of the divine lessons be not through your carelessness lost for the instruction of the hearers."[280] But {there is} more: "What you read with your lips, you must believe in your hearts and practice with your works"[281] etc. Reading the lessons {is} a function of the Church by which she *teaches* the faithful. The reader is bound to back up the truth of what he says by his own living example, in so far as he can. He is a *verbi Dei relator,*[282] both by word and by example. He is ready to earn a share of the reward given to all those who "have duly administered the word of God from the beginning."[283] That is to say, he participates in the glory of the prophets and saints whose words he reads in the assembly of the faithful. Hence the importance of diligent preparation. The singing of the lessons and responsories should not be regarded above all as a "musical" performance. The meters, puncta, etc. are *punctuation*—not just a "melody." The point is to convey the meaning of the text. In Church readings it is *never* proper for an individual to intrude his own personality on the hearers by emphasizing his own individual style. We will all retain our individuality, but merged into the universal and catholic character of the whole.

280. "*Studete igitur verba Dei, videlicet Lectiones sacras, distincte et aperte, ad intelligentiam, et aedificationem fidelium absque omni mendacio falsitatis proferre; ne veritas divinarum Lectionum incuria vestra ad instructionem audientium corrumpatur*" (*Pontificale Romanum Summorum Pontificum Iussu Editum a Benedicto XIV et Leone XIII Pontificibus Maximis Recognitum et Castigatum* [Mechliniae: H. Dessain, 1958], 19).

281. "*Quod autem ore legitis, corde credatis, atque opera compleatis*" (*Pontificale Romanum,* 19).

282. "a proclaimer of the word of God" (*Pontificale Romanum,* 19, which reads "*relatores*").

283. "*qui verbum Dei bene administraverunt ab initio*" (*Pontificale Romanum,* 19).

Example of Lessons and Responsories for III Nocturns:

First Sunday of August (Eighth after Pentecost[284]): to understand the first and second nocturns of the usual Sundays, we must remember that the Church aims at reading and commenting on practically the entire Bible in her offices throughout the year. Naturally, this would mean very long readings if the program were carried out in full in choir. In our Order, the ancient idea was that what was not read in choir should be *completed* in the refectory. As it is, the daily scripture reading in the refectory is taken at least from the same section of the Bible as the scripture reading in the nocturns. Hence, in Advent, we begin *Isaias*; after {the} Circumcision, {the} Epistles of St. Paul; after Septuagesima, Genesis, etc.; {during} Passiontide, Jeremias; {in the} Easter season, Acts, {the} Apocalypse, {the} canonical epistles; {from} Pentecost to {the} First Sunday {of} August, {the} Historical Books (Kings, Paralipomenon,[285] Esdras); {from the} *first Sunday* {of} *August*, {the} *Sapiential Books*; {from the} first Sunday {of} September, Job, Tobias, Judith, Esther; {from the} first Sunday {of} October, Maccabees; {from the} first Sunday {of} November, Ezechiel, Daniel, and {the} minor prophets. It is a good idea to make our private scripture reading fit in with this plan so that we really finish the books ourselves. The *responsories* during these times are from the same books.

Hence, in the first nocturn of {the} first Sunday of August, we begin the *Book of Proverbs*. Note: the readings from the Sapiential Books {are} recommended by the Church for "beginners"; {they} give us the best possible starting point for a true understanding of the divine office. The whole tone of the readings and responsories is set by the Sapiential Books: the desire for wisdom, which is found in the will and law of God, but above all, love and veneration for the Divine Wisdom Itself, God's own nature, His mind, with its divine plan for the creation, elevation and

---

284. I.e., August 4, 1957.
285. I.e., Chronicles.

divinization of man. The cult of divine wisdom is deeply mystical, not merely ethical. The Church seeks to enter into the great "mystery" of the Wisdom of God by cooperating with His love and letting His wisdom shine forth in her life. How? by judging according to His Law and living according to His Will.

READ Proverbs 1:1-22:[286]

a) {Note the} emphasis on prudence and justice, the right ordering of one's life, by *experience*—one's own and that of one's elders. {The focus is on} how to "judge," how to "interpret" and to understand, how to penetrate the wisdom of the ancients, how to enter into tradition as a vehicle of divine teaching. {One is to gain} maturity of judgement.

b) *The fear of the Lord is the beginning of wisdom.*[287] {This is} an all-important principle. It is not gained from book-learning alone, but by an interior change. "Fear of the Lord" changes the heart;

286. "The proverbs of Solomon, the son of David, king of Israel: That men may appreciate wisdom and discipline, may understand words of intelligence; may receive training in wise conduct, in what is right, just and honest; that resourcefulness may be imparted to the simple, to the young man knowledge and discretion. A wise man by hearing them will advance in learning, an intelligent man will gain sound guidance, that he may comprehend proverb and parable, the words of the wise and their riddles. The fear of the Lord is the beginning of knowledge; wisdom and instruction fools despise. Hear, my son, your father's instruction, and reject not your mother's teaching; a graceful diadem will they be for your head; a torque for your neck. My son, should sinners entice you, and say, 'Come along with us! Let us lie in wait for the honest man, let us, unprovoked, set a trap for the innocent; let us swallow them up, as the nether world does, alive, in the prime of life, like those who go down to the pit! All kinds of precious wealth shall we gain, we shall fill our houses with booty; cast in your lot with us, we shall all have one purse!'—My son, walk not in the way with them, hold back your foot from their path! For their feet run to evil, they hasten to shed blood. It is in vain that a net is spread before the eyes of any bird—these men lie in wait for their own blood, they set a trap for their own lives. This is the fate of everyone greedy of loot: unlawful gain takes away the life of him who acquires it. Wisdom cries out aloud in the street, in the open squares she raises her voice; down the crowded ways she calls out, at the city gates she utters her words: 'How long, you simple ones, will you love inanity, . . .'"

287. *Lectio* 2 (*Breviarium Cisterciense, Aestivalis*, 256).

{it leads to} conversion {and} compunction; {it} opens our eyes. Fools despise it. Holy fear makes us fly from sin as from death itself, and makes us value {the} experience of the wise.

c) "Let not sinners entice thee"—{that is}, the "fool" who secretly despises the will of God. They have specious arguments: do not listen to them. They *do not learn* from experience {but} are guided by their own will.

d) Wisdom crieth out in the streets: there is a *vocation* to Wisdom—she calls us and we must listen. Our reply {is found} in the ardent prayers of the responsories:

{In the} first responsory, Wisdom reveals herself (cf. Proverbs 8); who is Wisdom? God's own essence in so far as it contains His ideas and His plan for the world: "*In principio . . . ante omnes colles generavit me Dominus.*"[288] Is Wisdom the Logos? not exactly—but the Logos is Wisdom.

{The} third responsory {reads}: "Send forth, O Lord, Thy Wisdom from the throne of Thy majesty, that she may be with me and work with me, and that I may know what is pleasing to Thee at all times; Give me, O Lord, Wisdom Who stands ready by Thy throne . . ."[289]

{The} fourth, fifth responsories, etc. (also {used} in the Sunday procession): *Ne derelinquas me in cogitatu maligno . . . vanitatem et verbum mendacii longe fac a me.*[290] Our prayer {is} to have our thoughts purified and guided by Wisdom. To have bad thoughts, vanity, violence, lying, self-seeking, is to be immersed in darkness and folly. Bad thoughts spring from bad desires, which make us blind to the truth. How beautifully the Church meditates and prays in these responsories. How deep they are and how much they have to say—how universal, and yet how suited to each one's own needs. We could not have thought of

---

288. "In the beginning . . . the Lord brought me forth before all the hills" (Prov. 8:23, 25) (*Breviarium Cisterciense, Aestivalis*, 256).

289. *Breviarium Cisterciense, Aestivalis*, 257.

290. "Do not abandon me in evil thoughts . . . make vanity and a lying word be far from me" (*Breviarium Cisterciense, Aestivalis*, 257–58).

so many wonderful petitions by ourselves, yet they are just what we need. The first nocturn is penetrated with this sense of the fear of the Lord, and of the danger of having in one's mind a multitude of vain and evil thoughts. The same themes continue in the responsories of the three nocturns.

Second Nocturn: St. Ambrose[291] sketches out the beginning of a commentary: {he} takes these Old Testament themes of wisdom and folly and places them in the New Testament context: folly {is} love of the world; wisdom {is} love of the cross {and} renunciation of the world; {he explains} the vanity of Judaism: because it was zeal without knowledge. The Jews fasted, prayed, etc., but because they did not have wisdom, it was all vain. In other words, St. Ambrose shows us that what the Church is praying for when she prays for wisdom is the great monastic virtue of discretion, enlightened by docility and obedience.

This is a very Benedictine office, filled with the spirit of St. Benedict. As this happens to be the Eighth Sunday after Pentecost, then we have the Gospel of the Unjust Steward,[292] and it fits in as a very striking example of "wisdom." The children of this world are wiser in their own generation than the children of light. Paradoxically we have here ascended to the highest Christian spiritual wisdom, which consists in mercy and in forgiveness; and the highest is presented under a "low" and despicable form—that of a sinner, who is nevertheless praised by the Lord. This shows us that wisdom for the Christian is to be sought in lowliness and humility and mercy, and not in what the world respects and venerates as "wisdom" or even in what the world considers as virtue. The wisdom we seek is the wisdom of the cross and of the love of Jesus Christ, folly to the Greeks and scandal to the Jews.

The Te Deum ("Ambrosian hymn of praise"[293]) {is the} conclusion of nocturns on every feast {and the} transition to lauds. {By

---

291. *Sermo 5 in Ps. 118 (Breviarium Cisterciense, Aestivalis*, 257–58 [*lectiones* 5–8]).
292. Luke 16:1-9.
293. See Parsch, 159: "the so-called Ambrosian hymn of praise".

the} spirit of this hymn we have been filled to overflowing by the word of God in the nocturns and now there is nothing left but ardent praise. {This hymn was} not composed by any one author (certainly not sung by Saints Ambrose and Augustine after {the} latter's baptism[294]). {It is} a series of sections composed at different times by unknown authors and brought together, perhaps, into final form by Bishop Nicetas of Remesiana.[295] {It consists of} three parts:[296] v. 1-10 (with doxology) {are a} *hymn to the Father*, calling all the saints to praise Him; v. 14-21 {are a} *hymn to Christ* (of {a} later date: "Here we are given the glorious portrait that the ancient Church had of Christ": Parsch[297])—the King of Glory and conqueror of death; v. 22-29 {include} various petitions, {in} verses taken from psalms. "This hymn is one of the Church's grandest treasures . . . an exclusively Christian and Catholic prayer" (Parsch[298]).

The Gospel: {the} solemn reading of the Gospel by the abbot is the culminating point of feast-day vigils. All turn towards the *jube* and stand in ceremony, after the usual *Dominus vobiscum*[299] (its special significance {being that} the Lord is with us and is about to speak to us in His inspired Word; the Church firmly believes that it is Christ Himself Who speaks to her in the Gospel; also, the *Holy Spirit* is present in the midst of us to give us special light and understanding and to increase our faith). St. Benedict would have us listen "*cum tremore divino*."[300] An example {is} the Gospel of the *Feast of the Immaculate Heart of Mary*[301] (Luke 2:42-51): Our Lady kept "all the words" of Jesus in her heart. For our hearts to be perfectly pleasing to God, they should be like Mary's heart, filled with the words of Jesus. But notice that this refers to

---

294. See Parsch, 159.
295. See Parsch, 159.
296. See Parsch, 159.
297. Parsch, 160.
298. Parsch, 161–62.
299. "The Lord be with you."
300. lit. "with a divine trembling" (*Rule*, c. 50 [McCann, 116]).
301. *Breviarium Cisterciense, Aestivalis*, 607.

a mystery *which Mary did not understand*. It wounded her. It was a trial. We must be aware both of the intimacy and of the transcendence of the Divine Word. We all answer *Amen*—{we are} *responsible* for the seed that has been sown in our hearts.

Te Decet Laus[302] {is} another most beautiful hymn. Our only possible reaction after receiving with joy the *Verbum salutis*[303] is to burst forth into praise. Note the ceremonies: bow when the cantor take up *te decet hymnus*,[304] then go on the misericords after *"Sancto Spiritu."*[305] Here in brief is a beautiful example of the combination of rites, gestures, words and chant to make a perfect act of adoration with our whole being—if only we do it with understanding. Then {comes} the *collect* and the blessing of the *father abbot*.

The Morning Meditation

Vigils are followed by the morning meditation. This is the best time for mental prayer. It is a time of silence, darkness. The whole monastery is at peace. There is nothing for anyone to do (among the choir monks) except to pray. It is a time free from distractions, and furthermore the monk is already recollected; he has been chanting the psalms; he has heard the word of salvation; he is in the presence of God. This should normally be an ideal time for mental prayer, {for the} *cultivation* of the divine seed in our souls. It is also very conformable to the *Rule*, for St. Benedict prescribed that the time after vigils should be devoted to *meditatio psalmorum*.[306] In monastic tradition, after the psalms meditation was always practiced: psalms and meditations alternated, in the office of the desert fathers. The monastic tradition always associates liturgical prayer with mental prayer. Thus

---

302. "It is fitting [to give] you praise" (the brief hymn following the reading of the Gospel) (*Breviarium Cisterciense*, *Vernalis*, 34 etc.).

303. "word of salvation".

304. "It is fitting [to sing] you a hymn" (second line of the *"Te Decet Laus"*).

305. "[with] the Holy Spirit."

306. "meditation on the psalms" see chapter 8 (McCann, 48), where this precise phrase is not used.

we see that one leads to the other, normally and naturally. *Psalmodia* is a preparation for *oratio*. It is also associated with *lectio*. All together lead up to *contemplatio*.[307] If we are to profit by the morning meditation, we must form a truly monastic attitude towards mental prayer. Most of the failures in mental prayer flow from an unmonastic approach. Disjointedness, discontinuity, is the bane of monastic life and monastic spirituality. It should not normally exist in a monastery, where above all everything is ordered to unity. However, if we lead our monastic life under the domination of an unmonastic spirit, our day becomes broken up into fragments; everything is disjointed; we are going through a series of "exercises" which do not have any special connection with one another. They just become things which we do one after another. The bell rings, and that is what we do next. In fact, if when the bell rings we are seriously concerned about "dropping one thing and beginning another" we are subject to discontinuity and we have not yet gained the true monastic spirit. A true monk is always engaged in the *unum necessarium*.[308] But this requires considerable maturity. Others—less mature—are perhaps always immersed in the same fog, no matter what may be the "exercise" that is going on. This is not the monastic spirit either. It is not "continuity." If we are leading disjointed lives, we worry about what to do during "the morning meditation" as distinct from any other time. The key is to love *all the time*.

The connection between psalmody and meditation:

1) Both are ways of adoring and praising and loving God; both are nourished substantially by the *word of God* and by the *presence of God*.

2) In the psalmody, there is a greater element of *exterior* and *bodily* worship; the *imagination and senses* play a greater part. The effort is *communal*. The choir as a group rehearses in mind and

---

307. "psalmody . . . prayer . . . reading . . . contemplation".
308. "the one thing necessary" (Lk. 10:42).

memory the *magnalia Dei*,[309] the works, promises and revelations of God.

3) In the *oratio* this all goes deeper, becomes more personal, more interior; prayer descends from the lips and mind into the *heart*. But unless we have already been singing the psalms with our heart, the way is not fully open to mental prayer. From this it is clear what mental prayer is—and we must be clear about the nature of anything we try to do. The fact that people are so seldom aware of what "mental prayer" really is means that they fail. The term mental prayer is misleading. It is not prayer *in the mind* so much as prayer *in the heart*. Mental prayer is prayer in which we pray not so much by thoughts and words, by affections, etc., but by *the adoration of the inmost center of our being*. It is prayer in which we adore God, ideally, by finding Him in the depths of our own spirit, and by going out of ourselves to unite our spirit with His Spirit.

The purpose of mental prayer: in mental prayer we *digest* the nourishment that has been given to us by God in reading, psalmody, etc. We *assimilate* God's words to us—whether they have come to us exteriorly, through the teaching of books or of the liturgy, or through the words of our spiritual father, or through *experience* itself. One cannot be a true monk if he does not assimilate and *make his own* the teaching that is given him from morning to night by God our Father. We meditate formally at certain times, but this is only to give us the *habit of meditation*, the habit of "seeing" beyond the surface of things. A monk is necessarily a meditative, thoughtful man. He "considers" (*consideratio*). He does not jump to conclusions; he studies things from various angles; he penetrates their inner meaning. He plunges into the depths to find the wisdom of God in everything, but very simply.

{See} *Ecclesiastes*—a meditation on *life*. The monk should *meditate deeply on his own life* and his own experiences, his own failings, the providential help of God, the many instances of the

---

309. "the mighty works of God" (Acts 2:11).

mercy of God, the evident signs of the loving protection of God. The monk should know the meaning of life, and particularly he should *know the meaning of his own life.* After some years in the monastery, one should be able to thoroughly recognize and understand the "inscape" of his vocation. (Explain Hopkins' term "inscape"[310] and apply it here—the inner structure of a living, or organic, or even inorganic created being, the result of its gradual development under the secret action of nature—and the creative hand of God—the trademark of God imprinted in the *individual structure* given to a thing by its history, the mark of God's love and God's wisdom imprinted in the unique identity of a thing.)

We can then say that the purpose of meditation is threefold:

1) To *awaken man to the divine action and to God's teaching* and other providential helps for his salvation; to keep man alert, to help him to see and understand the meaning of God's word of salvation, of the teaching of the Church, of particular messages to him through others, and in a word to help him catch every important message that God would teach him. Here meditation is helped by *compunction* and *self-knowledge* and helps us to *cooperate with God's action our lives*. In order to preserve this inner vigilance of compunction:

a) we meditate on the *last things*—on God's merciful plan to save us from hell, on death as the final summing up of all, on judgement. *Meditation anticipates our judgement.* The meditative man has already judged himself, and has asked for mercy. The unwise man, who does not meditate, has gone through life without thought and without responsibility.

b) we meditate on the *life and passion* of Jesus in order to learn the reality of God's love for us, the infinite tender mercy of God

310. The term occurs almost fifty times in Hopkins' journal for the years 1868–1875, in a variety of ways, most often "to indicate the essential individuality and particularity or 'selfhood' of a thing working itself out and expressing itself in design and pattern" (John Pick, *Gerard Manley Hopkins, Priest and Poet* [1942; 2nd ed., New York: Oxford University Press, 1966], 33).

to us in Christ Jesus, to hate sin, and to fly with all confidence to the heart of our Divine Savior, to bury ourselves in His sacred wounds, and to hide from our spiritual enemies, to draw from the heart of Jesus soothing and cooling balm that heals the wounds of concupiscence and sin. We must always be very zealous in applying to our souls this medicine of Christ's love, and to wash ourselves repeatedly in the Blood of the Lamb of God Who takes away the sins of the world. Here, many beautiful ejaculations suggest themselves; we can spend our meditation prostrate at the foot of the cross crying, "Lamb of God Who takest away the sins of the world, have mercy on me."

c) we meditate on the economy of God's love—the sacraments, the Church, the aids He has given us and our use of these things, especially {the} Blessed Eucharist.

d) we meditate on Jesus' love in our own lives, as said above.

e) we meditate also on the divine attributes {and} seek to realize the *unfathomable* riches contained in each one, going beyond our poor analogy to the infinite reality of God Himself, {and} try to absorb something of this reality.

In this first kind of meditation, "thought" or *consideratio* plays an important part, but we must not suppose that this meditation is not also deeply affective. It is a matter of affective thinking, of thought impregnated with love and trust and humility. The fruits of our thinking increase the power of our affections, and the affections in turn give us light to penetrate more clearly into the inner meaning of the truths we behold. Our aim in all this is to REALIZE—to grasp a divine reality that is beyond our experience. The fruit of such prayer is normally in petitions for what we need or in "vows" as Cassian would say[311]—resolutions to do better, offering to God our good intentions in the humble sincerity of our hearts. Our mental prayer should sometimes have this dynamic and active character, even though it may normally be much simpler and contemplative.

311. *Collationes*, 9, c. 12 (*PL* 49, cols. 783A, 784A).

2) The second function of meditation is to enable man to *enter deeply into the school of life itself*, to make his whole life a meditation, a learning from God, a school of wisdom, *a clearsighted and humble cooperation with the wisdom of divine Providence in our lives*, a ceaseless effort to *please our Heavenly Father* by *receiving His secret instruction, in all events*, by learning from His holy will, and living constantly under His gaze. Meditation {is} not just playing with ideas but {being} fed by realities! Here, rather than thinking much, we *simply remain under the eyes of God* in an attitude of *docile submission*, reflecting in a general way on the action of grace and detecting as best we can the innumerable movements of divine love in our lives, *trying to respond at all times faithfully*. This prayer is characterized by great simplicity, and by frequent but simple, silent cries going up to God from the depths of our heart. Here we grow in knowledge of His love, not so much in exterior actions and things, but within ourselves. We realize that God seeks to dwell and rest in our souls, and we are content above all to open our hearts to Him and to give Him pleasure. We seek more and more the *simplicity of the intimate interior embrace which unites us to God in the depths of our being*. This kind of prayer is marked by a greater simplicity, by the absence of a large number of concepts and words. Thought is reduced to a simple, general apprehension of God in faith and love, and there is an increase of *darkness and unknowing*. Here we *no longer seek clear lights about God, clear intuitions, sensible graces, vivid consolations*. Everything has become dark and obscure. *God has receded from our minds, but paradoxically He is much closer to our inmost being*. If we can be content with the darkness of unknowing, we will be able to embrace Him within us purely in the mystery of faith. If we seek to grasp Him more clearly He will elude us and we will be left with agitation and disgust. Meditation fulfills this second function:

a) when it has enabled us to *unify our lives* so that all our life is more or less a continuous, simple meditation. Everything has meaning, but paradoxically everything has been simplified, and clear outlines have been blurred, so that there remains *the one great unity—our own life, impregnated with the love and action of God.* At the time of formal prayer, all else being put aside, we plunge into this general simplicity of love and attention and realize then more clearly that our life itself is a prayer.

b) This unification of our life is still ordered to *living and doing—here meditation flows from action and leads to action,* is intermingled with action. The fruit of this intermingling is that action is much simplified and purified, and thought is also impregnated with love and realism.

c) This meditative way of life is *essentially realistic and concrete.* That is why it is more simple. It discards cumbersome thought structures and patterns; it does away with lofty and abstract thinking to a great extent, *and reaches out to the simple reality that is present in life itself—our reality embraced in the supreme reality of the will and the love of God.* Here too there is less attention to elaborate patterns of feeling or to exuberant work of the imagination—all is peaceful and simple and matter-of-fact. This kind of meditation also promotes considerable spiritual *objectivity.* Although we are conscious of the reality of life itself, we are also less concentrated on ourselves. There is indeed here a kind of "introversion," but it is not at all what one would call introspection. There is no preoccupation with self. One lives and loves. Life and love are themselves the food of prayer.

3) To understand the *third and highest function of meditation* let us first look back over the other two:

a) In the first place, man becomes aware of things, concepts, words, truths, objects, as *filled with a divine meaning,* and passes through them to a deeper awareness of religious truth, and to a knowledge of God as He has revealed Himself to us—a knowledge of Christ Crucified, of God's plan for us, and how intimately it enters into our own lives. Here prayer is primarily *thoughtful, reflective, studious;* it inquires, seeks, finds, appreciates. There is concentration on particular subjects and aspects of divine truth, and there is a pleasant labor of investigation and admiration.

There is then a great *affective* quality about this thinking about God and it leads to a *realization* not only of the truths of faith but also of God Himself.

b) In the second place, passing beyond concepts and things, and no longer preoccupied with particular subjects and aspects of truth as much as before, the soul *makes its life a unified whole in which meditation penetrates everywhere*. Meditation has become *dynamic and practical*, a response to God's will, a constant preoccupation with pleasing God and uniting our will with His and thus *resting in His truth by our action*. Moments of formal prayer may be moments of affective seeking for the will or the good pleasure of God, {a} loving desire for the embrace of God in darkness, or simple resting in the peace of that embrace. The unity achieved by this kind of prayer is above all within ourselves. The soul is in order and at peace, and God can come and rest within us.

The *third function* of meditation is to take us even beyond this unity within ourselves, and to establish us, at least momentarily, *out of ourselves*, in God's own unity. Here we are no longer the masters of our prayer. We cannot decide to embrace this kind of prayer—it remains a mystery to one who is not actually enjoying it—even one who *has* tasted something of this prayer falls back into a sphere in which he realizes that the mystery of what he knew, in that brief moment, has evaded him. In this prayer, rather than finding sweet silence and peace within ourselves, *we lose ourselves entirely*; we lose touch with any point of reference that would make the experience fully intelligible to us. *Light is grasped in a supreme unknowing*, in which there seems to be no longer any knowing subject, but only "truth," "wisdom," or better still, reality itself. It is as if one had become one with the reality of all that is real, and had known the real by its own reality. One no longer can say how or why this takes place. Names, terms, distinctions, explanations, have little or no capacity to express what happens in this kind of prayer. As soon as one tries to explain, there arise innumerable occasions of error in one's expressions. For example, mystics have been tempted to explain this experience as one of "identification" with God.

Actually this term, which lends itself to misunderstanding, is practically meaningless here. Quibbling about the language of the mystics will only obscure the issue more completely.

What this prayer does is, it enters into the mystery revealed to Moses in the Burning Bush; it hears, as it were, the ineffable Name of God—"I am Who am"[312]—not in words and syllables, but in a supreme act of existing which has brought us into being beyond and above ourselves. One might say that this experience was a brief and transitory flash of the mystery of our own being as it is found not in ourselves but in God. In this prayer we rejoin the secret of our own being in the mind of God, and there indeed we "are" in the fullest sense—so fully indeed that it is no longer we who are but Christ Who lives and is in us. This third kind of meditation is of course far beyond all thought and discourse, and beyond every kind of merely human act no matter how spiritual. This is a divine enlightenment which gives us a momentary taste of what is really real, beyond and above the illusory "reality" which we perceive through the mist of everyday experience, a reality which does not belong to this world but to the world to come. Rather than boldly trying to push our way into prayer like this, we must humble ourselves more and more and purify our lives and forget every form of self-exaltation and self-preoccupation. If God wills to enlighten us, He will do so. The first two functions of meditation are normal and ordinary. In the second, one can say that there is already a notable element of passivity under the divine action, a kind of "ordinary" mysticism. In the third, we are over the threshold in the realm of purely mystical prayer, and here, no matter how wisely the theologians have written about it, we go beyond the reach of human discourse, man's "rules" and "degrees," and God alone is the guide and master in this kind of prayer. To respond faithfully to His action the soul can do nothing but abandon all other concerns and let the Divine Word espouse her to Himself, in His own way, and as He Himself pleases.

312. Ex. 3:14.

Further helps and hints in meditation:

1. We return again to the fundamental principle that what matters above all is our *attitude toward meditation*—what we think it is, what we think we are supposed to do. It should fit in with the rest of our life. Our whole life is a meditation of the Word of God. But also our whole life disposes us to *receive from God* the graces and helps without which we cannot go on. Hence our meditation, like everything else, should encourage us in an attitude of *submission, docility, receptivity, dependence on grace, humble faith, absolute trust.* Any way of meditation and prayer that produces these dispositions is good. Any other, no matter how suited for the active life, etc., is bad for us. Do not expect to *have great thoughts* or produce in yourself *a strong feeling of fervor.* Do not depend on your ability to make yourself feel this or that. Do not try too hard to stir up what you believe to be the proper psychological dispositions for the practice of virtue: that, yes, in due season—but it is secondary. *Our meditation should not aim at producing a psychological state.* We should not look at our psychological condition during or after meditation unless some special reason makes it necessary—ordinarily, no. This {is} against the advice of those who recommend much introspection and self-observation in connection with mental prayer. We should ordinarily not waste time thinking about our "degree of prayer." Those who have really advanced in prayer are aware of having no particular well-defined "degree" of prayer. They generally don't know where they are, and don't try to find out. They leave that to God.

2. It follows from the above that our meditation is valuable not for its psychological effects but for its *theological effects*; the best meditation is that in which we have had the greatest faith, hope, love for God. Faith, hope and love are strongest and purest in darkness: hence the value of trial and dryness. Very often when we are dry, we actually exercise more faith and are more humble and more dependent on God than we would be if we were flooded with "consolations." But also {we must} cultivate *positive* religious values. Look at {the} Face of God in Christ Jesus, not at self.

3. Meditation goes hand in hand with *lectio divina*. If our reading is good, then there will be good meditations in our lives, if not in choir, then at least at *lectio*. Our reading should be:

a) appropriate to us. Often our meditation is poor because we are reading things that don't apply to us and escape our understanding. {They are} too high, or otherwise unsuitable. *Beginners* should fill their imagination with images that drive out the memories and images of the world. They should accustom themselves to thinking about holy things, and "seeing" these realities, especially mysteries in {the} life of Jesus. IN THE BEGINNING, JUST LEARN TO SEE. Look. Watch. Absorb. The thinking will take care of itself. After you have done some thinking, in the end you will return to looking and loving—the preparation for contemplative prayer.

b) Our reading should also be solid. Often meditation fails because no substance is had in our reading. Solid means theological—the word of Christ: our reading should teach us to know Jesus, in His Reality, not just {as} an "idea"; not just "the Sacred Humanity of" Jesus, but the Person of Jesus, the God-Man.[313] We do not talk to and love a "Humanity" but a Person. Use of a book at meditation helps to keep recollected, and to provide a few thoughts to anchor on. But we should not just read or analyze the material in the book. Get enough to chew on, or something to look at.

4. *Prayer*: often we do not succeed in meditation *because we do not pray for help*. We kneel down to meditate and imagine that we know how to do it and ought to be a fabulous success, from the first moment, all by ourselves. Rather we should pray constantly and perseveringly for the grace to know how to meditate, {for} *faith that {the} Holy Spirit will guide and teach us, expecting all from Him and nothing from ourselves*. This will help us to advance a little, and will give material for our mental prayer itself. This attitude of dependence and "hoping" is the very heart of our

313. See Merton's article "The Humanity of Christ in Monastic Prayer," in Thomas Merton, *The Monastic Journey*, ed. Patrick Hart (Kansas City: Sheed, Andrews and McMeel, 1977), 87–106.

prayer. Note also that our failure to pray comes in part from a *lack of desire*, and this from *lack of interest*. We do not really want badly enough to learn how to meditate. But if we really seek God, and become convinced that in our meditation we will find Him, then we will be very eager to learn how to meditate, so that we can be with Him. The whole joy, the only joy really left in the life of the monk, is his union with God. We have left everything else. Unless we find all the satisfactions we have left and recover them in God, we will not be happy. It is in prayer, then, that we find peace, joy, strength, friendship. We are never less alone than when we are alone in prayer. We must learn how to find this joy in God, beyond all created things, a joy that no man can take from us. Beware of hidden pelagianism that seeks pleasure and satisfaction in activism and unrest: "What should I do next?"

5. *Visual Aids*: obviously we can often be helped by something to look at—a picture, a crucifix. Nearness to the tabernacle is a great help. In fact, one of the easiest ways to learn mental prayer is to remain near the tabernacle reflecting on Jesus' presence in the Blessed Sacrament. A picture of the Blessed Mother is always a great help for some. Just to look at her is often a completely satisfying way of prayer—particularly some really genuine image like that of Our Lady of Guadalupe. When we see such pictures, we truly see *her*. What more could we want?

6. Repetition of ejaculations or the slow recital of a vocal prayer or psalm {may be used}—or the Our Father: repeat the words slowly, pausing where you feel drawn to pause, and deepening the effect of the words, adding more faith and love to your thought on them. The "Jesus Prayer" ("Lord Jesus Christ, Son of God, have mercy on me a sinner"), in conjunction with slow, regular, deep breathing {is a similar method}.

7. Other points:

a) Our mental prayer will not be much good if we do not seek to pray outside the official time of prayer.

b) Distractions may come from negligence and lack of generosity outside the time of prayer. If one is habitually lazy and

tepid in controlling interior movements of various passions, especially anger, then these will be a great hindrance to prayer. *A
life of meekness and humility* is essential for a solid life of prayer.
A violent man cannot meditate. Neither can a grossly sensual
man; hence *mortification* is absolutely necessary for the life of
prayer; otherwise one will think about food or sensual pleasure
and comfort during mental prayer. Where your treasure is, there
will your heart be also. {There is a} necessity of detachment and
liberation from desires of all kinds to cut down on distractions. If
one is culpably unmortified, and negligent, then he is to some
extent responsible for distractions during mental prayer, even
though they may be involuntary at the time. If one makes generous efforts to lead a sincerely mortified life and tranquil life, then
even if distractions come during prayer, they have no bad effect
and should not even be noticed. The *will remains united to God*
beneath the surface of unwanted images, etc.

c) Do not be afraid to sit down if necessary. But avoid sleep.
Often mental prayer is spoiled by vain fear and human respect
on the part of those who are afraid of what others will think of
them. You are not praying to please men but to seek union with
God.

d) Avoid vanity and self-complacency in the interior life, for
this may turn your mental prayer into self-contemplation, the
ruin of true interior life.

8. *Progress in Mental Prayer*—Signs of Progress:

i. PEACE: you will not make progress by worrying about
progress. Anxiety will hold you back. Peace and trust, *tranquillity
and contentment with our own poverty* may be one of the best signs
of progress in mental prayer. Agitation ruins mental prayer. Even
though you have little tangible evidence of "getting anywhere,"
if you are able to remain at peace, content with the faith that Jesus
is near and that He loves you, you will then make much progress
in meditation. Forget about "getting somewhere" and think about
Jesus, love Him, be satisfied to abandon yourself to Him in all
your poverty. He will take care of the rest. Realize this.

ii. SIMPLICITY: as your prayer progresses, it becomes *simplified*. The acts are fewer and simpler; one is less and less aware of them. One is less and less able to see and measure what is going on. The imagination, reasoning and other cognitive faculties have *less* to do as mental prayer progresses. {There are} fewer thoughts, fewer images, or none at all. Some imagine things to be the exact contrary to this. They expect more and more thoughts, images, more brilliant lights, etc., and disturb their soul with untimely efforts to produce them. This hinders prayer greatly. The *affective* side of prayer is also greatly simplified. The emotions play less part in our prayer, or none at all. *Love* draws to itself and includes all the other affections: and love itself becomes more and more spiritualized and simple.

iii. OBSCURITY: *very often obscurity, dryness and trial are a sign of progress.* Paradoxically, in fervent souls who have previously meditated well, the *inability to make a discursive meditation* may be a sign of progress in prayer. A certain *incapacity, helplessness to make acts*, lack of desire to make formal acts may all be in fact an indication that one's prayer has become more spiritualized and simplified. In that case, *one should not strive to make acts* but just remain peacefully occupied with God, loving Him, abandoning oneself to His love, not asking to see results, trusting in Him alone, yielding to the secret instinct to be "drawn" to Him. If one remains quiet, he gradually becomes aware of a delicate interior tending to the invisible God. One feels oneself somehow turning to Him Whom one cannot see, and one feels that He turns to us also. This blind "turning to" God then becomes the whole essence of our prayer—a blind but trustful "tending" of the soul's instinct to love. "For who shall prevent God from doing that which He will in the soul that is resigned, annihilated and detached?"[314] (St. John of the Cross; read also *Ascent*, vol. I, p. 75–76[315]). Our

---

314. St. John of the Cross, *The Ascent of Mount Carmel*, Bk. II, c. 4.2, in *The Complete Works of Saint John of the Cross*, trans. E. Allison Peers, 3 vols. (Westminster, MD: Newman Press, 1949), 1.74.

315. "It is this that was meant by S. Paul when he said: *Accedentem ad Deum oportet credere quod est*. Which signifies: He that would journey towards union with God must needs believe in His being. As though he had said: He that would

prayer becomes a semi-passive yielding to grace in obscurity, a *consent* given without reserve and without hesitation to the action of God Whom we do not see. By this consent, and this yielding, we surrender the very depths of our being to God. He in return surrenders Himself to us in an ineffable way, in this same act of loving trust, an embrace in the darkness of loving faith!

iv. PURITY: the above conditions are not realized if our prayer is not pure. This demands a pure and detached heart. If our heart is still strongly attached to our own will, our own comfort, our own desires, our own little "possessions," then the sense of resting in God will probably be largely an illusion. Yet nevertheless, even a soul that is not yet perfectly detached may be invited to this obscure and restful prayer. For contemplative prayer is a *means of progress* and *not a reward for perfection*. However, this prayer should produce *fruits of humility and purity in our souls*. If

---

attain to being joined in one union with God must not walk by understanding, neither lean upon experience or feeling or imagination, but he must believe in His Being, which is not perceptible to the understanding, neither to the desire nor to the imagination nor to any other sense, neither can it be known in this life at all. Yea, in this life, the highest thing that can be felt and experienced concerning God is infinitely remote from God and from the pure possession of Him. Isaiah and S. Paul say: *Nec oculus vidit, nec auris audivit, nec in cor hominis ascendit, quae praeparavit Deus iis, qui diligunt illum.* Which signifies: That which God hath prepared for them that love Him neither eye hath seen, nor ear heard, neither hath it entered into the heart or thought of man. So, however greatly the soul aspires to be perfectly united through grace in this life with that to which it will be united through glory in the next (which, as S. Paul here says, eye hath not seen, nor ear heard, neither hath it entered into the heart of man in the flesh) it is clear that, in order perfectly to attain to union in this life through grace and through love, a soul must be in darkness with respect to all that can enter through the eye, and to all that can be received through the ear, and can be imagined with the fancy, and understood with the heart, which here signifies the soul. And thus a soul is greatly impeded from reaching this high estate of union with God when it clings to any understanding or feeling or imagination or appearance or will or manner of its own, or to any other act or to anything of its own, and cannot detach and strip itself of all these. For, as we say, the goal which it seeks is beyond all this, yea, beyond even the highest thing that can be known or experienced; and thus a soul must pass beyond everything to unknowing" (*Ascent*, II.4.4).

these fruits are not evident to us (they will probably *not* be evident to us), they will nevertheless be evident to our spiritual father, and we must trust his advice and approval. Another effect of this purity is to make the soul *less concerned with the externals* of the spiritual life. There will of course be a continued and unusual *fidelity* to all obligations, but this fidelity will not be scrupulous or legalistic. It will not be the fruit of an agitated attachment to externals, as if they had some independent value of their own. The soul will be more and more concerned with *pleasing God alone* and not with the external appearance of regularity which pleases men and gains their approval. The purity of the detached soul is related to humility and interior liberty. It means freedom from servility, from base human fears, from the craving to be approved and admired. But it is also united to a deep, self-despising humility which is not in any way attached to its own judgement, to its own methods, its own ways, its own views, its own "spirituality." In a word, the purified soul no longer concerns itself primarily with schools of spirituality and ways and means of perfection that are debated and praised by various groups. It seeks God alone, by a "little way" that is unknown and poor, and yet utterly common, for it is the way of the Gospel. The purified soul is not anxious to be unusual, to be different, to shine. It is content to be ordinary.

v. GENEROSITY: progress in mental prayer bears fruit in *generous effective charity*. But this generosity must be understood in terms of what has been said before. It is not a generosity of Martha who is "anxious about many things."[316] It is not a generosity which agitates the soul in the pursuit of many acts and virtues. It is not a generosity which flings itself into every opportunity for work, with an inordinate excitement. The generosity that flows from true prayer is humble, quiet and *persevering*. It is patient and unobtrusive. It is the generosity which *bears with everything* gladly and without complaint because it no longer stops to reflect that there is anything to bear. The generosity we speak of here has ceased to

316. Lk. 10:41.

measure, to count the cost. It does not compare itself with others. It minds its own business. It has forgotten the multiple concerns which used to attract it. It has renounced ambition. It takes magnanimity to be little in the spiritual life, because it takes magnanimity to offer oneself in a total holocaust to God. This generosity and totality is in fact inseparable from a great perfection in prayer and in charity. But this perfection may be almost totally invisible.

{9}.[317] *The Desire for Mystical Prayer*: much of what has been said already implies mystical (infused) contemplation, in which God is the chief agent and the soul remains almost entirely passive, or entirely so. It is perfectly licit to desire mystical contemplation, provided one does so with the right understanding and in the right way:

a) *with humility*. This means, right away, that one should not have a misplaced *ambition* to become a contemplative in the sense of "shining" as a contemplative. The desire to shine (even if only in one's own eyes) by reason of mystical experiences would effectively prevent the soul from preparing itself rightly for such graces.

b) *with a sense of due proportion*, realizing that mystical graces are secondary; they do not constitute perfection—without charity they are nothing. One should desire not mystical experiences (subjective) but *God*. One should retain his sense of humor and his common sense. A theatrical craving for mystical graces ruins the spiritual life. One should realize the *very special danger* of self-seeking in such matters.

c) *in complete abandonment to God's will*, realizing that He is the Master of His gifts, that He knows what is best for us, and that He alone knows how and when and where to give us the favors we need. We should leave all to Him, seek to please Him, and let Him do the rest. IT IS BEST NOT TO THINK TOO MUCH ABOUT BECOMING A "MYSTIC." You are more likely to become one if you forget all about it, and love God.

---

317. Typescript reads "8."

{The} Prayer of Simplicity and {the} Prayer of Quiet: in the last few years some authors have distinguished a prayer of "acquired contemplation,"[318] in which we reduce our own souls to simplicity and passivity, from {the} prayer of quiet, in which we remain passive under the action of God. It would seem this distinction might be misleading and had little practical value. In effect, contemplative prayer is more or less passive. We cannot "hold ourselves" in a state of passivity; this would lead to strain and illusion. But there is, truly, a sort of natural inclination to peace and repose. If united to a true call of grace, this natural repose will favor supernatural contemplation. If not, it will lead to sleep or to illusion.

The Office of Lauds

Lauds in General: We ended our discussion of meditation with a note on mystical prayer. This should not lead the monk into the fatal illusion that graces of contemplation are something he strives to acquire by and in mental prayer only. For us, the chief source of graces and lights of prayer remains the *liturgy* properly understood. By participating fully and normally in the great hour of praise which is lauds, we dispose ourselves admirably for lofty graces of prayer. The spirit of lauds is a spirit of *contemplative praise*. Lauds {is} the Church's ancient morning prayer, the most beautiful and solemn of all morning prayers. Note that the Church has two morning prayers and two evening prayers: lauds and prime, vespers and compline. Lauds and vespers are the ancient morning and evening prayer; prime and compline, though still ancient by our standards, are a relatively new morning and evening prayer. Both are due in large part to St. Benedict and the monks. St. Benedict calls lauds the *matutinorum solemnitas*[319]—the solemnity of *matins*. (In our office the night office is vigils, and lauds is "matins." This is as it should be. Matins means

318. For a discussion of this issue, see *Introduction to Christian Mysticism*, xxxiii, 235–45.
319. *Rule*, cc. 12 [title], 13 (McCann, 54, 56).

"morning office.") The name lauds {comes} from the term *laudes* applied to the last three psalms (148, 149 and 150), which are invariably sung and invariably give this office a dominant note of *praise*. Vigils are deeply reflective, filled with compunction and prayer; lauds {is} clear and joyous, {filled with} triumphant confidence in God (although there are also many psalms of "compunction" here also); {for} prime, {the} dominant note is of petition for grace in preparation for the day's work. Prime {is} an eminently *practical* morning prayer; lauds, on the other hand {is} a *contemplative* climax in the day's office. "I like to compare Lauds and Vespers to the first three petitions of the Lord's Prayer. These look to the increase and expansion of God's kingdom. Prime and Compline are more like the last three petitions, since they are concerned with deliverance from sin" (Parsch[320]). And Parsch goes on, quite beautifully: "I am tempted to say that Adam could well have prayed Lauds and Vespers in the Garden of Paradise; but only after his fall, in exile on this earth, could he pray Prime and Compline" (*idem*[321]).

What is the source of the character of lauds as a prayer of praise? It unites the waking of creation with the mystery of Christ's resurrection. Christ is the *"sol justitiae"*[322] Who, rising from death, illumines the world with the justice and truth and mercy of God. The material sun which rises in the morning is to us the symbol of the Lord triumphant over the darkness of sin, ignorance and death. This is particularly clear in lauds of Sundays (and great feasts). Lauds is above all a *festive hour*. It is always a celebration of the resurrection. But on feasts it also strongly brings out the celebration of the feast itself. Lauds and vespers are {the} two hours which keynote most strongly the character of the feast {being} celebrated. (Vigils of course with its long lessons and many antiphons, responsories, etc. is in a class by itself in this respect.) Prime and compline with us have little (prime) or nothing

320. Parsch, 212, which reads: ". . . Compline, however, are . . ."
321. Parsch, 212, which reads: ". . . am even tempted . . ."
322. "sun of justice" (Mal. 3:20).

(compline) to do with the theme of the feast celebrated. "In Lauds, the theme of the feast and the thought of the hour are intrinsically related" (Parsch[323]). Parsch concludes: "The themes of the feast and the hour coincide on Sunday. As a result, only the antiphon for the *Benedictus* and the oration vary."[324]

Lauds in the Rule of St. Benedict (chapters 12–13) begins with Psalm 66 *sine antiphona in directum*.[325] This is a preparatory psalm, an introduction like Psalm 3 in matins, and it is explicitly intended (c. 13) to enable "all to arrive in time for Psalm 50."[326] READ Psalm 66,[327] a beautiful morning prayer, chosen above all for the first line, which contains the words, "May He cause the light of His countenance to shine upon us and have mercy upon us." The light of day is a sign, almost a "sacrament," of the mercy of God. With the new day comes a blessing, and a renewal of divine mercy. According to the Prologue of the *Rule*,[328] each new day is to be regarded as a gift—a day more to amend our lives and turn to God, to hear His voice. For today we will hear His voice (cf. vigils[329]). The psalm continues: "That we may know *Thy way upon earth, Thy salvation in all nations.*" With the new day,

---

323. Parsch, 213.

324. Parsch, 214, which reads: ". . . theme for the feast and the theme of the hour . . ."

325. "straight through without an antiphon" (*Rule*, c. 12 [McCann, 54/55]).

326. McCann, 57.

327. "May God have mercy on us, and bless us: may he cause the light of his countenance to shine upon us, and may he have mercy on us. That we may know thy way upon earth, thy salvation in all nations. Let people confess to thee, O God: let all people give praise to thee. Let the nations be glad and rejoice; for thou judgest the people with justice, and directest the nations upon earth. Let the people, O God, confess to thee: let all the people give praise to thee: the earth hath yielded her fruit. May God, our God, bless us, may God bless us: and all the ends of the earth fear him."

328. "Having given us these instructions, the Lord daily expects us to make our life correspond with his holy admonitions. And the days of our life are lengthened and a respite allowed us for this very reason, that we may amend our evil ways" (McCann, 11).

329. I.e., Psalm 94[95]:8 (see above, n. 257).

we look out over the whole earth, and hail the coming of God's Kingdom, as He Himself has promised. The monk lives a life entirely oriented toward the great Day of the Lord when the whole earth shall be filled with the glory of the Lord and all nations shall praise Him. "Let the nations be glad and rejoice: for thou judgest the people with justice, and directest the nations upon earth." Here "judgement" is not regarded as a dreadful and horrible thing; it is the manifestation of the wisdom of Divine Providence in all things and all events of history, and the nations praise God for the fact that His wisdom was hidden even in their calamities and in spite of all, the "earth hath yielded her fruit." "May God, our God, bless us, may God bless us: and may all the ends of the earth fear Him." One of most beautiful of the psalms, we should make it our constant prayer and meditation.

Then follows Psalm 50 with an antiphon. Martène, summing up most of the ancient commentaries, says: "There is a special meaning [*mysterium*] in the fact that he wanted the fiftieth psalm, which is a psalm of penance and lamentation, to be sung with the alleluia, the song of joy and gladness, because this shows that the compunction of penance is always united with interior joy."[330] Another reason, perhaps more pertinent, is that the whole of Sunday lauds is made up of psalms which are "*alleluiati*" (Martène[331]). Psalm 50, the Miserere (read it[332]), is one of those which

---

330. Edmond Martène, *Commentarius in Regulam Sancti Patris Benedicti*, included in Migne's edition with the *Rule* (*PL* 66, col. 444D).

331. *PL* 66, col. 444D.

332. "Have mercy on me, O God, according to thy great mercy. And according to the multitude of thy tender mercies blot out my iniquity. Wash me yet more from my iniquity, and cleanse me from my sin. For I know my iniquity, and my sin is always before me. To thee only have I sinned, and have done evil before thee: that thou mayst be justified in thy words, and mayst overcome when thou are judged. For behold I was conceived in iniquities: and in sins did my mother conceive me. For behold thou hast loved truth: the uncertain and hidden things of thy wisdom thou hast made manifest to me. Thou shalt sprinkle me with hyssop, and I shall be cleansed: thou shalt wash me, and I shall be made whiter than snow. To my hearing thou shalt give joy and gladness: and the bones that have been humbled shall rejoice. Turn away thy face from my sins, and blot out all my

occur most frequently in monastic prayer. It is constantly on the lips of the monk: at lauds on most days, at lauds of the dead always, after dinner every day, at the asperges on Sundays, etc. It is the fourth of the penitential psalms. It plays a prominent part in the Ash Wednesday liturgy. *It is the psalm par excellence of Christian compunction.* A brief outline of this beautiful psalm must suffice us here, but it should be one of the monk's favorite themes of meditation:

a) verses 1-8 {focus on} the *sense of sin*, the deep sorrow of heart at having offended God; {on} the realization that even when we did not think of offending God at all, our sin was really an attack upon His love; {on the} realization that we are born in sins and that our actual sins follow after us everywhere, but that God Who loves truth allows our sins to happen precisely in order that He may show us who we are and Who He is, and His will is to blot out our iniquities "with the multitude of His tender mercies." {There is} joy in being able to say "I *know* my iniquity." The Church sees that in the confession of sin there is joy and peace— to get rid of morbid guilt and useless shame, {to} open our hearts to mercy, and to be in turn merciful to others.

b) verses 9-14: here we see explicitly stated what Martène observed—the union of penance and joy: joy of the penitent in his confident hope of pardon. Hope is of the very essence of Christian penance. Hell, where there is no hope, is not "penance."

---

iniquities. Create a clean heart in me, O God, and renew a right spirit within my bowels. Cast me not away from thy face; and take not thy holy spirit from me. Restore unto me the joy of thy salvation and strengthen me with a perfect spirit. I will teach the unjust thy ways: and the wicked shall be converted to thee. Deliver me from blood, O God, thou God of my salvation: and my tongue shall extol thy justice. O Lord, thou wilt open my lips: and my mouth shall declare thy praise. For if thou hadst desired sacrifice, I would indeed have given it: with burnt offerings thou wilt not be delighted. A sacrifice to God is an afflicted spirit: a contrite and humbled heart, O God, thou wilt not despise. Deal favourably, O Lord, in thy good will with Sion: that the walls of Jerusalem may be built up. Then shalt thou accept the sacrifice of justice, oblations and whole burnt offerings: then shall they lay calves upon thy altar."

"Thou shalt wash me and I shall be made white as snow. . . . To my hearing Thou shalt give joy and gladness and the bones that have been humbled shall rejoice." *God's pardon is not merely exterior, but it brings with it an interior* transformation: He not only blots out all our sins and forgets them, but He gives us His Holy Spirit, looks upon us with fatherly compassion, creates a clean heart in us, strengthens us "with a perfect spirit"—*a princely and a ruling spirit*: the Spirit of His love takes over and rules our lives. He thus becomes the shepherd of our souls again. Then we taste the joy of His salvation.

c) verses 15-21 {focus on} the fruitfulness of penance: the soul joyful in forgiveness will serve God fruitfully and humbly. We will convert other sinners by telling them of the mercy of God. We will praise God, for forgiveness will open our lips to praise Him. We will realize that our contrition and affliction of spirit were a pleasing sacrifice to God, much more pleasing than burnt offerings, for the God of truth desires us to know His truth in ourselves even though it may hurt us. Finally, Sion, the City of God, will be built up by penitents and the whole people of God will offer Him a pleasing worship in His Church.
Hence this is a most appropriate opening for lauds of ordinary days—a psalm of sorrow and of praise.

{Of} the other psalms of Sunday lauds, 117 is the most important: the last psalm of the Hallel, a *paschal psalm*, {expressing} thanksgiving for the deliverance from Egypt, and for the *pascha Christi*,[333] the Resurrection of Christ and our deliverance from Egypt by His power; it is a psalm which probably formed part of the "hymns" said by Christ and His Disciples at the Last Supper,[334] before His Passion. It praises the *victory of Christ* over death, and in our lives—in baptism and in the Eucharist. The psalms of lauds, particularly this one, are fine preparations for Mass and Holy Communion. Then {comes} Psalm 62: "a song of ardent

333. "the passover of Christ".
334. See Mt. 26:30; Mk. 14:26.

love and longing for God. Easy to understand and easy to pray, it ranks among our most beautiful psalms" (Parsch: see {the} commentary outlined by Parsch in *The Breviary Explained*, p. 215). The *Benedicite*[335] {is} a magnificent canticle of praise, in the spirit of the purest prayer. Without something of this spirit, we are not fully Christians. Note how St. Francis, one of the most Christ-like of saints, had this spirit perfectly.[336] Note the relationship to the *Miserere*—{it is} the other side of the same coin. In the *Miserere* the soul immersed in sorrow looks forward to joy. In the *Benedicite*, the three children in the fiery furnace praise God with no thought of their trial. Yet nevertheless it is somewhat of the same situation. The Church prays to God, Who saved the three children in the fiery furnace, to visit us in temptation and tribulation and deliver us from our passions. The Christian spirit of praise is a triumph over temptation by humility and trust in God. What is praise? What is glory? To *respond* to {the} goodness of God is to glorify God (LOVE!!). Recital of the *Benedicite* can, alas, too easily become a mechanical routine. It is an easy canticle to understand and our thoughts should follow the words and our hearts should truly reach out to embrace all creation and bring it with us into our chorus of exultation. The consideration of all these beings made by God shows us the goodness of God in them and awakens praise in our hearts. READ the *Benedicite*[337] (compare St. Fran-

---

335. Dan. 3:75-90 (the Canticle of the Three Young Men in the Fiery Furnace); the hymn in fact begins with vs. 52, but only the final sixteen verses are included in the liturgy.

336. Merton refers to the similarity of St. Francis' "Canticle of the Creatures" to this hymn.

337. "O ye mountains and hills, bless the Lord: praise and exalt him above all for ever. O all ye things that spring up in the earth, bless the Lord: praise and exalt him above all for ever. O ye fountains, bless the Lord: praise and exalt him above all for ever. O ye seas and rivers, bless the Lord: praise and exalt him above all for ever. O ye whales, and all that move in the waters, bless the Lord: praise and exalt him above all for ever. O all ye fowls of the air, bless the Lord: praise and exalt him above all for ever. O all ye beasts and cattle, bless the Lord: praise and exalt him above all for ever. O ye sons of men, bless the Lord: praise and exalt him above all for ever. O let Israel bless the Lord: let them praise and exalt

cis's *Canticle of the Sun*). Note {the} place of the *Benedicite* on Ember Saturdays, {in a} slightly different form.[338]

Laudate Dominum de Coelis[339] (Psalms 148-150): the name lauds comes from this last group of psalms, which counts really as one, the perfection of praise, the conclusion and summary of the psalter, the conclusion of every "night office." Even "lauds of the dead" ends with the *laudate*. This teaches us that praise is the peak and summary of everything for the Christian. Why? because of the victory of Christ; because all things are "made new in Christ";[340] because all creation has risen with Christ; because man, in Christ, is once again the high priest of creation, leading the choir of praise that rises from all creatures to the Father. When we call upon all creatures to praise the Lord, it presupposes *the full wakefulness of joy*, the full awareness of who God is and who we are, of the fulfillment of the Gospel message, in the gift of the Spirit to us. It presupposes that we have risen above the torpor and lethargy of the night and are filled with love and peace and ardor, for we have "seen" something of the wonder and greatness of God in our night vigils, meditations and praises. This then is the crown of all. But how can we summon inanimate creation to "praise" the Lord if we ourselves are

---

him above all for ever. O ye priests of the Lord, bless the Lord: praise and exalt him above all for ever. O ye servants of the Lord, bless the Lord: praise and exalt him above all for ever. O ye spirits and souls of the just, bless the Lord: praise and exalt him above all for ever. O ye holy and humble of heart, bless the Lord: praise and exalt him above all for ever. O Ananias, Azarias, and Misael, bless ye the Lord: praise and exalt him above all for ever. For he hath delivered us from hell, and saved us out of the hand of death, and delivered us out of the midst of the burning flame, and saved us out of the midst of the fire. O give thanks to the Lord, because he is good: because his mercy endureth for ever and ever. O all ye religious, bless the Lord the God of gods: praise him and give him thanks, because his mercy endureth for ever and ever."

338. *Missale Cisterciense*, 307 (response to the fifth reading); these verses are selected from Daniel 3:52-56, while the lauds reading is made up of selections from the latter part of the hymn.

339. "Praise the Lord from the heavens" (opening words of Ps. 148).

340. Cf. 2 Cor. 5:17, Rev. 21:5.

still sunk in torpor, if we are slouching in our stalls half-asleep and mumbling the words of this most beautiful of all psalms in a mechanical manner, or straining our heads over the pronunciation of the syllables and other material aspects of the psalmody? We must sing this psalm with joy, and strive to pay attention to what we are singing in order that there may indeed be joy in our hearts.

READ Psalm 148:[341] {in} vv. 1-6, we call upon the heavens, the angels, the stars, the firmament, to praise God. In them His will is reflected perfectly in their serene order: *Praeceptum posuit et non praeteribit.*[342] {In} vv. 7-14, the earth {and} all inanimate and brute creation is called upon to praise the Lord, then man—the kings and nations—and above all Israel entering into the presence of the Lord: *populo appropinquanti sibi.*[343] The whole sense of the psalm comes out in this dynamic progress: all creation, led by the Chosen People of God, is returning to Him. Note—we should here sing an alleluia. In the Bible each of these three psalms begins and ends with an alleluia. Psalm 149 follows logically from the above as though part of it. The Church praises God. God is pleased with His People, and the saints rest in Him waiting for the great day when they will openly triumph with Him in the

---

341. "Praise ye the Lord from the heavens: praise ye him in the high places. Praise ye him, all his angels: praise ye him all his hosts. Praise ye him, O sun and moon: praise him, all ye stars and light. Praise him, ye heavens of heavens: and let all the waters that are above the heavens praise the name of the Lord. For he spoke, and they were made: he commanded, and they were created. He hath established them for ever, and for ages of ages: he hath made a decree, and it shall not pass away. Praise the Lord from the earth, ye dragons, and all ye deeps: Fire, hail, snow, ice, stormy winds, which fulfill his word: Mountains and all hills, fruitful trees and all cedars: Beasts and all cattle: serpents and feathered fowls: Kings of the earth and all people: princes and all judges of the earth: Young men and maidens: let the old with the younger, praise the name of the Lord: for his name alone is exalted. The praise of him is above heaven and earth: and he hath exalted the horn of his people. A hymn to all his saints: to the children of Israel, a people approaching to him. Alleluia."

342. "He has made a decree, and will not revoke it."

343. "the people drawing near to Himself."

final victory over evil. {In} Psalm 150, finally our gaze is turned to the Lord alone, "in the firmament of His power,"[344] and each line repeats: *Praise Him! Praise Him!* The psalms of lauds thus end with a long series of *acclamations* and alleluias. We should feel at least something of this in our office. This part of lauds surely is not a time to relax in a mental stupor waiting for it all to end! In order to get something of this spirit of praise, perhaps one of the best things to do would be to make these three psalms a favorite private prayer, and recite them to ourselves when walking about in the garden and looking at the beauties of the forest and hills, especially in spring or fall, or on snowy days in winter, when God reveals His beauty to us in a more particular way. On Sundays, St. Benedict prescribes the antiphon *Alleluia*.[345] Nothing could be more appropriate than this song of the Lord's victory, the *Canticum Domini*, the "new song."

The Second Part of Lauds: in the *Rule*,[346] there now follows a very simple ending to lauds: {a} *capitulum* from the Apocalypse (*lectio de Apocalypsi una ex corde*[347])—one that was always more or less the same, evidently (*Benedictio et claritas et sapientia et gratiarum actio . . .*[348]). {Then follows} the *short responsory* (*Haec est dies quam fecit Dominus. Exultemus et laetemur in ea*[349]). Why this? because Sunday is a celebration above all of the Easter mystery, and Easter is the day of days, the day of eternity entering into time. The *hymn* of lauds in almost every office is a hymn to the new day, celebrating the coming of light as a symbol of the Risen Christ. The Sunday hymn for summer is very simple: Behold the darkness of night begins to wane—the dawn of the new light shines in splendor. With all our power let us pray the Almighty

344. Ps. 150:1.

345. *Rule*, c. 12 (McCann, 54).

346. *Rule*, c. 12 (McCann, 54).

347. "a lesson from the Apocalypse to be recited by heart" (McCann, 54/55).

348. "[Worthy is the Lamb who was slain to receive power and divinity] and wisdom and strength and honor and glory and blessing" (Rev. 5:12).

349. "This is the day that the Lord has made. Let us be glad and rejoice in it" (Ps. 117[118]:24).

that, as our God, He may have mercy on us and drive away all languor of spirit and by His Fatherly love grant us to enter the Kingdom of Heaven.[350] In winter the hymn[351] is more splendid, longer, more detailed, richer in theology—not because it is winter, but because the office is *longer* in winter. St. Benedict gives more time to the hymns when the nights are longer. The hymn hails Christ as the true Sun, the *diem Dies illuminans*.[352] He is the *Splendor paternae gloriae*,[353] He Who brings forth light from light, the "light of light and fount of light."[354] Thou true Sun, shine forth, blazing with eternal splendor, and pour forth into our souls the radiance of the Holy Spirit.[355] In the other stanzas the Church prays for strength in virtue, purity {and} faith, and sums up all her petitions in this: Let Christ be our food and let our drink be faith: in gladness let us drink deep the sober exultation of the spirit[356] (comment on the untranslatable term *sobria ebrietas*,[357] which became classical in patristic mysticism). The *versicle—Dominus regnavit, decorem induit, induit Dominus fortitudinem et praecinxit se virtute*[358]—{is} celebrating the strength and beauty of God, the Incarnate Word. The *Benedictus*[359] {is} one of the most beautiful canticles in the Scriptures; sung by Zachary at the birth of St. John the Baptist, it sums up all the promises of God in the Old Testament, celebrates

---

350. The reference is to the "*Ecce Jam Noctis*" ("Lo, Now [the Shadow] of Night"), attributed to St. Gregory the Great (*Breviarium Cisterciense, Aestivalis*, 40).

351. *Breviarium Cisterciense, Hiemalis*, 41.

352. "Day that lights up the day" (vs. 4).

353. "splendor of the Father's glory" (the opening verse of the hymn).

354. "*lux lucis et fons luminis*" (vs. 3).

355. "*Verusque sol, illabere / micans nitore perpeti, / iubarque Sancti Spiritus / infunde nostris sensibus*" (stanza 2).

356. "*Christusque nobis sit cibus, / potusque noster sit fides; / laeti bibamus sobriam / ebrietatem Spiritus*" (stanza 6).

357. "sober intoxication"; see *Introduction to Christian Mysticism*, 81, and note 438 below.

358. "The Lord has reigned; he has put on beauty; the Lord has put on strength; he has girded himself with power" (*Breviarium Cisterciense, Aestivalis*, 40; *Hiemalis*, 41).

359. Lk. 1:68-79.

their fulfillment in the coming of the Messias, and brings to a close the Old Dispensation. The full glory of the Gospels and of the New Testament is contained in this canticle. The Church sings at vespers and lauds the two canticles, *Magnificat* and *Benedictus*, which are bridges between the Old and the New and contain in themselves all the riches of divine revelation in the Scriptures. God has visited His People—He has raised up His power in the descendant of David, to defend His People against all their enemies. He has remembered all His Promises, and been faithful to His covenant with the Fathers. He has kept His oath to Abraham, that the People would at last be able to live at peace, in holiness and justice all their days. And John would be the prophet who would go before the face of the Messias and bring to the People of God the announcement of the forgiveness of their sins, and light from the mercy of God on high to them that sit in darkness. *Illuminare his qui in tenebris et in umbra mortis sedent ad dirigendos pedes nostros in viam pacis.*[360] How tragic to sing these words every day and not know what they mean, to go on acting as if we had not received the mercy of God, as if we were abandoned, as if we still needed something, struggling to "save ourselves," as if He could not save us! Note {the} importance St. Benedict attaches to the recital of {the} *Pater Noster* aloud after the *Benedictus* antiphon at lauds and *Magnificat* antiphon at vespers[361]—*propter scandalorum spinas*[362]. . . for fraternal charity. Forgiveness is always and constantly necessary in community life. It is by forgiveness that we bear one another's burdens. It makes our sacrifice of praise fully acceptable to God. What would be the use of praising God for hours in the night if our soul were sunk in the darkness of selfishness and unforgiving resentment towards others?

---

360. "to enlighten those who sit in darkness and in the shadow of death, in order to guide our feet in the way of peace" (vs. 79).

361. *Rule*, c. 13 (McCann, 56).

362. "on account of the thorns of scandals" (McCann, 56).

Private Masses and Communions

When the night office is finished, then, according to the *Rule*, begins a long period devoted to *lectio divina* (*Rule*, c. 8: *Quod vero restat post vigilias a fratribus qui psalterii vel lectionum aliquid indigent, meditationi inserviatur*[363]). In St. Benedict's time there were no private Masses, only the conventual Mass, and this was not sung every day, probably only on Sundays and feasts. After the twelfth century private Masses became more common in the monastic life. (Indeed, before this they were sometimes and in some places very frequent.) In our Order daily private Mass for every priest is a very late practice. Note that it is not the normal thing, according to the tradition of the Order, for every choir religious to go on to major orders. The traditional view of the Order is that of St. Benedict: the abbot can ordain *some* of the monks to be priests, whoever he judges fit.[364] It does not *restrict* the power of the abbot to get worthy candidates ordained, however, and if all·the choir monks are fit for holy orders, then they *may* be advanced to holy orders, at the abbot's discretion. The mere fact that one may be apt and fit for holy orders does not give a solemnly professed religious of our Order a right to demand that the abbot get him ordained. In any case, whatever may be the theoretical background, in practice all choir religious who are capable of receiving holy orders are normally advanced to orders in our houses at the present day, and the vocation of the "simple monk" has tended to become a rarity, whereas it used to be the normal thing. Since there are often many priests in the monastery, and since they will normally say Mass every day, there arises a problem: when are these Masses to be offered, and how do they fit into the life of the community? The *Ritual*,[365] fol-

---

363. "Let the time that remains after vigils be devoted to meditation by those brothers who are somewhat lacking in knowledge of the psalms and readings" (McCann, 48).

364. *Rule*, c. 62 (McCann, 140).

365. *Rituale*, 48 (II, iii, 2).

lowing the *Consuetudines*,[366] gives the earliest legislation of the Order on these points: a priest may offer private Mass *during any time set aside for lectio divina*. The spirit of this legislation is one of freedom. The matter is left to the priest himself. He needs no special permission, presumably. He needs only to make a sign to the sacristan, and to arrange with him so that he will be able to finish his Mass before the beginning of the next office. The sacristan prepares things, the priest gets a server, and says Mass. It is provided for, however, that when *three private Masses* are offered in succession on the same day (for instance, Christmas {or} All Souls), the priest requires the permission of the abbot to say the two extra Masses. This permission is always granted en bloc to all the priests by Rev. Father, the day before the feast, in chapter, and even if he should have forgotten to do so it is so much a matter of form that it could always be legitimately presumed (n.b. in point of fact the problem would never really arise since the three Masses would always normally be on one's Mass ticket beforehand anyway). Generally speaking it is *customary* to say the private Masses at the first free time of *lectio* after the night office, unless there is some special reason for waiting until later— for instance, visitors, sickness, etc. The fact that all the priests proceed immediately to the sacristy after the night office gives the impression of an officially regulated "exercise," but this is not the case. The Mass and communion that follow the night office *are in no sense a regular exercise*. Hence there is no *obligation* (according to {the} *Rule* or *Usages*) to say or attend Mass or to receive holy communion. Communion is indeed prescribed in the *Constitutions* and *Usages*[367] for certain feasts (see notes on {the} *Constitutions* #89[368]), but on these occasions the general communion

366. *Usus Antiquiores Ordinis Cisterciensis*, III.45 (*PL* 166, col. 1460B).

367. *Regulations*, 91 (n. 188), which simply refers to the *Constitutions*, nn. 89–90.

368. "The Monks shall receive Holy Communion on Sundays, on all Feasts of Sermon and of Two Masses, and whenever there is a Plenary Indulgence to be gained in the Order. These regulations, however, have only a directive force. For the rest, all shall follow the direction of their Confessor with regard to frequent

is prescribed at a *conventual Mass*. The practice of receiving at private Masses even on days when general communion is prescribed has now become common. These things need to be said in order that we may form our selves properly for what is in fact the greatest act of our day. The Mass offered by the priest monk, the communion by which the brother and novice or scholastic participates in this Mass, is in fact the sacramental heart of the monastic day. But due to circumstances, that sacramental center has been shifted from the *regular* center of the day, and hence Mass and communion come to have a curiously vague and confused place in our daily life. The following thoughts suggest themselves:

1) The fact that this sacramental act is the greatest we can possibly perform in our whole monastic day would lead some to treat it as if it were therefore "even more obligatory" than any other obligation we have. But this in fact confuses the issue greatly, first of all because it is not true, and secondly because the Church does not want us to take this attitude.

2) The priest offers his private Mass, the novice goes to communion, not because he *has to* but because he *wants to*. This spontaneity of course belongs to every act of a fervent monk. But it belongs in a special and peculiar way to the great act of love and worship which is the Eucharist. Indeed it is the whole spirit of the Eucharist to be one of love, spontaneous desire, sharing, and search for union, not in order to fulfill a formal obligation, but because this is the very essence of all that we live for.

Communion" (*Constitutions of the Order of Cistercians of the Strict Observance* [Dublin: M. H. Gill & Sons, c. 1924], 24–25). In "Constitutions of the Cistercians," a set of conference notes for a course given by Merton as master of novices and found in volume 15 of "Collected Essays," the 24-volume bound set of published and unpublished materials assembled at the Abbey of Gethsemani and available both there and at the Thomas Merton Center, Bellarmine University, Louisville, KY, Merton comments on this regulation, noting that plenary indulgences are given on Lenten Saturdays and certain feasts, some of which he lists, and that while daily communion is encouraged, it should not be received merely from routine or out of human respect (19–20).

3) The spirit of the Church and of the Order is to encourage frequent communion, indeed daily communion, and the priests all say Mass daily. Who would not wish to do so? Yet the fact that someone might perhaps absent himself from communion on a given day is nobody else's business. It should certainly not lead to rash judgements. (How often it turns out that the brother in question is only communicating at a later Mass, in any case!)

4) The last thing in the world that should creep into this, the heart of our interior life, would be a spirit of formalism and routine. Here above all we must remain spontaneous, be ourselves, give God the love of *our hearts*, and not just a *pro forma* external action. But the best way to avoid this is to focus our attention on the *real nature and meaning of the Eucharist* and to meditate frequently on it, reading about it, studying it, and making it our whole life. It is ignorance and wrong ideas of the Eucharist which, more than everything else, cause souls of sincere good will to grow confused and cold, and to participate in this great mystery with a sense of futility and fruitlessness for which there is no objective reason at all. A very common wrong approach to the great Eucharistic sacrifice is the *subjective* one which lays all the stress on what the individual *feels and thinks* at the moment when he approaches the holy table, or during his thanksgiving. The following problem arises: many are sincerely convinced that they are expected to "feel" and "experience" very special "elevations" of soul, or other interior dispositions, and that without these psychological side effects their communions are without love. The fact that, especially in our life, many are rather tired by the time communion comes round, makes this impossible for the majority. Hence many become secretly convinced that because they cannot "feel" certain things, they are not really pleasing to Our Lord and are not making good communions. This is complete nonsense, and can easily be dispelled by a more objective approach, which is the right approach, the approach of Holy Church.

5) Sometimes liturgical idealists tend to regret the fact that private Masses (and communion at these private Masses) tend to obscure the central importance of the conventual Mass. It is

certainly true that the logic of the monastic life would seem to demand that the conventual Mass should occupy its rightful place as the very heart of the monks' day, and that the monk should receive communion at that Mass. Many problems are involved however:

a) nowadays most monks need frustulum: {hence there would be the} difficulty of arranging {the} monastic horarium so that communion can be received at {the} conventual Mass;

b) communion at conventual Mass tends to prolong the Mass and encroach on {the} time of work (allowing for thanksgiving, etc.) or classes;

c) should one suppress the private Masses of the priests and make all receive communion at the conventual Mass? This would seem perhaps an extreme measure, one which probably would never be adopted in practice in our Order; but as long as there are numerous private Masses taking up most of the interval after the night office, it will be logical for non-priests to receive then.

It is possible that a satisfactory solution to some of these problems might someday be worked out. In practice we have to be satisfied with what we have at the moment. In any case, we can recall what is said in *Mediator Dei*[369] about private Masses:

369. See *Mediator Dei*, ##95–96: "Some in fact disapprove altogether of those Masses which are offered privately and without a congregation, on the ground that they are a departure from the ancient way of offering the Sacrifice; moreover, there are some who assert that priests cannot offer Mass at different altars at the same time, because, by doing so, they separate the community of the faithful and imperil its unity; while some go so far as to hold that the people must confirm and ratify the Sacrifice if it is to have its proper force and value. They are mistaken in appealing in this matter to the social character of the Eucharistic Sacrifice, for as often as a priest repeats what the Divine Redeemer did at the Last Supper, the Sacrifice is really completed. Moreover, this Sacrifice, necessarily and of its very nature, has always and everywhere the character of a public and social act, inasmuch as he who offers it, acts in the name of Christ and of the faithful, whose Head is the Divine Redeemer, and he offers it to God for the Holy Catholic Church, and for the living and the dead. This is undoubtedly so, whether the faithful are present—as We desire and commend them to do in great numbers

a) there are not sufficient grounds for disapproving of Mass offered without a congregation, for even then the sacrifice has by its very nature a public and social character;

b) there is no reason for disapproving of priests saying Mass simultaneously at different altars—this does not "separate the community of the faithful and imperil its unity."

These disjointed remarks having been made, let us pass on to a deeper meditation on our communion Masses. As we shall later consider the conventual Mass,[370] we shall here discuss chiefly those aspects of the Mass which bear more directly upon the Eucharist as sacrament, though even here the character of the Mass as sacrifice cannot be neglected.

THE HOLY EUCHARIST: OUR GIFT TO GOD AND GOD'S GIFT TO US. What takes place when we approach the altar after the night office, some to offer private Mass, others to serve or to assist at the Mass and receive communion? What are we doing? It is of the greatest importance here to reflect precisely what kind of action we are about to perform.

1. One might say: I am going to *pray*. True, the Mass is a prayer. Or, I am going to *meditate*. True, one does think what one is saying and doing and thus there is meditation in the Mass. But the Mass is not "a meditation"—nor is it "a contemplation." The Mass is not something which one exploits for subjective and psychological effects. It is true that there are all sorts of ways of assisting at Mass, and one need not necessarily follow the Mass with a missal; one may meditate or even "contemplate" when assisting at Mass. But one should avoid making one's assistance at Mass merely a matter of "waiting" in meditative prayer (more or less disconnected with the action going on at the altar) for Jesus to come to us in the Sacred Host so that then we may go on meditating and contemplating more profoundly, with Him in

and with devotion—or are not present, since it is in no wise required that the people ratify what the sacred Minister has done" (35–36).

370. Merton does not, in fact, discuss the conventual Mass, which would have been part of the second section of the course, which was never given.

our heart. The Mass is not merely a device to produce the Blessed Sacrament, to make Jesus present sacramentally in order that He may come to my heart and be adored there. That would be a reversal of ends and means, making the Holy Sacrifice a means to enable me to receive communion and "contemplate" with greater consolation. Putting the matter thus baldly is of course a caricature of the sincere approach of some well-meaning souls, but the fact remains, there is a kind of danger in treating the Mass more or less primarily as a "means of procuring" communion. This mentality is all the more likely to grow unconsciously when we habitually receive at "private Masses" at which one assists without serving and perhaps with an absolute minimum of active participation—barely aware of the principal parts of the Mass, lost in meditation or perhaps, alas, in a weary coma.

2. One will then go deeper into it and say: *the Mass is the Passion of Christ*. When I am assisting at Mass, I am present at the Passion. This is a deeper and more cogent variation of the above. The Mass becomes, in fact, a *meditation on the Passion*. This has indeed been the approach of many saints. It is characteristic of medieval devotion. The piety of the Middle Ages sought in various ways to see in the Mass various symbolic representations of the sufferings of Christ in the Passion. Naturally, since the Mass does *not represent symbolically* any of the sufferings of Christ, the representations thus found are far-fetched and misleading. For instance to see the fraction of the Host at the *Pax Domini*[371] as a symbol of the death of Christ would be theologically incorrect and lead many into serious errors. On the other hand, sound theology definitely tells us that the double consecration of the Body and Blood of Jesus, separate in the host and chalice, does indeed place the Divine Victim on the altar in a "state of sacrifice." But this is in no way allegorical or representational. A simple contemplation of the mystery of the Passion at Mass, not in the details of Jesus' sufferings, but as an *objectively present reality*—this is very good. There is nothing wrong with it, especially

---

371. "Peace of the Lord" (*Missale Romanum*, 358; *Missale Cisterciense*, 228).

if one remembers that one is *sacramentally participating in the Passion of Christ*—and focuses one's attention on the true meaning of the sacramental sign. It is highly praiseworthy to contemplate the Passion as *sacramentally* signified. Where souls go wrong is in seeking other "signs" and representations of the Passion which are not really there. *There is in the Mass no sacramental or allegorical or any other representation of the actual physical sufferings of Jesus.* In Fr. Lasance's *Blessed Sacrament Book*[372] we find a "method of assisting at Mass" which is a meditation on the Passion: at the Confiteor, we are to imagine Jesus retiring to the Garden of the Agony, and an act of contrition is then read from the book; at the Kyrie, we are to imagine Jesus taken and bound—other acts and prayers are then read; Fr. Lasance gives an epistle and gospel appropriate to this meditation on the Passion; at the offertory, we are to represent Jesus scourged, at the preface, crowned with thorns, and at the elevation we are to see Him hanging on the cross; at communion the pious Christian represents himself plunged into the wound in the Sacred Heart of Jesus, and after communion there is a long prayer to Jesus buried in the sepulchre—this last point is in doubtful taste and is very bad theology: Jesus present in our hearts in communion is certainly not "dead and buried" but *lives in us and we in Him*. In principle, this form of devotion has something to recommend it, and there is no doubt that some souls might be able to make use of it with considerable profit. There is no question of the reality of the Passion in the Mass. What one might question, however, is *this manner of approaching the reality of the Passion*. There is no doubt that this naive and artificial approach which nowhere indicates a deep understanding of the Holy Sacrifice, does not in fact come near the *objective reality* of the Sacred Mystery. At best it produces certain subjective dispositions, thoughts and devotions, which are in themselves good and pious and certainly dispose the soul for

372. Francis Xavier Lasance, *Blessed Sacrament Book* (Cincinnati: Benziger Brothers, 1913), 205–24: "Mass in Honor of the Five Wounds of Our Saviour and of the Exaltation of the Cross."

fruitful reception of holy communion. But the fact remains that in monks and priests one would desire a better understanding of the real nature of the Holy Sacrifice and a deeper sense of the true mind of the Church and of her liturgy. For this, we must keep much closer to the liturgical texts, and try to penetrate them and understand their inner meaning. As priests we must carry out the injunction of the bishop at our ordination: IMITAMINI QUOD TRACTATIS[373]—and emphasis is on the words QUOD TRACTATIS—not on a devotion or meditation which is somewhat outside the real center of the Mass, and remains peripheral to it. Let us study the missal itself and see what it tells us about the real nature of the Holy Eucharist. What do we actually do?

3. *The Ordinary of the Mass*: what does it tell us about the nature of Holy Mass? Nothing could tell us more clearly, simply, and concretely what we are "doing" at Mass than the prayers of the ordinary in the missal. Here we see the Church speaking to God and expressing in unmistakable terms just what she means. Note, however, in the ordinary we must distinguish two types of prayers: (a) those which the celebrant says more or less "privately," that is in his own name, in order to dispose himself to officiate worthily, and to keep his own dispositions on a high level; (b) those which he says in the name of the Church, formally officiating as priest—it is here in these prayers that we see most clearly what the nature of the Mass is. The prayers which the celebrant says *privately* (i.e. in his own name, in order to dispose himself) are of quite a different nature from those which he says formally as officiating priest in offering the Holy Sacrifice. Such "private" prayers are, for instance, the Confiteor and other prayers at the foot of the altar—of late date—a preliminary preparation for Mass (here the "people"—servers—join the priest in disposing themselves); the *Munda Cor*,[374] said by {the} priest (or deacon)

---

373. "Imitate what you hold" (*Pontificale Romanum*, 89, which reads: "*imitare quod tractas*").

374. "Cleanse [my] heart" (*Missale Romanum*, 274; *Missale Cisterciense*, 180).

before the Gospel; the *Lavabo*;[375] prayers just before communion.
It is well when offering Mass to be aware of this distinction. The
prayers have a different "tone"—they are personal. There should
be an alternation of emphasis and attitude as we pass back and
forth from the more solemn prayers of officiation, to the private,
interior acts of contrition and etc., before God in our own name.
{There is} a kind of inhaling and exhaling—a "rhythm" in which
a certain amount of subjectivity finds its rightful place—the priest
from time to time becomes aware of himself as an individual
person, then goes back to his public function as representative of
the *plebs sancta*[376] and of the divine High Priest. These prayers of
the celebrant in "his own name" tell us less about the real essence
of the Mass than the other prayers of the ordinary. Let us pass on
to these. We also pass over those prayers of the ordinary which
belong more properly to the people and to the choir (the Gloria,
Credo, etc.) and the other parts of the liturgy of praise and of the
divine word in the Mass of the Catechumens.

Beginning at the offertory, we find repeated indications and
expressions of the true nature of the Mass: it is a GIFT, an OFFER-
ING, a SACRIFICE, offered by the People of God to God Himself.
In the Mass we are *giving to God a Gift that is infinitely pleasing to
Him*. This is the real meaning of the Mass. This is absolutely
fundamental. If we have this in our minds, if we have this attitude, that we are *offering God a Gift*, then we know what we are
doing. We can start from there and include many other things—
v.g., meditation on the Passion. But if we do not have this mental
attitude of offering God a Gift, then no matter how much we may
meditate on pious subjects, even on the liturgical season, etc., we
are still wide of the mark, so this one point is absolutely fundamental. The Mass is an *objective Gift to God*. Our desire is to please

---

375. "I will wash [my hands in innocence]" (*Missale Romanum*, 277; *Missale
Cisterciense*, 183).

376. From the prayer after the elevation of the chalice: ". . . *nos servi tui,
sed et plebs tua sancta, . . .*" (". . . we Your servants, and also Your holy people
. . .") (*Missale Romanum*, 358; *Missale Cisterciense*, 228).

Him by the Gift we offer. Our prayer is that He will receive the Gift. We rejoice in fact that He does actually receive it. Our devotion will be proportionate to our realization of the nature and value of the Gift we offer. Our devotion at Mass should be centered above all in this desire to please God by offering Him a Gift which, we know, is in fact infinitely pleasing to Him. And why do we desire to please Him? because we love Him, of course. We offer Him this Gift in *thanksgiving* (*eucharistia*) for all His goodness to us. We shall enter into the details of this great mystery later on. For the moment, let us look at the missal.

{The} first word of the offertory in the ordinary {is} Suscipe: Receive . . . O Holy Father . . . this spotless host which I offer . . . for my own sins and for all here present."[377] Note this is *not* one of the prayers which the celebrant says as a private person, to dispose himself for the sacred actions he has to perform. Here he is explicitly officiating for the People of God—and for himself also. The gift offered by the priest is offered first for himself, then for all the people. We see already his privileged position. Offerimus:[378] then when the chalice has been prepared (the fact that the blessing of the water takes place at the epistle corner gives it a secondary and preparatory character) {he prays}: We offer to Thee . . . the chalice of salvation—that it may ascend with an odor of sweetness.[379] This expression clearly shows that our intent is to please God by this offering. The priest then renews the offering "in the spirit of humility"[380] and asks God to be pleased with it, and again he blesses the oblation, calling down the Holy Spirit to sanctify our gifts. Again {he prays} *Suscipe Sancta Trinitas*[381] (a later addition, recapitulating what has been said and pointing to the idea of the "memorial" of the Passion which will be stressed in the canon). *Orate Fratres:*[382] for what?

377. *Missale Romanum*, 276; *Missale Cisterciense*, 182.

378. "We offer" (*Missale Romanum*, 276; *Missale Cisterciense*, 182).

379. *Missale Romanum*, 276; *Missale Cisterciense*, 182.

380. *Missale Romanum*, 276; *Missale Cisterciense*, 182.

381. "Accept, Holy Trinity" (*Missale Romanum*, 278; *Missale Cisterciense*, 183).

382. "Pray, brothers" (*Missale Romanum*, 278; *Missale Cisterciense*, 183).

"that our sacrifice may be acceptable"; the servers reply: "May the Lord receive the sacrifice at thy hands," etc. The secret prayer, in the proper, frequently stresses this same idea, that we are offering God a gift with which we hope He will be pleased. "May the sacrifice of our devotion always be offered to Thee, O Lord . . . etc."[383] (Third Sunday {of} Advent); "Receive, O Lord, our offerings and prayers . . ."[384] (Friday, Advent Ember Days); "Look down favorably upon these sacrifices, O Lord . . . that they may be profitable to our devotion and salvation . . ."[385] (Fourth Sunday {of} Advent); "May the oblation of this day's festival be pleasing to thee . . ."[386] (Christmas—Midnight); "The gifts we offer do Thou, O Lord, sanctify by the new birth of Thine only begotten Son . . ."[387] (Christmas—Day Mass). To fully appreciate the mystery of the Eucharist we must realize the importance of the wonderful exchange that takes place as we offer "our gifts" to God, realize that during the offertory, *"haec dona"*[388] *means simply bread and wine.* After the consecration (in which Jesus Himself says *"Take* and eat . . . *Take* and drink"), these gifts have been transformed by God's own gift of Himself to us—the Body and Blood of His Son now replaces the substance of bread and wine. Some interesting *Secret* prayers (read them and comment) {include}: Octave of Epiphany: *Hostias tibi . . . deferimus suppliciter deprecantes ut sicut et ipse [Filius] nostrorum est auctor munerum ita sit ipse misericors et susceptor;*[389] Second Sunday after Epiphany *et*

---

383. *Missale Romanum*, 7; *Missale Cisterciense*, 6.

384. *Missale Romanum*, 11; *Missale Cisterciense*, 9.

385. *Missale Romanum*, 17; *Missale Cisterciense*, 12.

386. *Missale Romanum*, 20; *Missale Cisterciense*, 16.

387. *Missale Romanum*, 25; *Missale Cisterciense*, 19 (third Mass of Christmas).

388. "these gifts" (which actually occurs not during the offertory but at the beginning of the canon) (*Missale Romanum*, 349; *Missale Cisterciense*, 218).

389. "We bring to You our offerings, humbly beseeching that just as He [the Son] is the source of our gifts, so may He Himself mercifully be their receiver" (*Missale Romanum*, 50; *Missale Cisterciense*, 39).

alia: *Oblata Domine munera sanctifica . . . ;*[390] Ash Wednesday intimates the distinction between the "gifts" at the offertory which will become the "sacrament" at {the} consecration;[391] Easter Tuesday: "The sacrifice by which Thy Church is wonderfully fed and nourished";[392] Low Sunday: *"Suscipe munera, Domine, exsultantis Ecclesiae"*;[393] Corpus Christi: the bread and wine "mystically designate" the "gifts of unity and peace"[394] which we ask from God, and which we offer to God. *After study of the Secrets we conclude* {that} our gift is (a) {the} Body and Blood of Jesus Christ; (b) bread and wine to be transformed into His Body and Blood; (c) our virtues, our "fasts" (see Lent) in union with Christ; (d) our joys and sorrows, in union with Christ; (e) the unity of the Church herself.

IN THE CANON, the *Te Igitur*[395] is a solemn prayer that God may accept *"haec dona, haec munera, haec sancta sacrificia illibata"*[396] which we offer first of all for Thy Holy Catholic Church: HANC IGITUR OBLATIONEM SERVITUTIS NOSTRAE SED ET CUNCTAE FAMILIAE TUAE PLACATUS ACCIPIAS . . . . QUAM OBLATIONEM TU, DEUS, BENEDICTAM ETC. FACERE DIGNERIS . . .[397] Note the sober Roman tone of this prayer: we beg God to bless (*benedictam*), *"adscriptam"* (a technical legal

---

390. "Make holy, Lord, the gifts offered" (*Missale Romanum*, 52; *Missale Cisterciense*, 41).

391. *Missale Romanum*, 71; *Missale Cisterciense*, 55.

392. *Missale Romanum*, 374; *Missale Cisterciense*, 240 (actually Easter Wednesday).

393. "Accept, O Lord, the gifts of Your exultant Church" (*Missale Romanum*, 381; *Missale Cisterciense*, 246).

394. *Missale Romanum*, 429; *Missale Cisterciense*, 281.

395. "Therefore [we beg] You" (*Missale Romanum*, 347; *Missale Cisterciense*, 217).

396. "these gifts, these offerings, these holy, unspotted oblations" (*Missale Romanum*, 347; *Missale Cisterciense*, 217).

397. "May You be pleased to accept, therefore, this offering of our service and that of Your entire household. . . . May You deign, O God, to make this offering blessed . . ." (*Missale Romanum*, 350; *Missale Cisterciense*, 220); the text actually reads *"quaesumus, Domine ut"* ("we beg, Lord, that") following *"familiae tuae"*; *"in omnibus, quaesumus"* ("in everything, we beg") after *"Deus"*; and *"adscriptam, ratam, rationabilem, acceptabilemque"* ("approved, effective, right and acceptable") instead of "etc."

term {for which it is} hard to find {the} exact meaning: "legiti-mate" will have to do), "*ratam*" (*ratum habere* is to confirm, to guarantee acceptance), *rationabilem* (spiritual?), *acceptabilem* (all requirements of the law have been complied with). Note the striking thing about the consecration, in this connection, is that where the priest speaks *in persona Jesu Christi*,[398] nothing is said about gifts to God, but rather all is centered on Our Lord's gift of Himself to us. He lifts his eyes and *gives thanks* to the Father—we shall see in a moment that this is the key to the whole mys-tery—and then says: ACCIPITE ET MANDUCATE . . . ACCIPITE ET BIBITE.[399] He *gives us* His own Body and Blood in the consecrated species which have been transsubstantiated by His words. But these infinitely precious and holy Gifts, which we have received from Him, *we ourselves now offer to the Father. Unde et memores:*[400] {here is} the very heart of the canon, after the consecration: this prayer shows that in offering this Holy Sacrifice to the Father we are commemorating in the strongest possible sense the Passion, Res-urrection, Ascension (etc.—see {the} older *anamneses*[401]) of Christ. That is to say, these mysteries are sacramentally renewed and re-presented in the mystery of the Eucharist. With the full con-sciousness of this re-presentation, OFFERIMUS PRAECLARAE MAJESTATI TUAE DE TUIS DONIS AC DATIS HOSTIAM PURAM, HOSTIAM SANCTAM, HOSTIAM IMMACULATAM, PANEM SANCTUM VITAE AETERNAE, ET CALICEM SALUTIS PERPETUAE.[402] {This is a} marvelous prayer, {and} marvelous actions,

---

398. "in the person of Jesus Christ".

399. "Take and eat . . . . Take and drink" (*Missale Romanum*, 351; *Missale Cisterciense*, 221).

400. "And so, mindful" (*Missale Romanum*, 352; *Missale Cisterciense*, 222).

401. The "remembrance" or "commemoration" of the saving events of Christ's passion, resurrection and ascension, immediately following the consecra-tion (see Josef Jungmann, *The Mass of the Roman Rite: Its Origins and Development (Missarum Solemnia)*, trans. Francis A. Brunner, CSSR, 2 vols. [New York: Benziger, 1951, 1955], 2.218-26, which includes examples of early anamneses; see also Michael O'Carroll, CSSP, "Anamnesis," in *Corpus Christi: An Encyclopedia of the Eucharist* [Wilmington, DE: Michael Glazier, 1988], 12–14).

402. "We offer to Your splendid majesty, from the gifts You have given, the pure Victim, the holy Victim, the spotless Victim, the holy bread of eternal life,

which require contemplation rather than commentary. They are essentially simple and clear, but boundless in their depths. Note all the implications—which we will discuss later—gifts are offered to God *from among His own gifts to us*. This is essential. What have we that we have not received? This should be at the very center of priestly spirituality and priestly humility. The gift we offer is an infinitely pure and holy and spotless host. This, the Body of the Lord, is the Holy Bread of eternal life. This, the Precious Blood of the Savior, is the chalice of everlasting salvation. Here we must pause to consider the words of St. John, chapter 6: READ John 6:32 ff.: My Father giveth you true bread from heaven. . . . The bread of God is that which cometh down from heaven and giveth life to the world. They said therefore to Him, give us always this bread. Jesus said, I am the Bread of Life: he that cometh to me shall not hunger . . . . All that the Father giveth to me shall come to me. . . . This is the will of the Father: . . . that of all that He hath given me I should lose nothing, but should raise it up again at the last day. . . . No man can come to me except the Father draw him, and I will raise him up. I am the living bread—if any man shall eat of this bread he shall live forever, and the bread that I will give is my flesh for the life of the world. . . . He that eateth my flesh and drinketh my blood abideth in me and I in him. As the living Father has sent me and I live by the Father, so he that eateth me the same shall live by me. {There is a} tremendous mystery here: note how often the word "*give*" appears, and *it is always a question of God giving*: (a) the Father gives us true bread, His Son; gives us to His Son, that He may raise us up at the last day; draws us to the Son, to eat His flesh and drink His blood, that we may belong to Him; (b) the Son gives His flesh to be our bread, gives Himself to us to be our life, gives us to the Father in and with Himself. This throws a new and utterly supernatural light on the true mystery of the Eucharist. *In reality, it is God's greatest gift to us*. Our greatest gift

and the cup of everlasting salvation" (*Missale Romanum*, 352; *Missale Cisterciense*, 222–23).

to Him is to give Him His own Son, Whom He has given to us. But in order to do this, we must receive the Body and Blood of the Lord as the gift of the Father and of the Son to us. IN RECEIV-ING THIS GREATEST GIFT OF GOD WE IN TURN BECOME THE FATHER'S GIFT TO THE SON AND THE SON'S GIFT TO THE FATHER; AND MORE: GOD GIVES HIMSELF TO OUR NEIGHBOR THROUGH OURSELVES AND TO US THROUGH OUR NEIGHBOR. THE MYSTERY OF DIVINE LOVE AND DIVINE GIVING IS MANIFEST IN US WHEN WE LIVE AS WITNESS TO THE MYSTERY OF THE EUCHARIST WHICH IS OUR VERY LIFE. This is the meaning of our *offerimus*, which does not make perfect sense unless we fully participate in the mystery by RECEIVING the Lord in holy communion, at least spiritually.

Now we can continue with the prayers of the canon, and *our gift*, our offering of sacrifice to God. *Supra quae*:[403] we ask the Father to be pleased with our gifts and accept them as once He was pleased to accept the sacrifices of Abel, Abraham, and Melchisedec. {This is} a simple and childlike prayer, in which we have not an "out of place" comparison between sacrifices that cannot be com-pared with one another, but a straightforward recognition that the Blessed Eucharist fulfills the Old Testament types and is a "holy sacrifice, a spotless host."[404] In referring to *Abraham*, the prayer shows that the sacrifices of the Jews are fulfilled and included in the Mass. In referring to *Melchisedec* it brings out the astonishing fact that the Mass also fulfills and completes all the *pagan* sacrifices of the natural law in so far as they may have been good and fitting acts of worship; many of course were perverted and turned away from God by elements of magic and superstition.

Supplices te rogamus:[405] {this is} the climax of the sacrifice *as our gift* to God. It is here that we raise the holy offering up and place It in the hands of God. Note the error of those who think the elevation is the "offering" of the Host to God. On the contrary,

---

403. "Moreover" (*Missale Romanum*, 352; *Missale Cisterciense*, 223).

404. *Missale Romanum*, 352; *Missale Cisterciense*, 223.

405. "Most humbly we ask You" (*Missale Romanum*, 352; *Missale Cisterciense*, 223).

the true spirit of the liturgy, how much more wonderful and more truly "religious," is that we bow down and humble ourselves and offer the gift to God by the hands of the holy angels. This tells us much about the true spirit in which we should approach God in adoration and prayer and self-oblation. Note here that the *idea of the exchange* becomes evident. The *supplices* is the bridge between the consecration (sacrifice), and communion (our participation). Note that in most sacrifices, the element of union and friendship with God is symbolized by the sacred meal in which the worshippers share the good things of the altar with their Lord. "*UT:* . . . may the angels carry this gift to Thy holy altar IN ORDER THAT as many of us as by participation at this altar shall receive the most sacred Body and Blood of Thy Son may be filled with every heavenly blessing and grace."[406] {This is} the supreme prayer for grace and divine light and help and for perfect union with God. All possibilities of prayer of petition are exhausted here. Hereafter *prayer of petition* is uppermost—for the souls that "sleep in the sleep of peace,"[407] and for *Nobis quoque peccatoribus*[408] (asking a share in the blessedness of the saints). Then {comes} the magnificent climax of the canon—the *Per quem,*[409] etc. (the minor elevation).

COMMUNION:

a) Preparation for communion: naturally, there is no need to insist that one must receive communion well-prepared. If one has followed the Mass intelligently, as we have discussed it, and if one is full of ardent desire to please God with the sacred gifts which we offer Him as members of His Holy Church, then one is quite naturally prepared for communion. The gifts we have offered—the Body and Blood of Jesus—include the offering of ourselves and of our lives, the surrender of our hearts to the love

---

406. *Missale Romanum*, 352–53; *Missale Cisterciense*, 223–24.
407. *Missale Romanum*, 353; *Missale Cisterciense*, 224.
408. "us sinners also" (*Missale Romanum*, 353; *Missale Cisterciense*, 224).
409. "Through Whom" (*Missale Romanum*, 353; *Missale Cisterciense*, 225).

of God, to His Holy Will. Intelligent participation in the Sacred Mysteries means that we dispose ourselves for communion naturally and spontaneously by bringing to Mass *a consciousness of our needs*, a sense of our complete dependence on God, a realization of our utter helplessness without Him, our loneliness and isolation which seeks union with Him and with our brethren in the peace of Christ and in the bond of the Holy Spirit. We are also vividly conscious of the *needs of all*—all the faithful, all mankind. Before the consecration we pause to remember all the living, especially those near and dear to us or those for whom we have been inspired to pray. The *memento of the living* is by no means a distraction, {but a} sacred duty of charity—the salvation and sanctification of these souls is bound up with our Mass. If God reminds us to pray for them, it is because He wants to give them special graces through our prayer. Let His grace speak in our hearts! The greatest good you can do for your neighbor {is to} include him in your Mass. Think of those in concentration camps and prisons. The *memento of the dead* {reminds us} how the souls of the faithful departed depend on our Mass even more completely than those of the living. Seek out especially needy souls: special sinners, special groups, the poor, {those} who have no one to offer Mass for them. The fruits of many Masses *belong* to them and are assigned to them by Our Lady. N.B. {the role of} the Church Triumphant: the Mass {is} a supremely social act—{we experience the} joy and consolation of bringing in the saints at the *Communicantes*[410] and *Nobis quoque peccatoribus*. We bring, then, to Mass a sense of our own deficiencies but also a confident and loving *desire for unity* and for *peace in Christ's love*. In the three prayers before communion, the priest utters those sentiments which are most appropriate to dispose one immediately to receive the sacred Body and Blood of Christ. But right after the *Pater*, which includes all our petitions, there is the *Libera*, the keynote of which is the petition *for peace*, and deliverance from

---

410. "In communion with" (i.e. the commemoration of the saints preceding the consecration) (*Missale Romanum*, 348; *Missale Cisterciense*, 218).

all evils. It is simply an enlargement upon the last petition of the
Pater: *sed libera nos a malo*.[411] Libera nos . . . *ab omnibus malis,
praeteritis, praesentibus et futuris* . . . DA PROPITIUS PACEM *in diebus
nostris: ut ope misericordiae tuae adjuti, et* A PECCATO SIMUS SEMPER
LIBERI *et ab omni perturbatione securi*. . . .[412] Then the fraction of
the Host and the *Pax Domini*[413]—why? The dividing of the sacramental Body of Christ and its distribution to the faithful will
unite the faithful in peace and in love, and fill them with His
Presence and His Spirit. He is one in them all. They are thus one
in Him. Hence, the *kiss of peace* in our rite is a most important
part of our preparation for holy communion. READ Matthew
18:19[414] to the end: {note} the importance of agreement among

411. "But deliver us from evil" (*Missale Romanum,* 355, 357; *Missale Cisterciense,* 226–27).

412. "Deliver us from all evils, past, present and future . . . in Your goodness give us peace in our days, so that, aided by the richness of Your mercy, we
may be both free from sin always and safe from all disturbance" (*Missale Romanum,* 357; *Missale Cisterciense,* 227–28).

413. "Peace of the Lord" (*Missale Romanum,* 358; *Missale Cisterciense,* 228).

414. "'I say to you further, that if two of you shall agree on earth about
anything at all for which they ask, it shall be done for them by my Father in heaven.
For where two or three are gathered together for my sake, there am I in the midst
of them.' Then Peter came up to him and said, 'Lord, how often shall my brother
sin against me, and I forgive him? Up to seven times?' Jesus said to him, 'I do not
say to thee seven times, but seventy times seven. This is why the kingdom of
heaven is likened to a king who desired to settle accounts with his servants. And
when he had begun the settlement, one was brought to him who owed him ten
thousand talents. And as he had no means of paying, his master ordered him to
be sold, with his wife and children and all that he had, and payment to be made.
But the servant fell down and besought him, saying, "Have patience with me and
I will pay thee all!" And moved with compassion, the master of that servant re-
leased him and forgave him the debt. But as that servant went out, he met one of
his fellow-servants who owed him a hundred denarii, and he laid hold of him
and throttled him, saying, "Pay what thou owest." His fellow-servant therefore
fell down and began to entreat him, saying, "Have patience with me and I will
pay thee all." But he would not; but went away and cast him into prison until he
should pay what was due. His fellow-servants therefore, seeing what had hap-
pened, were very much saddened, and they went and informed their master of
what had taken place. Then his master called him, and said to him, "Wicked ser-

the disciples of Christ. What is important is not so much the objective faultlessness of their judgement, but the fact that their agreement is endorsed by God Himself in heaven. "For where two or three are gathered together in my name . . . ." {To} Peter's question, "How often shall I forgive?" {the} answer {is given}: seventy times seven. Finally {comes} the parable of the steward who throttled his fellow servant, and the conclusion: "So will also my heavenly Father do unto you if you forgive not every one your brother from his heart." The kiss of peace is not merely an outward ceremony. It implies serious inward dispositions, efforts to be meek, *cooperative*, obedient, humble. One who goes to the holy table harboring in his heart *envious* or unjustly *critical* thoughts, *resentments*, rebellions against authority, sullen determination to cling to his own will against another, refusals to give in to another reasonably, refusals to accept another interiorly: such a one is not really well prepared for communion. His communion may of course be a good one, if the matter is not seriously sinful, but there exist obstacles to the full cooperation of grace: hence the importance of this in our preparation. Cultivate meekness and non-violence—*seriously*.

b) Communion and its effects: what is communion? It is the *sacramental union of man with Christ*, in the real and actual reception of His Sacred Body (and Blood) in the Holy Eucharist. *Effectus hujus Sacramenti—UNIO HOMINIS AD CHRISTUM* (Decree for the Armenians [Denz. 698]).[415] Here it is well to recall a few basic facts about

---

vant! I forgave thee all the debt, because thou didst entreat me. Shouldst not thou also have had pity on thy fellow-servant, even as I had pity on thee?" And his master, being angry, handed him over to the torturers until he should pay all that was due to him. So also my heavenly Father will do to you, if you do not each forgive your brothers from your hearts'" (Mt. 18:19-35).

415. *Enchiridion Symbolorum Definitionum et Declarationum de Rebus Fidei et Morum*, 31st ed., ed. Henricus Denzinger et Carolus Rahner (Rome: Herder, 1957), 257: "*Huius sacramenti effectus, quem in anima operatur digne sumentis, est adunatio hominis ad Christum*" ("The effect of this sacrament, which takes place in the soul of one who receives it worthily, is to unite the person to Christ") (Council of Florence [1438–46]).

the *Real Presence*. One of the joys of the contemplative is the meditative study of this wonderful mystery of the Eucharist—see especially Vonier.[416]

(A) *What the Real Presence IS NOT*:

(1) The Eucharist is not merely bread and wine, used as a *symbol* of the Body and Blood of Christ. The consecrated Host is no longer bread; it no longer has the substance of bread. There has taken place the miracle of *transsubstantiation*, which means that the substance present is the Body of Christ. That is "what" is present. It is present under the accidents of bread. The substance of bread is no longer present.

(2) Hence, it is not true to say as Luther[417] said that the substance of the Body of Christ is present in the Eucharist *together with* the substance of bread, much in the same way that God is present in all things by His power, presence and essence.

(3) It is not true to say either, with Calvin,[418] that Christ is present in the Eucharist as a *power*, in the sense that those who receive with faith are given grace on the occasion of their reception, so that the Eucharist brings Christ to them by an increase of grace and in that sense only do they receive Him in communion. (Calvin also maintained that this "power" of grace was given only to the predestined when they received communion,

---

416. Anscar Vonier, *A Key to the Doctrine of the Eucharist* (Westminster, MD: Newman, 1946); Merton quotes from this work in *The Living Bread* (New York: Farrar, Straus and Cudahy, 1956), 59, 65–66; he also notes in his journal that he is reading Vonier on May 14, 1957 (*Search for Solitude*, 90).

417. On Luther's Eucharistic teaching, see L. Godefroy, "Eucharistie d'après le Concile de Trente," *Dictionnaire de Théologie Catholique*, 15 vols. (Paris: Letouzey et Ané, 1923–1950), 5, cols. 1340–41, 1346–47; E. C. Messenger, *The Reformation, the Mass and the Priesthood: A Documented History with Special Reference to the Question of Anglican Orders*, 2 vols. (London: Longmans, Green, 1936–37), 1.115-20; Darwell Stone, *A History of the Doctrine of the Holy Eucharist*, 2 vols. (London: Longmans, Green, 1909), 2.9-24.

418. On Calvin's Eucharistic teaching, found in the *Institutes of the Christian Religion*, Bk. IV, cc. 17-18, see Godefroy, cols. 1342–43; Messenger, 1.173-78; Stone, 2:50-61.

and the others got absolutely nothing but bread and wine, no grace.[419])

(4) It is not true to say that Christ is only present in the Sacrament as a kind of moral influence, so that we are merely expected to *act as if* we are in His presence when we are in the presence of the Blessed Sacrament, and this will aid our devotion and help us to practice virtue.

On the other hand,

(5) Transsubstantiation does not bring about a *hypostatic union* of the bread and the Divine Word. It is totally different, a sacramental union, unique in its kind.

(6) The real presence is not *strictly a local and natural presence*. The Council of Trent distinguishes between the "natural presence" of Christ at the right hand of the Father (*juxta modum exsistendi naturalem*[420]) from the sacramental presence in which, at the same time, He is really and *substantially* present in the Blessed Eucharist all over the world. The key to this distinction is the fact that Christ is not "locally" on the altar in the sense that there would be a *direct relation between His sensible dimensions* and the place where the host lies. The relation is indirect. The accidents of the host are localized on the paten, or in the tabernacle, and where these accidents are, Christ is *substantially*, and therefore really, in the strictest sense, present.

(7) Jesus does not *feel* and *see* with His senses in the host. His body feels nothing and does not suffer when the host is broken. He does not feel confinement within the tabernacle, or lack of air, etc. What we say of Him responding diversely to love or to indifference in the sacred host, refers to His Sacred Heart and not to His bodily senses. His perception of our love and other dispositions is attained by His *infused and beatific* knowledge and thus communicated to His Sacred Heart present in the tabernacle, not acquired by His human senses.

419. Calvin, *Institutes*, IV.17.33.

420. "according to the natural manner of being" (*Enchiridion*, 304 [#874; *Decretum de Eucharistia*, c. 1]).

Conclusion: two exaggerations must be avoided:

a) treating the substantial presence of the Body of Christ in the host *merely as a spiritual* presence. The Body of Christ is not present "merely" spiritually, but really and substantially, in its true and actual essence and being.

b) treating the presence of Christ's Body as a sensible local and natural presence, subject to sense impressions—and hence "dolorism," vain imaginings, false mysticism, etc. Avoid too much sentimentality in Eucharistic devotion, but cultivate sincere and humble love of {the} Sacred Heart.

What the Real Presence is:

1. Transsubstantiation is a *miracle*, by which there takes place an utterly unique change of the substance of bread and wine into the substance of the Body and Blood of Jesus. The *whole* substance of bread and the whole substance of wine become the whole substance of the Body and of the Blood of Jesus Christ. The following points are *de fide*:[421]

a) the substance of the bread does not remain present after transsubstantiation; the substance of bread is no longer there;

b) the accidents of bread and wine remain;

c) the whole substance of the bread is converted into the Body of Christ, {and} the whole substance of the wine is converted into the Blood of Christ;

d) the proper name of this unique change is trans-substantiation.

Clarifications: there is a real change of one substance into another, not the substitution of one substance for another; the substance of bread is more probably not to be thought of as annihilated and replaced by the substance of the Body of Christ. What is most important is Our Lord's reason for this special change, His reason for wanting the substance of bread to become the substance of His Body: because thus He gives us not merely a sensible indica-

---

421. i.e. defined dogmas, required to be believed.

tion of His presence, or a pious occasion of gaining grace, or an aid to devotion, but He desires to "fuse our bodies into His body by the fire of the Holy Spirit, He melts down the food proper to our body by the fire of the Holy Spirit and changes it into His own body" (Scheeben[422]). This *is* My Body!! Thus He is enabled to transform us into Himself, not only as individuals but also as a group—the Mystical Body. "The transformation of bread into the real Body of Christ produces and prefigures a supernatural transformation of Christ's mystical body by assimilating it to its Head" (Scheeben[423]).

2. Hence Jesus is present in the Blessed Sacrament really and truly and literally as the supernatural food of our souls, as the principle of unity for all His members in such a way that He can be really, substantially and wholly present in each member and in all of them together, in sacramental communion (because He is at the same time present in *all the hosts*, everywhere, without being divided; each one of us receives the whole Body of Christ). But the Body of Christ is hypostatically united to the Word of God. It is the Body and Blood of God Himself, made man, that we receive. This Body becomes to us then a principle of divinization and a life-giving Spirit.

3. The Body of Christ, being present *as a substance* in the Blessed Sacrament, cannot truly be imagined as it is present, because we have no way of adequately imagining the presence of a substance. It is therefore easier to "grasp" obscurely the truth of the real presence if we keep the imagination out of it, for imagination in this case is more of a hindrance than a help. What counts is *faith*, and a solid grasp of the terms of the dogma in their unvarnished simplicity.

---

422. Matthias Joseph Scheeben, *The Mysteries of Christianity*, trans. Cyril Vollert, sj (St. Louis: Herder, 1946), 500, which reads: ". . . bodies with . . . by that same fire . . ."

423. Scheeben, 501, which reads: "The transubstantiation of the bread . . . a supernatural and very remarkable . . ."

4. The soul and divinity of Jesus are present in the Blessed Sacrament *vi concomitantiae*[424] with His substance in the Host and the Precious Blood.

5. He is totally present in every smallest fragment, as long as it remains incorrupt.

6. He is to be adored in every fragment where He is present. In adoration of the Blessed Sacrament the species of bread and the Body of Christ are considered as one being.

7. In speaking of the real presence, whatever *refers to His presence* is to be predicated directly of the Body of Christ ("He is on the altar"; "He is received in communion"). What refers precisely to quantitative contact is predicated more properly of the species ("we touch the sacred species"—correct; "we touch Jesus"—less correct). What refers to eating {is} predicated more properly of the Body—we don't just consume the species.

The Fruits of Holy Communion: in order to make a fruitful thanksgiving, that is to say, in order to make a good *communion* (for communion and thanksgiving should really be one), we have only to realize the infinite riches of this most holy sacrament.

1. Holy communion not only brings us great graces, but the *Author and Source of all grace* gives Himself to us in this holy sacrament. All the graces which are conferred in the other sacraments are derived, like streams from a spring, from the Author of grace in the Blessed Eucharist. All the other sacraments lead to the Blessed Eucharist as to their end—all are consummated in the union with the Redeemer which is sacramentally effected in this sacred mystery: *Effectus hujus sacramenti*—unio hominis ad Christum.[425]

a) We are united to *His Most Holy Body* more intimately than in a bodily embrace. His sacred flesh sacramentally becomes our

---

424. "*vi naturalis illius conexionis et concomitantiae*" ("by the power of that natural connection and association") (*Enchiridion*, 306 [#876; *Decretum de Eucharistia*, c. 3]).

425. See above, note 415.

food, in order that through union with His flesh we may enter into a deeper and more mystical union with His *soul and His divinity*: *"in me manet et ego in eo"*[426] (St. John 6).

b) We are *united with His soul* in its worship and love of the Father, in its mysteries on earth, in its love of our brethren. *This embrace of hearts and souls with the Redeemer* is even more close and more ineffable than the union of our body with His. "Therefore let us enter into the closest union with Christ and strive to LOSE OURSELVES AS IT WERE IN HIS MOST HOLY SOUL AND BE SO UNITED TO HIM THAT WE MAY HAVE A SHARE IN THOSE ACTS BY WHICH HE ADORES THE BLESSED TRINITY WITH A HOMAGE that is most acceptable and by which He offers to the eternal Father supreme praise and thanks, which find an harmonious echo throughout the heaven and earth, according to the words of the prophet: *Benedicite omnia opera Domini Domino*," says Pius XII in the section of *Mediator Dei* (127)[427] in which he speaks of thanksgiving after communion. (How do we "lose ourselves in His soul"?)

c) *We are united with His Divinity*: St. Cyril of Alexandria clearly says that the *Word* in this sacrament is life to our souls. We receive in the Blessed Eucharist VERBUM . . . SECUNDUM NATURAM VITA CUNCTA VIVIFICANS. *Cum ex vivo Patre genitus sit, ipse quoque natura sua vita est: et quoniam vitae secundum naturam officium est vivificare, Christus omnia vivificat.*[428] Hence it is the Word as *Life* that we receive in this sacrament. But it is also the Word as LIGHT AND TRUTH that we receive. Scheeben says (*Mysteries of Christianity*, p. 525): "By partaking of His flesh we are illumined by the

---

426. "He remains in me and I in him" (Jn. 6:57).

427. *Mediator Dei*, 46; the quotation is from Daniel 3:57: "All you works of the Lord, bless the Lord."

428. "The Word, being Life in His very nature, giving life to all things. Since He is generated by the living Father, He is Himself Life by His very nature: and because the function of that which is life by nature is to give life, Christ gives life to all things" (*In Joannis Evangelium*, 3.6.32-33; J. P. Migne, ed., *Patrologiae Cursus Completus, Series Graeca* [PG], 161 vols. [Paris: Garnier, 1857–1866], vol. 73, col. 502AB); the translation is based on that found in *The Living Bread*, 109.

light of eternal truth, and are transfigured and transformed by its glory; *and in His Blood the ocean of eternal life and divine love floods our hearts.* By the divine power inhabiting the Lord's flesh we are *transformed in soul into the image of His divine glory*, and *in body into the image of His glorified* body, just as by *the power of the Holy Spirit coursing in our blood our souls and bodies are filled with the immortal and divine life.*"[429] *Habeo vere et adoro, quem angeli adorant in coelo* (*Imitation*, iv, 12[430]—READ context[431]). In receiving Christ in the Blessed Sacrament, we are as intimately united to the Word of God as if He were the soul of our soul and the being of our being. The Holy Spirit issues forth from the Word, received in us (*Verbum spirans amorem*[432]) and becomes a "torrent of divine life"[433] to our souls and to our whole being, *filling us with divine love.* (READ TEXTS in *The Living Bread*: pp. 110–114.[434]) Hence

429. Scheeben, 524–25, which reads: "Thus by . . . we are illuminated . . . His own glorified body, . . . in His blood . . . and our bodies . . . immortal, divine life" (emphasis added by Merton).

430. "I truly have and adore the One whom the angels in heaven adore" (*Thomae a Kempis De Imitatione Christi*, ed. J. Mooren, 2nd ed. [Coloniae: Agr. et Novesii, 1890], 384) (properly c. 11.2).

431. The chapter "*Quod corpus Christi et sacra scriptura maxime sint animae fideli necessaria*" ("That the Body of Christ and sacred scripture are most necessary to the faithful soul") (Mooren, 383–90) focuses on the impossibility in the present life of seeing the glorified Christ in his divine majesty, and the divine condescension of being present in the Blessed Sacrament, which will no longer be necessary in the life to come; but for the present, Word and Sacrament are the two tables providing spiritual nourishment for the soul in this world.

432. "the Word breathing forth Love" (Thomas Aquinas, *Summa Theologiae*, 1a, 43, 5, ad. 2, in *Summa Theologiae*, ed. Thomas Gilby, OP, *et al.*, 61 vols. [New York: McGraw-Hill, 1964–80], 7.222).

433. See Scheeben, 525: "He will completely flood us through and refresh us with the torrent of His love and His life"; this passage refers to the Word rather than the Spirit, but Scheeben later emphasizes that the Spirit "flows forth" from Christ and "pours Himself" into the faithful as "the flood and fragrance of the divine life" (528–29).

434. These pages, part of section 3, "Communion and Its Effects," of chapter 4, "I Am the Way," include two passages from Scheeben, the first (520, 524) focusing on the flesh of Christ as nourishment for the spirit and the blood of Christ as

Scheeben concludes: "What nourishes us in the Eucharist is properly *the divine energy of the Logos* inhabiting Christ's flesh."[435] "He unites His divinity to our souls in a way that resembles the union of His flesh and blood with our bodies."[436] Furthermore we must realize that this is not just a figure of speech: Jesus really gives Himself completely, body and soul, blood and divinity in the Blessed Sacrament to *be our permanent possession.*

d) Hence this possession of Christ is *a pledge of eternal life*—not only a promise, but even a mysterious and anticipated realization of what is promised. {See the} *postcommunion* {prayer} *of Corpus Christi*: "Grant us we beseech thee, O Lord, to be filled with the everlasting enjoyment of Thy divinity which IS PREFIGURED BY

---

pouring the Spirit into the soul (110–11), the second (520–21) stressing that sacramental union with the glorified flesh of Christ makes the soul a worthy sacrifice to God (111–12); a passage from St. Ambrose, *De Sacramentis*, 5.14-15: "You have therefore come to the altar and you have received the grace of Christ, His heavenly sacraments. The Church rejoices in the redemption of so many and exults with spiritual joy at the sight of the white-robed family. (He is addressing the newly baptized, who have received the Eucharist for the first time.) You will find all this in the Canticle of Canticles. In her joy the Church cries out to Christ, for she has a banquet all prepared which is splendid enough to be the banquet of heaven itself. Hence she says: 'Let my Brother come down into His garden and pluck the fruits of His trees' (Canticle 5:1). What are these fruit trees? You had become dry wood in Adam, but now, having been made fruit trees in Christ, you are bearing your harvest. And the Lord Jesus gladly accepts this invitation, and replies to His Church with a kindness that belongs to heaven: 'I have come down,' He says, 'into my garden. I have harvested my myrrh and my aromatical balsams. I have eaten my bread with my honey and I have drunk my wine with my milk.' 'Eat, my brothers,' he says, 'and be glad with wine' (Canticle, *ibid*.)" (112–13); and a passage from St. Cyprian, *Epistola* 63.11: "The chalice of the Lord inebriates men in such a way that they become sober. It brings their minds to heavenly wisdom so that each one loses his taste for this world and awakens to the understanding of God. And just as ordinary wine gladdens the mind and relaxes the soul and drives out all sorrow, so when we have drunk the Blood of the Lord and the saving chalice the memory of the old man is put out of our mind and we forget about our former conduct in the world, and the sad, dejected heart which was burdened with sins and anxieties, is filled with the happiness of divine pardon" (114).

435. Scheeben, 524, which reads: "What feeds and nourishes . . ."
436. Scheeben, 524.

THE TEMPORAL RECEPTION OF THY PRECIOUS BODY AND BLOOD."[437] Just as in the beatific vision, the immediate contact of the soul with the divine substance nourishes the soul with divine life and glory and truth, so in this Blessed Sacrament, in the darkness of faith, there is the same immediate presence of the divinity. St. Cyprian says that wine must be offered in the sacrifice rather than water, because water is not capable of signifying the reality of the divine presence which vivifies and inebriates our souls with a *sobria ebrietas*,[438] the pure and unearthly joy of the soul immediately united to Christ, Man and God, and filled with joy by His Holy Spirit of Love (cf. quote from St. Cyprian: *Living Bread*, p. 114[439]). The Fathers add that reception of the Blessed Eucharist in a mysterious way prepares and purifies even our bodies to dispose them for the glorious resurrection. In any case, the vivifying presence of Christ in the Blessed Eucharist acts on our souls as a TRANSFORMING AND DIVINIZING FORCE, ELEVATING AND SANCTIFYING OUR LIVES.

2. All the other effects of holy communion flow from this main one, union with Christ:

a) Naturally, as we have seen above, there is a *great increase of charity* in the well-disposed soul, quite apart from any feelings or conscious desires of charity. These of course may help to increase our union with Christ still further. But even in aridity and apparent frustration, our charity can grow greatly with each good communion. Indeed, it is likely that the *purifying effect of aridity*, raising us above the level of natural consolations, may greatly aid the increase of charity and fruitfulness of our communions without our being able to realize this fact. Avoid self-seeking in our life of prayer. In any case, the first and foremost effect of our sacramental union with Christ is A GREAT INCREASE IN SPIRITUAL AND SUPERNATURAL LIFE (that is, grace, charity). Intimately united

437. *Missale Romanum;* 429; *Missale Cisterciense*, 281.
438. See above, n. 357.
439. See n. 434.

to Him Who is love, united to Him in a union of love, we cannot help but grow in love if we are well disposed.

b) The growth in charity is accompanied by RENEWAL AND PURIFICATION. Innumerable texts of the liturgy show us this: *Cujus laetamur gustu,* renovemur effectu;[440] *Quos caelestibus reficis sacramentis;*[441] Mundet a crimine *et ad caelestia regna perducat;*[442] *Ut in me non remaneat scelerum macula* quem pura et sancta refecerunt sacramenta.[443] In what sense does it purify us from sin? (1) {it} certainly purifies from venial sin and remits punishment due to venial sin; (2) {it} would also purify from mortal sin in the case where the soul in good faith received communion with an unconfessed mortal sin—v.g. one that had been inculpably forgotten or not properly confessed due to invincible ignorance: cf. *Imitation,* IV:1: *In hoc sacramento confertur spiritualis gratia, et reparatur in anima virtus amissa, et per peccatum deformata, redit pulchritudo;*[444] Innocent III: *venialia delet et cavet mortalia;*[445] Council of Trent: *antidotum quo liberemur a culpis quotidianis et a peccatis mortalibus praeservemur.*[446] (N.B. for the Eucharist to remit venial sin there must be sorrow for that sin. Punishment is remitted

440. "may we be renewed by the effect of that whose taste makes us rejoice" (postcommunion: Monday, First Week of Lent [*Missale Romanum,* 82; *Missale Cisterciense,* 64]).

441. "those whom you refresh with your heavenly sacraments" (postcommunion: First Sunday after Epiphany [*Missale Romanum,* 48; *Missale Cisterciense,* 38]).

442. "may it cleanse from sin and lead to the heavenly realms" (postcommunion: Friday, Third Week of Lent [*Missale Romanum,* 125; *Missale Cisterciense,* 96]).

443. "that there may remain no stain of sin in me, whom the pure and holy mysteries have renewed" (prayer after communion while cleaning the chalice [*Missale Romanum,* 361; *Missale Cisterciense,* 232]).

444. "In this sacrament a spiritual grace is conferred, and the virtue that had been lost is restored to the soul, and that beauty deformed by sin returns" (*Imitatio,* 4.1.11 [Mooren, 345]).

445. "It wipes away venial sins and guards against mortal sins" (*De Sacro Altario Mysterio,* 5.44 [*PL* 217, col. 885B]).

446. "It is the antidote by which we are freed from daily faults and preserved from mortal sins" (*Enchiridion,* 305 [#875; *Decretum de Eucharistia,* c. 2]).

indirectly through the charity which is aroused in the commu-
nicant by his sacramental union with the Savior.) In any case the
reception of the Blessed Sacrament, bringing us increase in charity, removes obstacles to charity, destroys the remains of sin,
strikes at the roots of concupiscence. The reception of the Blessed
Sacrament with faith and love destroys the life of sin, of the old
man, and renews the life of charity, of the new man. Hence by
its reception we are *a vetustate purgatos*.[447] At our Christmas communion {we pray}: *Nova per carnem nativitas [Christi] liberet quos
sub peccati jugo vetusta servitus tenet . . .*[448] LIBERTY is an aspect of
this interior renewal and freedom from the burden of sin. *AB OMNI
VESTUSTATE PURGATOS . . . IN NOVAM TRANSFERAT CREATURAM . . . QUOS
TUIS MYSTERIIS RECREASTI.*[449] The mystery of the Eucharist is part of
a *sacramental re-creation* of man in Christ, restoring the old creation damaged and corrupted by the fall.

c) *JOY is an inseparable effect of this renewal and growth in divine
life.* A normal and natural effect of the sacramental grace of the
Eucharist, growth in charity, is the joy which belongs to charity.
Venite ad me, omnes qui laboratis et ego reficiam vos[450] (Invitatorium
{of} Corpus Christi[451]). How can we not taste joy and peace when
we rest in Jesus Who is our God and our all, Who is all our joy? *IPSE
ENIM EST SANCTIFICATIO NOSTRA ET REDEMPTIO; IPSE CONSOLATIO VIATORUM
ET SANCTORUM AETERNA FRUITIO (Imitation*, IV:1,12).[452] True, this joy
comes to us in the darkness of faith and sometimes is barely felt.

447. "cleansed from the old life" (postcommunion: First Sunday of Lent
[*Missale Romanum*, 80; *Missale Cisterciense*, 62]).

448. "May the new birth [of Christ] in the flesh free those whom the old
servitude holds under the yoke of sin" (collect prayer [n.b., not communion
prayer]: Third Mass of Christmas [*Missale Romanum*, 23; *Missale Cisterciense*, 18]).

449. "Having been cleansed from the old life, may it transform into a new
creature those whom you have recreated by your mysteries" (postcommunion:
Wednesday of Easter Week [*Missale Romanum*, 374; *Missale Cisterciense*, 241]).

450. "Come to me all you who labor, and I will give you rest" (Mt. 11:28).

451. *Breviarium Cisterciense, Aestivalis*, 194.

452. "For He Himself is our redemption and sanctification; He Himself is
the consolation of wayfarers and the eternal enjoyment of the saints" (Mooren,
346).

Sometimes indeed it is buried under the weight of our darkness, but nevertheless, no matter how anguished may be our interior life, Jesus always without fail brings comfort, and sometimes an almost miraculous comfort, to the soul that is abandoned to Him, and receives Him in self-forgetfulness and trust. (The great obstacle to joy in our communion is preoccupation with ourselves, worrying about our faults and limitations, coldness and lack of trust in Jesus, due to the excessive trust we have in ourselves, and our inordinate expectations of ourselves.) *Heu caecitas et duritia cordis humani* TAM INEFFABILE DONUM NON MAGIS ATTENDERE . . . (*Imitation, ibid.*[453]). *Dare* to have joy! Often we prevent ourselves from being happy by {our} unconscious conviction that joy is dangerous! Joy increases in proportion as we take our eyes off ourselves and admire and exult in the great goodness of God coming to us because He loves us and desires to be with us in the depths of our poor hearts, in spite of all their poverty and helplessness. Remember He is above all the *requies humilium.*[454] QUAM SUAVE ET JUCUNDUM CONVIVIUM, CUM TE IPSUM IN CIBUM DONASTI (*Imitation*, IV: 2,4;[455] cf. in our *Laudes Vespertinae:*[456] *O quam suavis est Domine Spiritus tuus* etc.[457]).

453. "Alas, the blindness and hard-heartedness of a person not to be more attentive to such a marvelous gift" (Mooren, 346).

454. "rest for the lowly" (line 23 of the hymn "*Christus Noster, Vere Cibus*" ["Christ Our True Food"]).

455. "How sweet and pleasant the banquet when You have given Yourself as food" (Mooren, 350).

456. I.e. hymns for Benediction of the Blessed Sacrament: see *Laudes Vespertinae: seu, Cantus Diversi ad Benedictionem SS. Sacramenti* (Westmalle, Belgium: Typis Ordinis, 1956), 8–9.

457. "O Lord, how sweet is Your spirit" (in addition to being used for Cistercian Benediction, this is the Magnificat antiphon of first vespers for Corpus Christi in the Roman rite [*Breviarium Romanum ex Decreto Sacrosancto Concilii Restitutum Summorum Pontificum Cura Recognitum cum Nova Psalterii Versione*, 27th ed. (Turonibus: Sumptibus et Typis Mame, 1952), *Aestivalis*, 365]): "*O quam suavis est, Domine, spiritus tuus, qui, ut dulcedinem tuam in filios demonstres, pane suavissimo de caelo praestito, esurientes reples bonis, fastidiosos divites dimittens inanes*" ("O Lord, how sweet is Your spirit, who in order to show Your sweetness toward Your children, having sent from heaven the most wonderful bread, fill the hungry with good things and send the disdainful rich away empty").

d) One of the great sources of joy in this sacrament is the fact that it is a PLEDGE AND FORETASTE OF ETERNAL LIFE. *FUTURAE GLORIAE NOBIS PIGNUS DATUR*[458] (office: Corpus Christi). The reception of the Blessed Sacrament is *a foretaste of the eternal joys of heaven*: *divinitatis tuae sempiterna fruitione repleri, quam pretiosi Corporis et Sanguinis tui perceptio praefigurat*[459] (postcommunion: Corpus Christi). In communion and in heaven we are directly united to God Himself—in communion sacramentally, in the darkness of faith and by charity; in heaven by glory. But in either case, it is God Himself who is substantially present to our souls and is Himself their joy. We have already spoken of this above.[460]

e) Another effect of the great increase of charity brought about by the Holy Eucharist *is strength to grow in all the other virtues*. {The} Council of Florence {declares}: *A malo retrahimur, confortamur in bono, et ad virtutum et gratiarum proficimus augmentum.*[461] For instance, in Lent, we pray that our communion may help us to be more generous and fervent in fasting: *continentiae promptioris nobis tribuat facultatem*[462] (secret: Friday after Ash Wednesday). It brings us the God Who strengthens and supports our weak steps: *nutantia corda tu dirigas.*[463] It brings us good desires: *desiderare quae recta sunt*

---

458. "A pledge of future glory is given to us" (Magnificat antiphon [vs. 4], second vespers, Corpus Christi [*Breviarium Romanum, Aestivalis*, 365; not in the Cistercian office of Corpus Christi, but also found in the *Laudes Vespertinae*, 11]); see below, n. 484, for the complete prayer.

459. "to be filled with the everlasting enjoyment of Your divinity, which the reception of Your precious Body and Blood foreshadows" (*Missale Romanum*, 429; *Missale Cisterciense*, 281).

460. See page 125.

461. "We are drawn back from evil, strengthened in good, and we progress toward an increase of virtues and graces" (*Enchiridion*, 257 [#698; *Decretum pro Armenis*, which reads: ". . . *proficimus incrementum*"]).

462. "may it give to us the power of more willing continence" (*Missale Romanum*, 76; *Missale Cisterciense*, 58); this and a number of the quotations that follow in this paragraph are also cited in *Living Bread*, 122.

463. "may You guide our inconstant hearts" (secret: Fifth Sunday after Epiphany [*Missale Romanum*, 57; *Missale Cisterciense*, 45]).

et desiderata percipere[464] (postcommunion: Fifth Sunday {after} Easter). In other places the Church prays that by our communions we may learn to pray for what God wills and to thus receive the answer to our prayers: *justa desideria compleantur.*[465] The Blessed Eucharist brings a great increase of *fervor*: *Praebeant fervorem . . . quo eorum pariter actu delectemur et fructu*[466] (postcommunion: Ember Saturday, Pentecost). It brings us light to protect our minds from error: *ut errorum circumventione depulsa, fidei firmitatem consequamur*[467] (growth in faith) (St. Justin: collect [{14}[468] April]). It protects us against temptation and other evils: *noxia semper a nobis cuncta depellat*[469] (postcommunion: Friday in Passion Week).

f) The fecundity and joy and virtue that come in the Eucharist come from the fact that together with the Body of Christ, we receive the HOLY GHOST AS A SPECIAL GIFT AND SOURCE OF STRENGTH in our communions. See especially the liturgy of Pentecost week: *Sancti Spiritus corda nostra mundet infusio, et sui roris intima aspersione fecundet*[470] (postcommunion: Pentecost). By the light of the Holy Spirit our souls are purified of sin in holy communion: *Sancti Spiritus illustratione emunda*[471] (secret: Pentecost). The Holy Spirit comes to us in communion as the "remission of

---

464. "to desire what is right and to obtain what is desired" (postcommunion: Fifth Sunday after Easter [*Missale Romanum*, 388; *Missale Cisterciense*, 252]).

465. "may just desires be fulfilled" (postcommunion: Sunday within the Octave of Christmas [*Missale Romanum*, 33; *Missale Cisterciene*, 29]).

466. "May [these mysteries] impart a fervor . . . through which we may be equally delighted by their celebration and their fruit" (*Missale Romanum*, 422; *Missale Cisterciense*, 275).

467. "so that having repelled the deceits of error, we might reach the steadfastness of faith" (*Missale Romanum*, 579).

468. Typescript reads "4".

469. "may it always drive away from us all that is harmful" (*Missale Romanum*, 161; *Missale Cisterciense*, 123).

470. "May the infusion of the Holy Spirit cleanse our hearts, and make them fruitful by the inward sprinkling of His dew" (*Missale Romanum*, 409; *Missale Cisterciense*, 265).

471. "purify by the illumination of the Holy Spirit" (*Missale Romanum*, 409; *Missale Cisterciense*, 265).

our sins": *quia ipse est remissio omnium peccatorum*[472]—a very deep and beautiful truth, {on} which we should meditate at length. As a result of all this, *we ourselves become a pleasing gift and sacrifice to God. Nosmetipsos perfice munus aeternum*[473] (secret: Whitmonday). Note that all these things do not come about *by magic*. The Holy Ghost is truly given to us; Christ Our Lord gives us His Body and Blood and is truly present to us. Charity is truly increased in our hearts whether or not we may be conscious of the fact—provided only that we are worthily disposed, that is to say, {in the} state of grace and {having a} right intention. However, the increase of fervor and virtue, the forgiveness of sins, the remission of punishment due to sin, the aid given against temptation, depends in large measure upon *our response*. This response is itself of course a gift of grace and a new grace. We can always be sure that the graces we have enumerated above are at *our disposal* when we receive the Body of the Lord—but we must reach out to take hold of them by our love: hence the value of stirring up our love when we approach the holy table. {The} fact remains that the best way to do so is to pay attention to the words and truths the Church herself utters in the liturgy, and to unite ourselves to them with all faith and fervor.

3. The Holy Eucharist: *Sacramentum unitatis*.[474] Read 1 Corinthians 10:15-17:[475] "For we being many are one body, all who partake of one bread." The Blessed Eucharist is at the same time the *sign of unity* and the *cause* of our unity in Christ. Christ Jesus on the cross was "lifted up that He might draw all things unto

---

472. "because He Himself is the remission of all sins" (postcommunion: Tuesday after Pentecost [*Missale Romanum*, 412; *Missale Cisterciense*, 267]).

473. "make of ourselves an eternal gift" (*Missale Romanum*, 410; *Missale Cisterciense*, 266).

474. St. Cyprian, *De Haereticis Baptizandis*, 11 (*PL* 3, col. 1116B).

475. "Judge for yourselves what I say. The cup of blessing that we bless, is it not the sharing of the blood of Christ? And the bread that we break, is it not the partaking of the body of the Lord? Because the bread is one, we though many, are one body, all of us who partake of the one bread."

Himself."[476] He did not merely wish to bring graces to each one of us individually, and to save us individually. He wanted us all to share together in His love, and to be one Body with Him. This is very important, and to miss this is to miss what is perhaps most essential of all in the sacrament of the Eucharist. St. Thomas says: "*Res hujus sacramenti est unitas corporis mystici, sine qua non potest esse salus*" (III, q. 73, a. 3).[477] Our communion is not merely a contact with Jesus Christ, person to person, but an *incorporation in Christ*. All of us who receive Him in communion are united in His life. We all live together by His Holy Spirit. We are united in one love, one faith, one hope. It follows that one of the main fruits of communion should be in fact fraternal unity, unity in belief, in thought, in cooperation. We must labor to put this into effect—overlooking differences—sharing with those who need something that we have, bearing one another's burdens. The Blessed Eucharist gives us grace to do this. The Eucharist {is} the perfect way of fulfilling the first and greatest commandment—to love God with our whole heart and our brother as ourself (in this way to fulfill all the commandments at once: love is the fulfillment of the Law: cf. Galatians 5:14 and Romans 13:10). READ John 17:9 ff.[478] and comment carefully.

476. Jn. 12:32.

477. "The thing signified is the unity of the mystical body of Christ which is an absolute requisite for salvation" (Gilby, 58.10/11, which reads: "*Res sacramenti*").

478. "I pray for them; not for the world do I pray, but for those whom thou hast given me, because they are thine; and all things that are mine are thine, and thine are mine; and I am glorified in them. And I am no longer in the world, but these are in the world, and I am coming to thee. Holy Father, keep in thy name those whom thou hast given me, that they may be one even as we are. While I was with them, I kept them in thy name. Those whom thou hast given me I guarded; and not one of them perished except the son of perdition, in order that the Scripture might be fulfilled. But now I am coming to thee; and these things I speak in the world, in order that they may have my joy made full in themselves. I have given them thy word; and the world has hated them, because they are not of the world, even as I am not of the world. I do not pray that thou take them out of the world, but that thou keep them from evil. They are not of the world, even

9: I pray for them thou hast given me; they are thine. {The} Father draws us to Jesus in communion: we all belong to the Father in Christ. {It is a} sign of love and of salvation—if we remain united to Jesus. But we know this if we remain united to one another.

10: Then He is glorified in us.

11: The Father will keep us so that we will be one as Jesus and the Father are one. This is most important, for if we do not preserve this unity, the work of Jesus is without fruit.

13: Thus His joy is able to abound and be full in us.

14: God does not take us out of the world, but because we live in Christ we are in the world, but no longer of the world.

19 ff.: Jesus sanctifies (i.e. sacrifices) Himself for us that we may be offered to the Father in truth.

21: That all may be one as Thou Father in me and I in Thee, that all may be one in us. And that thus His glory may be manifest in the world, (23) that the world may know that Thou hast sent me and hast loved them as Thou hast loved me.

St. Augustine says: "The faithful know the Body of Christ [in the Blessed Eucharist] if they themselves become the Body of Christ [the Church]. Let them be the Body of Christ if they wish to live by the Spirit of Christ. Only the Body of Christ lives by the Spirit of Christ."[479] It is useless to eat the Sacred Body of the Lord if we totally ignore all charity and fraternal unity in Christ which is the real expression of the Eucharistic life. It is useless to

---

as I am not of the world. Sanctify them in the truth. Thy word is truth. Even as thou hast sent me into the world, so I also have sent them into the world. And for them I sanctify myself, that they also may be sanctified in truth. Yet not for these only do I pray, but for those also who through their word are to believe in me, that all may be one, even as thou, Father, in me and I in thee; that they also may be one in us, that the world may believe that thou hast sent me. And the glory that thou hast given me, I have given to them, that they may be one, even as we are one: I in them and thou in me; that they may be perfected in unity, and that the world may know that thou hast sent me, and that thou hast loved them even as thou hast loved me" (Jn. 17:9-23).

479. *In Ioannis Evangelium*, 26.6.13 (*PL* 35, col. 1612).

receive communion without trying to live this Eucharistic life of
charity which is the great grace of the sacrament. St. Augustine
goes on {to say, in} a famous passage: *O sacramentum pietatis, o
signum unitatis, o vinculum caritatis! Qui vult vivere, habet unde
vivat, habet ubi vivat. Accedat, credat et incorporetur, ut vivificetur.
Non abhorreat a compage membrorum, non sit putre membrum quod
resecari mereatur . . . sit pulchrum, sit sanum, sit aptum, haereat
corpori, vivat de Deo: nunc laboret in terra, ut postea regnet in coelo."*[480]
He adds: This is the only food which makes those who receive
it immortal: *societas ipsa sanctorum, ubi pax erit et unitas plena et
perfecta.*[481] The Blessed Eucharist then is not merely an embrace
of Jesus alone, but an incorporation in the ineffable mystery of
the Body of Christ, sharing in the joy and the peace of the saints
in Christ, beginning already to taste on earth what we shall see
clearly in heaven, that *Christ is all in all.* The Eucharist is then
eminently a social sacrament, a sacrament of unity and love. But
Christ loved the whole world and died for the whole world. Love
for Christ, incorporation in the Body of Christ, knowledge of the
mystery of Christ, logically implies love for all those for whom
Christ died, the exclusion of none. But it does not mean a theoretical love for all mankind. It does not mean that we "wish well"
to all, and hope they will be saved, and in practice turn a deaf
ear to their needs, pay no attention to the injustices which they
suffer on this earth—which they suffer perhaps at the hands of
men who call themselves Christians, even at the hands of priests
of God. The meaning of the Eucharist is not clear, the glory of

480. "O mystery of piety, O sign of unity, O bond of charity! The one who
wishes to live has here the source of life, a place to live. Let him draw near, believe,
and be incorporated, that he might be revivified. Let him not shrink from the body
of members; let him not be a rotten member that deserves to be cut off . . . . May
he be a beautiful, healthy, and sound member; may he cling to the body, may he
live [for God] from God: may he now work on earth, so that afterward he may
reign in heaven" (col. 1613, which reads: ". . . *habet ubi* . . . *habet unde* . . . *credat,
incorporetur,* . . . *abhoreat* . . . *sit aptum, sit sanum* . . . *vivat Deo de Deo* . . .").

481. "the very society of the saints where there will be peace and full and
perfect unity" (26.6.17 [col. 1614]).

Christ is not visible in His Church, if it is merely a ceremony by
which we display *our union with our friends and immediate neighbors*
while at the same time remaining indifferent to those who belong
to a different class, a different race, a different society, a different
school of thought—even though they may also be Christians:
{cf.} the intolerable scandal of race prejudice among Christians,
white Christians (so-called), excluding those of another color
from their society (except in theory) {or} the even worse scandal
of mutual oppression and exploitation by Christians. The tremendous effect of this scandal {is that} it arms the enemies of the
Church with their most powerful weapons against her. They can
always point to instances of injustice, of unchristian behavior, of
Christians acting unconsciously not as members of Christ but as
members of a favored economic group. Naturally the enemies of
the Church twist and exaggerate everything they can get hold
of, but the fact remains that the carelessness and tepidity of those
who call themselves Christians too often give the enemies of our
faith a *fundamentum in re*[482] for their accusations. Our Eucharistic
life must be, then, a life of true love for others, of self-denial in
order to share everything with others, that no one may be un-
happy or oppressed on the face of this earth. No Christian should
be able to rest satisfied on this earth as long as there are other
men who are in want, who are abandoned, ill-treated, robbed
and oppressed by other men. Our Eucharistic life has reference
to this greatest of all duties, after our duty to God Himself—really
one and the same duty. All this can be summed up in a postcommunion which, significantly, is said twice—on two successive
days—at the very heart of the liturgical year: Easter Sunday and
Monday: *Spiritum nobis Domine tuae caritatis infunde:* UT QUOS SAC-
RAMENTIS PASCHALIBUS SATIASTI TUA FACIAS PIETATE CONCORDES.[483]

---

482. "basis in fact".
483. "Lord, pour into us the Spirit of Your love, so that You may make those
whom You have satisfied with the paschal sacraments of one heart through Your
care" (*Missale Romanum*, 367, 370; *Missale Cisterciense*, 236, 238).

The Eucharist is a *sacred banquet—sacrum convivium*[484]—agape—love feast. A "feast" in the natural order is the outward expression of unity and love. Normally we feast together with our loved ones and friends, and to invite one to a feast is a sign of friendship. In more primitive societies, a "feast" clearly retains this significance, which to some extent it has lost in sophisticated modern society (in which feasting is often done in a public restaurant or hotel, among strangers—and the character of *enjoyment* and *display* takes precedence over the more human and deeper matter of fraternal union). The essence of a feast {is} sharing good things (harvest fruits) with gratitude and joy—sharing the *fruits of common labor*, enjoying together the outcome of common struggle and victory. This is what the Eucharist is—a love-feast in which we enjoy together with Christ and all His members, particularly our own brethren, the joys and fruits of His victory, and share with Him, in anticipation, the joys of heaven and of eternal life.

How to "make a thanksgiving": when these dogmatic truths have been thoroughly meditated and assimilated, there should not be any special problem of "how to make a thanksgiving." Hence we need not try to work out some special "infallible method" for doing this. Just a few suggestions:

1. The Church puts on the lips of the priest after Mass the *Benedicite* and other prayers. This indicates the *spirit* with which we should make our thanksgiving—a spirit of praise, love, joy, thankfulness, in union with all creatures (n.b. learn {the} *Benedicite* by heart). The Lord Himself helps us to "make our thanksgiving"

---

484. "sacred banquet": opening words of a prayer ascribed to St. Thomas Aquinas used as the Magnificat antiphon for second vespers of the Feast of Corpus Christi in the Roman Breviary, and included in the Cistercian hymnal for Benediction (*Breviarium Romanum, Aestivalis*, 365; *Laudes Vespertinae*, 10–11): "*O sacrum convivium in quo Christus sumitur: recolitur memoria passionis ejus: mens impletur gratia: et futurae gloriae nobis pignus datur, alleluia*" ("O sacred banquet in which Christ is consumed; the memorial of His passion is celebrated anew; the soul is filled with grace; and a pledge of future glory is given to us, alleluia").

in the spirit of the *Benedicite* on spring mornings in the novitiate: we are there at sunrise. All is silent; the birds sing outside; we are united with our brothers in silence and peace. The air is filled with the scent of flowers, and is pleasantly cool. Everything speaks of the goodness and mercy of God, and thus we spontaneously unite our hearts with the praise that goes up to Him from all things. It is therefore no distraction to take note of these beautiful things, any more than it is a distraction to speak of them in the *Benedicite*. Distraction would come in, however, if we observed created things in a spirit of boredom and curiosity—seeking distraction in them, and seeking to escape from prayer. N.B. does the priest *have to* say the *Benedicite*, etc.? Jungmann (*The Mass of the Roman Rite*, vol. ii, p. 460) says that the rubric prescribing the recitation of the *Benedicite* etc. is *directive*. This means that it is simply a *norm* indicating the mind of the Church and that if one can meet this norm in some other way he is more or less free to do so, provided there is a good reason. *To omit the Benedicite and say nothing out of mere laziness would be sinful.* But if one is absorbed in the presence of the Lord and engaged in loving Him in one's own spontaneous way there is no strict obligation to recite the words of the *Benedicite* if these would be a mere external formality, in the circumstances. It is well to have the habit of reciting it, as an aid to devotion, and to cultivate above all the spirit of praise which it inculcates.

2. *Mental prayer* is of course the best form of thanksgiving. Jungmann quotes from a Dominican Ordinarium of the thirteenth century which says: *Terminatis vero omnibus potest sacerdos* orare secreto prout Dominus inspiraverit.[485] This gives the key: the Lord Himself should inspire our thanksgiving, and our job is to keep ourselves disposed and attentive with the fervor of love, that He may do so.

3. *Aids in thanksgiving*: the most important aids in opening our hearts to grace are the thoughts we have set forth above,

---

485. "When all is completed the priest can pray in secret as the Lord has inspired [him]" (Jungmann, 2.463, which reads: ". . . *orare sacerdos . . . prout ei Dominus . . .*).

about the *real presence*, the *fruits of communion*, our *union with one another in Christ*, etc. If we call these thoughts to mind, or one or other of them that specially attracts us, and dwell on it in the simplicity of faith, it will greatly help us to open our hearts to grace, and we will be more aware of the tremendous meaning of the mystery into which we have entered by our communion. Other aids {include} slow and pensive reading of chapter 17 of St. John; slow recital of the prayer to Jesus Crucified (*En ego* . . .[486]); slow recital of a psalm; making thanksgiving with and through Our Lady—abandoning ourselves to her love, confiding our weakness to her, and letting her thank Jesus for us and take care of our souls, bringing them the graces we need, uniting us more closely to her and to her divine Son.

4. *Avoid extremes*. We have to avoid two extremes: (a) sloth, sleep, inactivity, inertia, as a result of routine; (b) agitation, strain, {a} futile struggle to do things we are not meant to do, useless striving to stir up feelings. The simplicity of faith and true love will help us to avoid both these—also humility and deep trust in God.

5. *In practice*, the trials and difficulties of our daily lives, the obstacles we meet within ourselves and in our environment, all these *show to us our needs* and leave us little doubt of our relationship to Jesus as our Savior and Redeemer, without Whom we can

---

486. "*En ego o bone et dulcissime Iesu, ante conspectum tuum genibus me provolvo, ac maximo animi ardore te oro atque obtestor, ut meum in cor vividos fidei, spei et caritatis sensus, atque veram peccatorum meorum paenitentiam, eaque emendandi firmissimam voluntatem velis imprimere; dum magno animi affectu et dolore tua quinque vulnera mecum ipse considero ac mente contemplor, illud prae oculis habens, quod iam in ore ponebat tuo David propheta de te, o bone Iesu: Foderunt manus meas et pedes meos: dinumeraverunt omnia ossa mea. Amen.*" ("Behold, O good and most sweet Jesus, I fall on my knees in Your sight, and with the greatest devotion of soul I pray and beseech You that You might will to impress on my heart a lively sense of faith, hope and charity, true sorrow for my sins, and a most firm purpose of amendment, while with deep affection and sorrow I look upon and contemplate Your five wounds, having before my eyes what David the prophet put in Your mouth about You, O good Jesus: They have pierced My hands and My feet; they have numbered all My bones.")

do nothing. We hardly need to think how to pray to Him when we are in trial—our difficulties themselves dictate our prayer. Also, our graces and joys themselves take care of thanksgiving. In between the time of special grace or special trial, we should keep our efforts at prayer *simple, humble, calm, deep*. Gazing with the eyes of faith at the reality and content of the great mystery into which we have been introduced by the love of God—this is sufficient to keep our hearts aflame with hidden and obscure love that does not necessarily fill us with definite *feelings* of fervor but certainly unites us to our Lord in spirit and in truth.

Visits to the Most Blessed Sacrament: in connection with thanksgiving we might also speak of our daily visits to the Most Blessed Sacrament. Thanksgiving is only one aspect of a *full and well-integrated Eucharistic life*. Such a life is centered on the Mystery of the Eucharist—on the sacrifice and sacrament of the Mass, on the mystery of Christ present in the Christian community and His real sacramental presence in the tabernacle. The foundation {is} a vital, real, personal appreciation of the tremendous gift of God to us in the Eucharist—God with us! *Si scires donum Dei!*[487] This bears fruit in a love which expresses itself at all times, and seeks to nourish itself in every possible way, and is an integral part in a true life of contemplation. The great source of all "graces of prayer" {is} contact with Jesus in the Eucharist, the sacrament of love. Realize that there is a *special grace of love* that comes from and with our visits to the Blessed Sacrament—especially from those that are spontaneous and free—of our own volition. A soul that does not seek to be with Jesus alone at certain times during the day will also lack fervor in the official worship in the choir.

1. *Making visits*: in the first place, there is nothing prescribed, and there should be nothing prescribed. What follows is a matter of counsel, and it is important that it be regarded as such, precisely to *safeguard the freedom* of the personal visits we make—of our own spontaneous need to be with Jesus. If visits were "pre-

---

487. "If you knew the gift of God" (Jn. 4:10).

scribed," they might come to be a mere formality, and that is what we want to avoid. If a person does not have enough love for Our Lord to want to be with Him, then there is little use prescribing that he go to chapel anyway. On the other hand, it is imperative to *realize the importance of cultivating this love*. In practice, what will a good monk do? It seems to be the *normal thing in our contemplative life* for one to want to spend the *lectio divina* time more or less in prayer, reading and contemplation, or contemplative study. This includes a certain amount of time spent in private prayer or meditation or contemplation before the Most Blessed Sacrament. The normal thing—besides the thanksgiving after communion—is to spend *a fairly long time* (one would suppose twenty to thirty minutes, or in other cases ten to fifteen minutes) *at least once a day* in meditation, or affective or contemplative prayer, before the Blessed Sacrament. In other words, one longish visit a day would seem to recommend itself as almost a necessity in the life of the average contemplative monk. Circumstances alter cases, however, and this is something to be taken up in direction. It is completely normal for one to take a whole interval before the Blessed Sacrament, either regularly, or at times (especially on feast days). While one long visit a day would seem to be a normal thing, *one or more short visits* in addition to it would seem to be so well-established a custom that to *fail to make one short visit a day (five minutes or so) to the Blessed Sacrament would indeed be singular in a life like ours, especially when it is recommended by the Church* for all religious and clerics. In short, the novice should consider it a matter of prudence upon which his vocation and interior life practically depend, to cultivate the habit of making at least one good visit a day to the Blessed Sacrament. *The minimum would seem to be one five- or ten-minute visit* somewhere, as a rule. The normal thing would be a longish visit (of twenty minutes or so) and one or two shorter visits as opportunity presents itself. Naturally, presented in this way, the suggestion may look a little strange. It should not be necessary to give counsels in a form that seems to suggest hard and fast regulations. And the matter of time remains more or less arbitrary. In reality the individual should feel free to suit his own needs and meet with the inspirations of grace in his own case. However, in all simplicity, we felt it worth while to present something like a practical concrete norm, as a kind of standard of reference for newcomers to the religious life.

2. *How to make a visit*: about this there can and should be nothing definite. The whole idea of a visit is not to think about oneself "making a visit" but to think of Him Whom we are visiting. We do not have to draw up a formal program of what we are going to talk about when our parents come to visit the monastery. Nor should we have a formal program in speaking to Our Lord. *The heart should speak*—and it will find no difficulty in doing so if we remember the mystery of the real presence, and if we remember WHO IS PRESENT (!) and how much He loves us and understands us. We have come here seeking God; in the tabernacle, He Whom we seek is really and truly present, and sees us and knows us and is glad to lavish His love upon us and receive our love in return. This should be enough. In the relationship that is established by a *realizing love*, an I-Thou relationship, there is attained an ineffable spiritual reality which is the heart of our contemplative life: the reality of our love for Christ and His love for us. This reality is not seriously attained, in practice, without a fervent Eucharistic life. Take advantage of opportunities: the little visits that are more or less mandatory (and that are *not included* with the above one or two suggested as free and spontaneous) should be real visits—namely, the short visits in which we recollect ourselves before the beginning of office. The novices as a matter of course arrive in choir a little early, and together. They should regard this little period of prayer as a true visit to the Blessed Sacrament and unite themselves with Him in love, in preparation for the office. To enter and kneel down merely mechanically does little good—it just gets you there on time. If you form {the} habit of making a real visit here, then when you are professed you will want to make a regular practice of getting to choir a little before the office begins and make a short visit then. So too for the visits after meals, {the} short visit made by all after the official prayers. This should not

be a mere formality. When one has to go to {the} church or sacristy for something material, one should always make a serious little visit, even if only for a few moments. One can tell a good religious by the attention he pays to these things.

3. *Spiritual Communions*: these may profitably be included in our visits to the Blessed Sacrament. But also, one of the best ways of keeping recollected during the day, especially at work, is to make spiritual communions from time to time. First, realize that a spiritual communion is a *real communion* (in the sense of a real union of hearts, in love) although it is not sacramental. Failure to realize the *reality* of these communions makes us tend to neglect them. {It is} not necessary to imagine oneself receiving a host and go through the motions of swallowing! This has nothing to do with the reality of spiritual communion. But the essence {is a} union of hearts—receiving the love and Person of Jesus into the depths of our heart and surrendering ourselves in faith to the exigencies of His love, His will, His grace.

4. *Adoration of the Blessed Sacrament during Exposition*: we should of course pay special attention to opportunities to adore the Blessed Sacrament exposed: at Benediction, during Forty Hours, on days of recollection. A very special grace {is} to be able to spend two hours in night adoration, which happens only once a year in our life.

In conclusion, those who give themselves with love and faith to their desire for a more intimate penetration of this holy mystery are rewarded with an intimate sense of the presence of Jesus in the Blessed Sacrament and a more fervent love for Him—these are graces which imply love and deep faith. Without seeking and striving, without a modicum of generosity, these graces will remain unknown to us. But a very little good will and generosity on our part will open our hearts to graces beyond estimation.

LECTIO DIVINA—THE READING BEFORE PRIME:

Having now discussed communion and thanksgiving, we come to the first long period of silent, recollected reading or study in the monk's day. Understand the very great importance of *lectio divina* and particularly of this early morning interval of reading. We have used the word "interval," which was formerly customary among Trappists, for a time. *But it is misleading*. If the time of *lectio divina* is referred to as an "interval" one gets the impression that it is something of relative importance only, a *negative* time, when one is "not doing anything else"—not in choir, not working, therefore, practically speaking, "doing nothing." To regard *lectio divina* as something incidental or unimportant is *to miss the whole point of the contemplative life*. One who thinks of "intervals" instead of *lectio*—of blank spaces between things that "really matter"—will in fact never really understand or appreciate the divine office, and will furthermore not work with the proper monastic spirit because he will *lack a true monastic perspective*. READ Luke 10:38 ff.[488] {This} gospel of Martha and Mary {is} interpreted by patristic tradition, and especially St. Bernard, as referring to the contemplative life. Note that this text follows directly, in the context, upon the story of the Good Samaritan. Good works are necessary and good, but better than everything else is to sit at the feet of the Lord and to receive His doctrine of love. Without this peaceful resting in the Lord, our activity is full of solicitude and trouble and leads us less effectively to God. Our charity is less pure. *St. Bernard* and the Cistercian Fathers taught that Martha, Mary and Lazarus lived together in the monastery.[489]

488. "Now it came to pass as they were on their journey, that he entered a certain village; and a woman named Martha welcomed him to her house. And she had a sister called Mary, who also seated herself at the Lord's feet, and listened to his word. But Martha was busy about much serving. And she came up and said, 'Lord, is it no concern of thine that my sister has left me to serve alone? Tell her therefore to help me.' But the Lord answered and said to her, 'Martha, Martha, thou art anxious and troubled about many things; and yet only one thing is needful. Mary has chosen the best part, and it will not be taken away from her'" (Lk. 10:38-42).

489. See Thomas Merton, "Action and Contemplation in St. Bernard," in *Thomas Merton on St. Bernard*, Cistercian Studies [CS], vol. 9 (Kalamazoo, MI: Cistercian Publications, 1980), 42–44, 68–78. (The article originally appeared in *Collectanea Ordinis Cisterciensium Reformatorum* in three parts in 1953–54).

They are not enemies or rivals—they are one family. The monastic family is composed of these three types of monks: Lazarus is the penitent; Martha the active monk, the officer in the monastery, or the cellarer, etc.; Mary the contemplative, left completely free for the *otium contemplationis*.[490] "*Tria haec distribuit ordinatio caritatis.*"[491] In practice, each monk will combine in his own life elements of all three. All have to be penitents; all have some function in the monastery, a task to do, some responsibility however small. The ideal is not that one should be *absolutely without* any kind of task, because one must always contribute something to the common good, and in so doing he gains much for himself and attains to a deeper peace and union with God. His charity in more pure. The "Mary" ideal is not an ideal of complete withdrawal and inactivity. But on the other hand, this fact must not make us forget that to be *preoccupied* with active works and to give them the first place is to lose the spirit of our vocation. St. Bernard says "Mary" *is always to be preferred*: [*vita Mariae*] *omnino, quoad nos spectat*, eligenda.[492] Our preference {should be} for silent union with God, prayer, reading, contemplation. This does not imply a neglect of good works, but doing our work in such a way that it is *rightly ordered*, and remains entirely subservient to contemplation, *so that*, if the end of our work is not achieved, we are not troubled at all, or very little, since we were not working primarily to achieve any other end than to please God. Our eyes are on Him and not on any less ultimate purpose. It is when in fact our work becomes more or less the end we have in view that we lose sight of God, rejoice inordinately when we attain our temporal end, inordinately desire further success, and inordinately grieve over lack of success. *Hoc enim melius,* QUIESCERE

---

490. "the leisure of contemplation" (*In Cantica*, 67.9 [*PL* 183, col. 1054A]).

491. "The ordering of love is apportioned among these three" (*In Assumptione Beatae Virginis Mariae*, 3.4 [*PL* 183, col. 423B], which reads: ". . . *distribuerit . . . charitatis*").

492. "[the life of Mary], insofar as it applies to us, is always to be preferred" (*De Diversis*, 9.4 [*PL* 183, col. 566D], which reads: "*quod ad nos . . .*").

ET CUM CHRISTO ESSE (*Sermo* {46}[493] {*In*} *Cantica*).[494] To rest and to be with Christ! This is the Cistercian ideal (See St. Aelred: the "Sabbath" of divine charity[495]). Speaking to Pope Blessed Eugene III, St. Bernard tells him in very strong terms that even the duties and responsibilities of the papacy *come second* and the interior life is first.[496] Naturally, here again we must not suppose an opposition between priestly life and interior life. Even in his priestly activities the priest, and *a fortiori* the bishop (who is in the "state of perfection"[497]) is united with God in charity. But the temporal aspect of our activities must not warp our outlook and rob us of a spiritual perspective. The grace of God indeed endows active works with special power to unite us with Him and counteract the effects of distraction, etc. But on the other hand we must not become so immersed in work and attached to it for its own sake that we lose our spiritual perspective and no longer seek God above all in Himself. The rule St. Bernard lays down for Blessed Eugene {is}: *NON TOTUM TE, NEC SEMPER DARE ACTIONI: sed considerationi aliquid tui et cordis et temporis sequestrare* (*De Consideratione*).[498] By *consideratio* St. Bernard does not mean just any kind of prayer—for instance vocal prayer: he means inward reflection and meditation, not considered as a separate exercise necessarily, but in company with *lectio divina* or *psalmody*, or else leading more directly into *contemplatio*. The *otium Mariae*[499] IS NOT TO BE LOOKED UPON AS A LOSS OF TIME OR EFFORT—*Nec reputo perditionem unguenti hujus effusionem. . . .* Sapientiae otia negotia sunt,

---

493. Typescript reads "40".

494. "For this is better: to be quiet and to be with Christ" (*PL* 183, col. 1004B).

495. *Speculum Charitatis*, c. 18 (*PL* 195, col. 521AC).

496. All of Bernard's *De Consideratione* has this theme, but it is particularly the focus in Bk. II, cc. 8–13 (*PL* 182, cols. 746C–750B).

497. The idea of the bishop as "perfect" comes from the *Ecclesiastical Hierarchy* of Pseudo-Dionysius: see *Introduction to Christian Mysticism*, 140–41.

498. "Do not give yourself completely and always to action: but preserve something of both your heart and your time for consideration" (*De Consideratione*, 1.7 [*PL* 182, col. 736C]).

499. "the repose of Mary" (*In Cantica*, 40.3 [*PL* 183, col. 983A]).

et quo otiosior sapientia, eo negotiosior in genere suo (*De Div.* 90[500] and *In Cantica* 85[501]). Not only is resting in God, in thought, reading and contemplation, not a waste of time, but *the more we rest, the more we accomplish,* if our rest is the true repose of charity and wisdom, the repose which comes from casting away all temporal cares and all concern with ourselves in order to dwell in the love of God. *The purpose of our* lectio divina *is then to provide us with "contemplative leisure."* READ PSALM 30:21 (also read {the} context: vs. 20-25): "Thou shalt hide them in the secret of thy face from the disturbance of men: thou shalt protect them in thy tabernacle from the contradiction of tongues."[502] READ GENESIS 11:1-9: the Tower of Babel.[503] Comment: the builders of the Tower were mo-

500. "I do not consider the pouring out of this ointment as a loss" (*De Diversis*, 90.3 [*PL* 183, col. 709D]).

501. "Repose is the work of wisdom, and the more restful the wisdom, the more is accomplished in its way" (*In Cantica*, 85.8 [*PL* 183, col. 1191C], which reads: ". . . *eo exercitatior in* . . .").

502. These are vss. 21-22; vs. 20 reads: "O how great is the multitude of thy sweetness, O Lord, which thou hast hidden for them that fear thee! Which thou hast wrought for them that hope in thee, in the sight of the sons of men"; vss. 23-25 read: "But I said in the excess of my mind: I am cast away from before thy eyes. Therefore thou hast heard the voice of my prayer, when I cried to thee. O love the Lord, all ye his saints: for the Lord will require truth, and will repay them abundantly that act proudly. Do ye manfully, and let your heart be strengthened, all ye that hope in the Lord."

503. "The whole earth used the same language and the same speech. While men were migrating eastward, they discovered a valley in the land of Sennaar and settled there. They said to one another, 'Come, let us make bricks and bake them.' They used bricks for stone and bitumen for mortar. Then they said, 'Let us build ourselves a city and a tower with its top in the heavens; let us make a name for ourselves lest we be scattered all over the earth.' The Lord came down to see the city and the tower which men had built. And the Lord said, 'Truly, they are one people and they all have the same language. This is the beginning of what they will do. Hereafter they will not be restrained from anything which they determine to do. Let us go down, and there confuse their language so that they will not understand one another's speech.' So the Lord scattered them from that place all over the earth; and they stopped building the city. For this reason it was called Babel, because there the Lord confused the speech of all the earth. From there the Lord scattered them all over the earth."

tivated by human pride, human ambition, seeking to achieve divine dignity by their own power, seeking to make themselves equal to God: *eritis sicut Dii*,[504] as the tempter had suggested in Eden. Their futile efforts are confounded by God, and their efforts end in division and confusion. This is the fruit of ambition: the spirit of struggle, competition, fear, guile (politics), leading to mutual mistrust, servility, duplicity, and *constant agitation*. The spirit of Babel must not creep into the monastery; it is the spirit of the world. God has brought us to the cloister to protect us against this spirit, and to give us another spirit—His Holy Spirit. READ ACTS 1:4-5, 2:1-21: Pentecost.[505] The monastery is a cenacle,

---

504. "You shall be as gods" (Gen. 3:5).

505. "And while eating with them, he charged them not to depart from Jerusalem, but to wait for the promise of the Father, 'of which you have heard,' said he, 'by my mouth; for John indeed baptized with water, but you shall be baptized with the Holy Spirit not many days hence.' . . . And when the days of Pentecost were drawing to a close, they were all together in one place. And suddenly there came a sound from heaven, as of a violent wind blowing, and it filled the whole house where they were sitting. And there appeared to them parted tongues as of fire, which settled upon each of them. And they were all filled with the Holy Spirit and began to speak in foreign tongues, even as the Holy Spirit prompted them to speak. Now there were staying at Jerusalem devout Jews from every nation under heaven. And when this sound was heard, the multitude gathered and were bewildered in mind, because each heard them speaking in his own language. But they were all amazed and marvelled, saying, 'Behold, are not all these that are speaking Galileans? And how have we heard each his own language in which he was born? Parthians and Medes and Elamites, and inhabitants of Mesopotamia, Judea, and Cappadocia, Pontus and Asia, Phrygia and Pamphylia, Egypt and the parts of Libya about Cyrene, and visitors from Rome, Jews also and proselytes, Cretans and Arabians, we have heard them speaking in our own languages of the wonderful works of God.' And all were amazed and perplexed, saying to one another, 'What does this mean?' But others said in mockery, 'They are full of new wine.' But Peter, standing up with the Eleven, lifted up his voice and spoke out to them: 'Men of Judea and all you who dwell in Jerusalem, let this be known to you, and give ear to my words. These men are not drunk, as you suppose, for it is only the third hour of the day. But this is what was spoken through the prophet Joel: And it shall come to pass in the last days, says the Lord, that I will pour forth of my Spirit upon all flesh; and your sons and your daughters shall prophesy, and your young men shall see visions, and

a "tabernacle," where the silent community dwells together in peace, hidden from men, protected from the wrangling of tongues. Here, as we read, the Holy Spirit descends upon us, revealing to us the inner mysteries of scripture—not giving us gifts of tongues to utter prophecies, but enlightening us secretly with understanding to know Jesus and Him crucified. This is the spirit of our *lectio* and *contemplatio*.

Lectio and Silence: when we speak of *lectio divina* we naturally include and imply everything that belongs to the proper monastic atmosphere for *lectio*. *Lectio divina* is not just reading, nor just reading and thinking. One can read and think in a subway train or a crowded city bus. This is all right. But *lectio divina* means, ideally, reading and meditating and praying in *the silence of the cloister*, or of some other monastic and solitary place. The silence is part of the reading, a *positive element* in *lectio divina*, a factor that makes a very fruitful and positive contribution to our reading and prayer. Silence is not just negative—the absence of noise, the absence of talk. If we think of silence merely as a negation, we will naturally be very restless in it, and will not be able to settle down. Silence is a *positive presence*, the presence of Him Who is not heard, so that when all confused sounds and trivial noises are hushed, then the eloquent voice of reality, of God Himself, makes itself heard in peacefulness and in silence. Notice that silence is *not absolute*. The silence of *lectio divina* includes the presence of good natural sounds, the song of birds, or {sound} of rain, or wind; but it excludes useless or inordinate or artificial noises (radio; inane chatter; the agitation of many machines; the general atmosphere of restless noise and confusion that belongs to a place of business). We should be very much aware, as monks, of the value

---

your old men shall dream dreams. And moreover upon my servants and upon my handmaids in those days will I pour forth of my Spirit, and they shall prophesy. And I will show wonders in the heavens above and signs on the earth beneath, blood and fire and vapor of smoke. The sun shall be turned into darkness, and the moon into blood, before the day of the Lord comes, the great and manifest day. And it shall come to pass that whoever calls upon the name of the Lord, shall be saved. . . .'"

and meaning of silence, and of the significance of confused noise and chatter which is characteristic of "the world." The noise of "the world" is something inevitably flowing from the inane mentality of the world, that seeks flight from reality and from God into its own artificial chaotic atmosphere. Where there is noise and agitation, the mentality of the world, the mentality of selfishness and violence and falsity, is favored. Where there is silence, the mentality of the world cannot rest; it becomes disturbed; it makes noise; it seeks flight from silence. The monastic mentality does not grow where there is noise. The true monk, when he is mature, carries within himself enough silence and peace to be undisturbed even in the midst of the world: the superficial agitation of the world does not ruffle him too much, and in and through all the things going on around him in the world, he can see God as worldly people cannot. But this is because he is always attuned to the silence that is below the surface of agitation—this silence to which worldly people are not and cannot be attuned. But for a soul to become attuned to silence, the monastic atmosphere is necessary, and this is protected by our *rule of silence*. There is every reason for this rule to be taken seriously, very seriously, because without it we cannot be true monks; our life will be emptied of its true content; we will not have peace; we will not get down to the bedrock of the interior life and the presence of God, which is the real reason for our being here. Therefore to cultivate *lectio divina* means also to cultivate silence. The two are inseparable. Hence, it is necessary at this point to discuss our *rules on silence*. One who cannot give himself to reading and to silence and to meditation does not have a true monastic vocation. Silence is one of the great tests of our vocation. Silence, being one of the most important observances of the Order, is also one of those *most easily misunderstood*. How are we to properly understand monastic silence? It is not just a matter of *not talking*, and *not making signs*. Once again, the negative approach is fatal. It is a question of *inner desire*. By our monastic silence we learn to give up *the desire for communication* on a purely human level, except when such communication is demanded by charity or utility. And we replace this desire for unnecessary communication by a *desire for fruitful communication with God in silence*. Basically, the practice of true monastic silence is the love of an inner communication with God and with Life, without the medium of human language. True silence more or less stills even our interior chatter—but within reason of course. SILENCE THEN IS A QUESTION OF CHOICE. It is a preference—not for silence and the absence of talk (a negation) but for *inner communication* that is higher and better than communication by words; and on the basis of this inner communication, our talk and our words will themselves be more effective; our union with our brothers in charity, whether we speak or not, will be more perfect. To understand silence, we must understand *exactly what is the choice implied by monastic silence*.

{The} first WRONG IDEA {is} that by silence we choose God, and reject men. This is false. In our monastic silence we are also more closely united to our brethren as well as to God. For silence cuts away the *false and artificial* bond that is kept up by useless talk, flattery, insincerity and mere gossip. WHAT WE REJECT in choosing silence is not union with our brethren, or support by them, but the *false and useless support*, the "reassurance" that we get from hearing the sound of our own voice echoed by the sound of another's voice in inane gossip and laughter. The gossip means nothing; we have nothing to say, but what we seek is the reassurance of being apparently accepted and appreciated, which we think we get out of gabbing with another. {It is} something like looking at oneself in a mirror, using the interlocutor as a mirror in which we find ourselves reflected. We are comforted, and feel that we still exist, still have worth. Silence tests the reality of man's inner life: he is a monk if he can get along without the support of gossip. {The} second WRONG IDEA {is} that by silence we give up all human communication. This is false: we can never give up the communication presupposed by charity. Charity comes first, even before silence, so that where charity is in question, silence no longer binds. But remember, true charity is what considers the real interests of the other, and normally speaking there are few occasions in our monastic life where charity is served by *breaking* silence. Rather, silence is the guardian of true charity, because silence protects the inner life where charity grows and flowers. Monastic observance generously allows for all the occasions where charity normally requires speaking. There is free communication with one's director, or confessor, or superiors. One can obtain permission when necessary to speak to another about something important. One can write a note with permission. One can speak to a brother in the presence of a superior. These occasions are ample. Charity does not seek to add to them and magnify them, but rather to keep to the rule and preserve the interior life of the community, in which true charity flowers.

The Usages on Silence (nn. 323–331[506]): the most important and sweeping rule about silence is in n. 323, which covers practically everything. The rest is simply an explanation and application of this.

a) The religious shall have no communication with each other either by word of mouth or by writing . . .[507] What is meant here by "communication"? *the exchange of words*, and thereby the exchange of precise information, opinions, thoughts, etc. What is *not* excluded is *communion* or wordless and undefined sharing in the general peace and charity of the monastic community. But *direct talking*, conversation, or the exchange of notes, etc. is forbidden. This is one of the rules of the Order that are to be taken most strictly. *Notes* may only be passed with permission, given to {the} superior and passed on by him: in {the} novitiate, through Fr. Master or Undermaster (the latter when Fr. Master is not available); among the professed, through Fr. Prior, or, when Rev. Father is absent or Fr. Prior is not available, through Fr. Subprior. We should not develop the habit of writing long notes, or getting into a complicated correspondence by notes with another religious. This sometimes happens, with good motives and yet, quite often, with little real justification. Notes should be *only about practical matters*,

---

506. *Regulations*, 156–60 (Bk. VIII, c. 2).
507. *Regulations*, 156.

ordinarily, and quite brief: for instance, about a confession appointment, about getting shoes repaired, about work, or something that is needed for one's work. *Are personal notes permitted*? By personal notes are meant those which are simply an expression of friendship and good wishes. It is certainly not the intention of the *Usages* to exclude even personal notes when they are motivated by a good enough reason. On principle they should be *rare*, and *reserved for certain special occasions*: for instance, profession day (not the anniversary of profession, ordinarily); ordination day; jubilee; or when one is sick in the hospital or for a long time in the infirmary, etc. The custom in regard to such notes seems to vary. In the past they seem to have been more frequent than now. One should not write such notes just as a matter of form—as if one were "expected" to come across with a special note on a special occasion. These notes should be spontaneous and motivated by a real personal reason, not just by formal good manners. Note the danger of artificiality and insincerity when such notes are regarded as a necessary custom.

b) When they have anything useful to communicate they do so by signs.[508] What is meant by *useful*?

1. *Having a practical purpose*: signs are necessary for the smooth running of work, observances, special functions, etc. One should never hesitate to make signs when they are called for. Useful signs, made in the proper spirit, and in the right way, are edifying. They are an expression of monastic charity and courtesy; they indicate one's interest in helping one's brother to do things well, and are an evidence of thoughtfulness. To see a religious go by absorbed and unconcerned when there is something he should point out by sign, is not edifying. It does not give evidence of a really good monastic spirit. Of course, anyone can be taken up with thoughts and overlook something. But one should train himself in thoughtfulness.

508. *Regulations*, 156.

2. *Having a charitable purpose*: sometimes a sign may have no immediate practical purpose, but yet may be necessary from the point of view of community life—especially in the case of someone who is in difficulty, or who could use encouragement. Here again, one has to know when and how to make a sign. A purely formal and artificial sign, made out of conventionalism, is more useless than useful. In general there is likely to be a temptation to think that charity demands *more* signs than are actually called for. In our life, charity *does not mean a long sign conversation*. On the contrary, in view of the nature of our life, such conversations tend in the long run to defeat the purpose of charity. It is not charity to take up your brother's scanty reading time with a lot of trivialities; still less is it charity to attach him to yourself and take him away from something more important. In what sense {is it true that} long sign conversations are a real evil?

c) NOISES WITH THE MOUTH, ALTHOUGH INARTICULATE, AND USELESS SIGNS ARE EXPRESSLY FORBIDDEN.[509]

1. The problem of "noises"—the various hisses, grunts, growls, groans, plaintive cries, squeals, etc. that accompany the signs of some monks—{are} usually a matter of carelessness, lack of discipline, or weakness. One has to make a special effort to break such a habit, and it is worth while taking a lot of trouble to avoid picking it up. Extreme carelessness in this matter is sufficient reason for dismissal of a novice. Note: sometimes monks half-consciously develop irregularities which they feel to be amusing or attractive. They fool around and introduce into their fooling some half-spoken words, more as a joke than anything else. It may be amusing in a given case, but it so easily becomes a habit, and a bad habit, that in the long run it has very bad effects. It is necessary to see ourselves as others see us. We may think that our dissipation is very witty and that it makes us seem attractive. Invariably, those who more or less cultivate this kind of humor realize too late that they have become a pest, and that

509. *Regulations*, 156–57.

they are a penance to everyone, and that people often bear with them out of politeness and charity, but with great interior difficulty. It is very easy to become a crashing *bore* in the monastery by addiction to funny signs and pantomime.

2. *The problem of useless signs* is undoubtedly one of the great problems of the novitiate. It should be understood properly. It is natural for novices to want to try out their newfound skill. They are naturally communicative and usually have a lot to communicate. Their minds are still full of ideas and memories of the world outside; they have still not quite settled down to the life of prayer and reading; they are still stimulated by novelty; the new ones themselves make funny mistakes and give rise to comment. All this is understandable. Moreover, it is clear that the pleasure of useless signs and spontaneous fooling is the *one very definite form of recreation* which is still within reach. The danger is that all our need for every form of pleasure and recreation tends to seek an outlet by this one remaining safety valve. The trouble is that once one develops a firmly fixed habit, the thing is difficult to get rid of. Hence, one should try, from the beginning, *not to depend on this as a safety valve*. Otherwise one gets attached to it quite firmly. One comes to need it as a drunkard needs liquor—and then the thing really turns into a vice. It can become a real obstacle to the interior life. It has a bad effect on the whole community—making it a group of silly and empty-headed people without a serious aim in life.

3. *What signs are useless?* Any signs not definitely called for by immediate utility—work, observance, etc.—or by real fraternal charity (not imaginary charity)—are to be regarded as USELESS! The following are particular kinds of signs which can become a useless habit:

COMMENTS—especially in refectory or chapter, where they are most out of place: learn to mortify your desire to manifest your opinion about everything.

NEWS—passing on the latest gossip of the community, or even things of the world. Only in rare occasions can news really be considered useful. The usual gossip is matter only for useless signs—and a lot of the time it is not even true, or the signs are not properly understood—nothing so easily gets distorted as a piece of news that comes along the sign-makers' grapevine.

PERSONAL SIGNS—about other people or about ourselves:

a) Except in obvious cases when there is a matter of work or observance to be taken care of, *signs about other people are almost always useless*. Furthermore, when these signs become comments, or expressions of feeling and opinion about others and their acts, they quickly become a source of faults. One can distinguish signs that are simply useless from those which tend to be harmful. Useless signs about what others do, about their ways, character, etc., easily turn into *critical* signs which in turn open the way to *detraction*, which is severely punished in the Order and considered a sin to be fought against with special zeal by us. We should therefore be very careful not to make signs about others without real necessity, especially about superiors.

b) We should also be on our guard against the habit of revealing private and personal matters to others by signs. Even though the matter itself may be legitimate, this *is not the kind of communication which our rules foresee* and provide for. We are not supposed to make signs about our personal affairs. We have given up this kind of communication. If you want to communicate with someone about your personal, interior life, go and see your confessor, or a superior, or a director to whom you can speak. Do not discuss it with others to whom you cannot speak. In a very special case, if there is an important matter of a personal nature to be taken up with another member of the community (which would be a very rare case indeed), it would be better to get permission and talk frankly about it rather than try to get it across by signs. There are gradations in the material which we can communicate to others concerning ourselves:

(a) Our likes and dislikes, aspirations, feelings; this includes our opinions. Such material is harmless in itself. But we are not really supposed to make signs about such things, and in any case such signs lead to "conversations," etc. They must not be allowed to touch on other people.

(b) Our trials and difficulties: this is something more important and more interior. Normally, it is unwise to mention such things, or try to get them across by signs. It is understandable that one should seek sympathy and comfort, in time of trial. But a monk must learn to bear his trials in silence and to do without human sympathy, except in the ordinary ways in which it is provided for. One should avoid these signs and train himself to be a man and keep his troubles to himself and to his director. If you want a friend to sympathize with you, go and make a visit to Jesus in the Blessed Sacrament. NOTE: a novice would run the risk of sin if he freely communicated to other novices and postulants serious trials and temptations against his vocation. One must be very careful not to undermine or shake another's vocation. Above all, one should never under any circumstances try to communicate to others by signs, problems that are a matter of conscience and which should be reserved to the confessional. Very serious harm could be done in this way.

c) *Recreational signs*: one should try to make a habit of avoiding dissipated or recreational signs. Signs are not supposed to be a source of amusement. If one confines himself as far as possible to signs that are in the *Usages*,[510] he will not go far wrong. ALL LENGTHY SIGN CONVERSATIONS (over a minute or two) ARE TO BE REGARDED AS USELESS.

Continuing the Usages—On Silence:
n. 324:[511] TO WHOM DO WE SPEAK?

a) There are normally *two* people to whom one can speak, at any time: for the professed, the abbot and the prior; for the novices, the abbot and the Fr. Master. Since in our house it is rather hard to get to Rev. Father, there is more freedom in speaking

---

510. See "The Manner of Making the Signs Used in the Cistercian Order" (an alphabetical list) (*Regulations*, 317–39).

511. *Regulations*, 157.

to Fr. Undermaster. In practice, then, the novices have access to the Fr. Master and Fr. Undermaster at all times, EXCEPT *during the grand silence* (n. 330[512]) {and} in certain *forbidden places* (328[513]): church, cloisters, refectory, chapter, dormitory, cabinets (n.b. however, by reason of crowded space in {the} novitiate grand parlor, this last ends up by being an empty formality). Talking should be done as far as possible in rooms provided for the purpose. One should not talk indiscriminately around the paths in the garden, etc.—especially outside {the} professed grand parlor {while} waiting for work. Where are the recognized parlors? See notes above (regular places).[514] Talking is limited during the time of work.

b) When one of the superiors is absent, then a substitute is allowed to speak. For instance, if Fr. Abbot is absent, then Fr. Subprior can speak to the religious, etc. When Fr. Master or Undermaster is absent, someone else (a novitiate professed) *may* temporarily help out at least in speaking with postulants. Special permission is announced in each case—{it is} not automatic. (N.B. no provision is made for recreation in our rule, {which} presupposes that {the} ability to get along without recreation is a sign of {a} Trappist vocation.) {We} must not abuse speaking privileges. {We should take} care when we *do* speak to speak in a monastic manner. Problems of conscience {are} created by lack of silence {and} vocations {are} often ruined.

324–325 etc.[515]—RULES REGARDING SPEECH:

a) subordinate superiors do not speak to more than two at a time (except {in} cases of necessity);

b) *Benedicite* ({note} the origin of this: asking a blessing; WAIT for "*Dominus*");[516]

c) speak in the appointed places;

512. *Regulations*, 159.
513. *Regulations*, 159.
514. See pages 20–22.
515. *Regulations*, 157.
516. "Bless . . . Lord".

d) SPEAK IN A LOW TONE—you should be heard only by the one to whom you are speaking; many never cultivate this habit, which is nevertheless very important, especially in {the} novitiate;

e) KEEP TO THE SUBJECT on which you have been granted permission to speak;

f) avoid speaking to a third person to whom you do not have permission to speak;

g) keep to the terms of the permission (cf. n. 326[517]);

h) one does not have automatic permission to speak to anyone, even though that person may not be a member of the monastic community and may not know our signs;

i) avoid speaking if possible during the divine office;

j) "In order to prevent any temptation to speak, two religious ought never to remain near each other alone, without necessity, out of work time, whether in the cloister, Chapter or elsewhere" (n. 329[518]) (comment on {the} implications of this).

331—SILENCE IN GENERAL: finally, an important paragraph.[519] It is not sufficient to avoid speaking. The silence of God's house presupposes care in avoiding all *easily avoidable* noise. We do not have to make a fetish of silence and creep around on tiptoe. But there are all kinds of noises that can be avoided with a little care and thoughtfulness. {Concerning} *machines*, if one works while others are reading and studying, one should if possible stay away from them if using a machine. Take the long way round with your tractor rather than go right through the area where others are enjoying their *lectio divina*. {Concerning} *singing practice*, if one needs to practice reading and singing aloud, do so in a place and in a way that will cause {the} least possible disturbance to others. *Walking about*, closing doors, etc., one can be thoughtful and go quietly. It is a good thing to cultivate {the} habit of being quiet and poised in everything: {this} helps one's

---

517. *Regulations*, 158.
518. *Regulations*, 159.
519. *Regulations*, 159–60.

own interior life. N.B. {as for} laughing etc. in chapter—don't overdo it.

Lectio *during the Great Silence*

The Great Silence: after we have seen the importance of silence in general and what it consists in, we remember especially that there exists a time of special silence, the "night silence" or the "great silence." *Usages* 330 defines the limits of the Great Silence: "from the evening Angelus to the end of the collect of Prime."[520] Limitations of silence during this period {are as follows}: minor superiors may not speak (without special permission); all ordinary speaking permissions are revoked during Great Silence (note {the} special penalties imposed by Rev. Father); the first superior may still speak if he sees fit, but he is the only one—he can of course still give permission to speak; during the great silence, no signs are to be made, unless really important; we do not even salute one another during the great silence (cf. *Usages* 315 for places where we do not salute each other even outside of great silence[521]). It is obvious from this that the time of the great silence is a *time especially set apart and propitious for prayer and* lectio divina. The period between the night office and prime is the choice period of the day; that is why it is best for Mass and communion. After Mass and communion, and before mixt, there generally remains about half an hour for *lectio divina*. But note that on many occasions—when one is hebdomadary, or when one is saying a late Mass (for guests, etc.)—one then has free the *whole period* for *lectio divina*—and this period now amounts to *over two hours* when one is not saying Mass and taking mixt. It is clear that this can be a very fine opportunity to do some serious reading and thinking. We should therefore *prize above all* this morning *lectio*, with its special silence, its relative coolness in summer. Normally we should be able to read and

---

520. *Regulations*, 159, which reads: ". . . until the end . . ."

521. *Regulations*, 154: "church, dormitory, refectory, cabinets, and places of work."

think, refreshed and alert, during this time, though for some it seems to be a difficult time in which they have to fight sleep.

Problem of sleep: normally we get enough sleep in the dormitory. When one has had a partly sleepless night, or is ill, or in some other way indisposed, sleep can naturally become a *physical problem* during offices and *lectio*. Here there is a simple case of physical necessity and in such a case the simplest thing to do is ask permission, when feasible, to go to the dormitory and make up for the sleep that has been lost or is otherwise needed. The problem of sleep in offices and *lectio* is usually something other than physical. Generally it is psychological or even spiritual:

a) Sleep may accompany states of *spiritual aridity and acedia*. It may be a part of a *spiritual trial* and purification, a humiliation, a temptation. It may be the expression of inner spiritual conflicts.

b) Sleep may be an expression of *psychological conflict*—of resentment, of unconscious rebellion, of boredom with the spiritual life, of laziness and refusal of responsibility. It may be a form of *escape* from the problems of the life.

c) Sleep may be simply a sign that one is not adapted to the life, that one is not in the right place, that he needs activity, and that his contemplation tends to be little more than a "blank."

d) Generally we sleep when our interior life is not properly organized and when we are engaged in too many pursuits that we have chosen with unconsciously wrong motives.

In handling the problem of sleep when it is not a clear matter of physical need, there are various aids one can use:

a) Mechanical: changes of position, standing up, discreet movement, use of smelling salts (!); one must take care to be discreet and modest in the use of such means, and not make a spectacle of himself in the choir or scriptorium. Mechanical means are generally not much help. They can comfort one as a "proof" of good will, but they don't do much more than that.

b) Moral: one should of course be generous, and determined. Sheer will power is not enough. An earnest desire to keep awake is generally necessary if one is going to overcome constant sleeping.

But here again good resolutions are not enough. Prayer is important.

c) Psychological: generally the reason why we sleep or are tempted to sleep is because *our life is not properly balanced and regulated*. The simple fact is that when a person is fully interested in what he is doing, and is able to do it well, and carry out his functions fruitfully, he is not bored, or irritated by them, and he does not find them tedious. He does not sleep. One can mistakenly approach this problem by forcing on the person things which do not really interest him, *things he does not really understand*, and *ordering* him to be attentive. With all the good will in the world, he will not succeed.

MOST OF THE TROUBLE with sleep comes from the fact that:

a) in choir the novice is subjected to long offices where, if he has not a sufficient grounding in Latin, he understands little or nothing. Naturally he becomes bored, and sleeps. (It is not easy to keep up for long an independent train of mental prayer during a choral office—the prayer of the monk at that time should be nourished by the office itself.) We have to face the fact that sometimes the offices are objectively tedious—the Order has faced this fact in recently diminishing their length and cutting off a lot of useless accretions. The offices now are not overbalanced. On long offices on feasts of sermon major there will be tedium because of the length and because of the poor quality of the chant (dragging out responsories which the majority of the choir are not certain how to sing). This will naturally induce sleep in some. {The} REMEDY {is that} with a good grasp of Latin, understanding of the scriptures and of scriptural "contemplation" (through types, etc.), appreciation of the Fathers of the Church, appreciation of chant, the monk will know what he is doing and will enjoy it more {and} he will {be} better able to keep awake.

b) In *lectio divina* the monk *may be reading all the wrong things*. In *lectio* one has to acquire tastes for things he does not yet like, but at the same time one should have a fairly large proportion of reading in which one can take a *spontaneous interest*. It is better to read a light and "less spiritual" book which keeps one alert and interested, than to fall asleep constantly over a heavy "spiritual" tome in which one is not really interested, not yet capable of being spontaneously interested. {This is a} problem of students who overestimate their capacities and read books that are far beyond their intelligence and training—certain difficult Fathers of the Church. {The} same thing {is true} in the spiritual life {as elsewhere}: those who try to fly before they can walk—and do not understand what they are doing. PICK YOUR READING WISELY SO THAT YOU READ FRUITFULLY AND WITH INTEREST, AND YOU WILL NOT SLEEP DURING *LECTIO DIVINA*.

Scripture Reading before Prime:

St. Benedict says that normally the younger monks who are not yet thoroughly familiarized with the office will spend this time of *lectio* in *meditatio psalmorum*.[522] In accordance with this desire of St. Benedict we have always preferably given the *lectio* before prime to *scripture or the psalms*. It is a logical time for this. Normally, it is to be expected that the monk *set aside the best of his reading time* for what is objectively best in itself and also more germane to his vocation. This means scripture and especially the psalms. But this is not to be taken absolutely literally. Though the novice should strive as far as possible to give this best of intervals to scripture, he may devote it to something else at times if there is some necessity to do so—if he will keep awake and get more profit out of his reading. But the principle remains: we should learn to give the best of our time to scripture.

Importance of Holy Scripture: the reading of scripture is *lectio divina* in the best sense of the word. Other reading, no matter how spiritual, is less truly "*divina*" because it does not place us in direct contact with the mystery of the Revealed Word. The reading of scripture is more fitted than any other to arouse in us true love of God, because it tells us God's own message about

---

522. St. Benedict does not use this precise term, but speaks of meditating on psalms and readings in chapter 8 (McCann, 48); see above, n. 306.

Himself, but above all because all scripture, the revealed Word of God, is centered upon the great mystery of Christ the Incarnate Word of God. Hence the scriptures are as it were an extension of the Incarnation. The Church believes Christ to be present, in a certain way, in the scriptures, and she shows this by the special reverence with which she surrounds the book of the Gospels in solemn Mass. This is not of course to be taken too materially. But when the epistle is sung at solemn Mass, then the apostle (or prophet) is spiritually present in the church delivering his divinely appointed message. When the Gospel is sung, Christ Himself is present and speaks His own message. Hence the special reverence with which we listen (in ceremony). Note the importance of the sung Gospel in great monastic vocations such as that of St. Anthony of the Desert.[523] (Avoid superstition in these matters, however.) The words of scripture are *words of life*, not just in the sense of an ethical message that will teach us to be good, and thus merit an eternal reward, but dynamic and active words that add the seeds of new life, divine life, in our souls. If God has spoken, how eager we ought to be to hear His words. READ ST. MARK 4:3-20—the Parable of the Sower[524]—and comment

---

523. Hearing the Gospel of the Rich Young Man (Mt. 19:21) and later the words of the Sermon on the Mount, "Do not be anxious about tomorrow" (Mt. 6:34) led Anthony to his vocation: see Merton's discussion in *Cassian and the Fathers: Initiation into the Monastic Tradition*, ed. Patrick F. O'Connell, MW 1 (Kalamazoo, MI: Cistercian Publications, 2005), 32.

524. "'Hear! Behold, the sower went out to sow. And as he sowed, some seed fell by the wayside, and the birds came and ate it up. And other seed fell upon rocky ground, where it had not much earth; and it sprang up at once, because it had no depth of earth; but when the sun rose it was scorched, and because it had no root it withered away. And other seed fell among thorns; and the thorns grew up and choked it, and it yielded no fruit. And other seed fell upon good ground, and yielded fruit that grew up, made increase and produced, one thirty, another sixty, and another a hundredfold.' Then he said, 'He who has ears to hear, let him hear.' And when he was alone, those who were with him and the Twelve asked him about the parables. And he said to them, 'To you it is given to know the mystery of the kingdom of God; but to those outside, all things are treated in parables, that Seeing they may see, but not perceive; and hearing they

briefly: the great need we have to *hear* the word of the Lord, the word of salvation, not just materially, but with the ears of our inmost heart, to give ourselves to Christ. READ 1 CORINTHIANS 1:17-31[525]—the "word of the cross" which is foolishness and scandal

---

may hear, but not understand; lest perhaps at any time they should be converted, and their sins be forgiven them.' And he said to them, 'Do you not know this parable? How then will you understand all the parables? The sower sows the word. And those by the wayside are they in whom the word is sown; as soon as they have heard, Satan at once comes and takes away the word that has been sown in their hearts. And those likewise who are sown on the rocky ground are they who, when they have heard the word, receive it immediately with joy; and they have no root in themselves, but continue only for a time; then, when trouble and persecution come because of the word, they at once fall away. And those who are sown among the thorns are they who listen to the word; but the cares of the world, and the deceitfulness of riches, and the desires about other things, entering in, choke the word, and it is made fruitless. And those who are sown upon good ground, are they who hear the word, and welcome it, and yield fruit, one thirty, another sixty, and another a hundredfold.'"

525. "For Christ did not send me to baptize, but to preach the gospel, not with wisdom of words, lest the cross of Christ be made void. For the doctrine of the cross is foolishness to those who perish, but to those who are saved, that is, to us, it is the power of God. For it is written, I will destroy the wisdom of the wise, and the prudence of the prudent I will reject. Where is the 'wise man'? Where is the scribe? Where is the disputant of this world? Has not God turned to foolishness the 'wisdom' of this world? For since, in God's wisdom, the world did not come to know God by 'wisdom,' it pleased God, by the foolishness of our preaching, to save those who believe. For the Jews ask for signs, and the Greeks look for 'wisdom,' but we, for our part, preach a crucified Christ—to the Jews indeed a stumbling block and to the Gentiles foolishness, but to those who are called, both Jews and Greeks, Christ, the power of God and the wisdom of God. For the foolishness of God is wiser than men, and the weakness of God is stronger than men. For consider your own call, brethren; that there were not many wise according to the flesh, not many mighty, not many noble. But the foolish things of the world has God chosen to put to shame the 'wise,' and the weak things of the world has God chosen to put to shame the strong, and the base things of the world and the despised has God chosen, and the things that are not, to bring to naught the things that are; lest any flesh should pride itself before him. From him you are in Christ Jesus, who has become for us God-given wisdom, and justice, and sanctification, and redemption; so that, just as it is written, 'Let him who takes pride, take pride in the Lord.'"

to Greeks and Jews. Many of the saints and Fathers (especially
St. Jerome[526]) had trouble with the fact that the reading of scripture was not as delightful, from a literary and human viewpoint,
than the reading of secular and even pagan literature. The message of God comes to us in an especially poor and humble guise,
so that we will receive it with faith and humility, knowing that
God uses humble instruments and does not depend on the power
of man. If we have this faith, and devote ourselves to the scriptures with patience, we will gradually acquire the *taste* for the
Word of God and His message (*gustate et videte quoniam suavis est
Dominus*[527]). Then we will frequently experience the efficacy of
the divine Word in our lives. READ HEBREWS 4:9-16[528]—the word
of God, living and efficacious—and {its} context. The modern

526. Merton is no doubt recalling the famous dream of Jerome, related in
his Letter 22 (To Eustochium), in which he is brought before the divine judgement
seat and accused of being a Ciceronian rather than a Christian, an experience
that brings about a change of heart, so that he concludes his description: "After
that I read God's word with greater zeal than I had previously read the writings
of mortals" (Letter 22.30, in *Letters of St. Jerome*, vol. 1, trans. Charles C. Mierow,
ed. Thomas Comerford Lawlor, Ancient Christian Writers 33 [Westminster, MD:
Newman Press, 1963], 165–66). See also St. Augustine, *Confessions*, III.v.9: "I
therefore decided to give attention to the holy scriptures and to find out what
they were like. . . . It seemed to me unworthy in comparison with the dignity
of Cicero" (Augustine, *Confessions*, trans. Henry Chadwick [New York: Oxford
University Press, 1991], 40).

527. "Taste and see how sweet the Lord is" (Ps. 33[34]:9).

528. "There remains therefore a Sabbath Rest for the people of God. For he
who has entered into his Rest, has himself also rested from his own works, even
as God did from his. Let us therefore hasten to enter into that Rest, lest anyone
fall by following the same example of unbelief. For the word of God is living and
efficient and keener than any two-edged sword, and extending even to the division of soul and spirit, of joints also and of marrow, and a discerner of the
thoughts and intentions of the heart. And there is no creature hidden from his
sight; but all things are naked and open to the eyes of him to whom we have to
give account. Having therefore a great high priest who has passed into the heavens, Jesus the Son of God, let us hold fast our confession. For we have not a high
priest who cannot have compassion on our infirmities, but one tried as we are
in all things except sin. Let us therefore draw near with confidence to the throne
of grace, that we may obtain mercy and find grace to help in time of need."

popes have all insisted strongly that all the faithful should learn to read and love the scriptures—but this applies especially to monks. In Europe, there have been some very fruitful movements to initiate the faithful into the scriptures and make them love and discuss the scriptures in meetings. It would be a very sad thing if monks, men of God, men who chant the office, were less able to read and appreciate the scriptures; but this requires time and effort. Pope Pius XII says: "Men will more fully know and more ardently love the Author of Salvation, Christ, and more faithfully imitate Him, in proportion as they are more assiduously urged to know and meditate the sacred Scriptures, especially the New Testament, for as St. Jerome says, to ignore the Scriptures is to ignore Christ" (*Divino Afflante*[529]). In order to understand what the Church desires of us it would be well for all novices to read one or other of the encyclicals on sacred scripture. The best and most practical from the monastic viewpoint is *Spiritus Paraclitus*, on St. Jerome, by Pope Benedict XV.[530] Here we see clearly how the reading and knowledge of scripture is bound up very intimately with the holiness of the Christian life. A monastic life without meditation of the scriptures will be empty indeed. Hence the novice must learn this art. Later on, when one may be involved in many other studies (philosophy and theology), and may not be able to give his best time to the scriptures, he will nevertheless be able to return to them with a real thirst and draw from them real consolation which will refresh and greatly aid the spiritual life. Happy is the man who has received this grace, for then even if he cannot read the scriptures as continually as he

529. *Divino Afflante Spiritu: Encyclical Letter of Pope Pius XII on Promotion of Biblical Studies* (Washington, DC: National Catholic Welfare Conference, 1943), #57, which reads: "This the author of salvation, Christ, will men more fully know, more ardently love and more faithfully imitate in proportion as they are more assiduously urged to know and meditate the Sacred Letters, especially the New Testament, for, as St. Jerome, the Doctor of Stridon says 'To ignore the Scripture is to ignore Christ'" (25); the quotation is from *In Isaiam*, Prologue (*PL* 24, col. 17B).

530. *Spiritus Paraclitus: Encyclical Letter of Pope Benedict XV on the Fifteenth Centenary of the Death of St. Jerome* (Sept. 15, 1920) (Boston: St. Paul Editions, n.d.).

would like, he draws just as much fruit from reading them in the moments that are left to him. Ideally speaking the monk should always be a man of the scriptures. *Lectio divina* is one of the monk's main obligations, especially in this sense of meditation and reading of the scriptures. Notice that this obligation to read and meditate on the scriptures goes hand in hand with the divine office. However, as we shall see later, before one can *meditate on* the scriptures, one must know how to *read* them. False ideas of spirituality lead us to try to run before we can walk. We despise what is ordinary and simple and seek what is lofty and extraordinary. It is by our *lectio divina* and our study of scripture that we can come to penetrate more fully into the meaning and mystery of the choral office, and make it our own prayer as well as the prayer of the Church. The Church does not want monks who simply stand in choir and chant the psalms with blank minds, or with minds engaged on some private devotion of their own. The Church wants monks who can chant the psalms in full realization of the deep mystery which they contain, which is the life of Christ Himself in His Church, and the tension of the Church toward the final revelation of Christ at the Parousia. This is impossible to realize if we do not know the scriptures very well, through and through. To find Christ in the scriptures it is necessary to be thoroughly familiar with every book of the Bible and to be able to find, at all times, significant correspondences between one passage and another, especially those things in the Old Testament which have been cited as types by Christ and His apostles in the New. Thus we become able to read and understand the Old Testament as the apostles themselves approached it. {Regarding the} ascetic importance of scripture study, St. Jerome says: *Ama scientiam Scripturarum, et vitia carnis non amabis.*[531] Why is this? When we come to the monastery we need to find something rich and strong to feed our imagination, so that we will not be wandering always back to sensual and carnal images.

---

531. "Love the knowledge of the Scriptures and you will not love the vices of the flesh" (*Epistola* 125.11 [*PL* 22, col. 1078], which reads: ". . . *carnis vitia* . . .").

The scripture provides us with a solid nourishment in this matter, and spiritualizes our imagination in a way that cannot be done by reading, say, some abstract treatise on the spiritual life.

How to Read the Bible: it is true that the Bible is unlike any other book. It is the Word of God. But if we insist too much, in the wrong way, on this "difference" and this great loftiness of the Bible, we may lose all desire to read it. We may imagine that it is a book so different that it cannot be read like any other book. But precisely, that is the best way to begin: one should start *by reading the Bible like any other book*—that is to say, like any other book which is at the same time a *collection* of books. One can read it from cover to cover. This is not a bad idea. It should be done once in a lifetime. One can read the books that are indicated as most appropriate for the beginner. This is a better idea. One can take the following: Genesis, Exodus, Josue, Judges, Kings (I to IV), Ruth, Job, Tobias, Judith, Esther, Isaias, Jeremias, Ezechiel, Daniel, Jonas, Zacharias, Proverbs, Ecclesiastes, Ecclesiasticus, Wisdom, Canticle of Canticles, the Machabees; the Gospels, the Apocalypse, the Epistles of St. Paul, etc. One must first *read*. Read with a holy curiosity—to find out what is in the book, who the personages are, what happens, and why it happens. One should not *begin* by reading slowly and thoughtfully. Ordinarily one should read right along at a normal pace, to assimilate the contents of the book. One must *form ideas and opinions*. One must allow himself to be guided by interests and tastes. Some parts of scripture will appeal more than others. These will be occasions of special grace to us. We should read more thoroughly and intently what interests us genuinely. One must *not approach scripture with one's own preconceptions* about what is or is not "spiritual." Many readers despise scripture secretly because it deals with things that seem to them common and humdrum—the battles of the Jewish kings etc. This means that in fact they do not read scripture with faith and that their idea of spirituality is human and limited. They want the "devotions" and psychological insights that characterize modern spirituality. They are interested more in themselves than in the objective revelation made by God to the whole human race. One must *read with prayer and faith*. All our reading should be preceded by prayer, but especially the reading of scripture. Whenever we read any book we first kneel and pray facing the wall. When we read scripture we read a few verses on our knees to begin with. This should not be made a mere formality, but it should help us to realize that we are receiving a special gift from God, almost as if we were going to communion. This should give the right atmosphere for our scripture reading. One must *apply himself at times to study* the scriptures. Our scripture reading is not always a "study," but sometimes it must be. What is study? It is intellectual *work*, the striving to understand and to make one's own truths that are contained in the sacred books. Study seeks to answer these questions: what is being said here? what does it mean? what is important for my present objective? what should I retain? how should I retain it? *One cannot study without an objective*. Study is not just the acquisition of miscellaneous facts. It is the acquisition of truths that unite to throw light on something we are trying to discover. STUDY IS DISCOVERY. Without this element of discovery, we cannot penetrate any book. By study we proceed from what we know to the understanding of what we do not yet know. We advance in knowledge and understanding. The *ultimate objective* in the studies of the monk is the greater knowledge of God in order to love Him more and in order to enter more deeply into the plan of His love for the salvation of all mankind. The *objective of each individual* in his study is the realization of his own vocation, the carrying out of his own providentially appointed task in the work of God.

General objectives*: for each one of us, there will be *objectives we have in common*: to understand better the meaning of the divine office and liturgy; to understand better the ways of God with souls, particularly our own; to understand better the "spiritual life"—i.e. the action of the Holy Spirit in the Church and in ourselves; to "know Jesus Christ and Him Crucified."[532] In all our

532. 1 Cor. 2:2.

scripture reading we will be able to deepen our understanding of all these things, if we keep the objective in mind. But if when we open the Bible our only purpose is to spend a half hour reading the Bible, because that is what we have been told to do, we will soon find ourselves asleep.

Special objectives: each one will find by grace that special aspects of divine revelation offer themselves providentially to him, and arouse his interest and zeal. Some become interested in particular topics, for instance: the remnant of Israel that is to be saved; Jerusalem—type and antitype; the way the apostles interpreted and used the Old Testament; the character of Christ as portrayed in the Gospels. These are a few of thousands of special topics that one can start to investigate. Also, one may get interested in a special *field*: scripture and liturgy; Jewish history; history and archaeology of the Near East; Hebrew language, etc.; patristic interpretation of scripture (especially our Cistercian Fathers); the period of the patriarchs, their character etc.—life of {the} Near East at that time; {the} interpenetration of sacred history with history of the surrounding peoples. Above all, one will look for the *theological doctrine* contained in the scriptures. The topics listed above can tend to be more or less "hobbies," and may remain quite accidental and peripheral, though legitimate, in the monastic life. But the theological content of revelation is *essential*. One cannot develop his particular objective unless he knows what the scriptures say and what it means.

Introductions to Scripture: a class in scripture will enable you (after profession) to study the Bible more thoroughly. But even in the novitiate one ought to read some worthwhile *introduction* to the scriptures, to understand what is meant by inspired writings, and how these writings are to be interpreted (v.g. *Unless Some Man Show Me* by Jones[533]). One should learn a little of the geographical, etc. background. This can remain quite sketchy, but unless one has some clear concrete ideas of what it is all

---

533. Alexander Jones, *Unless Some Man Show Me* (New York: Sheed & Ward, 1951).

about, one cannot assimilate the literal meaning of the Bible. And without the literal sense, one cannot get at anything further. *The extent of one's study* of scripture will vary according to character, temperament, etc. Every monk should have some time devoted to *regular study* of scripture, but in one case the study may be quite simple and elementary, in another more advanced and developed.

1. A simple study plan would involve, for example, taking a book of the Bible, say *Judges*, {and} first reading an introduction to the book, thus finding out what the general idea and purpose of the writer was, and getting an overall view of the contents. Second, pre-read the book, with a map. Glance over the chapter headings, reading the opening paragraph here and there if it looks important; you will find familiar names like that of Samson; you will be oriented from the start. Third, read the book carefully from beginning to end, consulting {a} commentary if need be. Fourth, as you read the book, or perhaps on a later rereading, check references to characters like Sisera who are referred to in the psalms. Using {a} concordance, find the places in the psalms where events in Judges are referred to, etc. One can thus go through the Old Testament getting a good knowledge of the various books, and also correlating events described with references in the psalter; this will help us to understand the office better.

2. Another simple plan {is to} go through the Old Testament, making your own *historical chart* of the main dates and events, noting down these things as you come to them in your reading. In order to get the correct dates you will have to consult a history or a scripture commentary.

3. A more ambitious plan {is} going through the prophets, searching for references to Christ, noting down all their references to {the} Messias and Messianic times, and thus building up a composite picture of the Messias, etc. from the prophets. This would involve consulting writers on the prophets and other authorities. One might compare opinions in controversies on the point, etc.

Care must be taken to avoid complicated and over-ambitious stud-ies. Cistercian monks are not supposed to imagine themselves great scripture scholars and pioneers. They study for their own benefit; hence they simply make use of the work of others in order to acquire a few ideas of their own. One should keep his projects practical. They are practical if they remain consistently interesting and productive. Impractical projects get very in-volved; they branch out in all directions; they get nowhere, and instead of producing fruit and interest they bring only confusion and turmoil. When one studies wisely and discreetly, his study becomes a recreation, a joy, a help to the spiritual life and to prayer. When one studies unwisely, his study becomes a burden, a curse, a source of weariness and disgust, and leads to the ruin of the spiritual life and disgust with scripture. It produces agita-tion, bitterness, and the desire to fight with others over small useless points of controversy. Unsystematic study leads to weari-ness. *Lack of humility* in study leads to over-aggressiveness and attachment to our own opinion, and the desire to show off and humiliate others. ONE MUST ALWAYS REMAIN HUMBLE AND DIS-CREET IN ANY FORM OF STUDY, and not secretly imagine that he is acquiring knowledge that makes him "better than" someone else. Only a truly humble man can really engage in intensive study without suffering from it. Such a one knows his limitations and restrains a harmful eagerness that would lead too far. He studies not for his own sake, but because he loves truth. He studies not to admire himself but to lose himself in the light of truth.

MEDITATIO PSALMORUM: however all the monk's reading of scripture is not just study. Study is necessary to get a firm grasp of the literal meaning of the sacred text, but study is not an end in itself. The reading of scripture is not merely an intellectual exercise. Our *intelligence* applies itself to understand the meaning of the text and to clear up difficulties and perplexities. It smoothes the way. The main point *is love*. St. Bernard repeats over and over again that if we do not arrive at love for God in the scrip-tures, our knowledge of Him is vain and our studies have been useless.[534] The scriptures must become part of our life and in doing so must unite us interiorly, by love, with the Incarnate Word. READ from Sermon 73 *In Cantica* (Luddy trans., vol. ii, p. 363[535]). The literal sense is the "portion of the Jews."[536] By literal sense, St. Bernard means the scriptures understood intellectually without being penetrated by love. He does not oppose to the literal sense some obscure and recondite esoteric sense that also requires study by the intellect. He opposes to it rather *certain correspondences* which love, enlightened by faith and by the light of the New Testament, intuitively discovers. And through these correspondences love comes *to Christ Himself* in whom the true spiritual sense of the scriptures is centered. "I will search for treasures of spirit and life hidden in the profound depths of the sacred writings."[537] These treasures of spirit and life are our inheritance as Christians. They are "wholesome and savory food beneath the unprofitable and unpalatable letter."[538] The letter without the spirit is poison. "The letter ministers death to the

---

534. This is St. Bernard's basic objection to Abelard's approach to knowledge: "Even when his teaching is not false it is animated by a dangerous spirit. It is pride, always pride, that prompts reason to set out to understand what we ought rather humbly to accept by faith; to evacuate mystery is to evacuate our merit, since it is to refuse the act of humility that God requires of us if we wish to attain some day to the truth. The thing that makes Abelard's attitude so dangerous is therefore more especially his claim to see everything face to face and to give free rein to reason in dealing with mysteries that exceed its powers. . . . The only proper thing to do is to make our choice between the sciences with a view to salvation, that is to say so that we may acquire charity . . . . You will not learn to choose rightly in the school of Abelard, but only in the school of St. Benedict, in the school of Christ" (Étienne Gilson, *The Mystical Theology of St. Bernard*, trans. A. H. C. Downes [New York: Sheed & Ward, 1940], 64–65).

535. *St. Bernard's Sermons on the Canticle of Canticles*, trans. A Priest of Mount Melleray [Ailbe Luddy], 2 vols. (Dublin: Browne and Nolan, 1920); Merton proceeds to quote and comment on this passage.

536. Luddy, 363.

537. Luddy, 363, which reads: ". . . for the treasures . . . depths of these inspired utterances."

538. Luddy, 363, which reads: ". . . food of the spirit beneath . . ."

Jew—it becomes to me a source of life in the spirit."[539] How do we penetrate into the depths? by UNDERSTANDING—the love and humility which enter like the prodigal into the sacred feast to which we are invited by the Father's love (the lover of the letter alone stands outside like the elder brother of the prodigal[540]). One enters in *by love*. Again, READ from Sermon 74 (same vol., p. 374-375). In the "familiar images of earthly objects, as from chalices of vile material, [God] gives our human minds to drink things rare and precious, even the mysterious and invisible things of God."[541] "*Nostris affectibus, Deum dum figurat insinuat.*"[542] The translation is inadequate to convey the spiritual content of these words. {The} translation says the words of scripture "commend the Divinity to our love by investing Him with human affections."[543] {This is} quite off the target. In the human emotions and affections in which the divine message is clothed, *divine love is awakened and brought into being* in our hearts. We must respond then to the content of love that is there humanly expressed (specifically in the Canticle of Canticles) and realize that as we respond and "feel" the warmth of this love, the divine love of the Word is brought to life in our hearts. We have seen the functions of the *intellect* and the *will*, in the meditation of scripture. But we will not really understand what this meant to our Fathers until we realize *the key role played by the memory*. In monastic tradition, the understanding, study and love of the scriptures is always associated with *memorizing and using in prayer* the words of the scriptures. When St. Benedict prescribes *meditatio psalmorum* after the night office,[544] he creates a difficulty for some modern readers.

---

539. Luddy, 363, which reads: "the Scripture in the letter . . . becomes for me . . ."

540. See Luddy, 364.

541. Luddy, 375; the subject of this sentence is actually "Holy Scripture" (374).

542. *In Cantica*, 74.2 (*PL* 183, col. 1139C).

543. Luddy, 374, which reads: ". . . commends . . ." ("Holy Scripture" as subject).

544. *Rule*, c. 8 (McCann, 48; not a direct quotation).

Historically we realize that the term *meditatio* here refers to a
process of memorizing. Yet we feel that St. Benedict could hardly
have meant this, and we take it in our modern sense of "meditation." It would be quite difficult to make a formal modern
systematic meditation on a psalm, or on many other parts of
scripture. Actually St. Benedict did mean memorizing, but he
did not mean just a mechanical activity of "learning by rote." His
meditatio is a committing to memory of the scriptures, with
thought and reflection, and without systematic meditation, but
rather with the effort to penetrate the meaning of the psalm by
love and to make it completely and thoroughly one's own.

Memory and Heart: to understand this we must realize that in
the monastic tradition, there is a certain emphasis on one's inmost
being, the center on one's being. The function of the monastic life
is to open up this deepest center, where our human person opens
out into the mystery of God. The memory, for the Fathers of the
Church, was not just the faculty which preserves and recalls images and ideas. It is also the *consciousness*. It is awareness, potential
or actual, of our own being. Memory and recollection for the Fathers tend to go together—recollection in the sense of being interiorly clarified and brought to a focus in God, and not just "calling
to mind" past events. The "heart" provides a physical image for
all this. One can imagine the center of one's being as physical and
not only spiritual. The Fathers, especially oriental, spent time and
effort in "finding their heart" in prayer. St. Bernard did this also.
This was what he meant by recollection—to recover one's awareness of one's inmost being, who one is, what one is doing (*Bernarde,
ad quid venisti?*[545]), who God is. This is connected with the fear of
the Lord. Just as God searches the heart and the reins (*scrutans
corda et renes Deus*[546]) so too we must learn to enter into ourselves.

---

545. "Bernard, for what have you come?" (William of St. Thierry, *Vita Prima
Sancti Bernardi*, 4.19 [*PL* 185, col. 238A]).

546. "God examines the hearts and inmost parts [lit. kidneys]" (Ps. 7:10,
quoted by St. Bernard in *Epistola* 89, to William [*PL* 182, col. 208B], which reads:
"*. . . renes et corda . . .*").

In *meditatio psalmorum*, we enter into ourselves to "plant," so to speak, the word of God in the inmost depths of our being. For instance, take the line of the Psalm *Miserere*, {which is} very appropriate: COR MUNDUM CREA IN ME DEUS ET SPIRITUM RECTUM INNOVA IN VISCERIBUS MEIS.[547] *Meditatio* of the line does not involve simply memorizing the syllables so that they follow one another. On the contrary, it is a complex and integrated activity of intellect, memory and will, all three pointing to a *spiritual* activity beyond their own level. *Cor mundum crea in me*—understand the need for a pure heart, the very object of our monastic life because only the clean of heart see God.[548] {We must realize} that it must be "created" in us by God. This implies *an ardent prayer* for the action of His grace and love. At the same time, it is grace itself which opens my heart to realize that if I *really mean* this prayer, what I ask is already granted. Thus the inner depths of my being begin to open with love, gratitude and confidence. I repeat the words softly to myself, thinking of them being uttered, with all that they mean, in the very depths of my being, and uttering them with all the sincerity of my heart. (I have to enter deep into my heart in order to say these words with sincerity, fully aware of all that they mean.) This taking full cognizance of the meaning of the line for me, and thrusting it as it were deep into the inmost recesses of my own heart to make it perfectly my own, *unites me with Christ and His Holy Spirit*. For this is a thought of Christ Himself (though not a sinner, He takes upon Himself man's sin) and when it is perfectly my thought then He utters it Himself in me. Then my heart is hidden in His heart by virtue of the faith and love with which I make this line my own. The Father hears me as Christ Himself.

MIXT OR FRUSTULUM:

At 5:45 on ordinary days, 6:00 on feast days, the bell rings for mixt or frustulum. Thus, three and a half or four hours after

---

547. "Create a clean heart in me O God, and renew a steadfast spirit in my innermost self" (Ps. 50[51]:12).

548. Mt. 5:8.

rising, we take some nourishment for the body, when we do not fast. The morning refection of the monks is not strictly speaking a meal, and it should not become a meal. It is a light refection, something to "break the fast" and sustain the monk until dinner time at noon. The very essence of this morning snack is its *lightness and frugality*, whether in fast season or out of it. "*MIXTUM*": what is the meaning of the word mixt? The primitive sense of "*mixtum*" is mixed wine: *vini meri plenus mixto*[549] (Psalm 74:9 in the Vulgate). "*Merum*" is pure wine. *Mixtum* is wine mixed with other wine or with water. The verb "*miscere*," to mix, comes in medieval times to mean to mix wine and serve it. Then the noun *mixtum* comes to mean any drink, even beer, or water. In monastic usage, it is not clear whether *mixtum* from the beginning meant only a "drink" (of wine) (*biberes*) or a drink with some bread. St. Hildegard (twelfth century), commenting on the *Rule*, said that *mixtum* meant wine with bread dipped in it.[550] This would be a normal usage in northern climates. Boherius, a late commentator, says *mixtum* means the same as breakfast.[551] *The Consuetudines of Cîteaux* prescribed for mixt a quarter of a pound of bread and a third of a hemine of wine.[552] But note this was not for everyone: in the twelfth century, as according to the *Rule*, mixt was taken only by the reader in the refectory[553] and servants of the refectory,[554] and by those who had been bled. Those who ate dinner at the regular time took no mixt, even in summer. *The Usages of the O.C.S.O.* (n. 379) {says}: "The mixt consists of six ounces of bread with the ordinary drink or soup."[555] Extra bread, fruit etc. can be given for mixt, for a valid reason—for instance, extra work, or the heat of summer (cf. *Usages*, 369[556]).

---

549. "[a cup] of strong wine full of mixture".
550. Quoted in Martène, *PL* 66, col. 610B.
551. Quoted in Martène, *PL* 66, col. 610B.
552. *Usus Antiquiores Ordinis Cisterciensis*, III.73 (*PL* 166, col. 1448C).
553. *Rule*, c. 38 (McCann, 94).
554. *Rule*, c. 35 (McCann, 88).
555. *Regulations*, 179, which reads: ". . . drink, or of soup."
556. *Regulations*, 177.

Prayers, etc. for Mixt (see *Usages*, 390[557]): before {mixt}, bow
to the crucifix, say the *Largitor*, make the sign of the cross (over
the food if you are {a} priest, over {one's} self if not a priest). The
prayer {is as follows}: LARGITOR OMNIUM BONORUM, BENEDICAT CIBUM
ET POTUM SERVORUM SUORUM.[558] {This is} a simple blessing; {note the}
difference between "grace" and "blessing": grace ("*gratias*") signifies a prayer of thanksgiving *after* a meal. The meaning of {the}
blessing of food, drink, etc. {is that} all good things come to us
from God; they are good in their nature. But we ask them to be
blessed in order that we may make good use of them, that what
is in itself a gift may not be turned, by our wrong use, into a bad
thing for us. The blessing of the table is a *sacramental*, which has
the effect of actually blessing and making holy the food which
we take. Hence, after the blessing, our taking of food is a simple
and holy action, an act of worship for God, as well as a merely
natural act, good in itself, of bodily refection. We should pay
attention to the ceremonies and words of the prayer in order to
carry out consciously the intention of the prayer and eat devoutly,
humbly, thankfully, quietly, like children of God. The spirit in
which we take our food has an effect on our other actions during
the day. During mixt, and other meals, we are, ordinarily, covered, for the sake of: (a) warmth; {and} (b) recollection. We should
take our mixt quietly, peacefully, not looking around too much
and paying attention too much to everything that is going on.
(There is not much going on anyway, so why pay attention to it?)
Avoid curiosity during meals. But attend to your neighbor and
see that he has what he is supposed to have. If your neighbor is
missing what he ought to have at mixt, you may get it for him;
do not call the servant of the refectory at mixt. If someone spills
something he should go and get the rag or the mop and clean it
up himself. At other meals, call the servant of the refectory.

557. *Regulations*, 183.
558. "May the Giver of all good things bless the food and drink of His
servants."

Grace after mixt {consists of}: *RETRIBUERE DIGNARE DOMINE OM-*
NIBUS NOBIS BONA FACIENTIBUS PROPTER NOMEN TUUM, VITAM AETERNAM[559]
(note: {there is} no sign of the cross). All our graces after meals
are prayers, more or less long, for our benefactors living or dead,
as well as for deceased brethren, etc., after dinner. Here mention
is made not only of God Himself as our great Benefactor, but of
human instruments He uses in doing good to us. We are grateful
to men as well as to God. Why do we pray after meals for benefactors? We earn our own living, or we are supposed to. The
benefactors do not provide us with our meals, do they?

a) We have received a good gift in the natural order, and in
thanking God for it we remind ourselves of all the other good
gifts we have received. All monasteries in fact have benefactors,
and in the ancient monasteries sometimes benefactors left sums
of money to be used for "pittances" ("relief") to be served in the
refectory on certain days, and the monks prayed for them in a
special way in consequence. Pittances could be specified by the
benefactor—that the monks should have a dish of eggs, or even
of fish, or some wine of good quality, etc. Today benefactors or
friends of the monastery or parents of the monks sometimes
provide specialties for dinner—ice cream or candy—in the same
spirit. Even if the food has not been provided or enhanced by
some gift, we remember our benefactors after receiving the good
gift of bodily refection.

b) "All those who do good to us" implies not only benefactors in the sense of secular friends who give money or good
things to the monastery, but also our brethren due to whose care
we receive our mixt—the brothers who set out the bread, the
bakers, the one who cooked the coffee—prayers at least that the
Lord may have mercy on him (!)—and all who are good to us in
any way whatever. This implies that the monk should cultivate
a spirit of gratitude and appreciation towards everyone. The monk

559. "O Lord, deign to reward with eternal life all those doing good to us
on account of Your name."

should not let himself be hardened into a spirit of self-sufficiency and contempt for others, by taking everything for granted and assuming that he receives all as his just due and owes no one any thanks—on the contrary, that he has a right to reprove them and complain because what they have done for him is not good enough! Humility and gratitude go together in the monastic life, in our relations both with God and with man.

FRUSTULUM: on *fast days*, frustulum is permitted, but not prescribed (those who are not allowed to fast, take the mixt). {It consists of} two pieces of bread and some coffee. The *table reader* gets mixt outside of Lent, and frustulum in Lent. He should take them. His neighbor should see that it is given to him. Note: in winter season, mixt is given on the half-holydays and on such days everyone should take it, as it is prescribed. Frustulum may be omitted, with {the} approval of {one's} director or {the} superior. One should normally take the frustulum at least, during {the} first year of novitiate, until one knows his ability to fast. For those who can, fasting is recommended.

INTERVAL (the interval after mixt and those at other times of the day):

Recently (General Chapters {of} 1956, 1957[560]), we have been reminded to distinguish between the "intervals" and *"lectio divina."* This will avoid making the time of *lectio divina* a time for doing everything else together with perhaps a little reading. In order to safeguard the time for *lectio*, we must try to make use of the brief intervals for material concerns and unavoidable cares. Put them off until then. The intervals are brief periods, usually

---

560. "We will use the expression 'Lectio Divina' to designate the principal intervals of the day" (actually from the 1955 General Chapter, subsequently approved by the Holy See and published in 1956) (Notre Dame de Cîteaux, *Decisions and Definitions of the General Chapters of the Order of the Cistercians of the Strict Observance* [1953–1965] [multigraphed copies of translations of General Chapter decrees, Abbey of Gethsemani archives]).

wedged in between two other exercises, in which there is a moment for needs of nature, shaving, brushing teeth, and such unavoidable little concerns. *The interval after mixt,* daily, is the first opportunity for brushing one's teeth. We do not take time to brush our teeth on rising in the morning. The interval before prime may allow us a few minutes of leisure for some little spiritual thing, or some useful task. It is a good thing to know how to use very short periods profitably. A period of five or ten minutes is not long enough to get into a good book, but it is time for:

a) a short visit to the Blessed Sacrament;

b) checking up on some point of usages or rubrics;

c) thoughtfully reading a few lines from the *Rule* or *The Imitation of Christ;*

d) making a visit to the cemetery or to a statue of the Blessed Mother or of a saint—{note the} value of these little visits;

e) saying a few decades of the rosary, or psalms;

f) writing necessary notes, etc.

The Interval after Morning Work: in practice this interval does not exist in the novitiate because of the conferences and chant classes held at the end of morning work. But the holding of conferences during this time, instead of during *lectio divina,* enables the novices to take more time for *lectio.* Normally there is just time to change after morning work, in the novitiate. But for the professed, this "interval" exists and is useful for shaving, cutting fingernails, sewing on a button, or some such other thing.

The Interval after Mass on Sundays and Feasts is just long enough for needs of nature. One may also write a necessary note and place it in the box or give it to Fr. Master or Undermaster for delivery at dinner. One can make a brief visit to the cemetery. There is no need to leave church. The best thing would be to stay and continue the prayer that has been enkindled by the Holy Sacrifice of the Mass.

After the afternoon work, here there is no interval, but *lectio divina.* However, when one comes in from work it is the logical time for a shower, or a shave. {With regard to} *shaving*, we should shave at least twice a week, perhaps more if necessary. This is the will of our superiors. But we must take care not to waste too much time in little things that keep us from our reading, especially after work. It is good discipline to get out of the boot room as fast as possible after work and not linger around making signs. If you have to wait for {the} shower, take a book. *After supper*, this may be regarded as {an} interval but it is long enough for *lectio*, and time should not be wasted.

THE OFFICE OF PRIME:

Prime is the first of the little hours, and with prime the office begins to take on a new character, as we shall see. The daily office is divided into more solemn hours: vigils, lauds, vespers (the great offices of the day), in which the proper of the day is fully worked out, in which prayer is longer and more stately and more profound; the less solemn hours are the "little hours," most of them in the day, which are shorter, more active, while the longer hours are more contemplative. The little hours were intended for private recitation, for many years. In St. Benedict's time it is foreseen that one at least of the little hours, and perhaps others, are to be recited by the monks in the fields (sext).[561] The little hours are less formal; also they vary less. Prime and compline are the most recently instituted hours of the office. They are morning and night prayers of a more personal character, supplementing the solemn, universal and contemplative morning and night prayers of lauds and vespers.

The Structure of Prime and the Little Hours: prime, and the little hours, have in common the same simple structure (but in the case of prime there are special and unique additions, as we shall see):

561. See *Rule*, c. 48: "*hora secunda agatur Tertia; et usque Nonam omnes in opus suum laborent quod eis injungitur*" ("Let Tierce be said at that point [the end of the second hour], and from then until None let them all work at the tasks appointed to them") (McCann, 110/111).

. 1) the hymn of the hour (only at compline this hymn follows the psalms instead of preceding them);

2) three psalms;

3) one antiphon for the three psalms (except at compline);

4) a capitulum, followed by a versicle;

5) *Pater Noster*;

6) oration and conclusion.

In all the little hours except prime and compline, the antiphon and all that follows belongs to the proper office of the day. *At prime*, only the antiphon is proper; otherwise, every day the rest of the office is always the same, whether it be Christmas or a fast day—the only slight change being that there is one capitulum for feasts and another for ferial days. *At compline*, the office is exactly the same every day, except for changes in the hymn tone; not even the psalms of compline change. The only variation in compline comes in the last three days of Holy Week. At prime and the little hours of the day, special psalms are appointed. But the psalms of the little hours do not vary from Tuesday through Saturday.

The General Character of Prime: the "active" character of prime is highly emphasized. Prime is the most active office of the day, and is full of prayers and acts of good intention for the coming day. Prime is the beginning of the work day. By prime we seek to sanctify all the actions of the day and consecrate our work to God. We pray especially to be without sin. *Prime is divided into two halves.* In the monastery we really see the meaning of this division, because here the second half of prime is recited in the *chapter room*, the place originally destined for it. In the second half of prime there are special readings, the sermon of the abbot, even the chapter of faults, {which} are closely related to the office of prime. (Note: in some monasteries, notably among the Camaldolese, the chapter of faults is associated with compline.[562]) Prime has this in common with compline, that both

562. Actually, according to Camaldolese regulations, the chapter of faults is held following prime: see *Regola di S. Benedetto con le Dichiarazioni e Costituzioni dei Monaci Eremiti Camaldolesi O.S.B.* (Roma, 1957), 104: "216. Il P. Priore dunque,

have a division which takes place in chapter and includes special readings, but in compline the prayers said in chapter are reduced to a minimum.

1. *The First Part of Prime* (in church):

The Hymn: *Jam lucis orto sidere.*[563] Prime is the hour of dawn—hence the hymn, which is all concerned with the beginning of the day, and looks forward to the day's activities. The first verse is typically Benedictine in its spirit.[564] St. Benedict in the Prologue says that the monk should never begin anything he does without first praying to God for assistance: *ut quidquid agendum inchoas bonum, ab eo perfici instantissima oratione deposcas.*[565] This day is a gift of God. He has brought us to it, for our good. In this day He wishes to do us good. That we begin this day with prayers to Him is a grace. It is also a sign that He intends to give us many more graces during the day. We should not look forward to difficult things and try to visualize all their difficulty; we should simply trust in God to help us overcome all difficulties. {Note the} appropriateness of this prayer for the *hour of dawn*, one of the most beautiful hours of the day, and one which many people never see or appreciate. It is like the hour of the creation of the world, a new start: the coolness, silence, mist, birds beginning to sing, the sun rising over the woodlands to the east, the cows lowing, brothers starting out on wagons or tractors. It is a

---

convocati dopo prima i religiosi nel capitolo ogni sabato o in altro giorno della settimana e premessa una esortazione, chiami i fratelli a fare la propria accusa" ("Therefore the Father Prior, after calling together the religious in chapter after prime every Sunday or on another day of the week, and after delivering an exhortation, should call upon the brothers to accuse themselves").

563. "Now that the star of light has risen" (*Breviarium Cisterciense, Vernalis*, 2, etc.).

564. The rest of the stanza (quoted in part below) prays that God might keep them from all harm in their daily activities.

565. "With immediate prayer, you should ask that whatever good work you begin might be brought to completion by him" (McCann, 6).

great grace for us to be awake, alive, alert at this hour of the day. Remember and regret the days when we did not see the dawn. As the sun rises, *it is natural to pray*. Prayer at dawn is a feature of the most ancient natural religions, for example, a song from a sacred rite of the Mescalero Apache tribe (excerpt): The sunbeams stream forward, dawn boys, with shimmering shoes of yellow; / On top of the sunbeams {that}[566] stream towards us they are dancing. / At the east the rainbow moves forward, dawn maidens, with shimmering shoes and shirts of yellow dance over us. / Beautifully over us it is dawning. / Above us among the mountains the herbs are becoming green; / Above us, on the tops of the mountains, the herbs are becoming yellow. / Above us, among the mountains, with shoes of yellow, I go about among the fruits and herbs that shimmer . . . / On the beautiful mountains above it is daylight.[567] This song conveys in a primitive manner the sense of the beauty and sacredness of the dawn, as if the sunbeams and the new light were living, personal beings. We too know that the sun is a figure and a symbol of Christ our light, and it is a "word" of God, by which God communicates to us the idea of His grace which He is giving us, to begin this new day.

Deum precemur supplices . . . :[568] think of the prayer of the Moslem, prostrate toward Mecca at sunrise; *supplices*—we cast down our whole being before God (this the reason for the bow we make at this verse) begging Him to help us this day; that He may keep us from sin throughout the day (*a nocentibus*[569]) and from all harm, all scandal, all bad ideas, all temptations that might harm us. We beg him to turn trial to our advantage, to save us from the malice of our enemies (above all spiritual enemies),

---

566. Typescript reads "they".
567. *The Winged Serpent: An Anthology of American Indian Prose and Poetry*, ed. Margot Astrov (New York: John Day, 1946), 216, which reads: ". . . that stream toward us . . . I go around the fruits and the herbs . . ."
568. "Let us pray to God, supplicating" (l. 2).
569. "from harmful things" (l. 4).

to save our friends, our country. We say this prayer not only for ourselves but for the whole human race.

Linguam refrenans temperet . . . :[570] we ask God first of all to protect us in the most difficult struggle to overcome our quickness of tongue (or quickness to make signs). When we think of the infinite numbers of sins and evils performed by speech all over the world each day, and the wars that result from man's boastfulness and cruelty and pride, we will understand the meaning of the petition *ne litis horror insonet.*[571]

Visum fovendo contegat . . . :[572] we ask the Lord, as it were, to put His hand over our eyes to prevent us from seeing things that are worthless and distracting (*vanitates*); and we pray not to "drink in" (*hauriat*) these things.[573] A holy man does not dwell on the vain things that are presented to his vision by the world; think of the innumerable *vanitates* that surround a man in the world—the vapid and vulgar advertisements on all sides—how men are corrupted by them without realizing it: the press, cheap magazines, comic books, TV. Realize how fortunate we are to be delivered from all this in the monastery. To be constantly subject to such things would make the spiritual life all but impossible. We do not have to worry too much about seeing *vanitates* in the monastery. It would certainly be a great error to try to avoid seeing the hills, the fields, the woods, the flowers, etc. These things are given us by God as messengers from Him; they call us to seek Him; they speak to us constantly of Him. To try to avoid all this is a foolish form of pride (except in special cases where there is a special inspiration of grace, but this should be verified in direction). However the *vanitates* we should avoid in the community are seeing the faults and the mistakes of others (and laughing at them); idle curiosity about personal affairs or doings of others; watching others out of curiosity because of personal interest in

570. "May he govern and bridle the tongue" (l. 5).
571. "lest the frightfulness of disputing resound" (l. 6).
572. "May he cover our sight with a loving gesture" (l. 7)
573. *"Ne vanitates hauriat"* ("lest it drink in vanities") (l. 8).

them. At community exercises we should be discreet about gazing around and idle curiosity, because although what is around us is in general a help to prayer and a source of edification, yet we tend to make it a matter for vain curiosity, and turn what is good into *vanitas* by our perverse tendency to seek things we can criticize or admire in the wrong way.

Sint pura cordis intima . . . :[574] the second verse spoke of control of speech and of curiosity, both important, exterior things. The third verse goes deeper, into the inmost heart of the monk (*cordis intima*). *Puritas cordis,*[575] which means much more than chastity of heart, is the main objective of the monastic life. Blessed are the pure of heart because they shall see God.[576] This means having one's heart not only free from sinful thoughts, but also from useless and selfish and worldly thoughts. We know what a struggle this is. The heart that is full of anger, resentment, rebellion, dissatisfaction, may be very "pure" by the standards of chastity, but may be very vile and impure in the sight of God. What an important grace {is} this *puritas* of our inmost heart. What peace it implies! May God grant that we may always possess it and grow in it. Then we will be real monks. But this costs much suffering and patience. We must not be upset at our trials and distractions, because this is the only way we can become "pure" in this sense.

Absistat et vecordia:[577] *vecordia* is folly, madness. This is a prayer to protect us against the multitude of silly and crazy ideas that come through our heads and which often deceive us with a show of good sense—the wild schemes that sometimes occur to contemplatives, or the silly obsessions, the conviction that someone else is angry with them (projection), or the dizzy notions that

---

574. "May the inmost heart be pure" (l. 9).

575. "purity of heart"; for an extensive discussion, see *Cassian and the Fathers,* xxxv–xxxix, 204–10.

576. Mt. 5:8.

577. "and may folly cease" (l. 10).

make us dissipated, lead to practical jokes, sign conversations, and misplaced exhibitions of what we think is wit.

Carnis terat superbiam / Potus cibique parcitas:[578] we pray to be mortified in all our flesh; we pray to remain abstemious and to fast, so that the pride of our flesh may be tamed.

Ut cum dies abscesserit etc.:[579] thus when night comes again, we shall be pure because of our mortified lives and will give God glory.

The summary of the whole hymn: *the day is a grace given us by God*. Let us use it well; let us use it as He would have us use it. This means let us control our tongue, our eyes, our imagination, live as mortified and humble men, and this will make our whole day an act of worship giving glory to God.

The Psalms of Prime: St. Benedict distributed the psalms for the office in such a way that the whole psalter would be recited once a week.[580] He did not therefore expressly choose special psalms for their particular appropriateness in a given office. On Sunday at prime we begin Psalm 118; on Monday through Saturday we recite Psalms 1 to 19, skipping psalms like 3, which is said at the beginning of vigils, and 4, which is said daily at compline. (These were obviously picked for their special appropriateness—but they are exceptions.) Nevertheless there is a definite "slant" one can find in many of the psalms of prime which make

578. "May sparingness of food and drink / Wear away the pride of the flesh" (ll. 11–12).

579. "*Ut cum dies abscesserit, / Noctemque sors reduxerit, / Mundi per abstinentiam / Ipsi canamus gloriam*" ("So that when the day has departed / And the allotted course has brought back the night, / Pure through abstinence, / We may sing glory to Him") (ll. 13–16).

580. *Rule*, c. 18 (McCann, 66).

them appropriate for the beginning of the work day. (*Read and remark on Psalms 1*,[581] *6*[582] *and 14*[583] *in this light.*)

The Antiphons: the only part of the office of prime that is "proper" to any feast is the antiphon. Usually these antiphons suit the feast, but have nothing special to do with the hour.

The Prayers of Prime in Church:

a) *The Capitulum*: there is a slight variation in the capitulum, in that there is one for feasts and another for ferial days. There is never a proper capitulum, no matter on what feast. *On feast*

---

581. "Blessed is the man who hath not walked in the counsel of the ungodly, nor stood in the way of sinners, nor sat in the chair of pestilence. But his will is in the law of the Lord, and on his law he shall meditate day and night. And he shall be like a tree which is planted near the running waters, which shall bring forth its fruit, in due season. And his leaf shall not fall off: and all whatsoever he shall do shall prosper. Not so the wicked, not so: but like the dust, which the wind driveth from the face of the earth. Therefore the wicked shall not rise again in judgment: nor sinners in the council of the just. For the Lord knoweth the way of the just: and the way of the wicked shall perish."

582. "O Lord, rebuke me not in thy indignation, nor chastise me in thy wrath. Have mercy on me, O Lord, for I am weak: heal me, O Lord, for my bones are troubled. And my soul is troubled exceedingly: but thou, O Lord, how long? Turn to me, O Lord, and deliver my soul: O save me for thy mercy's sake. For there is no one in death, that is mindful of thee: and who shall confess to thee in hell? I have laboured in my groanings, every night I will wash my bed: I will water my couch with my tears. My eye is troubled through indignation: I have grown old amongst all my enemies. Depart from me, all ye workers of iniquity: for the Lord hath heard the voice of my weeping. The Lord hath heard my supplication: the Lord hath received my prayer. Let all my enemies be ashamed, and be very much troubled: let them be turned back, and be ashamed very speedily."

583. "Lord, who shall dwell in thy tabernacle? Or who shall rest in thy holy hill? He that walketh without blemish, and worketh justice: He that speaketh truth in his heart, who hath not used deceit in his tongue: Nor hath done evil to his neighbor: nor taken up a reproach against his neighbours. In his sight the malignant is brought to nothing: but he glorifieth them that fear the Lord. He that sweareth to his neighbour, and deceiveth not: he that hath not put out his money to usury, nor taken bribes against the innocent: He that doth these things shall not be moved for ever."

days: *Regi saeculorum . . . ;*[584] *on ferial days*: *Pacem et veritatem diligite . . . .*[585] These two beautiful texts, the first from St. Paul and the second from the Prophet Zachary, are even more beautiful in the simple contrast that exists between them. On feast days {there is} a more splendid, solemn text, {which} looks to God and declares His glory: "To the King of Ages, immortal and invisible, to God alone be honor and glory." It is an eloquent and lofty prayer. The ferial text is simple and humble; it considers more our own poverty and our daily trials. In these, if we would be servants of God and seek His glory, we must love peace and truth; and this is His own word to us. The ferial text is more ascetic (*bios praktikos*); the festive text is more contemplative (*bios theoretikos*). Meditate on the difference between them and we will see what the Church means by action and contemplation.

b) *Exurge Christe . '. .*[586] (the versicle): this does not change even on Easter Day.[587] Again, {it is} an active prayer: "Rise up O Christ." This does not refer to the resurrection, directly, but it is connected with the dawn and sunrise. Not only does the "rising up" of Christ bring us the help of His light, but He also comes to our aid with His power and springs to our defense. He comes as a guide, a teacher and a protector, but above all as our friend and deliverer (*Libera nos*[588]).

c) *The collect* carries on these same themes: O Lord Almighty, Who hast brought us to the beginning of this day . . . .[589] Reflect on this truth. The new day is God's gift. Without Him we would not have it as an opportunity to grow and develop and work. Save us by Thy power, protect us from sin, and grant that all our

---

584. "To the King of Ages . . ." (1 Tim. 1:17)—the entire verse is translated below (*Breviarium Cisterciense, Vernalis*, 4, etc.).

585. "Love peace and truth" (Zech. 8:19) (*Breviarium Cisterciense, Vernalis*, 5, etc.).

586. "Arise, O Christ . . ." (*Breviarium Cisterciense, Vernalis*, 5, etc.).

587. During the paschal season an "Alleluia" is added, however.

588. "Free us" (the response to the versicle: "*Et libera nos propter nomen tuum* [for Your name's sake]").

589. *Breviarium Cisterciense, Vernalis*, 5, etc.

actions may proceed to glorify Thee—our speech (*eloquia*), our thoughts (*cogitationes*) and our works (*opera*). And with this, and the usual responses, we proceed to chapter.

THE MORNING CHAPTER:

1. *The Second Part of Prime*: when we pass from church to chapter there is a change in the tempo of the daily life from contemplative to active (relatively, of course). In chapter we assemble not so much as a choir but as a family, not so much as a body of men dedicated specifically to the praise of God, but rather as a group engaged in a common life with common material and spiritual problems—as a *human* community. The human side of the community life has its center in the chapter (and ideally speaking in the cloister also—more usually in the scriptorium). The first thing we do on arriving at our places in chapter and sitting down is to *salute one another with a moderate bow*, meaning "good morning." This is the beginning of the day's family relationships, the beginning of the work day, the "social" day of the monk living together with his brothers in community.

The Martyrology: when all the community is assembled, the invitator uncovers and begins to read the martyrology. What is the martyrology? It is the book which contains the names and acts of the saints commemorated on the *following day*. The feast of the following day is announced first. {The} *purpose* {is} to enable one to look forward and prepare one's heart for the feasts or for the commemorations. Also, at the reading of the martyrology are announced *private feasts and commemorations*—for instance the dedication of the abbey church; a feast celebrated in the diocese only (or in the country: for instance, St. Thérèse and St. Joan of Arc in France, St. Patrick in Ireland); commemoration of the last deceased abbot of the monastery, etc. Note in the first pages of the martyrology notation of announcements for mobile feasts: Palm Sunday, {the} Ascension, etc. Some feasts are announced with special solemnity: on the vigils of all feasts of sermon of Our Lady, after the feast is announced, we rise and say an *Ave*, bowed profoundly; {cf.} *Usages*, 217: "When the Invitator has announced the Feast [of Christmas] in Chapter, we prostrate full length on the ground, at our place, and in that posture say the *Pater* and *Ave*."[590] *Usages*, 268: "On Easter Sunday, when the Cantor announces the solemnity in Chapter, we uncover, standing turned in choir with the sleeves raised [not in ceremony]. When he retires, we sit down and cover, and not until then do we salute each other."[591] Easter is the only feast on which there is a solemn announcement {on} *the day itself*. Formerly there was no martyrology in chapter on the last three days of Holy Week—all "martyrdom" was considered to be swallowed up in the great mystery of the Passion, the source and fountainhead of martyrdom and of all sanctity. The Easter announcement {is}: *Hac die quam fecit Dominus, solemnitas solemnitatum et Pascha nostrum, Resurrectio Domini nostri Jesu Christi secundum carnem*.[592] The Christmas martyrology[593] is much shorter and less elaborate than that of the Roman Rite (see Dec. 25).[594]

590. *Regulations*, 103, which reads: ". . . prostrate at full length . . ."

591. *Regulations*, 133.

592. "On this day that the Lord has made, the solemnity of solemnities and our Paschal feast, the Resurrection of Our Lord Jesus Christ in the flesh" (*Kalendarium Cisterciense, seu Martyrologium Sacri Ordinis Cisterciensis* [Westmalle: Ex Typographia Ordinis Cisterciensium Strictoris Observantiae, 1921], viii).

593. "*Jesus Christus Filius Dei in Bethlehem Judae nascitur, anno Caesaris Augusti quadragesimo secundo, hebdomada juxta Danielis prophetiam sexagesima quinta, Olympiade centesima nonagesima quarta*" ("Jesus Christ the Son of God is born in Bethlehem, in the forty-second year of Caesar Augustus, the sixty-fifth week according to the prophecy of Daniel, the one-hundred-ninety-fourth Olympiad"), followed by commemorations of Saints Anastasia and Eugenia (*Kalendarium Cisterciense*, 236).

594. See *Martyrologium Romanum Gregorii Papae XIII Iussu Editum Urbani VIII et Clementis X Auctoritate Recognitum ac Deinde Anno MDCCXLIX Benedicti XIV Opera et Studio Emendatum et Auctum* (Rome: Typis Polyglotis Vaticanis, 1948), 317–18, which gives the number of years (according to the traditional dating) from the creation of the world, the flood, the birth of Abraham, the Exodus and the anointing of David to the Nativity, along with the dating according to the prophecies of Daniel, the Greek Olympiads, the old Roman dating (from its founding) and the regnal year of Caesar Augustus (as well as notice of Saints Anastasia, Peter Nolasco, Eugenia and the martyrs of Nicomedia, also commemorated on December 25).

The Date: (note to {the} invitator: in chapter on December 24 you read the martyrology for December 25; remember that you read the saints of the *following day*, and they are given under their own date, not the date of the day when they are read out in chapter). The date is read out according to the Latin. Let us take for example the Feast of St. Benedict, 1959. We see in large letters the date in Latin, which does not vary of course: DUODECIMO KALEN-DAS APRILIS. This means the twelfth day before the kalends of April: the kalends are the first of the month (the nones are the fifth and the ides are the thirteenth). After the date we see in large letters LUNA, followed by a series of letters and numbers. In order to find the *luna* (the day of the moon), we look for the proper letter and number: the *"littera martyrologii"*[595] for the year is given at the beginning of the Ordo; in 1959 the *"luna"* for the feast of St. Benedict is *duodecima*:[596] this is very close to full. (The full moon will be on the 24th, Tuesday of Holy Week; this is the "Easter moon" and Easter is the first Sunday following this full moon. For details about finding the date of Easter consult your local liturgist.) Together with St. Benedict (read it[597]), there is also an announcement of the *natalis*[598] of St. Serapion, hermit and bishop of Thmuis in Egypt—a desert father; and St. Lupicinus, an abbot in the diocese of Lyons.

Commentary on the Martyrology: it is characteristic of liturgical piety to venerate the *days* on which the saints were born to eternal life. (This is a deep natural instinct of man, going back into the earliest primitive psychology—Mayan Indians believed that there was a god for each day, and by elaborate calculations they worked out how the "gods" came around in succession, bringing good

595. "the letter of the martyrology".

596. "twelfth".

597. *"In monte Cassino, natalis sancti Patris nostri, Benedicti Abbatis, cujus vitam virtutibus et miraculis gloriosam beatus Gregorius Papa scribit"* ("At Monte Cassino, the birth [into eternal life] of our holy Father Abbot Benedict, of whose glorious life, with its virtues and miracles, the blessed Pope Gregory wrote") (*Kalendarium Cisterciense*, 52).

598. "the birthday" (into eternal life).

and bad fortune.[599]) The saints and especially the *martyrs* are the ones in whom Christ has fulfilled His work, by dying and rising in them. Just as the feasts of the temporal cycle bring to us the *mysteries of Christ* in the Mass, so on the feasts of the saints the Mass is the celebration of Christ's victory in that saint. The martyrology announces the Mass of the following day, the celebration of a divine-human action of Christ in our midst, commemorating {the} victory of Christ in the life of someone else like ourselves, a frail human being, lifted up by the power of the Holy Spirit to share in the victory of Christ. Each day is a feast of charity in which we share, with some saint, joy at his passing into eternal life with Christ, and we also are reminded to ask him for his aid and to implore, through his intercession, graces for ourselves and others. Since we live thus in time, the Church has sanctified time for us, and we receive grace by successive renewals and fresh starts. Each day, with some new saint, we make a further step, a fresh start, in our journey to God. It is a matter of monastic piety to have a special love for certain saints and to rejoice as their commemoration comes round—even some that have no feast of liturgical commemoration, who are simply named in the martyrology; a few examples (sometimes the martyrology gives a brief history of a martyrdom or of the saint's virtues): St. Cuthbert (March 20);[600] St. Pancras (martyr at fourteen: May 12);[601] Felix and Adauctus (Aug. 30: Adauctus {is an} unknown man who was given this name because {he was} "added" to the crown of

---

599. See Maud Worcester Makemson, *The Book of the Jaguar Priest: A Translation of the Book of Chilam Balam of Tizimin, with Commentary* (New York: Henry Holt, 1951), 81–94 (a list of the days of the year, with the appropriate deity, each marked as lucky or unlucky); and chapter 3 of the commentary, "Gods and the Calendar" (137–59), in which the author notes: "it may be said that the 'cult of the calendar' reached its highest development in the Maya religion" (137). Merton would later use this volume as a source for his book-length poem *The Geography of Lograire* (New York: New Directions, 1969) (see "Notes on Sources" 143).

600. *Kalendarium Cisterciense*, 51.

601. *Kalendarium Cisterciense*, 84.

St. Felix);[602] St. Cassian (Aug. 13: stabbed by the pens of his pupils);[603] the Seven Sleepers of Ephesus (July 27);[604] Saints of the Order; Desert Fathers; commemorations of dedications of great abbey churches; etc, etc.

After the martyrology {we recite the} *Pretiosa in conspectu Domini.*[605] We stand up with a joyful and devout exclamation: Precious in the sight of the Lord is the death of His saints! {Here is} reverence, wonder, and a great sense of the *value* of the sacrifice of martyrdom in the sight of God. This is a truly beautiful versicle, filled with a spirit of monastic *piety* (i.e., reverent gratitude for the works, example and love of those who have gone before us, our fathers in the faith). The monk's whole day is thus permeated with pious remembrance of the martyrs and confessors and virgins who have left him an example of how to serve God in the spirit of perfect sacrifice and love.

The Prayers:

Sancta Maria:[606] right after the martyrology we ask Our Lady and all the saints to intercede for us before the throne of God, that we may receive His help and be saved by Him.

The triple *Deus in adjutorium*[607] follows this. Note the earnestness with which we pray God to *help* us during the labors and occupations of the monastic day. (Remember Cassian's stress on

---

602. *Kalendarium Cisterciense*, 158; Merton comments on the "mystery of liberality and generosity and joy" of the anonymous "Adauctus," who "stepped out of the crowd and declared himself a Christian when St. Felix was being led to crucifixion," and composes a brief prayer to this "great and unknown and nameless saint, whose name lives forever and forever in the secrecy of God," in a journal entry of August 30, 1956 (*Search for Solitude*, 76).

603. *Kalendarium Cisterciense*, 145.

604. *Kalendarium Cisterciense*, 134.

605. "Precious in the sight of the Lord [is the death of his holy ones]" (Ps. 115[116]:15) (*Breviarium Cisterciense, Vernalis*, 6, etc.).

606. *Breviarium Cisterciense, Vernalis*, 6, etc.

607. "O God, [come] to my assistance" (Ps. 69[70]:2) (*Breviarium Cisterciense, Vernalis*, 6, etc.).

the *Deus in adjutorium* as an ejaculation forming the basis of a whole life of prayer.[608])

The Pater: note its importance. It is not just an interval, a pause between other more important prayers. This greatest of all prayers is supposed to be said bowed and in deep silence for *special* recollection and earnestness. Too often, when it becomes part of a routine, we regard this simply as a kind of pause for rest, a blank.

Respice:[609] the prayers for help continue. *Look down upon Thy servants*: {this calls to mind the} creative power of the gaze of God. When God "sees" in this special sense, He *approves* (*Oculi Domini super justos*[610]); He watches with contentment. But he "turns His eyes away" from the wicked; or rather He sees them in another way—with a stony silence that does not bless their works (yet behind this is always His mercy desiring their conversion and working for it). These "human" expressions are not to be taken in an utterly serious human sense, yet they are serious and simple. The point is that not one of them is *exclusive of its opposite*; it depends how these expressions are taken in a given context. *And upon Thy works* (the men Thou hast created); *and direct their children* (the children of men); *and may the Splendor of God be upon us*. Our whole day is to be lived not simply under the approving gaze of God but also in His "splendor"—the light of the Word shines in our works, in proportion as we are united with Him by love. The splendor in this sense is the splendor of *truth* and of *love*. The more we seek to please God by conforming to His will and to His truth, the more His splendor will shine in our works, without our necessarily seeing or experiencing it. Nor will everyone else around us necessarily appreciate it. We must not expect this mystery to be confirmed by human approval. That

608. *Collationes*, 10.10 (*PL* 49, cols. 832B, 834A, 834B–836B); see *Cassian and the Fathers*, 253–54.

609. "*Respice in servos tuos, Domine, et in opera tua, et dirige filios eorum*" ("Look upon your servants, Lord, and upon your works, and direct their sons") (Ps. 89[90]:16) (*Breviarium Cisterciense, Vernalis*, 6, etc.)

610. "The eyes of the Lord are on the just" (Ps. 33[34]:16) (not in the "*Respice*").

is our error. Nevertheless, our light will shine before men—rather, not ours but God's. It will shine all the more in proportion as we are out of its way and do not block its shining with our self-seeking and self-preoccupation. Thus we beg the Lord to direct our works, and do not attempt to direct them by our own lights alone.

Dirigere:[611] *direct*, *sanctify*, *rule*—three intimate and all embracing actions, each one more penetrating than the last, by which we ask the Lord to take control of our whole self during this work day. Whom do we thus beg to help us? It is the "Lord God, King of Heaven and Earth." We call upon Him with an act of deep faith in His wisdom, providence and power, as the One Who truly controls everything that goes on. Aware that we can too easily withdraw from His control by our free will (though we will remain still subject to His power), we ask Him to keep us under the sway of His *love*. We ask Him to reach by His ruling and sanctifying power into our bodies, our hearts, our senses, our talk and all our acts. It is not sufficient however merely to offer this prayer and then let things take their natural course. We must also strive to think of God's will and His law in all our acts, thoughts, and more especially in our words. We ask Him to direct us according to His law and His will, that thus now and forever we may be *salvi et liberi*— "saved, or safe, and free." The *adjutorium nostrum in nomine Domini*[612] comes very appropriately at the end of this prayer.

We can see from these prayers that everything is now obviously prepared for what is to follow in the chapter. We have

---

611. "*Dirigere et sanctificare, regere et gubernare dignare, Domine Deus, Rex caeli et terrae, hodie corda et corpora nostra, sensus, sermones et actus nostros in lege tua et in operibus mandatorum tuorum; ut hic et in aeternum, te auxiliante, salvi et liberi esse mereamur, Salvator mundi: Qui vivis et regnas in saecula saeculorum. Amen.*" ("Lord God, King of heaven and earth, deign this day to direct and sanctify, rule and govern our hearts and bodies, our senses, words and acts, by Your law and the works of Your commandments, in order that here and in eternity we may merit to be saved and free through Your assistance, O Savior of the world, who live and reign forever and ever. Amen.") (*Breviarium Cisterciense, Vernalis*, 6, etc.).

612. "our help [is] in the name of the Lord" (*Breviarium Cisterciense, Vernalis*, 6, etc.).

prayed to know and to do the will of God. In reply to our prayers, God Himself every day gives us, *as a community, light to know His will in a more special way*. There is first the *reading of the Rule*, to remind us of some aspect of our obligations in general. This is followed by a *commentary on the Rule*. Traditionally, the idea was that the commentary would fit the passage just read, and apply it to the present situation. This would have certain advantages: it would lend more unity to the manifestation of God's will; it would highlight certain points in the day's reading of the *Rule* which the superior, as representative of God, felt ought to be brought out. This would make the reading of the *Rule* more intimate and concrete, less vague and impersonal. However, the *Rule* is not commented on every day. Sometimes, there is a *sermon*; at other times there will be *scripture, theological* or *liturgical* conferences. But in every case the emphasis should be on the idea that God is now manifesting to us His will. Then finally comes the *chapter of faults* where, very clearly, the divine will in regard to one or other individual member of the community is brought out. A fault is corrected, and *forgiven*. (The penance is an act of divine mercy wiping out all the debt of punishment for that fault.) The superior then gives advice which helps the individual and community to see God's will, in regard to that particular matter, more clearly. *In short*, all through the morning chapter we have a concrete and living development of what we have begun to ask for in the prayers. There is light given by God Himself, through His representatives, as to the will of God for us this day. In addition, in ancient times, the *work was distributed* by the superior in or after the chapter; and finally confessions were heard in the chapter in the early days of the Order (very often by the superior himself). The whole idea of the chapter is then this idea of God Himself teaching us His will, *manifesting to us and explaining to us the way of life*.

Note: on Saturday morning the reading of the *Rule* is followed by the *list of the weekly officers*—a formal and "liturgical" announcement of community functions. The names and offices are sung on the lesson tone—meter and punctum. Those senior to the reader are always "*nonnus*";[613] priests are always "*nonnus*"; non-priests junior to the reader and the reader himself are "*frater*."[614] This gives an added solemnity and dignity to simple jobs, which should remind us of their supernatural character: they are from God and for God. {Note} the *training in responsibility* that is given to novices and young monks by these obediences. Learn *to carry them out conscientiously and well*. This is the meaning of the moderate bow—acceptance. Those named on this list *do not ask permission* when they leave a community exercise to fulfill their functions.

The chapter is a *schola Spiritus*,[615] a *schola Christi*[616] (the expressions are frequent in St. Bernard and the Cistercian Fathers). Much may depend on the morning chapter. It is unhealthy for the chapter to become a routine and boring observance in which little of true spiritual life comes to the fore, and emphasis is almost exclusively on the dead letter of observances, in which there is little warmth of life, in which everything is highly impersonal and vague, in which all is formality and rigidity. If this were to happen it would be extremely sad. There should be an atmosphere of warmth, charity, life, attention, interest. The chapter gives the keynote to the whole spirit of a community.

2. *The Morning Chapter properly so-called: talks, announcements etc.*: the remaining prayers of prime being finished, the morning chapter meeting opens. We have seen above how important this is—a family gathering to hear the Word of God, in an atmosphere of charity and alertness, that we may learn better to know the

---

613. "father"; see *Rule*, c. 63 (McCann, 142) and Thomas Merton, *The Rule of Saint Benedict: Initiation into the Monastic Tradition* 4, ed. Patrick F. O'Connell, MW 19 (Collegeville, MN: Cistercian Publications, 2009), 105–106.

614. "brother".

615. "school of the Spirit" (St. Bernard, *Epistola* 341.1 [*PL* 182, col. 545C]; *In Festo Pentecostes*, 3.5 [*PL* 183, col. 332A]).

616. "school of Christ" (*Exordium Cisterciense*, 17 [*PL* 166, col. 1508C]; St. Bernard, *Epistolae* 320.2, 385.1 [*PL* 182, cols. 525D, 588A]; *In Nativitate S. Joannis Baptistae*, 1 [*PL* 183, col. 397D]; *De Diversis*, 121.1 [col. 743B]; Adam of Perseigne, *Epistola* 25 [*PL* 211, col. 670C]).

will of God in order to be more faithful to the Holy Spirit. We come to chapter to commune together in the Holy Spirit (*Congregavit nos in unum Christi amor.*[617])

The Spirit of the Chapter: one good way to find a summary of the whole meaning of the morning chapter is to look at the little lesson that is in the breviary[618] and which is read by one who misses the prayers in chapter, when making up the prayers privately, in place of the reading of the *Rule*. It is from St. Paul, 2 Thessalonians 3: "*May the Lord direct our bodies and our hearts in the charity of God and the patience of Christ.*" The whole purpose of the chapter is this: we come to open our hearts to the Word of God, that by faith, hope and love we may submit ourselves completely to the action of the Holy Spirit in ourselves and in the community, be guided by God in everything, in the charity of God Who is Charity—to "walk in love as most dear sons of God";[619] to "listen to the admonitions of our loving Father"[620] (*Rule*)—in the patience of Christ, that is to say, in union with the Passion of Christ: "by patience we share in the Passion of Christ" (*Rule*).[621] The whole atmosphere and spirit of the chapter is then one of self-denial, self-forgetfulness, in order to live more perfectly in Christ, that is to say, in love. We will treat the *Saturday mandatum* in its proper place,[622] but since it has so many texts to be sung about the life of the community in Christ, it will be appropriate to recall some of them here: "I give you a new commandment, that you love one another as I have loved you" (John 13:34). "If I your Lord and Master have washed your feet: how much more ought you to wash one another's feet . . . ."[623] "By this shall all men know if you are My disciples, if you have love

617. "The love of Christ has gathered us together" (l. 2 of the hymn "*Ubi caritas et amor, Deus ibi est,*" traditionally sung at the footwashing on Holy Thursday).

618. *Breviarium Cisterciense, Vernalis,* 6, etc.

619. Eph. 5:1-2.

620. *Rule*, Prologue (McCann, 6).

621. *Rule*, Prologue (McCann, 13).

622. This discussion is not included in the present text.

623. Jn. 13:14.

for one another. . . ."[624] "Let these three remain in you, faith, hope and charity, but the greatest of these is charity. . . ."[625] "Where charity and love are, there is God. . . ."[626] "The love of Christ has gathered us together; let us fear and love Christ our God"[627] etc. Note: this last is the key to the whole idea. The most important purpose of the chapter is *to manifest and to produce unity in charity*. The chapter is a sequel to our Eucharistic communion, and it should have a Eucharistic atmosphere (which it certainly does most of all on Holy Thursday evening after the Great Mandatum and the reading of St. John's account of the Last Supper). The *sacramental aspect* of the chapter {thus consists in} the mystery of the community with Christ in the midst of it. This depends on us. The presence of Christ is here not brought about by uttering the sacred words of consecration, but by that love which is the fruit of Eucharistic communion. Where charity and love are, *there is God*. The Roman Missal gives further development of these texts in the Great Mandatum; they illustrate our point well (see {the} Roman Missal[628]).

Chapter Talks: normally, each day the father abbot speaks to the assembled choir religious, and on Sundays and feasts to the entire community. Anyone else who speaks is normally either invited or appointed to do so by the father abbot. Hence everything that is said in chapter is spiritual nourishment provided for us by the father of the community. Naturally no one man expects to be able to tell his monks everything all by himself. Hence the abbot provides other speakers: {he} appoints priests of the community to preach on feast days, {and} invites guests to speak to the community, whether clerics or laymen, and especially other superiors of the Order.

---

624. Jn. 13:35.

625. 1 Cor. 13:13.

626. See above, n. 617.

627. The second line here combines vs. 4: "*Timeamus et amemus Deum vivum*" ("Let us fear and love the living God") and vs. 10: "*Et in medio nostri sit Christus Deus*" ("May Christ our God be in our midst").

628. See *Missale Romanum*, 202–204.

The Talks of the Father Abbot: the father abbot has a *special obligation and a special grace of state* to guide his community in the ways of the Lord, to lead them to salvation and to sanctification. This implies a special obligation on his part to be *doctus lege divina* (St. Benedict[629]) and to be immersed in the scriptures, the Fathers and the monastic traditions, especially of course our own *Rule*. We in our turn must look upon his teaching with the eyes of faith and receive it in a supernatural spirit. We should keep in mind the basic truth that since the father abbot has been put in his position by the Holy Spirit, the Holy Spirit will speak through him and use him, in ways that neither he nor we can foresee or understand. Indeed, it is possible that he may act as an instrument of God entirely beyond and outside his own conscious awareness and intentions, in a given case. Hence we should not take too human and exterior a view of his talks and teaching. It would be a mistake to demand a special kind of eloquence or learning that is not necessary for chapter talks, or to insist that the father abbot always preach a doctrine in conformity with our own needs and ideas at the moment. This is a manifest impossibility, and to expect it would indicate immaturity and self-centeredness in the religious. We must accept the subject matter and treatment chosen by the father abbot for the good of the greater number. As we go on in the monastic life, we may become quite familiar with many of his themes, and feel that we are not getting "anything new." The point is, if we are mature religious, we must realize that the father abbot is no longer preaching to us, but to the younger ones. He is not considering our needs, but theirs, which are more urgent and more elementary. Yet at the same time we must realize that the basic elements of the monastic life always apply to us also, and may indeed apply to us even more than to beginners, in certain times of trial: hence the need of *humility, simplicity, faith*. It is certainly a sign of lack of humility in a monk if he permits himself to sit in judgement on everything his abbot says, and to

---

629. "learned in the divine law" (*Rule*, c. 64 [McCann, 146/147], which reads: "*doctum*").

criticize the doctrine and the manner of presentation. Not only
is it pride but it is foolishness and a sign of a very worldly and
natural spirit which will cost the monk many graces which humility would guarantee him. Such a religious may perhaps have
in store for him grievous humiliations; perhaps a very serious
fall may be permitted by God to teach him the humility he lacks.
Simplicity and faith will teach us that in spite of the human ap-
pearances, even the most simple and unassuming, there may be
an important spiritual message for the most advanced and most
sophisticated of religious. We must never lose this humility and
spirit of faith. Read St. Paul: 1 Corinthians 1:17-24.[630] St. Paul
gives the Corinthians a lesson that applies to all of us. The Greeks
were in love with worldly wisdom and novelty, new and intrigu-
ing doctrines and elegant presentation were what they demanded, and they thought that spirituality depended on these
things. The Jews on the other hand were more spiritual but still
demanded signs and miracles, extraordinary manifestations of
God's action. The human approach {is} to seek what strikes curiosity and stimulates the mind. Paul preaches the Cross of Christ,
which is *foolishness to the human spirit*. Yet to those who are chosen,
it is salvation and the power of God. Let those who are tempted
to be bored with the apparent foolishness and simplicity of the
doctrines preached in chapter always remember this fact. God
can do what He wants.

   Parenthesis on Preaching: this does not absolve us from responsibility when we ourselves have *to preach {a} sermon* in chapter. We should do everything we can to make our sermons
interesting, lively and *full of good material*. We should be short and
to the point. {It is} useless to expect the community to listen for
more than twenty or twenty-five minutes. {There is} nothing
wrong with fifteen-minute sermons, provided they are good. It
usually takes about twenty minutes to develop a theme fully;
beyond that, time is wasting. It is fatuous to try to demand their
attention further. Who do you think you are? One has a *duty* to

---

630. See above, n. 525.

speak in a lively, interesting manner. It is a waste of time to drone out sentences that put everyone to sleep. {Sermons should consist in} good material, adapted to the hearers, {to the} common level of the community, {but} not talking down to them and patronizing them. *A little humor* is a good thing, but a preacher should not just aim to keep his audience in stitches; this is out of place anywhere, for a sermon—especially in a monastery. Remember our duty to the Church (souls) and to God's Word; the idea is to create a *living contact* between souls and God by faith, preaching the Word of God is such a way that souls will respond. *Preach to those who agree with you,* and let the others take care of themselves; do not try to convince real (or imaginary) opponents. Priests who are appointed to preach in chapter should remember the following: give common doctrine, not just their own opinions; follow the scriptures and use them freely: preach the Word of God—it is for this that everyone hungers; avoid what is lofty and obscure, or fantastic and exaggerated; avoid old wives' tales and far-fetched stories of wonders and revelations that tend to make the truth doubtful rather than more persuasive.

Problems and Temptations—some questions arise:

Does a monastery have an official spirituality to which everyone in the house has some obligation to conform? It is a mistake to think that everyone has some kind of obligation to take on the "official" spirituality preached by the father abbot and make his life conform to it in every respect. This is not the monastic idea. Neither does the monastery itself possess some clear-cut spiritual policy which governs the formation of everyone in small details. The house has its *spirit*, and that spirit is to a great extent determined by the father abbot. Everyone is free to let himself be moved and formed according to that spirit. If one places no deliberate resistance, the spirit of the house will spontaneously and naturally do its work for his sanctification. We should not be self-conscious about all this, and must not be attached to external questions of "spirituality." To treat spirituality as something official and obligatory is to kill it at the root. Let us be simple and humble and accept whatever we need from the environment, without trying to react against it. To resist and place obstacles would be a fault. If something does not suit our own spirit, it can be left to take care of itself; we will be unable to digest it anyway.

But is there not such a thing as Cistercian spirituality? And should the monk not seek to conform as far as possible to the spirituality of the Order? This must be understood correctly. It would be a mistake to insist that there is a clear-cut and definite norm of Cistercian spirituality, and to believe that in all things regarding prayer and the spiritual life we can appeal to certain definite norms that will enable us to say, without hesitation, "this is Cistercian"; this is "not Cistercian."

a) Note the semantic problem that immediately arises. "Cistercian" can become a word loaded with hidden associations and a vehicle for mere prejudice. A given group can make the word "Cistercian" the justification for its own limited ideas and desires; and they can use it as a standard for rejecting and unfairly stamping out what does not suit them or flatter their self-esteem.

b) There is a field in which we can define certain qualities that are in accord with the character of early Cistercian life: austerity, simplicity, humility, poverty, love of solitude (i.e. community away from men, in wooded and wild places), love of scripture. But these are not matter for a kind of Cistercian "party line." What one must learn to do is to develop a taste for the things that our Fathers loved, and to see and love these things in much the same way as they did. This can be arrived at spontaneously and without self-conscious insistence on "Cistercian-ism," simply by cultivating a taste for the writings of our Fathers and by studying the history of the Order.

c) The Order has no clearly defined and official spirituality which is of obligation for all the members. Ours is a *monastic spirit*, common to other monks, with particular modalities which flow from our *Rule* and observances. It is sufficient to love our *Rule* and observances, to love our house with its customs and traditions, and we will have the spirit of the Order. Individual differences may well remain, personal tastes and modalities in the spiritual life. Why should these be stamped out? On the contrary, to demand *absolute conformity* all down the line would be contrary to the spirit of our Order. There must always remain room for the Holy Spirit to do with souls as He pleases, and to lead them by various ways suited to their own needs and gifts.

Conclusion: if we are too set on forming an idea of the *perfectly correct norm* of spirituality, we will tend to judge everything that is preached and said in the chapter room, everything that is read, everything that is done in community, and we will very likely come up with the judgement that everyone else is wrong and "un-Cistercian" but ourselves.

What attitude should I then take? the attitude of simple faith which is presupposed by the *Rule*: *ausculta*—listen.[631] Do not let accidentals and trivialities stand in your way and prevent you from arriving at the essentials. The chapter room is a place in which God makes known His will and His graces. Anyone who is open-minded and docile, anyone who does not place obstacles in the way, will learn God's will and receive His graces. Do not let your attention be distracted by thoughts and projections that are beside the point, wondering: "Why is this being said? Is this directed at me? Is this for so and so? Is this an indication of some new policy? Is the abbot angry, or trying to 'get' somebody?" etc., etc. All these thoughts are unhealthy, and the devil easily uses such things in order to disturb the peace of individuals and of the community. Those who get in the habit of thinking this way will find the chapter a source of great trouble and will lose many opportunities to benefit by it. If this is in us we must do our best to get rid of such bad habits of thought.

"*Loquamur de ordine nostro*":[632] when the chapter talk or sermon has been completed, and when miscellaneous announcements have been made, we "speak of our Order." Haven't we been

631. *Rule*, Prologue (McCann, 6).
632. *Rituale*, 94 (III, viii, 2).

speaking of our Order all the time? What about the *Rule*, and the commentary on the *Rule*? and the announcements? Most often it is in the announcements themselves that we talk most about the Cistercian Order—about other houses of the Order, about the daughter houses, about news of what is going on here and there. To understand the phrase *"loquamur de ordine nostro"* we must remember some of the various meanings of *ordo*:[633]

1) Primarily it means a "way" (*modus, ratio*)—it appears thus in early medieval legal documents.

2) Then it means a curia or legislative group (again, {an} early use—in Theodosius[634]).

3) Then, order as a sacrament (holy orders).

4) Then, as a liturgical book, originally synonymous with that we would call our *rituale*.

5) Then, *ordo* in the sense of *rule*, religious rule.

6) (a) As far back as the eighth century we find it loosely used to correspond to what we would now call a religious order (*ordo monasticus*). But the monks were not an order in our modern sense. It is more a question of those who have embraced a state—the monastic state (*venire ad ordinem monachi*[635]).

(b) In the eleventh and twelfth century at Cluny, *ordo* can mean the monastery, the monastic community.

(c) Then, frequently, especially among the twelfth-century Cistercians, it means the *observance of the community*, or the way the monastic life is lived in the community. *Ordinem tenere*[636] means to be faithful to all the observances.

(d) Finally it came to mean the General Chapter, the highest legislative group; and *from this* it came to mean the "Order" in

---

633. Merton's discussion is based on the entry *"ordo"* in Charles Du Cange, *Glossarium Mediae et Infimae Latinitatis, editio nova*, ed. Léopold Favre, 10 vols. (1883–1887; Graz, Austria: Akademische Druck-u. Verlagsanstalt, 1954), 6.60–62.

634. I.e. the *Codex Theodosianus*.

635. "to come to the state of the monk" (*Chartularium S. Petri Neronis-villae*, fol. 15v, cited in Du Cange, 6.61).

636. "to keep the order" (Carthusian *Statutes* of 1261, cited in Du Cange, 6.61).

the modern sense of a religious institute considered as a whole, united under its supreme legislative body and carrying out the same observances everywhere (*Ordo niger*: the black Order, Benedictines; *Ordo albus*:[637] the Canons Regular; *Ordo griseus*:[638] the Cistercians—sometimes called the *ordo dealbatus*[639]).

Other meanings of *ordo* which came later {include}:

7) An advocate or judge.
8) A squad of soldiers.

In our chapter room, when the phrase *loquamur de ordine nostro* is uttered by the presiding superior, it has a more modern meaning, when it is taken to include news of deaths from other houses. But the original and proper meaning of this phrase is "Let us speak of our observance . . . let us speak of the way we are keeping our rule." It does not mean "Let us speak of what is confidential among ourselves," for the phrase is not used before a meeting of the (voting) members of the chapter.

The Chapter of Faults

Historical notes:[640] in Egyptian monasticism,[641] when a monk broke something or committed some external fault, he accused himself before the community *in choir*, or before the superior privately. Under St. Basil,[642] public accusation of faults was made at the end of the day. Today still, {the} chapter of faults is held by the Camaldolese in the *evening* chapter.[643] In the *Rule* of St. Benedict, no provision is made for accusation by others, but

637. "the white Order" (Du Cange, 6:61).
638. "the gray Order" (Du Cange, 6:61).
639. "the white Order" (Du Cange, 6:62).
640. See Philibert Schmitz, "Chapitre des Coulpes," *Dictionnaire de Spiritualité Ascétique et Mystique* [*DS*], ed. F. Cavallera *et al.*, 17 vols. (Paris: Beauchesne, 1932–95), 2:483-88.
641. See Schmitz, col. 483.
642. See Schmitz, col. 483.
643. But see above, n. 562.

only self-accusation,[644] not systematically done at any set time, but as opportunity offers itself (c. 46).[645] In the eighth century, there is reference to *canons regular* accusing themselves in their chapter—for convenience's sake, an appropriate time.[646] Regular chapters of faults as we know them began to appear systematically in the tenth and eleventh centuries. Formulas we know {were} introduced then: *quid dicitis?—mea culpa—surgite in nomine Domini.*[647] Proclamations also began at this time. Early monastic usages give precise rules on this point: (1) proclamations {are} to be simple and brief; (2) the one accused either asks pardon or states that he does not remember committing the fault; (3) the accuser can then go on to prove his point; (4) false accusations {are} severely punished. It is obvious that this could lead to bickering and abuse and turn the chapter into a court of law. The *proclaimers* were, first of all, certain special ones charged with watch over regularity, v.g. *circators*. This indicates that in monastic tradition, the duty of proclaiming belongs first of all to those who have certain definite responsibilities. For instance, one in charge of a certain job would have a special responsibility to proclaim those who interfere with its being carried out; or the sub-prior would have a special responsibility to proclaim those who are absent from choir without reason, or who do not report promptly for work, etc. {With regard to} penances, for grave faults the discipline was taken in chapter. This is still provided for in our *Usages*, as we shall see below.[648] The discipline could be taken by oneself or administered by others. Very often proclamations etc. were made *before* the abbot's chapter talk, and later the talk dealt with the faults committed and brought up in chapter. The morning chapter talk in that case was a kind of summary of the lessons

---

644. See Schmitz, col. 483.

645. McCann, 108.

646. See Schmitz, col. 484.

647. "What do you say?"; "through my fault"; "arise in the name of the Lord" (Martène [*PL* 66, col. 687B]; Schmitz, col. 485).

648. See page 250 below, and *Regulations*, 168 (n. 351), 173 (n. 363).

of the chapter of faults. Pope Paul V even enriched the chapter of faults with indulgences.[649]

The Cistercians introduced a special chapter of faults for the laybrothers to be held on Sundays.[650] The *Trappist* reform placed great emphasis on the chapter of faults. Abbot de Rancé believed in constantly humiliating and correcting his monks severely, at every opportunity.[651] His community accepted this in good faith and with good will, and La Trappe was edifying in consequence. Nevertheless it is generally admitted that Abbot de Rancé carried the chapter of faults to an extreme. He tended to *exaggerate and to dramatize* the chapter of faults beyond measure. Some typical practices of La Trappe {include}:

1) fiery and exaggerated tongue lashings in chapter, and severe penances for very slight faults, or even when there was no fault at all. Abbot de Rancé so believed in "humiliating his monks" that he would treat them as the vilest in creation on purpose, even when he knew them to be very good religious. He believed that they would appreciate this—and in general they shared his belief, and accepted it in good part. For instance, {he} treated with terrible severity a laybrother who presumed to speak to him (the abbot) before prime to notify him that the Mass *de Beata*[652] had not been said.[653] When a monk read a few words on a piece of paper he picked up by chance, Abbot de Rancé compared it to the "sin of Adam."[654] Often, Abbot de Rancé would make the whole community take the discipline for a fault (not

---

649. See Schmitz, col. 487.

650. See Schmitz, col. 485.

651. See Henri Bremond, *Armand de Rancé, Réformateur de la Trappe* (Paris: Librairie Hachette, 1929), 101 (ET: *The Thundering Abbot: Armand de Rancé, Reformer of La Trappe*, trans. F. J. Sheed [London: Sheed & Ward, 1930], 119; Merton uses the French version and provides his own translations).

652. I.e. of the Blessed Virgin.

653. See Bremond, 102 (ET: 120).

654. See Bremond, 103 (ET: 121).

necessarily grave) committed by one of the brethren, in addition to a very severe penance imposed on the one guilty.[655]

2) {The} extraordinary chapter of faults: when a fault came to his attention, Abbot de Rancé would immediately summon the entire community to chapter and denounce and penance the culprit in their presence. (This was done at Gethsemani by Dom Benedict[656] in the best Trappist tradition.) Once, when a retired abbot living at La Trappe had refused to let a monk light his way up the stairs with a candle, de Rancé proclaimed him in front of all, including the novices, and gave him a tongue-lashing for not accepting the favor.[657] (Note this principle—a good one—that monks should accept acts of kindness, and that de Rancé insisted on it.)

3) Note: humiliations outside of chapter were systematically encouraged and fostered at La Trappe. Abbot de Rancé would interrupt the reading in refectory to denounce the monks for "eating with too much avidity."[658] He would send a monk to eat among the pigs if his table manners were not good. (Dom Benedict of Gethsemani once slapped a priest who was preparing to say Mass, as a humiliation—presumably to help him say Mass with more fervor.)

With all due respect for the great work done by the reformer of La Trappe, we must admit that his idea of the chapter of faults,

---

655. See Bremond, 102–103 (ET: 121).

656. The reference is to Dom Benedict Berger, second abbot of Gethsemani (1860–1889), whom Merton described as "an abbot whose deliberate policy was to insult and humiliate his monks at every turn" (Thomas Merton, *The Waters of Siloe* [New York: Harcourt, Brace, 1949], 134); "In this powerful and unbending character there was a kind of thirst for humiliations; the ideal of De Rancé was his element. He would have reveled in the chapter of faults in the golden days of La Grande Trappe. That was what sanctity meant to Father Benedict Berger: the ability to receive outrageous insults, to be cursed, reviled, slapped in the face, spat upon, without twitching an eyebrow. That was his formula for his own sanctification, and that was to be his formula for the sanctification of others when he became abbot of Gethsemani" (*Waters of Siloe*, 129).

657. See Bremond, 103–104 (ET: 122).

658. Bremond, 104 (ET: 123).

though well meant, has had a bad effect. Admittedly, some of the stories told about him are exaggerated, but the above were related by his admirers.[659] It is no longer thought healthy to make use of exaggerated and artificial humiliations. Humiliation is no longer sought, so to speak, for its own sake, as a value in itself. We ought to remember, though, that the Trappist tradition is for the chapter of faults to be tough. *In receiving* proclamations that seem to us to be unjust or harsh or otherwise out of order, we should remember the tradition of fortitude and humility that belongs to our Order. But *in making proclamations*, a person would be very wrong to base himself on the precedent of La Trappe and argue that people ought to be treated harshly, for their own good. The duty of judging how tough to be on monks proclaimed in chapter belongs to the presiding superior. The duty of the one proclaiming is to be as simple and charitable as possible. *At the other extreme*, most other orders and congregations have dropped the chapter of faults altogether or at least have suppressed the practice of proclamations. Dom Delatte says, "Too easily a system of police surveillance sets itself up. How easy it is for petty jealousies, rivalries, vengeances and reprisals to mask under the regular proclamation! Doubtless, if the monks are all perfect, there is no danger—but then there is no need of the chapter of faults either."[660]

The chapter of faults today: this is a difficult and important topic. The observance of the chapter of faults must be properly understood to be properly used. Very often it is not properly understood, either by individuals or by communities. When the chapter of faults is wrongly used, it can do much harm. Often the harm done by a bad proclamation is much greater than the good that might have been done if the proclamation had been well made. Why is this? because the matters for which we make

659. Bremond relies on Pierre Le Nain's laudatory biography of Rancé (Paris: 1715); he himself hardly qualifies as an admirer.

660. Paul Delatte, osb, *Commentaire sur le Règle de Saint Benoît*, 2nd ed. (Paris: Plon-Nourrit/G. Oudin, 1913), 341, quoted in Schmitz, cols. 486–87, translated by Merton; a somewhat different version of the passage is found in McCann's translation, 300.

proclamations are generally external points of observance which involve no sin. But the one making a bad proclamation may be sinning against charity or justice and actively harming his brother's soul. Proclamations are sometimes greater faults than the faults proclaimed. Even when a bad proclamation is well taken (and therefore is turned to a good purpose by the one who receives it), it is a bad example and leads others to follow suit. A custom of making bad, uncharitable or exaggerated proclamations can easily creep in, and this does great harm to regularity, because it brings the *Rule* into disrepute. It is better to make no proclamations at all than to make bad ones. But at the same time it is often quite difficult to make good proclamations. It takes a great deal of thought, care, self-control, humility, to make good proclamations. Since we have an obligation to conduct the chapter of faults and to use it as a living and purposeful observance, not just a dead letter, we therefore have the obligation to learn how to make proclamations properly. Here, as everywhere, one learns by experience. But the trouble is that in this case we learn by practicing *on other people*, and this requires a spirit of discretion. Hence, as a starting point, we can take two principles as obvious beyond question, and try to remember them throughout:

a) *Charity always comes first.* I am supposed to be *helping* my brother. Hence I should always try to be as charitable as possible, not in the sense of being accommodating or flattering, but in the sense of avoiding all unkindness or harshness.

b) It is always better to say too little than to say too much. This flows from the above. In order to safeguard charity, in stating the fault it is better to "sin" by defect than by excess (the word sin is not meant seriously here, at least in the case of defect). It is better to state the fault in general and neutral terms, even if that means it will only be understood in a general way, than to state many details which will tend to make the proclamation too aggressive or even exaggerated.

Wrong ideas of the chapter of faults: the chapter of faults is not a court of law in which malefactors are brought in, convicted and punished. The proclaimer should not take upon himself the role of a judge or a policeman. There is a danger of doing this unconsciously when one imagines himself the divinely appointed custodian of regularity, dealing with a "tepid religious." As soon as one takes this attitude toward a fault he disqualifies himself immediately. *He no longer has the right to proclaim.* He is passing an implied judgement already, and simply seeking to have the offender punished. One only has the right to proclaim when he keeps himself on the same footing as the offender, realizing that *"in multis offendimus omnes."*[661] Others make the mistake of treating the chapter of faults as a kind of *recreation*. They get a kick out of making funny proclamations, and use proclamations as a means of teasing or kidding others in the presence of the community, or else to show off their own wit. They enjoy the element of excitement in catching others before being "caught" by them. It becomes a kind of game. It is one thing to be pleasant and kind in proclamations, and quite another to exploit the humor of the situation in such a way that others are hurt and humiliated by it. A childish attitude creeps in when proclamations are treated as a game. Those who take unconscious pleasure in "scoring" off others soon get into a very bitter game in which there is no longer a desire to play but a real need to hurt and to get even. Even when we are making our proclamation humorous in order to take out the sting, we must reflect that perhaps the humor will strike the one proclaimed in a different way, and may hurt him though our intention was to help him. It is true that laughter relieves the unpleasant tension of the chapter of faults, but the one proclaimed may well imagine himself laughed *at* rather than laughed *with*, and may resent it. {In} conclusion, even with the best intentions, it is better not to inject wit into proclamations. A straight, simple, unvarnished and kind statement of the fact is the only satisfactory proclamation.

There are some who mistakenly take the chapter as a place of *legislation and debate*, a place where customs and observances

---

661. "We all offend in many things" (James 3:2).

can be judged, interpreted and revised. They make proclamations which *call into question certain interpretations* of the *Rule* and observance. For instance, a father does something which is neither forbidden nor prescribed, but it seems to me to be contrary to the spirit of the *Rule*. I proclaim him in order to get the superior to forbid him this thing. Then my interpretation acquires the force of law. Is this the right thing to do? Is it not better to question the superior about it in private, and if there is nothing prescribed, to leave the question open? Why should each one try to impose his own views on everybody else, when there are already so many prescriptions in the book of *Usages*? We should never proclaim merely because someone interprets the *Rule* differently from ourselves, if there is room for a difference of opinion. My brother has a right to his opinion as much as I have a right to my own. Proclamations are to be based solely on black-and-white prescriptions in the *Rule* and *Usages*, or decisions of the superior, not on opinions, likes, dislikes or private interpretations.

Others take it upon themselves to make *analytical proclamations*. They think they have to proclaim in such a way that they bring to light hidden and undesirable motives in the one proclaimed. Such proclamations are made in such a way that emphasis is thrown on possible moral weaknesses or defects in the spirit of regularity. These proclamations are phrased in such a way that a simple action is heavily interpreted and slanted. Attention is drawn not to the act itself but to a supposed moral or spiritual defect which underlies it. This may be done with a good intention; one thinks he wants to help his brother become aware of an interior fault or deficiency. The trouble is that a proclaimer is in no position to do this, and a proclamation made in such a way will probably do more harm than good, even if the moral defect is really present. Most times the proclaimer is not able to judge correctly in any case. One who proclaims is not called upon to offer spiritual direction or psychotherapy to the one proclaimed. He is simply asked to point out an *external irregularity*, which the superior will then correct as he sees fit. It is certainly true that the chapter of faults brings out things which reveal a real lack of regularity and spirituality, even real moral faults in the one proclaimed. But then the duty of correcting these things falls upon the superior. If you think the superior has not understood the full meaning of your proclamation, and if you believe seriously that there is something wrong with the one proclaimed which the superior has not understood, you can make the matter known in private to the superior, and leave him to deal with the interior problem of the one proclaimed.

Still others treat the chapter of faults as a *mere formality*. It is wrong and harmful to regard the chapter of faults as a dead letter. The chapter is not useless in itself, and even though abuses may creep in, and proclamations may have been made badly, that is no reason for giving up the struggle and dismissing the whole thing as a farce. It is clear that the chapter of faults can serve as a very good way of keeping regularity and order in the community, and though this is purely external, it is by no means a mere formality. Regularity and order are important, and make a serious contribution to the peace of the community and to the contemplative life of the monks. But the function of the chapter of faults is not merely external. It is an ascetic exercise, and ascetic exercises are not to be despised and dismissed as foolish. A monk who cannot accept correction and put proclamations to good use cannot be a real monk. He should be able to practice the simple, elementary social virtues required of him in this exercise. To do away with the chapter of faults would deprive him of valuable opportunities. However it is a mistake to go to the other extreme and to imagine that the chapter of faults *by itself* can take care of all the problems of the community and prevent it from going downhill. The chapter of faults alone is of little value. It stands or falls with the general spirit of the community. The spirit of the community does not depend so much on the chapter of faults as the chapter of faults depends on the spirit of the community. The mere fact that a lot of proclamations are made and penances given will not guarantee that there is a good and regular community, unless the proclamations are *wise and well-made*, and the penances *effective* and *well-received*. But in a community with a defective or warped spirit, these things will certainly not be realized. The proclamations will not be well made or well received. When the community is good, the chapter of faults may help to keep it good and to make it better in certain accidentals. But if a community is bad, the chapter of faults will not suffice to reform it, because the chapter of faults will reflect the general level of the community, and indeed the worst will come out in chapter.

The purpose of the chapter of faults: the chapter of faults has two purposes: (a) to preserve regularity and order—an *exterior* function; (b) to provide an ascetic exercise for the monks—an *interior* and personal function; this ascetic exercise is twofold: on the part of the one *proclaiming* himself or another and on the part of the one *proclaimed*.

a) *The preservation of regularity and order*: here we must be careful. The rule is not an end in itself, but a means to an end. Hence the function of the chapter of faults is not the mere preservation of regularity for regularity's sake, but regularity for the sake of peace and the life of prayer, regularity for the common good, for the common purpose which has brought us all together to the monastery. But the purpose that has brought us to the monastery is *charity*. We have come here to love God and one another. Hence, if we see the rule as a means to living united in love and peace, we see it correctly. The idea of *charity*, unity and peace must be uppermost in the chapter of faults, both in its external and internal aspects. If we keep charity first and foremost in our minds, we will not go astray. It is an act of charity to the whole community to correct abuses and disturbances which upset the common life of prayer, labor, poverty, silence, etc. It is certainly not charity to merely tolerate abuses and errors and wrong interpretations of the *Rule*. Nor is it charity to permit new customs to creep in without justification when the old have worked well and still serve their purpose.

What is meant by regularity? Regularity is the faithful and prudent observance of laws and customs which have been officially adopted by the community; regularity is genuine when the observance is carried out in such a way as *to manifest and bring to life* in the community what is best and most vital in the monastic traditions. Hence, to preserve regularity is not merely to preserve the exterior observances, but to keep the observance functioning well, for the good of the community and of the monks. It follows from this that we proclaim only *real irregularities*. The following are not real irregularities: (a) a single slip in the rubrics, or usages; (b) an exception that may have been permitted by a superior on one or two occasions; (c) an exception which may have been taken by the subject on his own responsibility *on one occasion*, with subjectively good reasons. (Note: when many exceptions creep in perhaps without good reason, if they become habitual, one should consult the superior to find out if they were permitted. If he permits them and they still seem likely to lead to an abuse, take them up at regular visitation.) More examples of acts that are *not* real irregularities: (d) a single fault of weakness or inadvertence; (e) actions that are not forbidden by any rule or custom, but which merely seem to imply a false interpretation of the *Rule*; perhaps this may be a matter of opinion (see above); (f) it is customary not to proclaim a novice or young monk for faults committed in carrying out some function (v.g. servant of the church) when it is his *first appointment* to the function; obviously one can easily be confused and forget in such a case.

What are irregularities? Irregularities vary in importance. The most important are violations of the *Constitutions*. However, the legislation of the *Constitutions* is so framed that it seldom points directly at the actions of the individual. The *Constitutions* are directed to communities and superiors, and violations of the *Constitutions* are likely to be taken up more in the regular visitation, or in consultation with superiors. *The Rule* obviously is the great norm for "regularity." However, we must distinguish between the ascetic counsels of the *Rule* directed to the individual and regarding *interior* faults, and *exterior* faults against the *Rule*. {For} example, we would not proclaim a brother for "lacking humility," but we would proclaim him for arguing with the one in charge of the work and insisting on his own way. In such a case we would simply state the fact, and not attach any moral qualification to it, such as "disobedience" or "pride" (possible exceptions {would be} anger, laziness, dissipation). Matter for proclamations from the *Rule* {include}: contending with the abbot or other superiors (c. 3); manifesting anger or impatience (c. 4); murmuring, detraction (c. 4); excessive speaking, speaking without permission, etc.; lack of promptitude or zeal in carrying out commands (c. 5); dissipation in talk or signs (c. 6); particular friendship; complaining or refusing to accept something inferior, v.g. a less good tool at work, etc. (c. 7); notable singularity (c. 7); excessive laughter (c. 7); lack of modesty (c. 7); careless or slovenly use of monastic property (c. 32); proprietorship (independent use of common property—appropriation of common property) (c. 33); lack of attention to {the} needs of others (v.g. in {the} refectory) (c. 38); lateness or irregular attendance at common exercises, especially {the} office ({c.} 43); failure to make reparation for faults (c. 46); irregularity or lack of zeal in work (c. 48); levity or noisiness in church, etc. (c. 52); talking to or associating with guests (c. 53); violation of enclosure (c. 66); disputes and fighting (c. 69, 70); failure to be docile in relations with brethren (c. 71–72) (v.g. {a} case of one who would be arrogant or imperious or too demanding). These are some examples of the "regularity" which the chapter of faults preserves: prompt and punctual obedience, attendance at community exercises, silence, work, kind and charitable relations with brethren, poverty, modesty. In general, these are *important*, and the chapter of faults should pay special attention to these things. But irregularities in such matters do not necessarily arise every day, though in a big community one might expect to find many such.

The Usages are the main source of material for proclamations:

a) They contain further details on the above matters from the *Rule*. The *Usages* interpret and apply the *Rule* in our Cistercian life today. (Note that at the moment the *Usages* are *being revised*.[662])

662. The revision of the *Usages* was commissioned at the General Chapter of 1958 but the completed text was not published until 1964, and then only in a mimeographed version because of anticipated changes due to the Second Vatican Council, still in session: *Usages of the Cistercian Monks of the Strict Observance*

b) The *Usages* also prescribe many ceremonies and other actions. Proclamations on these matters may be said to be more or less routine proclamations; they form the usual substance of the chapter of faults. {For} example, READ *Usages* 104,[663] on the different kinds of *bows* in choir. The *manner* of making the bow is often deficient. The bow at the *Gloria Patri* is often truncated. {The} bow before turning {one's} back on {the} high altar {is} sometimes omitted. The proper bows at the presbytery step, etc., etc. {are often deficient}. Here we have examples of small, routine matters of observance which nevertheless are to be practiced with loving attention because of the dignity and order which they give to the divine service. *These may be very small things, but they are nevertheless important* and their importance must not be neglected. Often the fervor and genuine spirit of a religious and of a community can be connected with these things, and *attention to them is a real help*. It is not just mere formalism. It is a great and harmful mistake to simply dismiss all these things with a wave of the hand and pay no attention to them at all, or to slight these little observances. Contempt for them would certainly not be the work of grace and would not help anyone to adapt himself happily in the monastery. A novice who could not learn to perform these things well, but would treat them as ridiculous, would soon lose his vocation. They do in fact have quite a lot to do with our monastic spirit. *They are acts of obedience and acts of worship*, and by expressing certain spiritual acts, they can help us to elicit these acts interiorly. But of course a chance failure to make a bow properly is not to be interpreted harshly.

(Monte Cistello [Rome]: [Cistercian Generalate], 1964); for details, see Augusta Tescari, OCSO, Marie-Gérard Dubois, OCSO and Maria Paola Santachiara, OCSO, eds., *The Cistercian Order of the Strict Observance in the Twentieth Century*, 2 vols. (Rome: Cistercian Order of the Strict Observance, 2008), 1.263-64.

663. *Regulations*, 50–51; the chapter distinguishes the different types of bows and specifies when they are to be used: the profound bow, "made by bowing with the hands crossed on the knees"; the moderate, which "consists in a moderately profound inclination of the head, and a sufficiently pronounced bending of the shoulders"; and the slight, a "bowing of the head."

Making and Taking Proclamations: we shall now consider the actual making and taking of proclamations, more from the *interior* point of view—as an ascetic exercise for both the proclaimer and the proclaimed. What has been said so far treats of the *objective* character of the proclamation and how the chapter should be taken in its essence. Here we deal with the *subjective* dispositions of the ones involved, and the practical details of their conduct. In general all who take part in the chapter of faults should do so in a spirit of *faith*. This implies the perspectives we have outlined, not making trifles into great irregularities, and not treating offenders as criminals. When the chapter is abused, the spirit of faith declines and it becomes a futile formality, or worse. But with the spirit of faith, and in the presence of God, we stand a better chance of seeing things in their right perspectives. We will try to make proclamations that will really help our brother, and really help the community, and we will accept proclamations as expressions of the will of God, even though they may be off the beam in some cases.

The Ceremonies: the *Usages* begin, exceptionally, with a paragraph on the dispositions of those participating in the chapter. (I do not refer to the small print, which also stresses the importance of supernatural motives and zeal for the chapter. One gets the impression that the fathers of the Order are afraid the practice might die out.) N. 342 of the *Usages* reads: "The brethren should only proclaim one another in a spirit of charity and zeal for the glory of God; they should be faithful to this practice"[664] (commentary {on this will come} later). N. 339 {indicates that} chapters of faults may be held on any day except Sundays, holydays and feasts of MM.[665] (This does not exclude the Sunday chapter for brothers, which is traditional in the Order.) Then the different groups who participate are outlined: oblates, novices, non-stabiliated professed, professed of the community.

Accusing oneself: those who have to accuse themselves *prostrate at their place*. Do not prostrate if you have no fault on your

---

664. *Regulations*, 165, which reads: "they ought to be . . ."
665. I.e., of two Masses (*Regulations*, 163).

mind. Prostrate for faults committed only in the last week or so, or since the last chapter of faults if there was not one in the last week. Do not prostrate for faults that have already been taken care of in the external forum, v.g. for which you have already been penanced by the Fr. Master, or for which you have been corrected by a superior. {The} meaning of the full prostration {is that} it is an expression of sorrow and humility. We should not prostrate merely as a formality. If you are not sorry for your fault, why prostrate? The act of prostration indicates not just "I am eligible for a proclamation," but more than that: it shows that one has committed a fault which he *regrets and which he wishes to expiate.* This implies *faith in the value of the chapter of faults.* He who sincerely accuses himself of and regrets his faults against the *Rule* is pardoned and will receive no other punishment in time or eternity once his penance has been performed. We should prostrate with this deep faith in our hearts, anxious to get rid of any monastic faults in this way, rather than waiting for purgatory to do so! The value of the chapter does not consist in the external routine but in the interior dispositions which it supposes. The superior says, *Quid dicitis?* Those who prostrate reply *Mea culpa.* This too should have meaning. If we don't mean that we are sorry for our faults, why do we say this? *Surgite in nomine Domini*: even here, in the "name of the Lord" {means} we don't just get up, but arise in the name of the Lord, that is, as an act of faith, with the sense that He is present. The superior calls out the ones whose accusations of themselves he wishes to hear. They come out singly, and accuse themselves with a profound bow before and after. If only one prostrates, he comes out immediately, without being called. Note: the only other occasion when one would come out without being called would be: (a) if one had committed a fault that scandalized the novices, or members of another group, in which case one would prostrate with them and come out immediately on rising, even though others were waiting to be called; {the} same {is the case} for the brothers' chapter; (b) sometimes a professed comes out in this way in the professed chapter. In either case one should not come out spontaneously unless the fault is *externally serious*, and really gave notable scandal. One would expect such a fault to be at least apparently a sin of some sort, for instance a violent public expression of anger or disobedience, or some negligence that disturbed the whole community.

N. 340: the *Usages* give some details:

a) "We acknowledge our external faults, without making known the secret motives which prompted them."[666] Even in accusing ourselves, we stick to external acts; {there should be} no mention of motives. N.B. there is a practice here of objecting when someone says, "I forgot . . . such and such a thing" as if this were an expression of a secret motive or, in other cases, as if this were an excuse. This is hair-splitting. What the rule means is that one should not mention purely interior faults (distractions in choir) or any interior *hidden* motive. But when the motive is apparent in the fault itself, then one can hardly avoid mentioning it—for instance, manifesting anger, or impatience, or unchari-tableness, etc. One should not say, "I wanted to help so and so, and therefore I did this . . ." "I thought the superior said so and so, therefore I . . ." Explanations, whether they extenuate or aggravate, are out of place. They open the door to excuses and self-justification. *Note*: there is a style of self-accusation which is in reality accusation of another. This may be well-meant, but it smacks of a certain hypocrisy: v.g. "I caused Frater so and so to fly into a rage . . ." Here one is publicly performing an act of virtue (self-accusation) which turns out to be a slam at a brother's fault, and not a self-accusation at all. However, objectively, in such a situation, it is simplest just to accuse oneself *and the brother*, and to try to formulate the proclamation so that the blame is evenly distributed: "I was careless and Frater X became impatient, . . ." etc.

b) "Vague and general accusations are forbidden."[667] How vague? Here are examples of vague proclamations: "I accuse

666. *Regulations*, 164.
667. *Regulations*, 164.

myself of my irregularities"; "I accuse myself of lack of zeal";
". . . of laziness." To make the proclamation *specific* one has only
to enter into the precise species of the irregularity: which rule
did I break? silence? enclosure? attendance at choir? When was
I lazy? at work? oversleeping in the dormitory? sleeping in community exercises? In order to make the proclamation quite specific and give it the full effect, a circumstance may be added:
where, when, etc. Then the accusation will have its full effect; the
fault will be recognized by those who were disedified; reparation
will be made; all will be well.

c) Further points: after the accusation, {make} another bow,
then receive humbly the reprimand of the superior. Usually it is
not really a "reprimand." But remember that perhaps it ought to
be one, that if we have not deserved to be reprimanded for this
fault, there are others more serious for which we have not been
reprimanded. Hence accept it humbly and with a certain degree
of seriousness. The acceptance of the remarks of the superior on
our fault should not be merely a matter of routine. We should
pay attention because what is said is after all an indication of
God's will in our regard. The penance {follows}: the faults for
which we are proclaimed in chapter are "penal," which means
that though they are not in themselves moral faults or sins, they
do oblige us at least to perform the penance assigned for violation
of them. A *strong reprimand* (341[668]) {requires that} if the superior
makes a strong reprimand, or himself accuses the one proclaimed
of a different fault, the one proclaimed should *prostrate again*.

Accusing Others: the sections on proclaiming others in the
chapter are preceded in the *Usages* with a paragraph in small print,
which means that this is an important and difficult matter for
which special ascetic advice is considered necessary. The following
main points are made: (a) the *matter* of proclamations (cf. 344[669]);
(b) the supernatural spirit with which proclamations should be

668. *Regulations*, 164.
669. *Regulations*, 166.

made: {in} faith and charity; (c) the importance of making proclamations: "They hold, together with silence, the first rank among
the observances of our Order [a characteristically *Trappist* obser-
vance]. They are the support, both indispensable and infallible, of
all regular observance."[670] One wonders if this paragraph will not
need to be revised and stated with greater reserve in the new edition of the *Usages*: infallible??? In any case, without haggling over
words, it is clearly the intention of the fathers of the Order that
proclamations be made generously and constantly. We should not
shirk this obligation. But above all let us understand it properly.
What is said in the small print is said more succinctly and definitely
in n. 342 (quoted above page {228}). The simplest procedure here
is to comment in detail on the words of the *Usages*:

N. 342:[671] the brethren should only proclaim one another *in
a spirit of charity and zeal for the glory of God. Spirit of charity*: this
covers a lot of ground and merits much thought. A proclaimer
should never make a proclamation unless he has previously
considered, in his heart, and sincerely, *whether his motives are really
charitable*. Hence, unless one is sure that he is habitually charitable
in this matter, spur-of-the-moment proclamations may prove to
be uncharitable or rash, and ought perhaps to be avoided until
one is grounded in charity and can make them well, spontaneously. The spirit of charity *excludes* all proclamations of the following type: harsh, bitter accusations; exaggerated wording;
language that implies contempt or destructive criticism of {a}
brother; excessive eagerness to punish a brother; desire to get
even with a brother. Before we make a proclamation we should
examine ourselves to see if there is any resentment or grudge
present, and if there is, then we should be slow to make a proclamation unless it is really necessary to do so, and then we should
make it with care. It is necessary to be careful of unconscious

---

670. *Regulations*, 165, which reads: "Considered as a monastic observance,
they hold . . . among those of . . ." (this is the material in small print mentioned
above).

671. *Regulations*, 165.

grudges and resentments, even when our conscious motives are very noble. {We should} take our motives with {a} grain of salt. Mockery is also excluded by charity. We must not make proclamations that heap unnecessary ridicule upon a brother. {We should be} careful not to raise a laugh at the expense of {a} brother—though sometimes there will be laughter. Pride in the proclamation is a great obstacle to charity: that is, if the proclamation implicitly or explicitly states a judgement of the brother as an inferior person. Many other examples could be quoted. We should reflect on these things carefully for ourselves. In order to *cultivate charity in proclamations*, reflect on the ways to *help* our brother by proclamation. This means trying to put ourselves in his place. This is a very important element in proclamations, and because few understand it the chapter of faults loses its good effect and often does harm.

How to *put yourself in your brother's place*:

1) There is a difference between putting my brother *in my place* and putting *myself in his place*. I may see a fault committed, and think: if I did that, it would be pride. But this is *projection* of ourselves into the brother, usually done unconsciously. It is putting *myself* in his place. It is in reality condemning in him what I hate in myself, and what I hate in myself may not even be present in him. Projection is one of the worst sources of uncharitableness in a monastery. Actually it implies lack of love, and complete self-centeredness. The brother does not really exist as a separate person. I simply see in him a projection of myself, and I pin onto him what I dislike in myself. What I love in "me" I keep to myself. What I hate in "me" I foist onto others. This is a very bad situation which, at least, represents great emotional immaturity.

2) Putting myself in {my} brother's place requires *empathy*. Empathy is a kind of insight by which I am able to see and experience things from the point of view of another, by which I experience things *his* way rather than just my own way: for example, a mother who "understands" the fear her child has of the dark by experiencing it in herself, though she herself does not fear the dark. Hence

she doesn't just dismiss it as silly, but intuitively finds a way to explain that there is nothing to be afraid of, an explanation that will fit the experience of the child and calm its fears.

3) *Empathy* requires maturity and especially *maturity of love*. A selfish and insecure person cannot feel empathy. He is too concerned with himself, his own feelings, emotions, passions, needs, fears, etc. He cannot get "out of himself" long enough to appreciate the sentiments and needs of another. *Empathy* presupposes *sympathy*. It is a deeper form of sympathy, and yet it is less tinged with emotion, more "detached" and able to do more for the other. Both empathy and sympathy imply love. Begin by cultivating *sympathy* ("feeling with"—compassion): this is very important. I cannot correct others or even begin to help them in any way if I feel no compassion for them in their predicament. Where there is lack of sympathy, a hard and resistant attitude which simply judges, condemns and rejects, the other feels it immediately and reacts with hostility or fear. Such motives prompting a proclamation or punishment have no good effect. If you want to make useful proclamations you must *constantly and habitually* cultivate sympathy and compassion for your brother. If we feel genuinely sorry for him in his faults, as if they were our own faults, we will instinctively realize the right way to approach them. In correcting the fault of another, after preparing the way by putting myself in his place, understanding his fault, and seeing that perhaps he is, from his viewpoint, largely inculpable, I will frame my proclamation accordingly. (N.B. it is not possible to read the minds of others, and there may be all kinds of doubts as to what his motives really are. We can only interpret them by exterior signs. But we must be careful to interpret those signs in a charitable way, and soft-pedal everything that prompts a harsh judgement.)

Making the proclamation: in formulating the words of the proclamation, we might ask ourselves: "How would I like this proclamation *if I were the one being proclaimed and he were the one proclaiming*?" This is nothing but a simple and obvious application of the golden rule, but it is so obvious that most people overlook it. This simple rule would in itself be sufficient to guarantee that most proclamations would be fair, just, discreet and charitable. {With respect to} *other accidentals*, one should also take care of important features like tone of voice; control of haste and impatience—in getting your man on the floor, avoid {any} appearance of eagerness; try to control nervousness and harshness, which are in fact expressions of aggressive feeling and perhaps of hostility. When this has been taken care of, "zeal for the glory of God" will receive its due share automatically. God cannot be glorified by harsh, unjust, prejudiced and silly proclamations. On the contrary, when the chapter of faults is carried on in a childish and petty spirit of resentment and zeal for punishment, it brings the whole monastic state and the monastic community into disrepute. Hence zeal for the glory of God must not be interpreted as zeal to punish offenders and to "avenge the *Rule*." This may be very laudable in theory but those who in practice see things in such a light are very easily *misled by passion masking as zeal*. History has taught us the immense harm done by bigotry and prejudice, in which hatred and hostility masking as virtue and zeal have led to persecutions, all carried out in "good faith" for the "glory of God." When such bigotry and prejudice appear in a monastery, very great harm is done to souls. It is one of the serious dangers that must always be guarded against in the chapter of faults. In practice, zeal for the glory of God in the chapter of faults should take the form of empathy, described above, and of *humility, meekness, kindness* and *truth*. These are the things that edify in a well-made proclamation. In our proclamations a large place should be given to plain common sense and ordinary politeness. These natural qualities have a very important connection with the supernatural spirit which gives "glory to God." Pig-headed obtuseness and vindictiveness can never give glory to God.

Taking proclamations: for many monks it is easier to take proclamations than to make them. That is because the process is *passive*—one does not have to do or say anything. That makes it at once more difficult and more easy. If one has a strong reaction and has nothing to "do" but remain silent and humble, he may feel his reaction very strongly and for a long time. It may be painful. But if one does not react very strongly, then the "acceptance" of proclamations has no special difficulty and is indeed very easy. But the fact that one reacts should not be taken as a bad sign or as a humiliation, for that makes the reaction worse. There is nothing wrong with being sensitive at the beginning of one's religious life. And certain temperaments will remain sensitive *all* their life. The important thing is not to be dominated by, or guided by, one's hurt feelings. A few points on the acceptance of proclamations:

1. *Before the chapter of faults*: we might as well enter the chapter of faults prepared for a proclamation. But how? We should not come with fear, already cringing and dreading a humiliation. A person who lets himself be overcome by such fears will suffer unnecessarily from the chapter. Indeed, exaggerated fear is unworthy. One should not allow himself to dread such a small thing as a proclamation, and one should overcome these feelings—that will be possible in the average person at least. We may be sensitive. All right, accept the fact and shrug it off. It is of no special importance. We must not take ourselves too seriously. If we feel proclamations, there is no harm in that; perhaps it is a good thing. It gives us a chance to humble ourselves. We are not stolid and insensible. However, the best thing is to tell ourselves *not to exaggerate* and not to make a mountain out of a molehill. Before the chapter of faults we should reflect:

a) that we have committed faults for which we deserve to be proclaimed, and we may not recognize the fact. Someone else may have noticed something in us that we have not realized.

b) It is a *good thing* to be proclaimed. We should value proclamations. They are a help to us, or can be a help to us. If we are so lacking in balance and virtue that they become a stumbling block, then we must work to overcome this.

c) We should be prepared to *make an effort* to bear the proclamation gracefully and well, and to accept it fully in our hearts—again, taking our sensitivity with a grain of salt, and *not exaggerating* this "trial." It may be ridiculously small.

This "prevision" of the chapter will help us to be prepared, and if we are generously resolved to make a serious effort to take proclamations well, this will be a real help. Whether we are proclaimed or not, we will already have acted virtuously and given glory to God.

2. *When proclaimed*: while waiting in line for the proclamation, forget yourself and the one proclaiming you. Listen to the others' proclamations. Listen without showing any special reaction. Don't look around at the proclaimer. Listen attentively and humbly, and suppress various manifestations of surprise, indignation, disagreement, scorn, contempt, mockery, etc. Be sure to listen to the penance. Sometimes people are so concerned with the proclamation that they are too dazed to hear what the superior is telling them to do about it. Do not occupy your mind with the justice or injustice of the proclamation, or its exactitude. Be prepared to understand and forgive exaggerations, failures of charity, inexactitude. For this two things are necessary:

(1) Recognize that you are prejudiced in your own favor. Do not waste time trying to justify yourself in your own eyes. Completely disregard that aspect of the thing. Simply resolve to do the right thing, whether you have violated the rule or not. You will keep it in the future—that is all.

(2) Unite yourself with Christ Our Lord and practice His meekness, humility and charity.

(3) Again, recognizing that proclamations are a good thing, be grateful for the good that has been done you. Thank God for it, and pray for the one who proclaimed you.

3. *After the proclamation*: be careful not to show resentment or to make any signs whatever about the proclamation to anyone. When the chapter is over, the fact of the proclamation should be forgotten. One should simply remember to keep the rule concerning which one was proclaimed. If there is some question or problem raised by the proclamation, see your Father Master about it, or if professed, see the prior or Rev. Father, not in order to justify yourself, but in order to clarify the point and find out exactly

what is God's will in your regard. (This case may arise when there are varying interpretations of the rule. Sometimes a proclaimer does not interpret the rule in the same way as the superior, and this has not been made clear. The superior has accepted the proclamation without realizing that it raises a conflict with his own orders or policies. One should then check with him and find out what he wants done in this particular case. {For} example, one is proclaimed for working overtime, when one has a job, given by obedience, which cannot be done without overtime work.) It is good, in the novitiate, to ask the full meaning of proclamations and find out exactly what one has done wrong, in order to understand the rule better and know what to do in order to improve one's regularity. Do not try, directly or indirectly, to excuse or justify yourself in the eyes of superiors, but if there is something that needs to be said about your conduct, make it known with simplicity, and rest with the judgement of the superior on the point. Remember to carry out your penance with a modicum of seriousness. A penance is not just a formality. It makes reparation for your fault, such as it was. If there was any moral failure, your penance takes care entirely of any debt that remains in the eyes of God. That is one fault you will never again have to worry about, in this life or in purgatory.

Conclusion: the chapter of faults is an important and characteristic observance in our Order. Let us not be discontent with it and try to change it or get rid of it. That would reflect a bad spirit. It is true that sometimes proclamations are silly, immature, uncharitable and even unjust. It is true that the spirit promoted by the chapter is sometimes wanting in common sense and breadth of vision. But let us make it a school of religious maturity, patience, broad-mindedness. If we insist that everybody else should be broad-minded and use common sense, let us be the first to practice these things, especially when we ourselves are proclaimed. Sometimes those who have the most arguments against the chapter of faults as an institution are simply the ones who have no idea how to profit by it, who get upset and rattled by the mere thought of proclamations, who are hypersensitive and complain of everything. Sometimes these are the least charitable people in the community, {who} backbite everyone else, criticize everyone, and do not accept any criticism themselves. When they argue that the chapter of faults is silly or antiquated, they are simply trying to get around an observance that requires more generosity and effort than they are willing to give to it. Let us accept the chapter of faults as it is, with its imperfections, and be content. The Lord will bless this attitude, much more than the attitude of those who are so eager to change everything that soon they will leave nothing whatever of the Cistercian life intact.

Public Penances (see *Usages*, nn. 351–363[672])

The section of the *Usages* on penances, particularly public ones, naturally follows the part about the chapter of faults. Here again, we come upon a typically and characteristically *Trappist* observance, which perhaps is not too well understood at the present time. Is it possible that today we do not really see the meaning and the value of these public penances? In any case, they were certainly strongly emphasized by Abbot de Rancé, who attached a very great importance to them. It is possible that the early Trappist reformers exaggerated the importance of public penances, but it is equally likely that we underestimate them.

In general, what are these public penances? Essentially they are *punishments* inflicted by the community, or rather by the superior in the name of the community, upon an individual member who has violated the rules and has in some way disturbed the order and regularity of the common life. A punishment is supposed to have a threefold effect:

a) to correct the erring brother: this is the principal purpose. Our punishments are all primarily *medicinal*.

b) to make reparation for a fault, especially a public fault. {It is} a restoration of balance and of order, which has been violated.

672. *Regulations*, 168–73.

c) to remind the other members of the community of the meaning and seriousness of faults, of their obligations to the community and to God.

Hence public penances are supposed, ideally, to fit in seriously to our life of charity, our life of seeking God, our life of regular discipline and self-denial, and our life of worship. *They are the acts of a monk seeking sanctity.* They are acts of worship. It is very important to see penances as acts of love and of worship. Otherwise they will turn out to be meaningless. But this requires *faith* and *attention.* The efficacy of penances in bringing about the three effects described above depends *almost entirely on how the community looks at them.* If the punishments are regarded as an annoying or ridiculous formality, imposed by a misguided superior or prescribed by an outmoded rule, they will certainly not correct the one who is penanced. He will simply regard himself as the victim of a tiresome custom. Generally, religious have a little more respect for the rule than this, and do not regard penances, at least consciously, as absurd formalities. (But in effect, if they are not treated with the proper good sense, they do become mere annoying formalities.) A purely subjective view of penances is sometimes taken: a penance is just a challenge to the individual, to see if he can "take it." This is a limited and misleading view. It throws the emphasis on the individual's attitude. It can induce a certain spirit of self-conscious bravado. In that case it is not medicinal. But even more, it lacks the power to be an act of worship and a help to the community. When one has received a penance, he must regard it as an act of worship of God, like praying or going to communion; and he should perform his penance for the glory of God, out of love for God, in the same way as he sings the office or assists at Mass. This act of worship has its own special character, because it is a *penance.* It is an act of reparation for a *fault.* Hence it implies the sincere, interior acknowledgement that I am at fault, a sense that I have, however slightly, displeased God, or at least have failed in an opportunity to please Him. And then I will be eager to please Him and honor Him by this act of public penance and reparation. But this means *seeing objectively* whatever there is in the penitential act that can give glory to God, or serve as an expression of worship. In our consideration of public penances, then, we shall try to some extent, if possible, to find out what there is about these various prescribed acts which has an element of worship. It would be very desirable to see penances performed in a spirit of mature, serious simplicity as acts of worship. At the present time one feels that they are simply done with the maximum possible good humor. One tries to be a good sport about the whole thing; that is all. Well, that is something, but it isn't very much. {A} further note on penances in general: simplicity and common sense are above all necessary if penances are not to look stupid, and thus lose their effect. One should not be tragic about public penances, or abnormally austere in one's approach, taking a kind of undertaker's attitude toward them. It takes virtue to perform public penances simply, humbly and seriously as acts of worship. (Note: human respect sometimes interferes with this, especially in the case of novices who want to be sure that they are liked and accepted. In that case, one gives in easily to those who try misguidedly to make light of the whole thing, and to turn the penance into an occasion for laughter.)

What are the public penances? Basically, the penances are all traced back to St. Benedict's penal code, on excommunication, etc. We might briefly look over those chapters of the *Rule* (23–30, 43–46) here:

23[673] takes up the general matter of *excommunication*. In general {this is} the *most serious punishment*—exclusion from the life of the Church, from fraternal encouragement, from the grace of Christ, {being} turned over to the devil. Every penance, no matter how slight, even kneeling at the door of the church, is related basically to this idea of exclusion, excommunication. That is, of course, that the symbolism of the act, by which one is set apart, suggests the ultimate end of the process. The one kneeling at the door of the church is not of course really excluded, but that is

673. See McCann, 72.

what the act signifies, in a very small way. St. Benedict here retails what he considers serious faults, mostly boiling down to pride and contumacious disobedience in some form or other. Serious penances are for those who *despise* the order and peace of regular life and prefer their own will (*contemptor regulae*[674]). (Hence the meaning of public penances; normally they are supposed to make us reflect on how much we lose by following our own will and cutting ourselves off from the common charity which is the life of Christ in the community.)

24–25[675] {describe the} varying degrees of excommunication: (a) light: eats apart from the others; does not intone psalms or read lessons in choir; (b) grave: complete exclusion from the community.

26–27[676] {describe} how others are to act towards the excommunicated.

28[677] {asks} what about those who do not correct themselves?

29[678] {asks} what about those who run away from the monastery? They have three chances to return.

30[679] {considers} the punishment of children.

43[680] {describes} small penances for minor irregularities, especially *lateness* in choir or refectory: *stand apart to be seen by all*: this is considered sufficient; taking {one's} meal alone, without wine. (Read chapter 43.[681])

---

674. "one contemptuous toward the *Rule*" (McCann, 72, which reads: "*sanctae regulae et praeceptis seniorum suorum contemptor*" ["contemptuous toward the holy rule and the directives of his superiors"]).

675. See McCann, 72, 74.

676. See McCann, 74, 76.

677. See McCann, 78.

678. See McCann, 78, 80.

679. See McCann, 80.

680. See McCann, 102, 104.

681. "At the hour of the divine office, as soon as the signal has been heard, having put away whatever had been in their hands, they should hasten with the greatest speed, yet with seriousness, so that misbehavior may not find an incitement. Nothing, then, should be put before the work of God. If anyone should arrive at the nightly vigils after the *Gloria* of Psalm 94, which we wish to be said

44:[682] here we come to precisely the *public penances* by which the excommunicated satisfy for their faults. They must not only be excommunicated, but they must perform certain *symbolic actions* which indicate interior conversion. Penance is not a mere exterior formality. The external gestures must indicate an inner change of heart. They must in all truth declare that the person is sorry for what he has done and will not do it again:

a) prostrating at the door of the church after office, so that the brethren step over the body as they go out; this is part of the fact of his exclusion from the common prayer;

---

on this account slowly and pensively throughout, let him not stand in his place in choir, but stand last of all or in a place apart which the abbot has designated for such negligent persons, so that they may be seen by him and by all, until he does penance by making public satisfaction once the work of God is ended. We have determined that they should stand in the last place or a place set apart so that, having been seen by all, they may amend out of shame itself. For if they remained outside the oratory, perhaps there might be someone who would either go back to bed and sleep, or at least sit down by himself outside, and waste time in tales, and an opportunity would be given to the evil one; but let them come inside so that they do not lose the whole time of prayer, and may use well the time that is left. During the day hours, let one who has not arrived at the work of God until after the verse and the *Gloria* of the first psalm which is recited after the verse, stand in the last place according to the rule which we have set forth above. Let him not presume to join the choir of those chanting until he has made satisfaction, unless perhaps the abbot by his pardon allows him to do so. Nevertheless such a culprit should make satisfaction. For a meal, anyone who has not arrived before the verse, so that all might say the verse and pray together and approach the table at the same time—who has through his own negligence or fault not arrived, should be corrected for this up to a second time. If he still has not reformed, let him not be allowed to take his place at the common table, but set apart from the company of all, let him eat alone, and have his portion of wine taken away until he has made satisfaction and mended his ways. Likewise one who is not present for the verse which is said after the meal should endure the same punishment. And let no one presume to take any food or drink before the assigned hour, or after it. But if anything is offered to someone by a superior and he refuses to accept it, at the time when he desires what he had earlier refused, or anything else, let him receive nothing at all, until there has been a suitable amendment."

682. See McCann, 104, 106.

b) asking the prayers of all in the oratory, when rejoining the community;

c) even when he returns to choir he still does not intone anything until special permission is given;

d) prostrating at the end of the office, at his place.

The penitential acts are all first of all *very visible*. They single the person out, in a humiliating position and posture. They are continued from day to day until the abbot says "enough."

45[683] {considers} smaller faults—the "little satisfaction." *Read* chapter 45.[684] Note corporal punishment for children, for mistakes in {the} office, {a mark of} St. Benedict's extraordinary zeal for perfection in the recitation of the office.

Read our *Usages* (nn. 136–142[685]):

136[686] {considers the} satisfaction made by {the} bell-ringer who gets {the} community up late; satisfaction for lateness at office (note {the} positions to take at {the} presbytery step when there are several); what to do when one arrives with {the} abbot, late for office; what {to do} when arriving late for office but not before {the} *Gloria Patri* of {the} first psalm; how much of the office to make up; when {the} office is not made up. *When no satisfaction is* made for lateness: those who have said or served a community Mass; {those who} have been praying beside {the} dead or receiving guests; weekly officers after returning from their function; one who has left choir with permission; those who arrive after the *Kyrie* of {the} office, unless another office or Mass follows immediately (n.b. not walking in choir when all are on

---

683. See McCann, 106.

684. "If anyone, while reciting a psalm, responsory, antiphon or reading, makes a mistake, unless he has humbly made satisfaction there in front of all, let him undergo a greater punishment, for he is certainly one who was unwilling to correct in humility what he had committed in negligence. However, for such a fault let children receive a beating."

685. *Regulations*, 63–65: "Of Satisfaction in Choir" (Bk. III, c. 8).

686. *Regulations*, 63.

misericords); lateness for compline; how long to remain?[687] Who does *not* make the satisfaction:[688] servant of {the} refectory on days of two meals; those who have been in adoration before {the} Blessed Sacrament during supper or compline reading.

140 {discusses the} little satisfaction for mistakes in office (note: not when the "mistake is general"[689] {and} not during {the} office of {the} dead).

141 {considers the} mistakes by those who have to intone in office—"considerable noise"[690] (*quid*?[691]). (Note: be careful if you have something else to sing right away; prostrate only after you have done all you have to do here and now.)

Penances in the strict sense (*Usages*, 351-363[692]): here we deal with the sections of the *Usages* which contain the usual public and private penances. Many of these are in fact no longer performed, or performed very seldom:

351:[693] Penance for {a} grave fault, corresponds to St. Benedict's excommunication. This is simply the application of chapter 44 of the *Rule*[694] to our present form of life. It contains all the essential elements, and adds one thing which was not in St. Benedict, namely the discipline in chapter.

352[695] is also an application of St. Benedict: meals apart from {the} community (excommunication *a mensa*[696]); no intoning in choir (excommunication *in oratorio*[697]); prostrations or bows at

687. "until the end of the Credo" (*Regulations*, 64 [n. 139]).

688. See *Regulations*, 64 (n. 139).

689. *Regulations*, 65.

690. *Regulations*, 65.

691. "What?"

692. *Regulations*, 168–73: "Of Penances" (Bk. VIII, c. 6).

693. *Regulations*, 168–69.

694. See McCann, 104, 106.

695. *Regulations*, 169.

696. "from the table" (*Rule*, c. 44; McCann, 104).

697. "in the oratory" (*Rule*, c. 44; McCann, 104, which reads: "*ab oratorio*" ["from the oratory"]).

{the} presbytery step at the end of each hour of the office, from the *Kyrie* to the end.

353[698] {considers} *penances in the refectory*: here we come to the more familiar penances. {The} general norms {specify that these are} never performed on Sundays or holydays, or at supper, or in the presence of seculars; holydays includes feasts of two Masses on which there is no work in the morning, and of course feasts of sermon. {They are} not {undertaken} in {the} presence of seculars unless by special order. Seculars sometimes are invited to eat in {the} refectory of {the} community, {though} rarely here. The text of the *Usages* as we have it at present is a little confusing because 354,[699] dealing with penances at {the} door of {the} refectory, breaks the sequence that has been begun in 353:

a) *For any penance in {the} refectory*, first remain standing before your place, uncovered with hands "in sleeves" (i.e. up) until {the} signal to begin the meal, that is, the knock at which all uncover their bread and spread {the} napkin. Here we have an exception: since kissing {the} feet of {the} community is delayed here until the coffee pourers etc. are out of the way, we do not stand in front of our place; one can either sit down or wait elsewhere.

b) *Praying before {the} superiors' table* (seldom done today {as there is} no room); see 355:[700] {with} head uncovered, go and kneel when {the} signal {is} given to begin {the} meal, say {the} prayer, bow and depart.

c) *Reading something aloud*: sometimes it is a useful medicinal penance to give someone a few sentences of {the} *Rule* to read, which apply to his needs or case. This is done, kneeling, bareheaded, in {the} "middle of {the} refectory,"[701] that is, in the center, near the reader's pulpit. It is done after the end of the Latin reading of scripture. {The} same {is done} for {an} accusation in {the} refectory.

698. *Regulations*, 169–70.
699. *Regulations*, 170.
700. *Regulations*, 170.
701. *Regulations*, 170.

{d)} *Eating on the floor* (356):[702] when {the} signal is given to begin {the} meal, take {a} knife, fork, etc., bread and {a} jug of water, and go to get {the} little stool kept under {the} reader's pulpit usually; place yourself with {your} back to {the} center pillar of {the} refectory, opposite {the} reader's stand, spread {the} napkin on {your} knees. {The} servant of {the} refectory should get your portions. When finished, return to {your} place, put your dishes at {your} place, then go back to {the} center of {the} refectory and remain standing to {the} end of {the} meal.

{e)} *Begging a portion* (357):[703] this is no longer done here for the time being, because of the problem of space. (Note that all these penances lose their true character in a cramped and crowded space where everyone is milling around in confusion. To be properly understood and to have their genuine effect, one must visualize them in a broad open refectory where there are tables around the walls, but a wide space in the middle, such as in our French monasteries.)

(a) On entering {the} refectory, make {a} sign to {the} servant to get you an empty bowl.

(b) At {the} signal for {the} meal to begin, go to {the} superior, bow, kneel, and present {the} basin with both hands; rise; bow; do {the} same to {the} prior {and} subprior, then down the side on which the penitent himself sits, asking from two at a time; kneel before each pair. Those who give a "contribution" rise, give one spoonful, bow and sit down.

(c) After getting a full portion, go to {the} superior, kneel and hold up the bowl, and wait for his signal to retire. Then dig in heartily—you probably have a much bigger portion than anybody else by this time.

(d) Two religious ought not to perform this penance on the same day, say the *Usages*,[704] prudently concerned for the diet of the other brethren.

702. *Regulations*, 170–71.
703. *Regulations*, 171.
704. *Regulations*, 171 (n. 357).

{f)} *Kissing the feet* (358):[705] normally, begin with {the} abbot, then {the} prior, then the religious on your own side, afterwards the other side. Here there are modifications—we don't do all in one day. Consult {the} prior or Father Master about {the} arrangement. {It} may be done in two or four shifts. Here {the} work blouse is worn for penances that involve kneeling in {the} refectory, because of {the} danger of soiling {the} robe in spilt food, etc. Kiss *one foot* only. Those whose feet are being kissed {should} remember to cover the proper foot with {the} cloak or cowl and extend it somewhat. {Make a} profound bow to {the} abbot before and after, {and a} moderate bow to each pair of religious *after*. "This penance should not be performed by several on the same day" (*Usages*[706]).

Prostrating at {the} door of {the} church or refectory (354, 359):[707] we seldom prostrate at {the} door of {the} refectory, sometimes at {the} door of {the} church. Get to {the} door of {the} church or refectory a minute or so ahead of {the} community, prostrate full-length with feet turned toward the side where {the} community arrives. Obviously only one can do this at a time.

Kneeling at {the} door of {the} church or refectory: our most common penance has practically lost its penitential character because {it is} so familiar. Remember one point: open the door of the church when you arrive there before kneeling down; kneel uncovered; do not sing the psalm with the community; rise when {the} community has passed; enter to make a visit, normally, if at church.

Prostrating at conventual Mass (360):[708] leave your stall toward {the} end of {the} preface so as to prostrate full-length at {the} presbytery step at {the} *Sanctus*; remain until the *Per Omnia*,[709]

---

705. *Regulations*, 171–72.

706. *Regulations*, 172.

707. *Regulations*, 170, 172.

708. *Regulations*, 172.

709. i.e. *"per omnia saecula saeculorum"* ("through all the ages of ages"), which concludes the minor elevation immediately before the recitation of the *Pater Noster*.

which precedes the *Pater*; thus you prostrate during the Canon; when returning, you must go on the misericords at {the} first stall, and remain so until after the *Pax Domini*.[710]

Deprivation of the habit: one may be in secular clothes, or oblate habit; in either case, one is always in {the} last place and intones or reads nothing.

Discipline (see nn. 362, 363):[711] the discipline is the only instrument of penance whose use is formally prescribed in our Order. We make less use of penitential instruments than most other Orders. Our manual labor and the poverty of our life should normally compensate for this. However as there is a growing spirit of comfort and a dwindling of the sense of mortification, we should not neglect to take this penance generously. It is the one occasion when we actually punish our flesh. There is no harm in doing so. It would be foolish and exaggerated to see in the moderate and simple exercise a "perversion" or an ascetic deviation. It is just a matter of course in a life that is supposed to have a character of penance about it. The fact that it is formal and so to speak cold-blooded should be no objection. One should preserve a sense of the objective, quasi-liturgical nature of the penance on Friday mornings. Admittedly it is a medieval practice, remote from the early spirit of the liturgy. It has its limitations, but there is no point in making a big fuss over them. The simplest and most obvious thing to do is to take the penance as it is given to us, in a spirit of humility, mortification and faith. We should remember the Lord cruelly scourged for our sins, particularly our sins of the flesh. We should take the discipline generously in a spirit of reparation, and with the desire to earn grace for sinners as well as for ourselves who are not in a state of sin but are nevertheless "sinners" like everyone else, and capable of every excess. It will do us no harm to remember these things. There is also an element of obedience, and no small element. We take the discipline only when told, and only as long as the rest of the community, starting and

---

710. "Peace of the Lord".
711. *Regulations*, 173.

stopping at the signal of the superior. Some might find it easy to do much "better" when acting spontaneously on their own. But actually the element of obedience is also important. If the penance is distasteful because of its formality and artificiality, well, take that too. We owe it to the Lord to submit to the rule and common practice in this matter, in the right spirit. For the discipline in chapter, {see} 363: it is taken kneeling, surrounded by religious with their backs turned to the penitent; he stops at {the} signal of {the} superior. Remember that in the old days it was common for a religious to be scourged by one of the brethren as an ordinary penance at the chapter of faults. Note that the Order prescribes this penance for a choir religious who detracts against a superior in a grave matter. It is also prescribed for a fugitive or apostate when received back into the community (see n. 47[712]).

Thus we conclude the section on public penances. They should remind us that faults against the rules were taken very seriously by the early fathers of the Order. But then, too, real faults were meant, not just slips and oversights in fulfilling small observances. But the spirit engendered by the fact that these penances exist and some are onerous, should remind us not to take rules lightly and not to disregard the importance of religious observance. However one must observe the rules in a spirit of sanity and love, not out of fear of being caught and punished.

End of Part One—Notes on Observances.

---

712. *Regulations*, 25–26.

APPENDIX {1}

Contents of

SPIRITUAL DIRECTION IN THE MONASTIC SETTING

SPIRITUAL DIRECTION
IN THE MONASTIC SETTING

Preface

Though not absolutely essential for monastic perfection, spiritual direction, in the sense of continuous guidance by a director who knows one's soul, is of the greatest value to the monk. Direction in the sense of occasional guidance, and aid in the solution of notable problems, is not as hard to find as continuous guidance. Even then it is not always easy, even in a monastery, to find a director who really helps one's soul to make progress, whether occasionally or continuously.

However we must not expect too much from spiritual direction. Some who may imagine it is hard for them to find a director, are in reality not looking for a director but for a miracle worker who will solve all their difficulties as if by magic. This is not what direction is really supposed to do. Nor is the director one who takes our dreams and wishes, and turns them into reality ("the will of God") by giving them his approval. The director is not there to assume responsibilities which we ourselves ought to shoulder. He is not supposed to live our lives for us, or to make our decisions for us. He is there to tell us that our decisions seem to him to be prudent, and seem to him to be in accordance with the will of God, or not. But it is up to us to lead our own lives and make our own decisions—in the light of docility and prudence, and paying attention to all warnings against the danger of self-will or of capriciousness.

The monk has to achieve the delicate balance between docility and spiritual freedom. He must at the same time distrust his own judgement and realize how easily he can be blinded by his passions, and yet he must take responsibility for his own life and make his own decisions—with the proper precautions, and with due humility.

These notes, taken in large part from the article on *Direction* in the *Dictionnaire de Spiritualité*,[713] aim mostly at giving the traditional monastic concept of spiritual direction, with a few practical observations that might be of use to the modern monastic reader. They do not pretend to cover the whole subject exhaustively, or to treat modern controversies and solutions, for instance the modern consensus of theologians that one should never make a vow of obedience to the spiritual director. This we thoroughly endorse, without however discussing it in these pages.

> Choir Novitiate
> Abbey of Gethsemani, 1958

---

713. "Direction Spirituelle," *DS* 3, cols. 1002–1214; Merton draws particularly on Irénée Hausherr, "II. Chez les Chrétiens Orientaux," cols. 1008–1061.

SPIRITUAL DIRECTION IN THE MONASTIC SETTING

I. *The Life-giving Action of Jesus in His Church*

Our Lord Jesus Christ came to give us a share in His own divine life. He does so by sending into our hearts the Holy Spirit. The Spirit descends upon us at baptism, making us sons of God in Christ, and we are pleasing to the Father, united to Him in His beloved Son. Living in us by His Spirit, Jesus communicates Himself to us and moves us with the sentiments and thoughts of His own Sacred Heart, transforming us in His likeness. *All the actions of Jesus in the Church* tend to diffuse and increase His life in souls, to bring them more and more under the sway of His life-giving action, through His Spirit in their hearts.

The Sacraments are the chief channels of this life-giving action, for they are instruments for the direct communication of grace. But Jesus also and very especially acts on us through *men*, through our superiors and directors (not to mention parents). It is necessary that He act on us from without through men. If left to purely interior inspirations, we can lose the sense of the difference between nature and grace. If left to our nature, we remain infinitely far from Him. He is good; we have fallen away from His goodness. He is light, we darkness. He is life; we tend daily to death. He is justice; we work iniquity. He is holiness; we are plunged in sin. There is no possibility of finding Him if we are left to ourselves and to our own blindness. We can never be quite sure that even the best of inspirations is really a good one for us. How can we be sure whether or not it is God's will? whether it comes

255

from Him, from our nature, or from our enemy? As we are members of the Mystical Body of Christ, we must trust God to sanctify us through the Church and through His visible representatives in the Church, as well as by the direct action of grace within our souls. If our interior inspirations are confirmed by a wise spiritual father, then we can follow them in all security.

We must therefore *desire Christ to act* on us through our superiors and directors. If our spiritual fathers merely flatter our whims, the action of the Holy Spirit is defeated. *Abbatem sibi praeesse desiderant*[714]—our abbot is not only a benevolent friend but an authority who binds and looses. Only when we are stripped of our own desires by the action of Christ through those who guide us do we have true security and true illumination.

Authority of Jesus in His Church: the divine authority in the Church embraces man in his entirety, in all the reaches of his life, private and social. It plunges even into the depths of conscience, imposing *obligations* which cannot be evaded. It is not a mere external disciplinary power; *it demands internal assent*, and it can *impose obligations which we are no longer free to disavow*. It can overrule our most intimate choices, and exact submission. But this submission is to God, not to man, and its purpose is our liberation from slavery, not our subjection to an arbitrary human authority. The purpose of all this authority is still only to liberate our souls and bring them fully into the light of the truth which "makes us free."[715] We must see, by faith, that submission to the representatives of Christ is necessary if we are to be truly free. Submission is not the end in view—it does not in itself constitute perfection. But it opens the way for us to attain perfection by the free gift of ourselves in love.

Corresponding to this power given by God to His human representatives, is a *divine guarantee* that their God-given authority is not a mere arbitrary exercise of human power. "I am with you all days, even to the consummation of the world" (Matt.

714. "They desire an abbot to be over them" (*Rule*, c. 5 [McCann, 34]).
715. See Jn. 8:32.

28:20). The authority of the Church is the divine authority of Christ the Lord visibly exercised in the society of His saints.

Enlightenment of Souls by Jesus in His Church: the Lord enlightens us not merely by teaching us truths and doctrines, through the medium of His representatives. The Holy Spirit lives and works in the Church in two ways:

a) Exteriorly, guiding and directing human instruments who will teach and preach the word of God, who will govern and guide souls. This exterior action is twofold:

1) Ministerial (hierarchical)—through popes, bishops, priests, and all those ordained to carry out special functions for the Church and for souls.

2) Charismatic—independent of the established hierarchical framework, "free gifts" of the Spirit to preach and spread the word can be and are given to ministers of the word, and also to others who have no official ministerial function. It is sometimes said that *all* have some charism, some special gift to reach particular souls with whom they come into contact.

The exterior action of the enlightening Spirit is seen in preaching, writing, liturgy, sacred art, etc. The liturgy is the "embodiment of the faith of the Church in visible acts"[716] and rites, in "visible mysteries,"[717] and taking part in these we are moved by the Spirit to show forth the truth and light of God even though we may not be fully conscious of the fact. So, too, in preaching, writing and in works of art. *Prayer*: by our prayer and penance

716. Source unidentified.

717. "*Praesta nobis, quaesumus, omnipotens et misericors Deus: ut, quae visibilibus mysteriis sumenda percepimus, invisibili consequamur effectu*" (postcommunion: Ascension [*Missale Romanum*, 396; *Missale Cisterciense*, 257]) ("Grant us, we beseech Thee, O almighty and merciful Lord, that what we have received as our nourishment in visible Mysteries we may enjoy in its invisible effect": translation as found in Thomas Merton, *Bread in the Wilderness* [New York: New Directions, 1953], 79, in which the third chapter of Part III, "*Sacramenta Scripturarum*," is entitled "Visible Mysteries" [79–84], and is focused on participation in the Eucharist as a sharing in the redemptive death and resurrection of Christ).

we become instruments of the Holy Spirit, secretly bringing light to other souls. Here the exterior and interior action of the Spirit are united.

b) *Interiorly*—by all manner of graces and gifts, the Holy Spirit *heals* souls in sin and makes them capable of receiving light; *purifies* them to receive it; *sanctifies* them to be able to bear it; *instructs* them that they may grow in it; *enkindles* them to love the light; *moves* them to put into effect His teaching, and this in turn makes them more capable of seeing and loving the light; *strengthens* them to grow in capacity for holy action and contemplation; *anoints* them with divine graces that prepare them for transformation; *transforms* and *unites* them in the light.

II. *The Spiritual Director*

A most important agent in this work of the Holy Spirit is the *spiritual Father*, in whom are united the *power of authority*, the *life-giving action* of the priesthood, through ministry of the sacraments, and the *sanctifying* and *teaching* power of the Spirit. As a manifestation of His great love and care for souls, God united all these great powers and special gifts in the instrument He chooses to cooperate with the action of His Divine Spirit in their souls. In the spiritual Father, God gently adapts and tempers and adjusts all His divine power, light, love and wisdom to the needs and circumstances of the struggling soul, here and now. *The spiritual Father is in the place of God to the soul*, not only in the sense that God will support his decisions, but also in the sense that *all the power and love, light and truth, wisdom and sanctity of God are concentrated in him, to guide this soul who has come to him*. He is the instrument God has chosen in His all-wise Providence to lead this Christian to sanctity, to *filter through* to him the divine light, power and wisdom.

Providence selects instruments purposely with this in view, in order that God may reach the Christian in a way that will not trouble, frighten or disconcert him, but will effectively and as it were naturally, sweetly and easily guide him on towards sanctity. The director is, in all truth, Jesus for the faithful Christian. He is a "sacrament," a "mystery" of Christ, in whom the Holy Spirit acts in a very special manner for our sanctification.

Who Is the Director? What has been said above is *only completely true if there exists in the fullest sense a bond of spiritual sonship between the subject and the director*, that is to say, if the director is really the *Father*, spiritual and charismatic, of the subject. It often happens that a Christian cannot find a director, or that having a director, the charismatic bond does not exist except in an inchoate manner, as the director lacks the capacity to understand and penetrate the soul, and his decisions do not have the proper effect, do not inspire confidence, do not bring light. Or it happens that between the soul, moved too much by emotion, and the director, likewise dominated by emotion, there grows up a *false bond*, which is not spiritual and charismatic, and which ends with bad effects in the soul due to *mis-direction*.

How does it happen that God allows a Christian to be without a director, or to find a bad director? These are questions which it is hard to answer and perhaps presumptuous to raise. It is sufficient to say that God allows causes to be followed by their normal effects. Where there is a warped or false spirit, where directors themselves are malformed, He allows them to communicate some of their malformation to others. But He also protects the Christian against bad directors, and the reason why one cannot find a director is perhaps that for many reasons one is better off without one, or that one does not deserve to find one (motives for seeking one being wrong—vanity, self-seeking, overestimation of one's own "spirituality" and importance, etc.).

The Canonical Director: the spiritual director, in the ordinary sense of the word, is a guide, usually a priest, who is freely chosen by the Christian, after adequate prayer and consultation, one who then undertakes, on the basis of a quasi-contract, the guidance of his soul.

But in certain situations, for instance the novitiate, the Church places a Father and director over the novice. Here the director is chosen *by the Church*, for special reasons. The Father Master is the ordinary director of the novices. He has a *juridical* function to help them decide their vocation, to select or reject them, to form them for their religious life. But he alone has a *charismatic* function, in regard to their decision to stay or to leave, and in regard to their formation.

In this situation, the Holy Spirit guarantees special lights and graces to the Father Master, in order that he may fulfill his functions. It is explicitly stated (Canon 561, n. 1[718]) that the Master of Novices *alone* has the right and the obligation to watch over the formation of the novices and to run the novitiate, so that no one else is allowed in any way to interfere with him in these functions, except superiors and visitors. The novices therefore do not, as do the professed, choose for themselves a director among the confessors. The only way in which a confessor enters authoritatively into the question of a novice's vocation is when there is something in the internal forum that makes the novice unfit for profession—then {the} confessor can and must tell him to leave. But the confessor is not the director or spiritual Father of the novice, although of course in practice he may exercise a great influence for good and contribute to the novice's spiritual formation (which he will do best if he works along the same lines as the Father Master).

The Father Master's position is not only juridical but also *charismatic.* He has a very special grace of state to select vocations and to guide them towards the goal of their vocation. This is true even when perhaps there may be a lack of spontaneous human sympathy between the novice and the Father Master. Even though

---

718. See John A. Abbo and Jerome D. Hannan, *The Sacred Canons: A Concise Presentation of the Current Disciplinary Norms of the Church,* 2 vols. (St. Louis: Herder, 1952), 1:579: "The master of novices alone possesses the right and duty of supervising the training of the novices and only to him belongs the government of the novitiate; no one else, therefore, may intervene in these matters, under any pretext whatsoever, except those superiors to whom the constitutions entrust this authority and except the visitators. In reference, however, to matters affecting the house at large, the master of novices and the novices are subject to the governing authority of the local superior." For the original Latin see *Codex Iuris Canonici,* ed. Petrus Cardinal Gaspari (Westminster, MD: Newman Press, 1957), 190.

the Father Master may not perfectly understand the novice in everything, he will have grace to guide and form him. But of course here, too, there can be limitations!

This does not mean that every utterance of the Father Master is a divine oracle. He is human and fallible, and can easily be mistaken. But no one can sin in accepting what he says formally and officially in regard to vocation and the necessary steps to be taken to fulfill it. His decision represents the will of God. We shall see that the important thing is *lively faith* which can see God in and through the Father Master—this faith can overcome all obstacles, and it wins special graces for the Father, as well as for the novice.

III. *The Spiritual Father in Monastic Tradition*

1. *The place of the spiritual Father is of primary importance in the monastic life*. The first words of St. Benedict's *Rule* affirm this: *Ausculta, o fili . . . admonitionem pii Patris libenter excipe et efficaciter comple.*[719] The whole monastic life is contained in this idea of the son carrying out the teaching of the Father.

2. *Difference between "Father" and "Director"*: a director simply guides and teaches, according to an externally codified rule, or according to spiritual books. A *spiritual Father* (this concept evolved in the days of purely oral tradition) *embodies in his life and teaching* the whole doctrine of Jesus and the Apostles, as handed down by the monastic "Fathers." He *communicates this life* by teaching, precept and example to his disciples and *sons*. As the heavenly Father makes us His sons by communicating to us, with His Son, the sanctifying Spirit, so the spiritual Father makes us sons of God by imparting to us his own life, his own spirit—this is a real participation in the divine paternity (cf. Ephesians 3:14-15). This paternity is not without suffering, participation in the cross. It is not by any means the fruit of a mere natural zeal to teach others or to form them, nor of a human need to be

---

719. "Listen, O son . . . freely receive the instruction of a caring father and carry it out effectively" (McCann, 6).

supported and completed by disciples. *It is the fruit of a divine mission and its efficacy is entirely from the cross of Christ.* If Matthew 23:9 says no man is to be called "Father," it is because God alone is the true Father, *and one is our master, Christ*—the Master both of the Father and of the novice—Christ Who teaches us and forms us both by our interrelationship in His Church (cf. *Rule* of St. Benedict, c. 2,[720] and James 1:17).

3. *He must be "Spiritual"*: the term *spiritual director* means "director in spiritual things." The term *spiritual Father* throws emphasis, first of all, on the fact that the Father is himself spiritual—like Christ and in Christ he is "life-giving Spirit."[721] He engenders a higher spiritual life in his children and of course inspires and commands a more spiritual mode of action. The term "comparing spiritual things with spiritual"[722] applies here not to the fact that the son judges the counsels and teaching of the Father in the light of other spiritual teachings, but that he accepts spiritually, in the spirit of sonship, the teachings of the Father, responding to them with the piety and love of a son, thus understanding and apprehending their meaning in his heart. (Spiritual how? not by *nature* nor by *gnosis*—but by charity and the Holy Spirit and by a more perfect union with the "Spirit of the Church"—having the mind and heart and outlook of Christ. But he can retain human imperfections and limitations. The highest proof of perfect charity—of "spirituality"—for the early Church was martyrdom, in which charity overcame the weakness of the flesh. "Greater love hath no man than this, than that he lay down his life for his friends."[723] The "spirituality" of the Father is then measured by sacrifice—the Gospel of the Good Shepherd.[724])

---

720. See McCann, 16: the abbot is called father as a representative of Christ.
721. 1 Cor. 15:45.
722. 1 Cor. 2:13.
723. Jn. 15:13.
724. Jn. 10:1-21.

4. *The Qualities and Functions of the Spiritual Father*:

a) *Love* unto complete self-sacrifice—as above. The job itself brings with it sacrifice.

b) Prayer: he must be a man of prayer, close to God; he must pray to be full of the Holy Spirit, since he is a mediator and channel of grace; he must plunge entirely into the life of God, in order to transmit the divine life to others; he cannot sacrifice his life of prayer (except *ad tempus*[725]) for his sons, as all depends on this; his prayer is the *chief source of light and grace*—he is above all an *intercessor* rather than an adviser. This comes in a lower place! All the effectiveness of spiritual direction is attributed in oriental tradition to the prayer of the Father. For our part we also include the prayer of the spiritual son.

c) *Discernment* of spirits: direction, insofar as it implies guidance and teaching, is above all the practice of this discernment. It means the ability to identify and show up hidden motives—to detect the action of the devil or of nature under the surface of what appears to be good; to find out the wrong motives, or the useless motives, that mask as indifferent or good tendencies; to find out where the person is not being true to himself or to grace, while deceiving himself; in a word, to find out what is wrong with the mentality of the one directed, not only in formal moral faults, but above all in illusions and self-deceptions, under the guise of good. Things are not what they appear to be, and it is impossible for any individual to analyze himself and find out all that is in him. The director is there to show him his inner motives as in a mirror, so that he will come to *know himself*. The eyes of the director penetrating into the soul, are illumined with the light of Christ, to see what is according to the Spirit of God and what is contrary to it. This is a charism frequently given to directors; at least it was frequently given in ancient times. A director can rightly hope for this gift and ask for it, not for himself but for the good of the souls entrusted to him. *Note that for this penetrating*

725. "for a [limited] time".

discernment to operate, the director must be detached and supremely humble. The subject also must remain humble, docile and detached from himself. He must not try to manipulate his guide. Usually the hidden motives which activate a soul, under a mask of good, are motives which are kept hidden for a serious (though perhaps unrecognized) reason. The soul resents these motives being known, and resists their unmasking by the director. Sometimes a whole mechanism of psychological forces comes into play, to keep the director from exercising his true function. Without thinking or reasoning about it, the subject unconsciously tries to keep direction on a certain plane in which he himself appears in a good light, in which he is respected, approved, admired, and praised, in which his requests are all granted and his desires are never thwarted. Often the subject unconsciously does all that he can to avoid letting anyone see into the depths of his soul, because he does not want to see into those depths himself. He is afraid of them; they are too much for him to face. If the depths are to be laid open, he wants to have the satisfaction of making the revelation *himself*, and showing how much he knows himself. Then he will be praised and approved for his cleverness and spiritual insight. But to have the depths penetrated against his will, by another—this is something he resents and resists with all his power. Sometimes, then, direction causes uneasiness and trouble. The soul thinks, "This director does not understand my problems; he upsets me. I ought to seek another director who does not trouble me and throw me into confusion." But perhaps the trouble and confusion are salutary at this point. Perhaps it is necessary for the soul to be disconcerted, humbled, brought to recognize its own defects, and its own fundamental insincerity! It is useless to run to another who conveniently does not see, and who confines himself to comfortable generalities, one who never asks any sacrifice and never comes out with a "hard saying." The "opening up" of the soul is something the subject resists not only because he fears to see himself as he is, but because he fears the consequences—the efforts and sacrifices that will be unavoidable if he admits he has to change. Often a whole life is built on a foundation of sand, and the subject prefers to pretend everything is solid in order to avoid having to reconstruct everything from the ground up, on a new foundation. Direction consists not only in *showing* the weaknesses, but in imposing sacrifices that *force the issue* and make the struggle to change unavoidable. Faith in the spiritual Father means readiness to accept any sacrifice he may impose. The demands he makes are an indication of God's will for us. A most valuable attitude, this faith compensates for the lack of other virtues, and guarantees rapid progress. *It is the key to real generosity with God*—generosity which cannot be found merely by forcing ourselves to carry out self-imposed sacrifices. At the same time a director must know when and when not to open up a sensitive wound. No good can be done by unveiling depths that the subject is not capable of seeing. On the contrary this may ruin a vocation. All things have their season. A good director knows how to wait for things to come out more or less spontaneously, at the moment willed by God. Do not expect a good director to *force* you onward to sanctity by violence! Hence the next necessary gift of the spiritual Father:

d) *Patience and meekness*: patience is most necessary in the point just mentioned: when the spiritual Father sees or suspects a weakness, an illusion, and realizes that the illusion is the source of a lot of tiresome and unnecessary work for him! He is moved by natural impatience to clear the way immediately, but no, he must be willing apparently to waste time, apparently to indulge the weaknesses of the one directed, until the time comes to make these faults known. This is time especially when it is a matter of listening to a lot of nonsense which the subject thinks important, and which is simply dictated by his own self-love. He seems to be wasting his time and the director's. Yet the time is not really wasted. It is necessary to deepen the bond between the son and the Father. Also, this "nonsense" is in itself significant, and a good director will see its meaning. When the director is patient and enlightened, he sees that *everything* is significant. The meekness and kindness of the spiritual Father are not indulgence; they are *necessary for the Father to come to know the son by love—by empathy, by finding his way into the heart of the son, not with the cold light of scientific analysis, but with the humble sympathy of love that identifies itself with the sufferings of another.* This cannot be done without a real and sincere good will, and this depth of sincerity is not possible without *time.* One cannot sincerely identify himself with all the weaknesses and trouble of someone he has not yet had time to know and to understand.

e) *Firmness*: the director must balance sympathy with firmness—he must not be severe about repented faults. Sometimes the subject himself may want to concentrate on the past—but this may well be only an evasion of the present. The director's eyes are on the future, and his main task is to give the subject *strength* and *courage* to bear up in the struggle that lies ahead. The firmness of the director is, then, not firmness in defense of the rule so much as *firmness in support of the soul.* He is unyielding not so much because an abstract rule is at stake, but because of the concrete spiritual need of the soul actually present. Where there is a choice between the abstract principle and the concrete good of the soul, a true spiritual Father prefers to seek the concrete good of his son in Christ. The sabbath was made for man, not man for the sabbath. Usually he will see that to support the claims of the rule and to strengthen the soul are in fact the same thing. The rule is not for its own sake, but precisely in order to aid and form souls. Sometimes it is necessary to be very firm: St. Anthony of the desert is an example. When one monk asked him to pray for him, Anthony replied, "Neither I nor God will have pity on you if you do not get down to business seriously yourself, especially in this matter of prayer."[726] Severity should not mean *hardness* so much as *frankness* and *clarity* in making known the truth. But above all the director strives to be firm in sustaining the soul and strengthening it against discouragement.

726. *Apophthegmata*, Anthony #16 (*PG* 65, col. 80C), quoted in Hausherr, col. 1031.

IV. *The Nature and Efficacy of Spiritual Direction*

The ancient monastic concept of spiritual direction {is that} it is a *means to attain purity of heart. By the manifestation of our inmost thoughts, to a spiritual Father, we are enlightened to see the illusions and deceptions of the devil or of self-love*, and by obedience to his direction we are strengthened to overcome the assaults of the enemy. This implies a certain definite concept of what goes on in the soul. Spiritual direction is not so much the remedy against sin, as against illusions and temptations and trials. For sin, there is sacramental confession. Spiritual direction does not concern itself with past sins except indirectly—insofar as they may still have an influence in our present illusions and temptations. Direction aims at producing purity and strength that will guard against future sins and falls. As regards the past, direction shows us how to accept it wisely and humbly and use it in ordering our conduct for the future. Mental attitudes, ways of judging and deciding matters in the spiritual life, have a very potent influence on our whole life—in fact our spiritual life *depends on the way in which we think. It depends on our attitudes*, which condition our thinking from the very beginning, by giving it an orientation of their own. For instance, the monk who thinks himself very important and unusual will take himself too seriously in everything that happens to him, and will even be proud and self-important in his attempts to practice humility, in his self-accusations, in his manifestations to his director, in his idea of perfection. In such a case, the aim of direction will be to reach down and correct this fundamental attitude, from which everything else flows, and by which all the monk's thinking is vitiated.

The direction given by the spiritual Father aims, then, *not simply to correct overt acts*, to punish infractions against the rule, to warn against passion and sin, to block evil tendencies, to unmask hidden and subtle temptations, but also and above all *to correct the most fundamental attitudes of the soul* and to *change the thinking* and the very *manner of judging* on spiritual things, to give a new outlook, a "new mind" and a "new heart" in conformity with the

Mind and Heart of Jesus—the *sensus Christi*.[727] (N.B. this applies only to the extent that a change is seen to be necessary. The director does not change the soul merely for the sake of change.) A change of interior attitude is usually much more necessary, in monks, than a change of exterior life. Direction does not mean advising a lot of new and different "practices," but rather giving light on the meaning and possibilities of one's ordinary everyday life, as it now is. Here is where the spiritual paternity of the Father of souls really comes into play—in engendering a new spirit which is the Spirit of Christ Himself—removing obstacles by discretion, gaining grace by prayer, enlightening by precept and counsel, so that the Holy Spirit can take ever fuller possession of the soul!

Hence it follows that there are many *inadequate notions of spiritual direction*. All notions of direction that presuppose that the inmost soul *of the beginner* does not need to be changed in some way, is inadequate. The required inner transformation will be more or less profound, in proportion as grace has already more or less achieved mastery over the soul. But even where a person is sinless, that does not mean that he does not have to be corrected and strengthened within himself by direction—assuming that proper direction be available. (If it is not, the Holy Spirit Himself will supply.) Many good souls in the monastery vegetate and become warped through lack of deep and constructive direction that would release their inner capacity to love God. But the "director" sees they have "no sins" and while recognizing perhaps (one hopes!) the futility of their misguided attempts to advance themselves in spirituality, makes the mistake of treating them as if no advance needed to be made. In effect, these souls, while "good," are still imprisoned in their own nature and narrowed by their own petty human outlook and attitudes. Even in their sincere efforts to be "more perfect" they manage, in fact, to enmesh themselves more tightly in the net of human imperfections because of their limited outlook and faulty way of thinking. This is not their fault. It comes from lack of experience and of discre-

---

727. St. Ambrose, *In Psalmum 118 Expositio*, 11.8 (*PL* 15, col. 1351A).

tion. It is the job of the director to *liberate* these souls and set them free to follow the Holy Spirit Whom they cannot yet sufficiently recognize, and Whose action they are afraid to follow because it is unfamiliar, and does not fit the only moral standard they know—that of their own human outlook and human values. Direction will then be entirely inadequate if it is:

a) Merely *an attempt to prevent deliberate sin*. In the case of sinners, of course, direction on this point will be united to confession *as a matter of duty*. But the monastic idea of direction presupposes a soul *free from habits of sin*, at least deliberate. The occasional *acts* of sin into which a monk may fall call for direction insofar as his reaction to these falls affects his interior attitude, or insofar as his outlook makes such falls possible.

b) Merely *general discourse on the spiritual life*, an instruction given by the director, a pious meditation on the current liturgical season. Sometimes spiritual directors who are also confessors acquit themselves of the duty of direction by simply appending a few words on the Mass of the day to their exhortation in confession. This is not, strictly speaking, spiritual direction.

c) Merely *an exhortation to virtue*. Direction does not consist only in telling the subject to practice a virtue which the director sees he needs to cultivate. This of course is good and necessary, but it is not yet sufficient to make for real spiritual direction. It does not go deep enough.

d) Merely *a warning against hidden tendencies and weaknesses*, although this, too, may be obligatory and vitally important.

These concepts of direction are inadequate because such things can be done *without the manifestation of conscience* that is necessary for true direction. They can be carried out on the basis of a confession of sins (insufficient for true direction), or on the basis of the accusation of faults in the external forum, or the observation of the monk in community or at work. For real spiritual direction there must be a manifestation of one's inmost attitudes and drives—and for some characters this is difficult, because they have trained themselves not to see themselves—

they have trained themselves to say: "This is the way I ought to have acted, ergo this is the way I *have* acted." Direction in the incomplete sense is of course necessary and valuable. But it is not, properly speaking, true direction.

Such direction as the above may be given by *superiors* as such, when they have no access to the interior of the soul. It is their right and obligation to give at least this direction. The Father Master can and must give to all novices such direction as this, whether they ask it or not. It can and sometimes must be given by the confessor in the sacred tribunal. It is the *bare minimum of guidance which every soul should* receive from the ministers of the Church in order to live the life of the Church. What a tragedy it is that some souls do not even receive this minimum; and again, what a tragedy that in religion such direction is customarily regarded as amply sufficient, as fulfilling all the needs of those striving for the highest perfection, while, in fact, even this minimum is not available to many sincere souls in religious communities. Such direction as the above may be given in public, in conferences, sermons, or in formal interviews with a superior. Adequate personal and interior direction is impossible without the manifestation of soul willingly made by the subject in order to avail himself of the light of a spiritual Father.

Manifestation of soul means more than a plain confession. It is not simply the declaration of faults. It is the revelation of one's inmost tendencies. *Particularly it is the revelation of one's most characteristic tendencies with a view to guidance and support in striving for perfection.* This last distinction is of the greatest importance. Some subjects do not know how to make known the interior of their soul. Confusing direction with confession, they think they are supposed to reveal problems, temptations and sins, so that when they come to direction, if they have "no problems" they are completely at a loss. The director does not want to know just your sins, or your faults, or your temptations, or your problems. He wants above all to know *you*. It is much more important for him to get a good idea of your character and of your most individual and personal attitudes, than it is for him to know your faults and your sins. These may, in fact, be separated from what is most personal in your soul, or, in any case, it is quite likely that the knowledge of them does not necessarily lead to the knowledge of who you really are. To know sins is not to know a person. To know a problem is closer to knowing a character, but in any case what really matters is the knowledge of the person, in his individuality, how he thinks, how he judges, how he reacts, what he loves, what he hates, what he *thinks* he loves and hates (when in fact his inmost motives may be different from what he thinks).

However, there are other *faults to avoid in penetrating the inner depths of the soul*:

a) Knowledge of a person is something more than classification of a person in terms of temperament, character structure, personality type, etc. Spiritual direction is not a mere *classification* of characters.

b) Direction is something quite apart from psychotherapy or psychoanalysis. It is a good thing for the director to be acquainted with these sciences, in case of need. But he is not a psychiatrist, and it would lead to disaster if he simply tried to analyze his subject. The director is not concerned primarily with subconscious drives, still less with emotional problems that have a neurotic tendency. His relationship with the subject is quite different from the relationship of an analyst with his patient. The director should sedulously avoid "playing around" with a science which is utterly beyond his sphere and has nothing to do with his real mission. He is not concerned with neurotic drives but with normal passions, with conscious moral and ascetic activity, and with the hidden action of God's grace. He will need to recognize a neurosis when he sees one. He will need to avoid ways of acting that encourage a neurotic response in the subject. He will retain a healthy respect for the unconscious, instinctual life of the Christian whom he guides. But direction can never be psychoanalysis.

c) In order really to know a person, the director must learn to identify himself with that person's interests and inmost strivings, in order to experience in and for himself what goes on in the heart of the other. Hence direction cannot be a merely *impersonal and objective* thing, although it must always preserve an objective quality, too. But it must have something more. It cannot be cold, a mere matter of business or science. Only charity and paternal affection can give a real inner knowledge of souls. In order truly to know a person, one must love that person, one must appreciate all the good in him, even though that good be hidden. One must sympathize with his difficulties as if they were one's own. One must, moreover, see that soul through the eyes of Jesus Christ and love him with the heart of Christ. In a word, one must be a true *spiritual Father*, as well as a teacher and physician of souls. In order for this fatherhood to come into being, there must be a true harmony of wills between the Father and the son. It is not sufficient that the director on his side have a paternal affection for the subject, or that the subject feel filially disposed towards the Father. What matters most is the act by which the son places himself entirely under the guidance of the Father *by complete and confident self-manifestation* in a spirit of total trust in God, a spirit of supernatural faith and confidence in the action of the Holy Spirit through the visible representative whom Christ has sent, in the person of the spiritual Father. Let us now consider the nature of this manifestation.

V. *Openness*

It is not sufficient to have good will, trust in God, and confidence in direction and the director. *One must know how to manifest one's inner self, and be able to do so with a certain amount of freedom.* This is an art which is sometimes difficult to learn. First of all, what is to be manifested? We have seen that the Father needs to know the whole character and interior life of his spiritual son. Therefore, everything is to be manifested that gives an idea of who we are.

a) Sins: a general idea of past sins is of value, but by no means of exclusive importance. To give spiritual direction is not to rake up the coals of old fires that have gone out, or to pore over the refuse of past years. However, the important sins of one's past should be known by the director, at least in a general way, since this is necessary to estimate our character correctly. More valuable than the mere number and seriousness of these forgiven sins, is a *knowledge of the motives and attitudes by which they were accompanied, at least in a general way*. It makes a great difference if, for instance, a scrupulous soul, with a high desire for perfection, fell into many imaginary sins against purity, or if a person fell frequently out of weakness, or if one who had a deliberate disregard for the spiritual life seldom fell at all, through coldness. However, these things are not to be too thoroughly investigated. A brief indication suffices.

b) Temptations, trials, problems: *especially in their motives*, in the attitude that goes with them. It is usually better to discuss frankly the concrete situation than to treat of the case in vague general terms. This must, however, be done without offending charity.

c) The most characteristic material for direction (tradition-ally) is one's inner impulsions that go against grace or the will of God (cf. the Instruments of Good Works, nn. 50–51: *Cogitationes malas suo {cordi} advenientes mox ad Christum allidere et* seniori spirituali patefacere![728]—and the fifth degree of humility;[729] other traditional sources: St. Benedict says only evil thoughts; Cassian [*Coll.* 2] says that the fundamental test of humility is that *all actions to be performed and all one's thoughts* are submitted to the scrutiny of one's spiritual Father[730]).

d) *All the movements of our soul are matter for manifestation.* St. Basil (*Long Rules*, 26) says:

728. "At once to dash against Christ [the rock] evil thoughts arriving in one's heart and to reveal them to a spiritual director" (*Rule*, c. 3 [McCann, 28]); copy text reads "*corde*."

729. *Rule*, c. 7 (McCann, 44), which concerns revealing to the abbot all evil thoughts and secret sins; see Merton's discussion in *Rule of St. Benedict*, 190–93.

730. *Collatio* 2.10 (*PL* 49, col. 538); see Merton's discussion in *Cassian and the Fathers*, 224–25.

Every subject, if he intends to make any progress worth mentioning and to be confirmed in the mode of life that accords with the precepts of Our Lord Jesus Christ, ought not to conceal within himself *any movement of his soul*, nor yet utter any thoughtless word, but he should reveal the secrets of his heart to those of his brethren whose office it is to exercise a compassionate and sympathetic solicitude for the weak. In this way, that which is laudable will be ratified and that which is worthy of rebuke will receive the correction it deserves, and by the practice of such co-operative discipline, we shall by a gradual advance attain to perfection.[731]

Note the implications of all this:

1) The reason for making known *all* our thoughts is that we do not yet realize which are good and which are evil. It therefore makes an immense difference if we reserve to ourselves the judgement on this preliminary point, and simply submit "humbly" what we think is evil to the judgement of another. It is a more perfect and more realistic humility to realize that we may be wrong even in this judgement, that we may not know ourselves at all, and that the judgement of another may be necessary even to tell us what is right and wrong in ourselves. The resolve to accept and abide by such judgement, and to be enlightened by it in our search for God, is the basic humility that characterizes the monk's relation with his spiritual Father. It is *essential to the monastic ascesis*.

2) This revelation is not made thoughtlessly or indiscriminately, but only to the representative of God.

3) It is a revelation: that is to say, it should be *clear* and *exact* insofar as this is possible to us. This does not presuppose an ability to analyze ourselves, but rather the sincerity and simplicity to make known the movements of our soul just as we experi-

---

731. St. Basil, *Ascetical Works*, trans. Sister M. Monica Wagner, CSC, Fathers of the Church, vol. 9 (Washington: Catholic University of America Press, 1950), 288-89, which reads ". . . a mode of life . . . , ought not conceal . . ."

ence them,* so that the Father can be able to experience vicariously what we experience ourselves, so that he may "know connaturally" what is going on within us. Then he will give the decision that he would make himself in the circumstances. Thus there is a deep communion of soul between the Father and the son; the Father takes upon himself the son's difficulties and weaknesses (assumes responsibility to a great extent), and in return gives the son light, grace, strength, to discern his own movements and assume responsibility for them himself. The aim of this direction is not and cannot be merely to reduce the son to helpless and passive subjection to the Father. On the contrary, its aim is to make him mature, to help him grow and form his own judgement and his own will, guided step by step by the experience and the grace of the spiritual Father.

4) This revelation is to be supernatural (cf. the texts quoted by St. Benedict[732]). *Revela Domino viam tuam*[733]—to make known our ways, our thoughts, to the spiritual Father is to make them known to the Lord. But the Lord already knows them? Certainly. But this is an acknowledgement in practice that He really sees all; and it is an act of faith in the Church, and in God's will to work through His ministers, to expect help from God most of all through the spiritual Father whom He has given us.

*Every soul, as it really is, is interesting, lovable, important—the image of God. It is the false self that is tedious and uninteresting—saying not what we are but what we think we ought to be—no life in there—no mystery—no reality—hollow. But a real soul—real mystery—is always fascinating. The joy and consolation of seeing the real self come out. The interrelation of Father and son—mutual help and inspiration—wonder of God's action in souls.

732. *Rule*, c. 7 (McCann, 44/45): Benedict quotes Ps. 36[37]:5: "Make known thy way unto the Lord and hope in him"; Ps. 105[106]:1: "Confess to the Lord, for he is good, and his mercy endureth for ever"; Ps. 31[32]:5: "I have made known my sin to thee, and my faults I have not concealed. I said: I will be my own accuser and confess my faults to the Lord, and with that thou didst remit the guilt of my sin."

733. "Reveal your way to the Lord" (Ps. 36[37]:5).

Danger of not Manifesting One's Thoughts: the humble manifestation of one's thoughts to the spiritual Father protects us in
the most efficacious possible manner against the illusions of the
devil. Cassian (*Instituta*, 4) says, "With all his subtlety the demon
would not be able to delude or to overthrow a novice except by
prompting him to hide his thoughts either out of pride or out of
shame. Hence the Fathers say that a universal and evident sign
that a thought comes from the demon, is the fact that one blushes
to reveal it to his spiritual Father."[734] Abbot Poemen said: "No
one so much rejoices the enemy as he who refuses to manifest
his thoughts."[735] When an inner movement has developed to the
point of coming out in an exterior action, the manifestation of it
is *too late*. "The more one hides his [bad] thoughts, the more they
multiply and grow strong," says a Greek Father, and "He who
manifests his thoughts is soon cured. But he who hides them
becomes sick with pride."[736]

The purpose of manifesting one's thoughts is not merely to
bring thoughts to light, but to *submit our own will to the judgement
and correction* of another. Hence we must understand that in manifesting our thoughts, we are also and at the same time renouncing
our own will. To manifest our thoughts purely speculatively, as
an exercise of the mind, would be useless if we did not also intend
to do what the spiritual Father tells us. The manifestation of our
inner thoughts implies the renunciation of our own will even in
the search for perfection. In the *Apothegmata* we read: "If you see
a young man climbing up to heaven by his own will, take him
by the foot and pull him down again, because it is of no use to
him."[737] In effect, there is no true monastic perfection without
complete self-renunciation, and this self-renunciation depends
most of all on the humility with which we place our own will in

734. *Instituta*, 4.9 (*PL* 49, cols. 161–62), quoted in Hausherr, col. 1034.
735. *Verba Seniorum*, 3.177 (*PL* 73, col. 798C), quoted in Hausherr, col. 1034.
736. Hausherr, col. 1033, quoting Paul Evergetinos, *Synagogè*, 54.1, c. 20.
737. *Verba Seniorum*, 5.10.111 (*PL* 73, col. 932BC), quoted in Hausherr, col.
1035; Merton includes this saying in *The Wisdom of the Desert: Sayings from the
Desert Fathers of the Fourth Century* (New York: New Directions, 1960), 47 [#62].

the hands of another, even in matters concerning our own spiritual perfection. The very heart of that "self" which we must sacrifice, is our will. And this renunciation is the most solid evidence of perfect faith. Barsanuphius says: "It is lack of faith that keeps you from giving up your own will, and lack of faith comes from your desire for human glory. . . . Get rid of these three things: self-will, justification of yourself, and the desire to please; and then compunction will come to you in all truth."[738] To seek a spiritual Father who does not make us give up our own will is to seek an accomplice, not a Father and guide.

Advantages of Self-Manifestation: but if we renounce our will, and let our Father guide and form us, we are led from slavery to liberty, *by the substitution of God's almighty will for our own will*. This liberty brings with it perfection of interior peace, freedom from all care, *amerimnia* (forgetfulness of care), says Climacus, etc.: "Freedom from care in all things, whether reasonable or unreasonable."[739] "Whosoever gives himself up to obey his Father possesses this freedom from care and this interior peace."[740] When this condition is realized, then *all graces can come to the son through the prayers of the Father*, because this docility to the representative of God opens the way for the unimpeded action of the Holy Spirit in the soul, and it is the Spirit Who sanctifies, guides and forms the soul, rather than the spiritual Father, who is merely an instrument and mediator. Barsanuphius again says: "The saints do not speak from their own depths, but it is God Who speaks in them as He sees fit, sometimes clearly, sometimes obscurely. He speaks as He wills, not as they will themselves."[741] This obedience to the Father contains within itself all the other virtues: "He who questions the Fathers fulfills the law and the prophets"[742] (Evagrius).

738. *Letter* 236, quoted in Hausherr, col. 1035.
739. *Scala Paradisi*, 27, quoted in Hausherr, col. 1046.
740. Dorotheus of Gaza, *Doctrina*, 1.17 (*PG* 88, col. 1640D), quoted in Hausherr, col. 1046.
741. *Letter* 885, quoted in Hausherr, col. 1049.
742. Quoted in Hausherr, col. 1049.

Résumé on the Efficacy of Direction: the spiritual Father is a mediator, a representative of God, "life-giving Spirit"[743] to his spiritual son. These potentialities will not be realized if the Father himself does not strive to be holy and to be a man of prayer. But he will remain imperfect in many respects. The disciple must close his eyes to the human imperfections of the Father and see only God in him, to accept his words as the words of God, to submit his will to him as to God, to be guided by him as by God Himself. Where there is such faith, God will surely give great graces through the action of the spiritual Father, graces which the Father himself will scarcely realize, of which perhaps he will know nothing at all. On the contrary, if the relation of Father and son is based purely on human sympathy, on esteem for human gifts, and natural infatuation, the Spirit will not be able to work as He desires. The mutual love, sympathy, respect, and the veneration of the son for the Father should be entirely supernatural and based on faith. The Father is not a miracle worker who can do wonders according to his own fancy. Everything depends upon the faith of the son and of the Father, permitting God to work in them.

743. 1 Cor. 15:45.

APPENDIX A
Textual Notes

Additions and Alterations Included in Mimeo

1   MONASTIC OBSERVANCES] *not in typescript; mimeo only*

3   CONTENTS . . . End of Part I] *not in typescript; mimeo only*

5   Our observances] *preceded by x'd out* Dangers to
        breath] *preceded by x'd out* action
        love for God] *typed interlined*
        rites] *preceded by x'd out* symbolism

6   with its] *preceded by x'd out* b)
        monastic tradition] *preceded by x'd out* Order

7   traditional] *interlined above x'd out* disposition of the
            monas
        meaning] *added in left margin to replace cancelled* plan
        each] *preceded by uncancelled* a *and x'd out* differe

8   instruction] *followed by x'd out* even though all other
            masters are not heard.

10   side of the quadrangle] *preceded by x'd out* or east
        N.B. when . . . Chapter.] *added in lower margin*
        read . . . p. 39] *added on line*

11   Everywhere . . . in church.] *added on line*

12   *screen] followed by x'd out* (Gen Chap

13   original . . . hall] *added on line following x'd out* There
            are too [*sic*] kinds of basilicas in the
        is signalized] *interlined above cancelled* consists *followed*
            by x'd out usuall
        Sepulchre] *followed by x'd out* and of the N
        been favorable] *preceded by cancelled* always

14   etc., etc.] *added on line*

15   This is a . . . bad taste.] *opposite page*
        today: DDT] *added on line*
        In a word, . . . sacristy.] *interlined*
16   The cemetery] *interlined above cancelled* It
        in English] *followed by x'd out* here
17   It is guarded . . . angel.] *added in left margin and marked*
                for insertion
        perseverance] *preceded by x'd out* perpetual
        those who] *preceded by x'd out* who
        dost cause] *preceded by x'd out* does *and followed by x'd out*
                permit the
19   St. Peter . . . world."] *typed on line and marked for*
                insertion
20   we do not . . . cloister (*Usages*, 328)] *added on line*
21   stairs] *followed by cancelled* Point for proclamation!
        accessible.] *followed by x'd out* The monks would go
                down a f
22   matters"] *followed by x'd out* The tendency in
23   supernatural] *preceded by x'd out* family life in which
                the members are united in the
24   exercises] *preceded by x'd out* is prescribed
25   In some . . . stands.] *added on line*
26   laudable . . . proclamations] *added on line*
        sorts of] *followed by x'd out* odds a
27   paragraphs] *followed by x'd out* regulate the
28   wandering around.] *followed by x'd out* When entering
                coming in or going
29   especially the fire escapes!] *interlined*
        without . . . reason.] *interlined and marked for insertion*
        then . . . blouse] *added on line*
        the way you use] *typed interlined and marked for*
                insertion
30   "Where two . . . of them."] *added on line*
31   faith] *followed by x'd out* respond
        by these bells] *typed following* earth *and marked for*
                transposition
        If we go . . . our prayer.] *interlined*

32   Thus we make . . . evil things.] *opposite page*

34   belfry] *preceded by x'd out* tower

      main idea] *preceded by x'd out* chief

35   -nine] *followed by x'd out* large (middle) bell on l

      feast,] *followed by x'd out* three on

36   ablutions] *preceded by x'd out* Pater of the conventual

      small bell] *preceded by x'd out* Pater *and followed by x'd*
         out rung

37   tolled for a *Pater*] tolled *typed below x'd out* rung

      space?] *preceded by x'd out* length o

40   light work] *followed by x'd out* with

41   St. Bernard, *loc. cit.*] St. Bernard *interlined and marked*
         for insertion

42   AS THE FERVOR] AS *interlined below cancelled* THAN

      purpose of the] *followed by x'd out* choir is to make all

43   affairs] *preceded by x'd out* history of the development

44   needed by] *followed by x'd out* the Church

      before all] *preceded by x'd out* above all

45   *Importance*] *preceded by x'd out Relation*

      interior and] *preceded by cancelled* both

      all exterior] *all interlined with a caret*

46   drawn] *followed by x'd out* to

      call to] to *altered by x'ing out from* into

47   consists] *followed by x'd out* of

48   attitude] *preceded by x'd out* bearing

49   in the wrong way] *typed interlined and marked*
         for insertion

      look down] *preceded by x'd out* etc.

50   near the statue] *preceded by x'd out* around

51   are made in] *preceded by x'd out* that

      hearing a] *preceded by x'd out* private mass

52   Instead of] *preceded by x'd out* One

54   walking when others] *preceded by cancelled* Private prayer
         in Church (see later). Rules for those who wear a
         calotte—see Usages 90.

      such times] *followed by x'd out* and when

      choir without] *preceded by x'd out* Church without

(exception: . . . lamps)] *added on line*
sing when] *followed by x'd out* out of their sta
choir: why?] why? *added on line*

55 Closing {of} books] books *interlined below cancelled* them
and {the} office . . . dead] *interlined with a caret*
(93–100)] *followed by x'd out* The rank has the hierarchi
avoid] *preceded by x'd out* beware

56 throne of God.] *followed by x'd out* In the
place of highest] *preceded by x'd out* highest place

57 three principles] three *interlined above cancelled* two
novices] *following* laybrothers *and marked for
transposition*
laybrothers] *preceding* novices *and marked for
transposition*
turned] *preceded by x'd out* waiting

58 Bouyer,] *followed by x'd out* in the

59 greatness] *preceded by x'd out* wonder

60 "We recognize] *followed by x'd out* His voice

61 *Domine quid*] *preceded by x'd out* The Invitatorium.

62 The psalm introduces . . . strength.] *added in lower
margin*

63 pasture] *preceded by cancelled* hand
Attention . . . corde."] *added on line*
For the . . . 20:2-13] *interlined*
and forge . . . rest.] *interlined*

63–64 Parsch says: . . . praise."] *opposite page*

64 some part] *preceded by cancelled* the
{I} Sunday] *added in left margin*

66 St. Pius V] St. *typed interlined and marked for insertion*
Discuss . . . Sundays] *interlined*

67 particular office.] *followed by x'd out* (Examples later).

68 14–21] 4 *interlined above cancelled* 6
Every time . . . fulfilled . . ."] *added on line*
lectorate . . . concerned.] *interlined*
lectorate] *preceded by cancelled* Order of

69 intelligibly] *preceded by x'd out* intelligently

share] *followed by x'd out* with

of the whole.] *followed by cancelled Example of Lessons—*
Feast of St James the Great I Nocturn—I Corinthians
4:1-14. The apostolic vocation—The Apostles are
"ministers of Christ and dispensers of the mysteries
of God". Yet though they are the greatest of the
saints, they are called to greater humility and they
have within themselves the reason for humbling
themselves before God and men—for God Himself
has humbled them—Hence Paul cares no more
whether he be judged by men, and he does not even
judge his own self. (cf Guardini's beautiful Chapter
on God seeing our hearts, in the *Living God.*)

Christ] *preceded by x'd out* God

judged by] *followed by x'd out* God or by

70   is taken] *preceded by x'd out* follows

It is a good . . . ourselves.] *interlined*

Note: . . . office.] *opposite page*

71   How? . . . His Will.] *added on line*

by *experience* . . . elders.] *interlined with a caret*

maturity of judgement] *added on line*

72   Holy fear . . . of the wise.] *added on line*

They *do not* . . . own will.] *added on line*

Bad thoughts . . . truth.] *added on line*

73   enlightened . . . obedience.] *added on line*

The TE DEUM] *preceded by* (Te Deum—Gospel—Te decet
laus) *interlined and cancelled*

74–75   *The Gospel:* . . . *father abbot.*] *opposite page*

75   he has heard . . . salvation] *interlined below and marked
for insertion*

cultivation . . . souls] *added on line*

76   which do not] *followed by x'd out* become connected
merely because we

It is not "continuity."] *added on line*

If we are leading . . . *time.*] *added on line*

78   in a word] *preceded by x'd out* the

learn] *preceded by x'd out* teach our

79   especially . . . Eucharist] *added on line*

e) . . . reality.] *added in lower margin*

Our aim . . . experience.] *interlined*

80   The second . . . meditation is] *interlined and marked for insertion*

silent] *added in right margin*

81   introspection.] *followed by x'd out* One of

82   *makes its*] *followed by cancelled whole*

momentarily,] *followed by x'd out* our

known the real] *preceded by x'd out* vanished

83   Bush] *followed by x'd out* It knows the

The first two . . . pleases.] *opposite page*

84   fundamental] *followed by x'd out* idea

But also . . . at self.] *added on line*

85   especially . . . Jesus] *added on line*

Our reading . . . be] *interlined with a caret*

85–86 This attitude . . . prayer.] *added on line*

86   Beware . . . next?"] *interlined*

Jesus'] *interlined below cancelled* His

regular] *preceded by x'd out* breathing

lack of] *preceded by x'd out* care

87   satisfied] *preceded by x'd out* with

88   reasoning and] *followed by x'd out* lower

cognitive] *preceded by x'd out* such faculties

"For who . . . 75-76] *opposite page*

89   an embrace . . . faith!] *added on line*

90   and approval.] *followed by x'd out* The director

pleases] *followed by x'd out* and

human fears,] *followed by x'd out* the

In a word,] a *altered from* an

primarily] *preceded by x'd out* with

92   Prayer of Simplicity . . . to illusion.] *opposite page*

reduce] *preceded by cancelled* are

might be] *interlined with a caret above cancelled* was

We ended . . . praise.] *opposite page*

ended] *preceded by cancelled* have

94   of the *Rule*] *added in right margin*
vigils] *preceded by x'd out* Matins

95   the song of] *preceded by x'd out* because
(READ it)] *added on line*

96   joy . . . iniquity."] *added in left margin*
The Church . . . others.] *added in lower margin*

97   We will convert] We *typed in left margin before x'd out* It
We will praise] We *typed in left margin before x'd out* It
it is a psalm] *preceded by x'd out* we renew
are fine] are *interlined above cancelled* and

98   What is praise? . . . (LOVE!!).] *opposite page*

101   psalms of lauds] *preceded by x'd out* psalms and

102   sums up] *preceded by x'd out* ends

103   Note . . . others?] *opposite page*

107   other interior] *preceded by x'd out* moral dispositio
rather tired] *followed by x'd out* and

108   It is possible . . . moment.] *typed before* c) *and marked for
transposition*

109   chiefly] *typed above x'd out* only

109–10 with Him in our heart.] *added on line*

110   merely] *added in left margin and marked for insertion*
various] *preceded by x'd out* all

110–11 A simple . . . of Jesus.] *opposite page*

111   in the Mass] *interlined with a caret*
of Jesus] *followed by cancelled* in the Mass.
then read] *preceded by x'd out* given
bound] *followed by x'd out* and scourged
this last point . . . in Him.] *added on line*
to make] *followed by x'd out* of
this manner] *this altered from the*
deep] *interlined above cancelled* real
come] *followed by cancelled* anywhere

112   in monks] in *interlined above cancelled* for
What . . . do?] *added on line*
in his own name,] *preceded by cancelled* to say

to officiate] *preceded by x'd out* for

113   they are personal.] they *interlined with a caret*

v.g., . . . Passion] *added in left margin*

114   private person,] *followed by x'd out* for hi

115–16 To fully . . . Church herself.] *on verso*

116   become the "sacrament"] *followed by cancelled* after

transformed into His] His *interlined above cancelled* Him

119   IN TURN] *preceded by x'd out* ARE

OUR NEIGHBOR.] *preceded by x'd out* OUR BROTHER THROUGH
    EACH ONE OF US

perfect] *typed interlined and marked for insertion*

In referring to *Abraham*, . . . superstition.] *opposite page*

Melchisedec] *followed by cancelled* we are astonished

120   consecration (sacrifice),] *preceded by x'd out* sacrifice and
    communion in

worshippers] *followed by x'd out* sit down at the table with
the minor elevation] *added in lower margin*

121   We are also . . . *peccatoribus*.] *opposite page*

122   why?] *added on line*

He is . . . in Him.] *added on line*

123   real and actual] *interlined with a caret*

125   and this will . . . virtue.] *interlined*

7] *added in left margin before cancelled* but

infused and beatific] *added in left margin before cancelled*
    divine

126   Conclusion:] *added in left margin before cancelled* Note
    however that

local and natural] *interlined with a caret*

remain;] *preceded by cancelled* only

127   This *is* My Body!!] *interlined*

129   How do . . . soul"?] *interlined*

132   Avoid . . . prayer.] *interlined*

133   *Ut in me* . . . *sacramenta*.] *added in right margin and
    marked for insertion*

133–34 cf. *Imitation* . . . Savior.] *opposite page*

134   through the charity] *followed by cancelled* that

CREATURAM] *followed by x'd out* QUOS CAELESTIBUS REFICIS
135 Dare . . . dangerous!] *interlined*
     Remember . . . *humilium.*] *interlined*
136 We have . . . above.] *added in lower margin*
     Council . . . *augmentum.*] *opposite page*
137 *justa*] *preceded by x'd out desideras quae recta sunt et*
          desiderata percipere
     pariter] *preceded by x'd out actu*
138 and fervor.] (union notes *added in lower margin*
          and cancelled
140 without fruit.] *preceded by x'd out largely*
     able] *preceded by x'd out fill*
     faithful] *followed by x'd out will*
141 *pietatis,*] *preceded by x'd out unitatis*
142 *neighbors*] *followed by x'd out and our*
     one and the same duty] duty *added in lower margin*
143 strangers] *preceded by x'd out utter*
     assimilated] *preceded by x'd out grasped*
     n.b. learn . . . heart] *opposite page*
144 and seeking . . . prayer] *added on line*
     directive.] *preceded by x'd out prescriptive (this is the*
          common
     meet] *preceded by x'd out fulfil*
     nothing] *followed by x'd out or to*
145 Other aids] *preceded by x'd out Twofold*
147 *fail to*] *preceded by x'd out omit at least one five minute visit*
          a day to the Bl. Sacrament would
     one or two] *preceded by x'd out a shorter or*
     be necessary] *preceded by x'd out 2—How to*
148 is glad] *preceded by x'd out enjoys*
     spiritual] *preceded by x'd out reality*
150 monk's day.] *followed by x'd out We will talk later*
151 "Tria . . . *caritatis.*"] *interlined*
153 *provide*] *preceded by x'd out lead*
     (also . . . 20-25)] *interlined and marked for insertion*
154 efforts end] *preceded by x'd out tongues and*

1:4-5] *interlined with a caret*

156   favored] *followed by interlined and cancelled* Worldly
           "peace" is for the
       Therefore] *added in left margin*

157   he is a monk if he can] *interlined with a caret above
           cancelled* he
       get] *altered from* gets
       human] *interlined with a caret*
       few] *interlined above cancelled* no

158   *the exchange*] *preceded by x'd out* Passing to
       (the latter . . . available)] *added on line*

159   observances,] *followed by x'd out* etc.
       are an evidence] *preceded by x'd out* to consider
       It does not give] It *interlined above cancelled* and

160   necessary] *followed by x'd out* for the poi
       In what . . . evil] *added on line*
       Extreme . . . novice.] *added on line*
       irregularities] *preceded by x'd out* funny
       it so easily] *preceded by x'd out* in the lo

161   difficulty.] *followed by x'd out* One
       funny signs] *preceded by x'd out* sings and
       It has . . . in life.] *interlined*

162   *almost always*] *interlined above cancelled usually*
       material] *followed by x'd out* about
       to others] to *typed interlined above x'd out* with
       includes] *preceded by x'd out* resembles what has

163   touch on] *interlined below cancelled* verge on
       It is understandable] *preceded by x'd out* Under pressure
           of great interior
       ways in which] in *typed in left margin before x'd out* for
       keep] *preceded by x'd out* bear thing
       sin] *typed interlined above x'd out* a serious fault
       far wrong.] *followed by x'd out* But even then

164   Special . . . automatic.] *added on line*
       Rules Regarding] *preceded by x'd out* How to speak

165   especially . . . novitiate.] *added on line*

SUBJECT on] on *typed interlined above x'd out* for

paragraph] *interlined above cancelled* chapter

using] *altered from* uses *preceded by cancelled* one

machine.] *preceded by cancelled* noisy

enjoying] *interlined below cancelled* having

165–66 one's own] *preceded by x'd out* the interio

166 don't overdo it.] *added in lower margin below cancelled ne
   quid nimis*

relative] *added in left margin and marked for insertion*

167 It may be a form . . . life.] *added on line*

d) Generally . . . motives.] *added in lower margin*

salts (!)] (!) *added on line*

awake] *followed by x'd out* will sometimes

168 mistakenly] *interlined with a caret*

novice] *interlined above cancelled* monk

if he has not] if *interlined with a caret above cancelled*
   because

are objectively] *preceded by cancelled* themselves

accretions.] *followed by x'd out* Nevertheless, there are

169 same thing . . . doing] *interlined*

PICK] *preceded by x'd out* One should also face the fact
   that much that has been written about the spiritual
   life and about scripture is in fact *tedious and useless*
   for monks—elaborate pseudo-scientific studies of
   minor points of *scripture*, pedestrian and stupid commentaries, "verbalizing" the interior life in pseudo-
   ascetic and mystic treatises, etc.

Scripture . . . Prime] *interlined above cancelled Meditatio
   Psalmorum*

time to scripture.] *followed by x'd out* This

Importance . . . Scripture] *typed in left margin*

170 Avoid . . . however.] *added on line*

If God . . . words.] *interlined*

171 give ourselves] *preceded by x'd out* apply

173 monastic life] *preceded by x'd out* life

his best] *preceded by x'd out* him

174   However, . . . extraordinary.] *opposite page*
175   One can read the books] *preceded by x'd out* But
      One can take] *preceded by cancelled* In the Old Testament,
          and followed by cancelled in order,
      to IV] *preceded by x'd out* and
      thoughtfully] *followed by cancelled* necessarily.
176   what should . . . retain it?] *interlined*
      One cannot] *preceded by cancelled* To start with the last.
      General objectives] *interlined*
177   for instance] *added on line*
      enable] *preceded by x'd out* be
      after profession] *interlined above cancelled* later on
178   in one case] *preceded by x'd out* his study
      the opening] *preceded by x'd out* a significant
          paragraph.
179   monk's reading] reading *typed interlined above x'd*
          out study
181   translation says] *preceded by x'd out* They say that
      meditation of scripture] scripture *typed interlined above*
          x'd out the psal
182   with thought] *preceded by x'd out* but not in
183   The Father . . . Himself.] *added on line*
184   noun] *typed interlined above x'd out* verb
      climates] *followed by cancelled* but perhaps was not what
          was directly intended by St Benedict.
      quarter] *typed interlined above x'd out* third
186   DIGNARE] *interlined with a caret*
      (note . . . cross)] *interlined*
      certain days] *followed by x'd out* in exchange for the
          prayers of the monks
      those who] *preceded by x'd out* for t
187   Put . . . then.] *added on line*
188   in the morning.] *followed by* It is a custom of the house
          not to shave or take showers before prime without
          a special reason (v.g. guests or going out early for a
          doctor's appointment, etc). *marked* do not copy *in*
          left margin

going *followed by x'd out* to town early)
The interval before] *preceded by cancelled* Hence
value . . . visits] *added on line*
e) . . . psalms] *interlined*
f) . . . etc.] *added in left margin and marked for insertion*
to take] *followed by x'd out* to

189   stately] *typed interlined below x'd out* solemn
"little hours,"] *preceded by x'd out* day hours

190   The only . . . Week.] *added on line*
readings,] *followed by cancelled* and
abbot,] *followed by cancelled* and
of faults,] of *interlined with a caret*

193   quickness to] *preceded by cancelled* in
error to] *followed by x'd out* think we
(and laughing at them)] *added on line*

194   although what] *preceded by x'd out* this
heads] *preceded by x'd out* hearts and

196   any feast] *typed interlined above x'd out* it

197   Easter Day] *followed by cancelled* (though it would seem
that it should. At all the other hours except compline
we sing Haec dies quem fecit Dominus alleluia)
bring us] *followed by x'd out* help, but also he comes to

198   relationships] *followed by x'd out* It marks the end
Ascension, etc.] *followed by x'd out* On two great feasts of
the year, Christmas and Easter, there is a solemn
announcement in chap
vigils] *preceded by x'd out* feasts

199   day itself.] *followed by cancelled* The last three days of Holy
week there is *no martyrology* and thus Easter does
not have an announcement on Holy Saturday. And
this is as it should be. It would not fit in with the
liturgy, and would be in a sense an absurdity.
25] *preceded by cancelled* 24

200   remember] *preceded by x'd out* It is always given
this full moon] *followed by x'd out* before the kalends
of Apri

201   victory] *preceded by x'd out* a the

203   *The Pater:] preceded by x'd out* After
         Nor will] *preceded by x'd out* But
204   bodies,] *preceded by x'd out* hearts
205–206 Note: . . . their functions.] *opposite page*
         Those senior . . . "frater."] *written above and marked for*
              insertion
206   may] *added in left margin and marked for insertion to replace*
              cancelled should
         If this were] *preceded by x'd out* This is
         interest.] *followed by cancelled* This does not depend only
              on the ones listening but also and above all on the
              one speaking. This
         The chapter] *added in left margin*
         2] *added in left margin*
         properly . . . etc.] *added on line*
207   one good] *preceded by cancelled* a)
         We will treat] *preceded by cancelled* b)
208   guests] *preceded by x'd out* other
210   a theme] *followed by x'd out* adequately.
210–11   One has a . . . opponents.] *opposite page*
211   arise] *followed by cancelled* Supposing some preacher, or
              even the Father Abbot himself, chances to make a
              theological error? Do not pounce on it and try to
              exploit it to make trouble. If the error is serious, it
              may be discretely [*sic*] brought to the attention of the
              one concerned. Usually there are minor slips or mis-
              takes of emphasis which do not deserve a moment's
              attention. They will soon be forgotten and most
              people have not noticed them. Not charitable to dis-
              cuss these things among ourselves, though if a prob-
              lem arises one may ask his director for enlightenment.
              Very often there are merely misunderstandings and
              errors of interpretation on the part of the hearer.
         itself possess] *preceded by x'd out* The spiri
212   To resist] *preceded by x'd out* This too is a
         of the Order?] *followed by x'd out* not

213 everyone] *altered from* everything *by x'ing out* thing *and adding* one *on line*

thoughts] *preceded by x'd out* things

such bad] *preceded by x'd out* the

214 eleventh] *preceded by x'd out* 10th and

217 Pope Paul . . . indulgences.] *interlined*

Abbot de Rancé believed] Abbot de Rancé *added in left margin before cancelled* He

been said.] *followed by cancelled* To us this appears not only extreme but more [ ], even a fault on the part of Abbot de Rancé.

Adam."] *followed by cancelled* A bit [ ]

218 immediately] *interlined with a caret*

slapped a priest] *followed by x'd out* before he

219 had a bad] *preceded by x'd out* left a bad

healthy to] *followed by x'd out* exaggerate

We ought] *preceded by x'd out* It will serve

wrong to base] *preceded by x'd out* much at fault

own good.] *followed by x'd out* That remains at the disc

surveillance] *preceded by x'd out* spying sets itself up

much harm.] *followed by x'd out* Often a bad proclamation does much

220 and this does . . . disrepute.] *added on line*

properly.] *followed by x'd out* But in this matter,

221–22 There are some . . . interpretations.] *typed opposite page*

222 my interpretation] *preceded by x'd out* it ac

to light] *typed interlined below x'd out* out

drawn] *followed by x'd out* to

defect] *interlined below cancelled* irregularity

223 unless] *preceded by x'd out* because

224 or warped] *interlined with a caret*

prudent] *preceded by x'd out* wise

by the community;] *followed by x'd out* and

225 preserve the] *followed by x'd out* outer shell of

have been permitted] *preceded by x'd out* perhaps

More . . . irregularities] *interlined*

inadvertence] *followed by x'd out* Rare or single faults
do not constitute irregularities. One would only
proclaim in such a case, if the person committing
the fault obviously thought he was

appointment] *preceded by x'd out time*

attach] *preceded by x'd out* qualify

226 possible . . . laziness, dissipation] *added on line following*
x'd out Irregularities

particular friendship] *added in lower margin*

docile] *followed by x'd out* and

brethren] *followed by x'd out* failure to atone for injuries
or insults

71–72)] *preceded by x'd out* 72)

day] *interlined above cancelled* week

are the main] *preceded by cancelled* which

proclamations] *followed by x'd out* first

They] *interlined*

227 are to be . . . attention] *interlined and marked for insertion*
below cancelled have their importance

of a religious] *followed by x'd out* can

be connected] *preceded by x'd out* be judged

It is not] It is *interlined below and marked for insertion*

treat] *interlined above cancelled* take

But of course . . . harshly.] *added in lower margin*

228 In general] *followed by x'd out* both

(commentary . . . later)] *added on line*

229 in time or eternity] *added in left margin and marked for*
insertion

with a profound] *preceded by x'd out* after

230 purely interior] *followed by x'd out* thoughts

They open . . . self-justification] *added on line*

"Vague . . . forbidden."] *quotation marks added*

231 The acceptance] *preceded by x'd out* It sh

233 situation which,] *followed by x'd out* for the leas

234 formulating] *preceded by x'd out* forming th

236 However, . . . molehill] *interlined*

again, . . . small] *interlined*

237 mockery] *preceded by x'd out* rage
to anyone.] *followed by x'd out* Forget it, enter
the rule] the *altered from* that
concerning] *interlined with a caret*
which . . . proclaimed] *added on line*
question or] *followed by x'd out* difficulty
238 promoted] *preceded by cancelled* of regularity
239 requires] *preceded by x'd out* is
240 But this . . . attention.] *added on line*
bringing] *preceded by x'd out* carry
attitude.] *preceded by x'd out* power to
241 simply done] *followed by x'd out* "with a good"
43–46] 43 *altered from* 44 *and* 46 *interlined to replace
cancelled* 6
242 43 . . . wine.] *added in lower margin*
Read chapter 43] *added in left margin*
246 signal to begin] *followed by x'd out* to me
247 d)] c) *in typescript; corrected in mimeo*
e)] d) *in typescript; corrected in mimeo*
248 f)] e) *in typescript; corrected in mimeo*
Per Omnia,] *preceded by x'd out* end of the Pater
249 doing so.] *followed by x'd out* The moderation of this
exercise is certainly
250 common practice] *preceded by x'd out* desires of

Additions and Alterations Not Included in Mimeo

38 The *Angelus* tends . . . fervent.] *added in lower margin*
reminder] *preceded by cancelled* relic of the
42–43 The essence . . . above all.] *opposite page*
43 Note the . . . of death.] *opposite page*
56 Let us . . . men.] *interlined*
74 spirit of this hymn] hymn *interlined above cancelled*
selection
80 Meditation . . . realities!] *interlined*
100 and ends] *interlined below and marked for insertion*
116–17 Note the . . . complied with] *opposite page*

124   One of . . . Vonier.] *interlined*
164   N.B. no provision . . . ruined.] *opposite page*
165   comment on . . . this] *interlined*
199   Formerly . . . sanctity.] *opposite page*
214   (holy orders)] *added on line*

Additions and Alterations in Appendix

251   APPENDIX . . . V.   Openness] *omitted*
253–54   IN THE MONASTIC SETTING . . . Abbey of
         Gethsemani, 1958] *omitted*
255   SPIRITUAL DIRECTION IN THE MONASTIC SETTING]
         omitted
         I. *The Life-giving Action*] I. *Life-giving action preceded by*
         Let us consider Christ's action in His Church, espe-
         cially how His light comes to us through His
         Church, and *most particularly how He acts upon us*
         and enlightens us through the ministers He has chosen
         to be our guides.
         Our Lord Jesus Christ] Jesus
         have fallen . . . goodness.] are evil.
         we tend daily to death.] we death.
         justice; we work iniquity.] justice, we iniquity.
         we are plunged in sin.] we are sin.
         finding Him] union
         and to our own blindness] *omitted*
255–56   We can never . . . security.] *omitted*
256   must therefore *desire Christ*] must *desire Him*
         through our superiors] in our Superiors
         and directors] *omitted*
         spiritual fathers] Superiors
         our abbot is not only] not merely as
         friend] *followed by* who says yes to everything we want
         an authority] as a Superior
         those who guide us] our Superiors
         Authority of Jesus in His·Church] *followed by* Jesus rules
         visibly in His Vicar, who possesses all the authority
         of the Christ, on earth, and who shares that author-

ity with the hierarchy and priests. All authoritative actions of the hierarchy flow from the authority of Christ. This authority establishes a supernatural bond between souls and Jesus, through the hierarchy. It is necessary for the union of souls with God in the mystical Christ, and its supreme end is the sanctification of souls, their transformation in Christ, and their perfect union with the Father. (Even where the Superiors themselves may be human, may be in error, Jesus works.)

obligations] *obligation*

Submission . . . in love.] *omitted*

human power.] *followed by* The Pope has infallible authority in doctrine, and the hierarchy is divinely assisted in the exercise of its rule.

257 authority of Christ the Lord] authority of Jesus

society of His] society of the

saints.] *followed by* (Colomer)

the Lord enlightens] Jesus enlightens

His representatives.] *followed by* Above all we must understand that the light that Jesus gives us is His own Truth, His own Holy Spirit, and Himself in and with the Spirit. In receiving as our gift from God the divine Spirit, we receive into our hearts the very substance of divine life and divine truth. The Holy Spirit is not merely a passive "object" deposited in our hearts. He is Pure Act—Light, Life, Love.

The Holy Spirit lives] He lives

in the Church] in His Church

Exteriorly,] *Exteriorly,*

through popes,] Popes,

and all . . . for souls.] and their co-workers.

established hierarchical framework] established framework

are given] is given

no official ministerial] no ministerial

is sometimes said] is said

some special] *omitted*
reach particular] reach some
with whom . . . contact] *omitted*
sacred art,] art,
preaching] *followed by* and
and in works of art] *omitted*

258   become instruments] are instruments
through ministry] and ministry
united] places
great powers and special gifts] powers and gifts
power] *followed by* and
light] *followed by* and
wisdom] grace
the struggling soul, here and now.] the soul.
to the soul,] to the soul,
love] *followed by and*
truth] *followed by and*
guide this] *guide the*
who has come to him] *omitted*
lead this Christian] lead the soul
the divine light] the light *followed by* and
wisdom] *followed by* of God.
reach the Christian] reach the soul
frighten or] and upset and
disconcert him,] disconcert it,
naturally] *followed by* and
guide him] guide it
faithful Christian.] soul.

259   *only completely true*] only fully true
if there . . . director,] if there . . . director,
Christian cannot] subject cannot
do not bring light.] etc.
much by emotion,] much by nature,
dominated by emotion,] dominated by nature,
false bond,] false bond,
allows a Christian] allows a soul
protects the Christian] protects the soul

vanity, self-seeking,] *omitted*
"spirituality"] spirituality
chosen by the Christian,] chosen by the subject,
undertakes,] takes upon himself,
guidance of his] guidance of the
over the novice.] over the subject.
Here the director . . . reasons.] *omitted*
Father Master] *followed by* in the novitiate
260   But he alone . . . formation.] *omitted*
visitors.] *followed by* (Superiors—Abbot).
can and must] *preceded by* then
for good] for the good
261   limitations!] *preceded by* lacks and
He is human . . . mistaken.] *omitted*
no one can] *preceded by* it does mean that
sin] err
His decision . . . of God.] *omitted*
as well as for the novice] *omitted*
teaching of the Father.] *followed by* Commentators won-
     der who is the Pius Pater—God? St. Benedict?
     Both. And more. The Father is:
     a) *God*—the heavenly Father, Whose Son Jesus does
       all the things that are pleasing to Him. Monastic
       life outwardly reproduces the relations of Father
       and Son in the Holy Trinity.
     b) *Jesus*—Who came from the Father to give us the
       sanctifying Word of the Father.
     c) *St. Benedict*—who resumes the Gospel teaching
       for monks.
     d) *The Abbot*—who applies and interprets the Rule.
     e) The Spiritual Father—in immediate contact with
       the monk (if there is some other Father than the
       Abbot) through whom all these "Fathers" in one
       reach the individual monk.
A *spiritual Father*] The *Father*
(this concept . . . purely oral tradition)] belonging
    more to the time of oral tradition,

by teaching] *followed by* and
a human need] any need
262   supported and completed by] supported by
Father, *and*] Father, and
He engenders] Then he engenders
in his children] *omitted*
263   transmit the divine life] give life
in oriental tradition] *omitted*
For our part . . . spiritual son.] *omitted*
charism] charisma
it was frequently given] *omitted*
264   *supremely humble.*] *omitted*
The subject also must] *and the subject must also*
humble, docile] *humble and docile*
He must not . . . guide.] *omitted*
his true function.] his function.
in which his . . . thwarted.] *omitted*
to face.] to handle.
revelation *himself,*] revelation himself,
Then he will . . . insight.] *omitted*
will, by another] will,
But perhaps the trouble] But the trouble
are salutary] *followed by* and necessary
Perhaps it is necessary . . . insincerity!] *omitted*
one who . . . saying."] *omitted*
whole life is] whole is
265   struggle to change] weaknesses
The demands . . . for us.] *omitted*
the lack of other virtues,] many other virtues
On the contrary . . . vocation.] *omitted*
at the moment . . . violence!] *omitted*
the spiritual Father sees] one sees
and realizes] and one realizes
tiresome] useless
for him!] for the director!
natural impatience] nature

he must be willing] one must be willing
these faults known.] them known.
This is time especially when it is a] Especially in the
self-love. . . . be wasting] self-love: wasting
everything is significant.] everything is significant.

266   sincerely identify himself] sincerely identify oneself
weaknesses and trouble] weaknesses and troubles
of someone he] of someone one
to know and to understand.] *followed by* (A parenthesis
on *transference*:)

> Transference—the term is sometimes met with in a
> good sense—in which the subject being counselled
> by a psychiatrist "transfers" his worries and bur-
> dens to the shoulders of the psychiatrist and lets
> him take care of them. This notion is inadequate.
> The more usual and more scientific use of the term is
> in a *bad* sense in which the subject (of analysis) seeks
> to block the action of the one helping him by fixing
> on him emotions and drives, the function of which is
> to allay the anxiety aroused by the fact that the doctor
> has touched upon sensitive and vitally important
> points, and has aroused a sense of danger.
> What happens in transference?
> a) A powerful emotional reaction (it matters little
>   which emotion—it may be love, hate, joy, desire,
>   fear, etc.)
> b) The emotional reaction is focussed principally on
>   *something that is not there*—in the director. The direc-
>   tor is assumed to have an attitude which he does
>   not have. Example: "You are trying to throw me
>   out of the monastery." "You have got it in for me."
>   This is explained as a "transference" of some-
>   thing that happened before, in the past of the
>   subject.
> c) In trying emotionally to re-live some past situa-
>   tion in terms of the present, the subject *falsifies*

the present in order to keep it *comprehensible* and in order to *avoid changing*, to avoid giving up whatever has to be given up about himself.

He is indeed menaced, and he recognizes it. But what is menaced is his illusory self and his unsatisfactory attitudes towards life. Instead of facing the necessity to give these up, he transfers the whole situation, says something else is menaced: "his vocation", "his reputation", "the Catholic Faith", "the spirit of the Order", etc. His emotions and anxieties are then *rationalized* on the basis of this false assumption. Transference is a way of setting up a smoke screen, under which one makes his escape.

What has to be done?

The director must avoid forming a countertransference—because then the whole situation will become incomprehensible and nothing can be done.

He must understand what is going on, interpret it as far as possible.

He must bring in help from whatever quarter possible.

He must avoid all resentment.

Continue helping, trying to give light, patiently, gradually, until the subject realizes the truth, *realizes he is not menaced*, that everything is all right and will come out for the best.

repented faults.] past faults.

that lies ahead] *omitted*

a true spiritual . . . for the sabbath.] he gives the good of the soul preference.

he will see that] he must see how

firm: St. Anthony . . . example. When] firm. (v.g., St. Anthony, when

yourself, especially] yourself, and especially

matter of prayer."] matter of prayer.")

not mean *hardness*] mean less *hardness*

so much as *frankness*] than *frankness*

But above all . . . discouragement.] *omitted*

267   *means to attain*] means to attain

Direction aims] Of course, direction aims

sins and falls] *followed by* as a result of our evil
     passions.

As regards . . . future.] *omitted*

Mental attitudes,] The psychology behind direction is
     this: that thoughts, mental attitudes,

ways of judging] *preceded by* ways of thinking,

important and unusual] important and special

manifestations to] relations with

vitiated.] conditioned.

The direction given by] Direction of

268   ordinary . . . now is.] ordinary life.

soul *of the beginner*] soul of the beginner

misguided attempts] mistaken attempts

This is . . . discretion.] *omitted*

269   *liberate*] liberate

as a matter of duty.] as a matter of duty.

These concepts . . . such things] All the above inade-
     quacies come from the fact that they

without the . . . conscience] without the manifestation of
     the soul

270   the way I *have* acted."] the way I have acted."

Direction in the] This direction in the

above may be given] above is given

soul *should* receive] *soul must* receive

life of the Church] *followed by* and remain united to
     Christ.

is not available] is denied

religious communities] *followed by* —at least in a
     personal and individual form.

above may be given] above is adequate insofar as it
     may be given

a plain confession.] manifestation of conscience.

with a view . . . perfection] *omitted*

temptations and sins,] temptation, and sins,

271   motives may be different] motives are different
       classification of characters.] *classification* of case histories.
       something . . . psychotherapy] more than psychiatry
       lead to disaster] lead to error
       to analyze his subject.] to unravel complexes in his
             spiritual direction.
       The director is not . . . never be psychoanalysis.]
             Direction goes beyond mere psychological study.
             It is more than *analysis*.

272   preserve an objective] preserve its objective
       Only charity . . . of souls.] *omitted*
       appreciate all the good] appreciate the good
       even though . . . hidden.] *omitted*
       One must sympathize] one must sympathize
       love him with] love it with
       under the guidance of] at the disposition of
       good will, trust] good will, and trust
       in direction and the director.] in the directional
             situation.
       character and interior life] character and person

273   trials, problems:] *followed by* and again
       general terms.] *followed by* (I am tempted to impatience
             at work, etc.)

274   be necessary even] even be necessary
       should be *clear*] is *clear*

276   hide his thoughts] hide his thought
       an inner movement] the inner movement
       is *too late*.] *comes too late*.

277   Barsanuphius again says:] Barsanuphius again:

278   in many respects. The disciple] in many respects and
             the disciple
       of which perhaps] perhaps which
       know nothing at all.] know nothing about at all.
       and natural infatuation,] and so forth,

APPENDIX B
For Further Reading

Other Writings by Thomas Merton
on Topics Treated in *Monastic Observances*

Cistercian Monastic Life

Basic Principles of Monastic Spirituality. Trappist, KY: Abbey of
  Gethsemani, 1957.
Cistercian Contemplatives: A Guide to Trappist Life. Trappist, KY:
  Abbey of Gethsemani, 1948.
Contemplation in a World of Action. Garden City, NY: Doubleday,
  1971.
Gethsemani: A Life of Praise. Trappist, KY: Abbey of Gethsemani,
  1966.
The Monastic Journey, ed. Brother Patrick Hart. Kansas City:
  Sheed, Andrews & McMeel, 1977.
Monastic Life at Gethsemani. Trappist, KY: Abbey of Gethsemani,
  1965.
Monastic Peace. Trappist, KY: Abbey of Gethsemani, 1958.
The Rule of Saint Benedict: Initiation into the Monastic Tradition 4,
  ed. Patrick F. O'Connell. Collegeville, MN: Cistercian Publica-
  tions, 2009.
The Silent Life. New York: Farrar, Straus & Cudahy, 1957.
The Waters of Siloe. New York: Harcourt, Brace, 1949.

Monastic Office

Bread in the Wilderness. New York: New Directions, 1953.
Praying the Psalms. Collegeville, MN: Liturgical Press, 1956.

Liturgy

"Christian Worship and Social Reform." *The Merton Seasonal*, 34.4 (Winter 2009), 3–11.

Seasons of Celebration. New York: Farrar, Straus & Giroux, 1965.

Spiritual Direction

An Introduction to Christian Mysticism: Initiation into the Monastic Tradition 3, ed. Patrick F. O'Connell. Kalamazoo, MI: Cistercian Publications, 2008: 251–332.

"Spiritual Direction." *The Merton Seasonal*, 32.1 (Spring 2007), 3–17.

Spiritual Direction and Meditation. Collegeville, MN: Liturgical Press, 1960: 3–42.

"The Spiritual Father in the Desert Tradition." *Contemplation in a World of Action*: 269–93.

INDEX

Aaron: 33
abandonment: xxxi, 87–88, 91
Abbo, John A.: 260
abbot: xix, xxi, xxiii, xxvii, xlii–xliv,
    8–9, 16, 20, 24–25, 29, 34, 37, 52,
    56–57, 74–75, 104–5, 163–64, 166,
    190, 198, 200, 208–11, 213, 216–18,
    226, 237, 243–44, 248, 256, 262, 273;
    as representative of Christ: 23–24;
    authority of: 24
Abel: 119
Abelard, Peter: 180
Abraham: 103, 119, 199
abstinence: 195
abuse(s): 216, 223–25
acceptance: xxxi, 206, 236
accidentals: 213, 224, 235
accusation(s): 142, 215–16, 229, 231,
    246, 269; bitter: xlv, 232; general:
    230; harsh: xlv, 232; self-: 229–30,
    267; vague: 230–31
accuser: 216
acedia: 167
act(s): 47, 90, 161, 190, 204, 222, 225,
    229, 240–42; external: 230; formal:
    88; human: 83; natural: 185; overt:
    267; penitential: 241, 244; pre-
    scribed: 241; sinful: 269; social: 121;
    spiritual: 83, 88, 227; visible: 257
action(s): xlii, 47, 49, 81–82, 152, 176,
    190, 197, 204, 207, 222, 225, 227, 262,

273, 278; divine: 56, 78, 83; exterior:
    80, 107, 257–58, 276; hidden: 271;
    holy: 185, 258; interior: 258; life-
    giving: xlvii, 255, 258; liturgical: 5;
    of God: xxix, 81, 89, 92, 210, 275; of
    grace: 256; of nature: 78; of Spirit:
    53, 269, 272, 277; sacred: 114; sym-
    bolic: 243
activism: 86
activity: xxviii, xxxi, 150, 152, 167, 191;
    ascetic: 271; formal: xii; moral: 271;
    spiritual: 48, 183
Acts of the Apostles: 70
Adam: 93, 131, 217
Adam of Perseigne, Abbot: 206
adaptation(s): xvii, xix, xxiii
Adauctus, St.: 201–2
admiration: 81
adoration: xxviii, 44, 63, 75–77, 120,
    128, 245; Eucharistic: 149
Advent: 66, 70, 115
advertisements: 193
advice: ascetic: 231; practical: xxx
adviser: 263
Aelred of Rievaulx, St.: 152
aestheticism: 6
affection(s): xxix, 77, 79, 145, 181; pa-
    ternal: xlix, 272; spiritual: 18
affectivity: 82, 88
affliction: 97
agape: 143